Chronicles and Its Synoptic Parallels
in
Samuel, Kings, and Related Biblical Texts

Chronicles and Its Synoptic Parallels
in
Samuel, Kings, and Related Biblical Texts

John C. Endres, S.J.
William R. Millar
John Barclay Burns

Editors

Corrine Patton
Pauline Viviano
James Fitzgerald

Contributors

Roger W. Uitti

Project Design

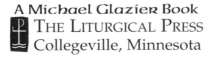
A Michael Glazier Book
THE LITURGICAL PRESS
Collegeville, Minnesota

A Michael Glazier Book published by The Liturgical Press.

Cover design by David Manahan, O.S.B. Illustration: "The Temple of Jerusalem" from a Passover Haggadah. Printed at Amsterdam in 1695.

1   2   3   4   5   6   7   8   9

Library of Congress Cataloging-in-Publication Data

Chronicles and its synoptic parallels in Samuel, Kings, and related
   biblical texts / John C. Endres, William R. Millar, John Barclay
   Burns, editors ; Corrine Patton, Pauline Viviano, Jim Fitzgerald,
   contributors ; Roger W. Uitti, project design.
        p.   cm.
    "A Michael Glazier book."
    Includes bibliographical references.
    ISBN 0-8146-5930-6 (alk. paper)
    1. Bible. O.T. Chronicles—Relation to Samuel. 2. Bible. O.T.
Chronicles—Relation to Kings. 3. Bible. O.T. Samuel—Relation to
Chronicles. 4. Bible. O.T. Kings—Relation to Chronicles.
5. Deuteronomistic history (Biblical criticism) I. Endres, John
C., 1946–   . II. Millar, William R., 1938–   . III. Burns, John
Barclay, 1943–   . IV. Patton, Corrine, 1958–   . V. Viviano,
Pauline A., 1946–   . VI. Fitzgerald, Jim.
    BS1345.2.C57   1998
    222'.606—dc21   98-25616
                                                                          CIP

Contents

Preface

This book represents the fusion of two distinct interests among its co-authors: the importance of synoptic parallels for study of the Hebrew Bible and the emergence in recent decades of fresh energy for study of the books of Chronicles. Our journey has taken nine years and the route has veered in one direction or another several times.

The seed for the book was sown by Roger Uitti, who devoted at least one sabbatical leave to the preparation of the outline of an Old Testament Synopticon, a collection of all parallel texts he could locate within the Hebrew Bible. This detailed and careful work provided the outline of all of our work, and it seemed providential that Roger and several others of us were invited by Loren Mack-Fisher to a meeting of the Hebrew Bible Seminar, which formed one unit of the Westar Institute in Sonoma, California, founded and directed by Robert Funk. At biannual meetings of the Westar Institute we planned and discussed theory and practice of the creation of synoptic parallels for study of the Bible. One extremely helpful resource was Robert Funk's own work, *New Gospel Parallels,* and its sequel, a new series.

We devoted considerable time to the study of various books of synoptic parallels, especially for study of the Gospels in the New Testament. Comparative study of many different approaches helped us to refine our own goals and ideas, which we utilized in our study of the various parallel versions of Samuel–Kings and Chronicles. Results of that study appear in sections of the Introduction.

Questions of translation also occupied much time. When we began our work—the New Revised Standard Version of the Bible was then being awaited—we considered using one of the available English translations and simply formatting it appropriately for our parallels project. Several factors militated against this procedure; most important, no available translation proved usable as a "synoptic" translation, where the same Hebrew expressions in both Chronicles and Samuel–Kings were consistently translated in the same fashion. So we reached a significant consensus, to translate the text "synoptically" ourselves, at least for all the texts in the books of Samuel, Kings, and Chronicles. So we devoted considerable energy and many vigorous discussions to a workable set of translation principles; the results of that process also appear in the Introduction. As always, a group translation project runs the perilous risk of widely divergent styles, so the entire translation has been checked several times and finally reviewed for general consistency of style by John Barclay Burns.

Initial hopes to produce a parallels version for scholars, with Hebrew, Greek, and Latin texts gradually narrowed to a different audience: students who do not read biblical languages but who can certainly learn a great deal about Chronicles by using a synoptic parallels book. The use of gospel parallels books for study of the Synoptic Gospels had long ago proven the benefits of such study. All of the authors teach such students, and some have used portions of this work-in-progress with classes at the seminary and undergraduate level and also in church Bible study. We hope that the visual format of the book and its straightforward presentation of textual materials can prove useful to both students and their teachers.

It has been our experience that reading Chronicles in a synopsis, or with one in hand, allows us to reach many of the fine judgments contained in commentaries and monographs on Chronicles, and also to read them with a critical sensibility which leads to some new hypotheses and approaches to particular questions and problems. In one sense, then, we produced the kind of tool we will enjoy using with our students. At the same time, however, we learned much about the theory and practice of translation and the careful comparison of biblical texts and ways to present this information visually—more than we can ever articulate. We also experienced the joys and frustrations of collegial projects, but we are convinced that only a type of consensual learning and wisdom could have brought us to this point.

We are grateful to students who assisted our work, both in our classes and as research assistants. We appreciate the consideration and counsel of other colleagues who traveled part of the journey with us, as well as friends and relatives who have asked when this book will ever be finished. We are grateful to the Association of Theological Schools which supported the work of John Endres, S.J., for a sabbatical leave in 1990 to work on this project, as well as to the Jesuit School of Theology at Berkeley, which provided valuable research assistance during these years of preparation. We thank the editors at The Liturgical Press, and especially Linda Maloney, for their sage advice and assistance in producing a manuscript with such complicated structure.

Project Participants

Editors:

JOHN C. ENDRES, S.J., is associate professor of Old Testament at the Jesuit School of Theology at Berkeley, California. He did his graduate work at Vanderbilt University. He was an editor and translator for the project.

WILLIAM R. MILLAR is professor of religious studies at Linfield College, McMinnville, Oregon. He did his graduate work at Harvard University. He was an editor and translator for the project.

JOHN BARCLAY BURNS is associate professor of religious studies at George Mason University, Fairfax, Virginia. He did his graduate work at the Universities of St. Andrews and Glasgow in Scotland. He was an editor and translator for the project.

Contributors:

CORRINE PATTON is assistant professor of Old Testament/Hebrew Bible at the University of St. Thomas, St. Paul, Minnesota. She did her graduate work at Yale University. She was a translator for the project.

PAULINE VIVIANO is associate professor of Old Testament at Loyola University of Chicago, Chicago, Illinois. She did her graduate work at St. Louis University. She was a translator for the project.

JAMES FITZGERALD is a product designer at Prototype Solutions, Portland, Oregon. He is a graduate of Linfield College and has co-authored two books on computer-aided design, *AutoCAD Release 13 for Beginners* and *Inside AutoCAD Release 13,* both from New Riders Publishing. James teaches AutoCAD at Mount Hood Community College. He created all of the charts in this book.

Project Design:

ROGER W. UITTI is dean of studies and professor of Old Testament at Lutheran Theological Seminary (ELCIC), Saskatoon, Saskatchewan, Canada. He did his graduate work at the Oriental Institute, University of Chicago, and the Lutheran School of Theology at Chicago. In addition to supplying the underlying pericopal unit titles and substructures for this project, Roger also served as one of the translators and early editors.

Introduction

This book encompasses two spheres of interest in Hebrew Bible study: two distinct texts (1–2 Chronicles and the Deuteronomistic History, especially in 2 Samuel and 1–2 Kings) and a particular mode of study, comparison of parallel texts. We address first the phenomenon of parallels in the Hebrew Bible and then point to the paramount example of such parallelism, the relationship between Samuel–Kings and Chronicles, which repeats and reworks much of the material familiar from the earlier history. We survey presently available tools to assist the study of parallel texts, assess their usefulness, and then demonstrate the contours of a new tool for study of these two blocks of biblical literature which can prove particularly useful for study of 1–2 Chronicles. Issues and principles of translation are explained and the format of this book is presented for the reader. Finally, we offer some suggestions and guidance for different kinds of questions and problems that one can study with the assistance of this *Chronicles/ Samuel–Kings Parallels.*

1. *Parallel Study in the Old Testament/ Hebrew Bible*

All but the most casual readers of the Bible begin to notice that some narratives and poems occur more than once in the Hebrew Bible. Some of the best-known examples occur in the Pentateuch.

Torah (Pentateuch)

—two creation accounts (Gen 1:1–2:4a / Gen 2:4b-25);
—three stories of a wife/sister in danger (Gen 12:10–13:1 / Gen 20:1-18 / Gen 26:1-11),
—two versions of the Decalogue (Exod 20:1-17 / Deut 5:6-21).

> **Torah = Pentateuch:** the first five books of the Hebrew Bible

Countless students of the Hebrew Bible have considered these parallel passages as part of the important "evidence" for different sources or tradition-strands within the Pentateuch.

How widespread is the phenomenon of parallel passages in the Hebrew Bible? The usual practice of reading one book of the Bible will not help to answer this question because it is so easy to fasten onto one of the several parallel versions of a story, especially if they appear in different books. For example, most people know the Ten Commandments from the Decalogue in Exodus 20:1-17; only the most diligent students have also examined the parallel text in Deuteronomy 5:6-21. In fact, parallel texts occur within each major section of the Hebrew Scriptures. Some examples follow.

	The Former Prophets (Deuteronomistic History)
Former Prophets = Deuteronomistic History: Deuteronomy, Joshua, Judges, 1–2 Samuel, 1–2 Kings	—two accounts of Saul's death (1 Sam 31:1-6 / 2 Sam 1:1-6) —parallel accounts of the reign of Ahaziah of Judah (2 Kgs 8:25-29 / 2 Kgs 9:14-16, 29)

The Former Prophets (Deuteronomistic History)

—two accounts of Saul's death (1 Sam 31:1-6 / 2 Sam 1:1-6)

—parallel accounts of the reign of Ahaziah of Judah (2 Kgs 8:25-29 / 2 Kgs 9:14-16, 29)

Former Prophets = Deuteronomistic History: Deuteronomy, Joshua, Judges, 1–2 Samuel, 1–2 Kings

Latter Prophets (Writing Prophets)

—similar oracles (Isaiah 2:2-5 / Micah 4:1-4 [with reversal in Joel 4:10])

—similar oracles (Obadiah 1–4 / Jeremiah 49:14-16 and Obadiah 5–6 / Jeremiah 49:9-10)

Latter Prophets = Writing Prophets: Isaiah, Jeremiah, Ezekiel, The Twelve (minor prophets)

The Writings (Poetical Books)

—Psalm 14=Psalm 53

—Proverbs 14:12=16:25; 18:8=26:22; 12:11 / 28:19

Writings = Wisdom and Poetic Books: Job, Psalms, Proverbs, Song of Songs, Ruth, Lamentations, Ecclesiastes, Esther, Daniel, Ezra, Nehemiah, 1–2 Chronicles

In each of these cases we can imagine different tradents or writers from similar social-scribal settings presenting similar or identical traditions.

There are also significant parallels between texts in *different parts* of the Hebrew Bible. Consider the following.

—Psalm 18=2 Samuel 22

—Psalm 104 / Genesis 1:1–2:4a

—1 Chronicles 16:7-36 / Psalms 105:1-15; 96:1-13; 106:1, 47-48

Of course, the scribes and communities that produced the Writings were reflecting on the contemporary significance of both the Torah and the Prophets for their era, so some close parallels are bound to occur in these texts.

Many students of the Bible, however, know only one of the parallel traditions. In the case of the history of Judah and Israel, for example, most people read and study the books of Genesis through 2 Kings, plus Ezra and Nehemiah. Only the most curious readers also study Chronicles, even though major sections of 1–2 Chronicles parallel the "history" in 1–2 Samuel and 1–2 Kings.

In addition, it is difficult to assess how much "parallelism" there is in the Hebrew Bible. One way to describe the extent of parallelism in the Hebrew Scriptures comes from statistics. One could count the number of parallel verses in the Hebrew Bible, but we prefer larger units, which are sometimes called pericopes. When Roger Uitti prepared the text for parallels study he adapted a list of section units provided by the United Bible Society for their translators, and his complete list contains 1323 pericopes.[1] For our system of division of the Hebrew Bible into pericopes, consult the appendix, *Synoptic Parallels in Chronicles and Samuel-Kings*. For comparative purposes, note the number of units in each major division.

Pericope: Greek, literally, "something cut around"; a discrete, self-contained unit of biblical text

—Genesis–Numbers   nos. 1–281   (281)

—Deuteronomy–2 Kings nos. 282–698   (417)

—Prophets   nos. 699–1036   (338)

—Writings   nos. 1037–1323 (287)

At least 25 percent of the sections in this list seem to exhibit some kind of clear synoptic parallelism, even though in some instances only a few verses are involved. The majority of synoptic parallels occur in the Former Prophets/Deuteronomistic History (nos. 282–698). These 417 sections contain approximately 41 percent of all synoptic parallels within the Hebrew Bible. Most of the pericopes parallel to the Deuteronomistic History occur in 1–2 Chronicles. The parallel "histories" (Chronicles and Samuel–Kings) display the most clear and extensive case of parallelism in the Hebrew Bible, so the comparative approach can best be used to help study Chronicles, a text that now enjoys newfound interest among scholars.

The identification of parallel texts allows the reader to approach the text in new ways. For instance, one can compare the parallel texts to answer questions about historical, textual, compositional, and theological matters. As a result, study of parallels is a basic tool of the biblical scholar; but many students of the Bible do not read parallel biblical texts in the synoptic fashion so fruitfully used by scholars, so they rely on secondary literature instead of studying parallels and arriving at their own conclusions. The importance of independent consideration of the parallel material can be demonstrated if we turn to some ways that scholars who have studied parallel texts in great detail describe (1) the Deuteronomistic History [Deuteronomy through 2 Kings] and (2) the Chronicler's History [1–2 Chronicles].

2. *Parallels: Types and Principles*

Parallels occur when more than one "text"—whether clauses, sentences, verses or longer sections—manifests similar language, tone, or structure. Parallels may be verbatim, nearly verbatim, structural, within the same book of the Bible, between different books in the Bible, between a biblical and a nonbiblical book (from other Jewish literature, such as the Pseudepigraphal or Apocryphal books, or from broader ancient Near Eastern texts). In this book only parallels from the Hebrew Bible will appear.

> **Parallel**: more than one text displays similar or same content, language, structure

2.1 *Viewing Parallels Synoptically*

Synoptic parallels occur when one can "view together" two or more "texts" because they are so similar. In biblical studies, scholars have long spoken of "Synoptic Books," that is, those which can actually be viewed together because they exhibit so many similarities. In New Testament studies, the Gospels of Matthew, Mark, and Luke can be viewed synoptically, so they have been described as the Synoptic Gospels (to distinguish them from the Gospel of John). In Hebrew Bible studies, the books of Samuel, Kings, and Chronicles are often considered to be synoptic books.

Perhaps the easiest way to compare parallel texts and interpret their significance is to view them synoptically, that is, in visually matching sections. One might view them in parallel columns on the page of a book, in matching "windows" on a computer screen, or as one would view pieces of visual art placed together on a wall or screen.

> **Synopsis**: Greek, literally "viewing together." Arrangement of texts in parallel columns to see where texts agree or disagree

> **Synoptic parallel**: parallel text[s] so close in content that one can study them together by comparative means

From the world of art emerges an example of the beauty and value of synoptic viewing. Many visitors to the Van Gogh Museum in Amsterdam have been amazed by a room devoted to the "Potato Eaters." That famous painting appeared together with a large number of preparatory sketches that preceded it—various studies of peasants in their fields and homes, some focusing on faces and others on gnarled hands. Spending time with all of these works arranged in this manner informs the viewer in two ways: first, one gets a sense of the various images, motifs, and portraits that preceded the final work of art known to us today; second, one can see how the painting combines aspects of all these images in a new visual relationship, providing each character or image a new meaning in the total picture. In biblical terms, one gains insight into Van Gogh's sources, but also appreciates the artist's composition in a fresh way.

2.2 *Various Parallel Relationships*

Various types of biblical parallels can be described according to the ways in which various texts resemble each other. In the Hebrew Bible there appear both primary and secondary parallels. **Primary parallels** are materials in a text which resemble each other in either a verbatim or nearly verbatim manner. **Secondary parallels** are those materials in a text that exhibit similar content, thrust or theme, but not in any kind of verbatim manner. Such secondary parallels include material found elsewhere in the Hebrew Bible, as well as in the New Testament, Josephus' *Antiquities of the Jews,* and other ancient works.

> **Primary parallels**: the resemblance is nearly verbatim

> **Secondary parallels**: resemblance in terms of content or theme, but not verbatim

Internal parallels = vertical parallels: parallel texts within the same book/document

External parallels = horizontal parallels: parallel texts in two or more documents

Biblical parallels are also distinguished in terms of their sources. Those who study biblical texts find parallel texts in various locations: within the same biblical book, in different books of the Bible, or even in nonbiblical texts. **Internal parallels** are those which occur within the same book of the Bible (e.g., Genesis 12, 20, 26: the wife/sister in danger). We may also call them vertical parallels because one needs to move up or down the normal page to find them. **External parallels** describe parallels between a text in one book and a text in [an]other book[s] or documents. When they are viewed next to each other on a page or screen we speak of them as horizontal parallels.

Primary parallels may be twofold: internal parallels and external parallels. Internal primary parallels are those which repeat a line, phrase, or even paragraph within the same pericope or source document (see 557, 567, 627). External primary parallels are portions of the Hebrew Bible where one observes an actual verbal correspondence when viewing two or more different source documents horizontally (see 575 or 645). In this book the majority of primary synoptic parallels come from the books of Samuel, Kings, Genesis, Exodus, Psalms, and Jeremiah.

In this handbook our division into smaller sections has been carried out with a sensitivity to the standard partitioning already done by members of the translation team of the United Bible Society. As a result, the pericopes or textual units in this book reflect with some modification the subdivisions and titles already developed by the United Bible Society for use by Bible translators.

3.   *The Chronicler's History and the Deuteronomistic History*

The books of 1–2 Chronicles, 2 Samuel, and 1–2 Kings offer excellent material for comparative study. These five books present Israel's history for later generations from two distinct viewpoints: the History of the Deuteronomists [Deuteronomy, Joshua, Judges, 1–2 Samuel, 1–2 Kings] and the Chronicler's History [1–2 Chronicles; some would add Ezra and Nehemiah]. Although Chronicles covers much of the history found in Samuel and Kings, there are enough differences in content, outlook and focus to suggest that they are works from distinct times, places, and writers. Taken together, these books provide the basic materials for discerning the history of the monarchic era.

3.1   *Contents of 1–2 Samuel, 1–2 Kings, and 1–2 Chronicles*

The books of Samuel and Kings contain a history-like story, a narrative of the life and times of monarchic Israel during the era of the monarchy, from Saul and David (around 1000 B.C.E.) to the last king of Judah, Jehoiachin (587 B.C.E.). They include events and persons in both of the two kingdoms that emerged from the division after the death of Solomon: Judah in the south and Israel in the north. The books of Kings conclude with a description of Babylon's conquest of Judah and a sketchy view of life after the destruction of Jerusalem and during the exilic era.

The writer of 1–2 Chronicles creates a theological history which spans the time from the creation of the world through Cyrus' termination of the Babylonian exile in 538 B.C.E. Not all periods of Israel's history are treated in the same fashion. For example, in 1 Chronicles 1–9 the Chronicler uses extensive genealogies to present the period from the creation of the world to the time of King Saul; no stories are included. When this history describes the rise of David and his rule, it pays more attention than the Deuteronomist to the king's concern for the construction of the future temple and provision of its personnel [1 Chr 22–29]. Second Chronicles begins with Solomon's reign, viewed as a wonderful era for later Israel to remember and to anticipate again. The remainder of 2 Chronicles focuses almost exclusively on the southern kingdom, and especially the exemplary reigns of Kings Jehoshaphat, Hezekiah, and Josiah. The Chronicler regularly speaks of "all Israel," suggesting his hope for a reunion of all Israel, that is, both the southern and northern kingdoms. In summary, the Chronicler's history covers the Pentateuch by way of genealogies and the history of the Deuteronomists by rewriting the story with special emphasis on David's royal line.

3.2   *Biblical Story and Interpretation in Samuel and Kings*

1–2 Samuel and 1–2 Kings contain a complete story. They include collections of written and oral traditions, combinations of stories and legends, all reshaped to address the contemporary needs of their composers and audiences. Smaller stories have been combined to form larger sections of narratives; they are often recognized because they focus on a particular institution, person, or notion of God. Other sections are identifiable through their unique style of language and theology: sometimes stories are interspersed with sermons or hortatory sections.

The books of Samuel and Kings, then, consist of narratives which retell Israel's monarchic history and reflective sections which sermonize on the events of history, explaining God's role and the people's covenant obligations. Very ancient narratives are found embedded within later interpretations: the biblical history attracted further nuances in later centuries while it was still being reformulated and retold in Israel. Generally, biblical scholars assumed that history-like narratives were written close to the time of the events which they describe, while the interpretive sections reflect later interpretation.

3.3   *The Deuteronomistic History*

In the Jewish Scriptures the books of Samuel and Kings together with Joshua and Judges are called the Former Prophets. But they also exhibit genuine affinity with the book of Deuteronomy, which seems closer to the books that follow it than to the books of the Torah which precede it (Genesis, Exodus, Leviticus, and Numbers). Since Deuteronomy shares vocabulary and theological perspective with these later books, this distinctive perspective has led scholars to call this whole collection of writings the Deuteronomistic History. This title combines the historical character of these books with the theological flavor of Deuteronomy.

> **Deuteronomistic Historian:** person who collected Israel's historic traditions and wrote the "history" in Deuteronomy, Joshua, Judges, Samuel, and Kings

Even if we consider the history as a single work, we do not claim that a single person authored it. Rather we envision a final group of writers whose theological insight and prodigious labor shaped these books into their present form. Although there are good arguments to support the conclusion that the present version of these books comes from the time of the Exile to Babylon, when people were searching for an explanation for their catastrophe, many scholars believe that the bulk of this material was composed before 587 B.C.E. Perhaps a first version or edition was composed during the reign of King Josiah (ca. 622 B.C.E.), who strove to reform worship and political life of the southern kingdom of Judah. Groups of preachers and teachers exhorted Judeans to reform their lives, promising salvation for Torah obedience, but destruction for infidelity to the Mosaic covenant. Perhaps Deuteronomy came to light during these years (Cf. 2 Kings 22, and the narrative of Huldah the Prophetess). For these reasons, scholars call these preachers and teachers the Deuteronomists.

> **Deuteronomistic History:** term referring to the larger history in the books of Deuteronomy, Joshua, Judges, Samuel, and Kings. Scholars use the sigla Dtr[1] and Dtr[2] to refer to a 7th century B.C.E. and a later exilic edition of the DtrH Deuteronomistic history respectively

When we speak of Deuteronomic interpretation and history, we generally refer to their vision and religious program, which can be discovered by studying how they retold and interpreted older stories, some of them dating as far back as the reign of Solomon. For these Deuteronomists, Josiah modeled right conduct with regard to the temple, its worship, Torah, and prophecy. The style of Deuteronomy is appropriate to its setting: a sermon Moses preached to Israel before entering the Promised Land. This homiletic style characterizes significant sections of Samuel and Kings: sermons, homilies, and theological reflections in 1 Samuel 12, 1 Kings 8 and 2 Kings 17 have been identified because they share the distinctive language and vision of Deuteronomy. Once their patterns become familiar to a reader, many shorter passages and brief comments

> **Deuteronomic:** term referring to the core stratum, the Book of Deuteronomy

fit a similar pattern of stylized language and similar theology. Many such phrases are repeated regularly throughout Samuel and Kings; occasionally they will be indicated in a parallel column. However, the Deuteronomist's process of redacting earlier traditions must be studied through the normal procedures of source and redaction criticism. One must notice the differences in vocabulary, style, and theology, and then analyze the similarities and differences; in general it seems there were earlier sources which the Deuteronomists incorporated into their patterned "history." The process resembles many studies of the Pentateuch in the modern era.

Similar to studies of the Pentateuch, the formation of the books of Deuteronomy, Joshua, Judges, 1–2 Samuel and 1–2 Kings has occupied critical scholarship since the emergence of the historical critical method of interpretation. The success achieved by source critical analysis of the Pentateuch in the eighteenth and early nineteenth centuries led scholars to view the formation of these "historical" books in much the same way. The sources of the Pentateuch (J, E, P, D) were traced into Joshua, Judges, and the books of Samuel and Kings; each of these books was thought to have been a compilation of these sources by a later Deuteronomic editor.[2] However there was little agreement about the scope or dating of these sources. Only with the publication of Martin Noth's *The Deuteronomistic History* in 1943[3] were serious advances made on the issue of authorship of Deuteronomy through 2 Kings. Noth recognized that these seven books form a unified whole, for which the book of Deuteronomy serves as an introduction; thus he called this collection the Deuteronomistic History. He differs from his predecessors by insisting that the history is the work of an author, not simply an editor. Noth allows that this author, whom he called the Deuteronomist, certainly used sources; however, the overriding unity of the work argues against the view that some editor simply pieced the history together from various preexisting versions of a history.

The Deuteronomist, Noth argued, has imposed a literary and theological unity on his work. That unity is most apparent in the speeches and essays which are found at critical junctures in the history of Israel, and also in the overarching framework that unites the work from Deuteronomy through Kings. He demonstrated that there are speeches (e.g., Josh 1:11-15; Josh 23; 1 Sam 12; 1 Kgs 8:14-61) and essays (Josh 12; Judg 2:11-23; 2 Kgs 17:7-23) that are related to one another in vocabulary, style, and theology. These speeches and essays look back to where Israel has been and point forward to where Israel is moving. Both the events of the past and those yet to come are explained in terms of Deuteronomic theology: obedience to the Deuteronomic Code (Deut 12–26) has brought or will bring success; disobedience has led or will lead to failure.

3.4   *Biblical Story and Interpretation in Chronicles*

The books of 1–2 Chronicles also present a history-type presentation, containing several different kinds of texts, including genealogies, historical narratives, prayers, sermons, speeches and descriptions of ceremonies. Some of these materials have been considered sources for the historian, especially genealogies and some prayers, but the most important source of Chronicles is the library of "books" of the Bible which the writer apparently knew and used, especially the Pentateuch and the Deuteronomistic History (focusing on 1 Samuel 31 through 2 Kings 25). So, one excellent approach to the study of Chronicles and its author is to use a synoptic parallel approach, comparing its text with the sources its author utilized, especially 2 Samuel and 1–2 Kings. Observing the similarities and differences and analyzing their patterns offers an excellent method to discern how the Chronicler rewrote and interpreted his sources, especially in utilizing materials from the Deuteronomistic History and the Pentateuch.

3.5 *The Chronicler's History*

The biblical text in 1–2 Chronicles often follows the presentation of Samuel and Kings very closely. If one compares the text of Chronicles with a variety of texts from Samuel, Kings, Genesis, and Psalms, the similarity in many parts of Chronicles is staggering: whole sections of Chronicles seem to be nearly verbatim replications of its source material. From this fact, that one can look at Chronicles and at Samuel–Kings placed next to each other and find that the later text (Chronicles) seems almost a word-for-word citation of the source (Samuel–Kings), we use the term "synoptic parallel." Even in the genealogies of 1 Chronicles 1–9, where the author did not follow the Deuteronomistic History, there exists significant correspondence between the information in these genealogies and the narratives and genealogies of other biblical books, especially Genesis.

Parallel study helps to identify the sources and to make comparative studies. The way in which the Chronicler understands and presents materials suggests how the various source materials were appreciated and evaluated. Even slight variations between Chronicles and Samuel–Kings may hint at this author's view of the older story. For example, after David entered Jerusalem, King Hiram of Tyre sent him massive amounts of building materials. The Deuteronomist in 2 Samuel mentions that David's family increased greatly in numbers, perhaps implying a connection between house construction and family size. But the text in 1 Chronicles differs.

> **Chronicler**: one who redacted earlier traditions and composed Book of 1–2 Chronicles

> **Chronicler's History**: history found in the Book of 1–2 Chronicles (some also include Ezra and Nehemiah)

2 Samuel 5	*1 Chronicles 14*
[13] And David took more concubines and wives from Jerusalem after he came from Hebron; and more sons and more daughters were born to David.	[3] And David took more wives in Jerusalem, and David begot more sons and daughters.

In each text the next verse names the children born to David in Jerusalem. However, Chronicles offered two more names than 2 Samuel, but makes no mention of David's concubines. While the Chronicler offered a fuller (more accurate?) list, one might ask why he omitted mention of David's concubines—to protect David's character, or to assure the legitimacy of his children, or for some other reason? The numerous examples of interpretative technique in Chronicles suggested to some early scholars that Chronicles should be described as a "midrash" on the biblical text, that is, as a careful explanation and commentary of some type. Some have even described the Chronicler as the first midrashist, establishing a type of writing which became important in Jewish rabbinic circles in the early centuries of the Common Era.

The Chronicler used many other techniques to retell the Deuteronomistic story. Sometimes the Chronicler added names and emphasized roles and offices held by people, especially for the Levites, who find new prominence in Chronicles. An overall study of Chronicles' differences from its sources, and the patterns of presentation of the material suggests that the Chronicler intended to present another "history of Israel," one with a very definite theological viewpoint and emphasis. Those scholars who see the presentation of the "story" as the Chronicler's major emphasis usually speak of the Chronicler's History as an alternative history in the Bible, comparable to the Deuteronomistic History and the Pentateuch together, which some have termed the Primary History.

This author rewrote history in order to make ancient sacred traditions applicable to contemporary issues and needs, a process we describe as "contemporizing" the ancient tradition. Such updating helped to emphasize a life program for people of the Chronicler's generation in fifth- or fourth-century Palestine. The Jewish community which lived there had experienced difficulty reconstituting itself after the return from Babylon. Because these Jews experienced the political impotence of several vanquished peoples in the Persian empire, the Chronicler created for them a spiritual center and focus to help them maintain their identity through religion. The temple and its personnel —priests and Levites—were viewed as a rallying point for Israel since the monarchy had never reappeared after the Exile. The Chronicler recast the David of 1–2 Samuel as the originator and the spiritual head of the temple and its worship, reinterpreting their early history to suit present circumstances. At the same time he acted like a preacher, issuing a powerful exhortation to remain faithful to temple worship in Jerusalem. By listing the various ministers and their functions in his genealogies, with special attention to their duties and accomplishments, he encouraged and legitimated these various groups, especially the Levites. In 1–2 Chronicles the exhortatory tendencies point to a life vision or spirituality to which the Chronicler was inviting postexilic Jews resettled again in and around Jerusalem.

4. *Need for a New Parallels Version of Chronicles, Samuel and Kings*

Comparative study of Chronicles vis-à-vis Samuel and Kings has long profited from a synoptic display of parallel texts. A brief "history" of synoptic parallels versions of these books will demonstrate their usefulness for biblical research as well as some features that should be included in this edition.

4.1   *Harmonies*

Our review begins with harmonies. A harmony intends to aid the historical study of an era by offering parallel texts in such a way that all available biblical texts concerning an event or era may present a fuller picture for the reader. An excellent example is:

> William Day Crockett, *A Harmony of Samuel, Kings, and Chronicles* (Grand Rapids, Mich.: Baker, 1951; 1985 reprint).

Harmony: book of parallels that aims to give a unified, consistent story/narrative

This harmony provides a reference guide to the history of the kingdoms of Judah and Israel. Crockett reconstructed the English text: some passages appear in parallel, but all of the units are arranged chronologically. This harmony occasionally rearranges the order of events in either or both books in order to present a particular chronology. For example, Crockett rearranges verses in 2 Samuel 8 to produce a coherent biography of King David: in no. 86, "Decisive Campaign Against Hadadezer," Crockett presents the lead text, 2 Samuel 8:3,4,7,8 and its parallels. In no. 87, "Subjugation of Damascus," he extracts verses from the previous section, 2 Samuel 8:5-6.

A synopsis, by contrast, respects the literary order of the text, even if that means forsaking a clear-cut chronology of events. The second example of a harmony moves in this direction.

Synopsis: a book that arranges similar texts in parallel columns so that one can easily see where they agree and disagree

> James Newsome, *A Synoptic Harmony of Samuel, Kings, and Chronicles With Related Passages from Psalms, Isaiah, Jeremiah and Ezra* (Grand Rapids, Mich.: Baker, 1986).

This synoptic harmony presents 1 Samuel 31 through 2 Kings as the lead text, on the left side of each page; parallels from Chronicles and other books appear on the right side. When the lead text has no synoptic parallel, it expands horizontally to cover the entire page. In a few places, Newsome uses three columns for the parallels. This edition, however, omits significant sections of 1–2 Chronicles, suggesting much higher esteem for the text of these Deuteronomistic books (Samuel–Kings) and history.

Newsome uses the translation of the Revised Standard Version (RSV), but he finds it necessary to make occasional changes in the RSV translation to bring out or accommodate parallel verses. Two common situations in the RSV result in translation changes in Newsome's edition: sometimes different English expressions are given for identical Hebrew expressions; elsewhere, different Hebrew expressions are rendered the same in the English translation. In both cases his alterations identify parallels and differences much more clearly. This volume is a very accessible tool for general student use, especially for study oriented to the Deuteronomistic History.

4.2   *Synoptic parallels*

Synoptic comparisons to date include also a number of volumes of synoptic parallels. For many biblical scholars, serious study of synoptic parallels brings to mind the older volumes of Vannutelli, extending to over seven hundred pages.

> Primus Vannutelli, *Libri Synoptici Veteris Testamenti seu Librorum Regum et Chronicorum Loci Paralleli* (Rome: Pontifical Biblical Institute, 1931–34).

This work displays the Hebrew and Greek texts[4] of the parallel passages on facing pages, with Samuel–Kings on the left and Chronicles on the right. On the two-page folio the Hebrew Massoretic text (MT) appears on the left page, while the Septuagint Greek (LXX) version appears to the right. In addition to these primary texts, there also appear a text-critical apparatus, a Vulgate text (Latin) and pertinent citations from Josephus' *Antiquities of the Jews* (Greek).

In Vannutelli's synopsis, Chronicles generally functions as the lead text, though some inconsistencies have been noted.[5] His text sections are organized according to content, and when large blocks of material have no synoptic parallel, he regularly includes only a summary of its contents. The two-column format (that is, four columns across the folio of two pages) is used consistently.

This work facilitates textual and redaction-critical study by its use of two visual indicators of difference: (1) there are gaps, spaces in the printed line to indicate words without a parallel in the comparable text; (2) only the lead texts have full vocalization (addition of markings which identify the vowels in Hebrew), so that vowel pointing appears in the parallel text only when it differs from that in the lead text. Both of these features—spatial gaps and differences in vowels—provide powerful visual tools to identify similarities and differences between parallel texts. This synopsis also provides some help for the study of parallels within the biblical book and developments within a single text, especially by references forward or backward in the biblical text. But this volume does not provide complete texts either of Chronicles or of Samuel–Kings.[6] Furthermore, it is accessible only to those who read biblical languages (including Latin). Finally, it has long been out of print.

Vannutelli's book provides assistance for text-critics, especially by its presentation of the Septuagint text (Codex Vaticanus), the Vulgate, and the selections from Josephus. These parallels help one to observe and identify textual differences, the first step in text-criticism. Contemporary text-critics need additional materials, including some readings from the Dead Sea scrolls, which were discovered a generation after Vannutelli's work.

In the same genre as Vannutelli is a smaller, less expensive volume published in Israel.

> Abba Bendavid, *Maqbilot baMiqra [Parallels in the Bible]* (Jerusalem: Carta, 1972).

This Hebrew volume prints the text of 1 Samuel 31 through Ezra 2 as its lead text, in the right hand column (typical of books printed in Hebrew). Chronicles is fully presented, in a left column, and primary parallels from other books also appear, sometimes in a middle section. Like Vannutelli, Bendavid facilitated comparison by: (1) word-gaps (though all parallel texts are fully vocalized); and (2) red coloring to indicate minor differences in the spelling or pointing of the parallel. Although there are no section numbers or titles, catchwords (in Hebrew) in the margins help to guide the Hebrew reader. This volume is especially recommended because of its trim size, but it cannot be used for text-critical work or by students not versed in Hebrew.

A synopsis especially designed for German university students has been prepared by Jürgen Kegler and Matthias Augustin.

> Jürgen Kegler and Matthias Augustin, *Synopse zum Chronistischen Geschichtswerk*. Beitrage zur Erforschung des Alten Testaments und des Antiken Judentums, Band 1. Frankfurt am Main: Peter Lang, 1984.

Here Chronicles is the lead text, in the right column, while the left column contains parallel texts from Samuel and Kings; other parallels from the Hebrew Scriptures fall into a middle column. All biblical texts appear in Hebrew. The authors have divided the text into form-critical units, which they explain and identify. In this volume texts appear in full block format, that is, like regular paragraphs. Block presentation of text, however, makes it more difficult for readers to notice small and precise differences. Yet the most appealing feature of this volume is its focus on Chronicles.

4.3   *Important Features for a New Synoptic Parallels Version*

Notwithstanding their excellent features, the volumes of synoptic parallels described above lack several elements critical for contemporary biblical study by English-speaking students. First, students should have an English translation that shows with precision the synoptic relationships between parallel texts. Second, in order to respect the literary integrity of each text, both the Chronicler's History (1–2 Chronicles) and its parallels in the Deuteronomistic History (2 Samuel and 1–2 Kings) should appear in full. Third, the format should present a readable text which also allows observation of synoptic differences.

5.   *Features of The New Chronicles Samuel–Kings Parallels*

5.1   *Translation*

This book utilizes a new synoptic translation of 1 Chronicles 10–2 Chronicles 36 and its parallel texts (especially Samuel–Kings and Psalms). For the spelling of Hebrew proper names it follows an accepted tradition used in the New Revised Standard Version (NRSV). Since most of the text in 1 Chronicles 1–9 is composed of genealogies and lists of names, we have utilized the NRSV translation in those chapters. In a few places we have changed the NRSV translation to reflect a synoptic parallel in the Hebrew where that translation obscures it: each *change* in the translation appears in our text in italics.

Tetragrammeton (YHWH): the four Hebrew consonants representing the name of God. Often appears as LORD in English translations

The Tetragrammeton, the Hebrew name for God which consists of four consonants, presents a special problem. Since the name ceased to be pronounced at some time after the Babylonian exile, Jews began to substitute another word for it when reading the text aloud, and it is still pronounced as Adonai. The closest English equivalent of this word is LORD, which is the translation found in most English translations (e.g., New Revised Standard Version, Revised Standard Version, New American Bible, New International Version, Jewish Publication Society). Since the Hebrew consonants transliterated into English are YHWH, we have chosen to write those four letters whenever their equivalent, the Tetragrammeton, appears in the Hebrew text. This practice allows the reader[s] to determine how to read it—LORD, Adonai, etc.—but preserves the difficulty of the Hebrew text itself. In passages from the NRSV we have substituted YHWH for LORD whenever it appears, though these changes are not marked each time.

5.1a   *Synoptic Translation*

The biblical translations mentioned above and others are usually translated by committees, where individuals are assigned books to translate according to certain stated translation principles. Then a committee reviews the material and attempts to regularize the translations received. We have operated in this fashion, but with one apparent difference: instead of assigning books to individuals, each member of the translation team took responsibility for sections of Chronicles, including the synoptic portions of the text. This practice emerged from our goal: providing a translation that facilitates synoptic study of the texts. The result is a translation that helps one to pinpoint in English the similarities and differences between synoptic portions of the Hebrew text. If the Hebrew parallel passages are the same, the English will be the same. If the Hebrew texts use different words in a parallel passage, the English translation of those words will be different.

5.1b   *Translation of Nonsynoptic sections*

Another way of describing parallels is to use the terms "horizontal" and "vertical." Horizontal parallels are those one can see looking across the page, that is, a synoptic parallel. Vertical parallels are those one might notice reading forward or backward in the same book, that is, moving in a vertical line up or down the page. While it is essential for our purposes to translate horizontal parallels synoptically, we also attempt to standardize the translation of vertical parallels, that is, those in the same book, of which there are numerous occurrences.

This procedure, however, does not mean that a Hebrew word will always be translated by the same English word, wherever it occurs. Literary context is always a factor in determining the particular nuance of a word, so a particular Hebrew word might be rendered differently in different parts of a book. In general, we have attempted to adhere closely to the Hebrew text, while retaining an English idiom, particularly in passages for which there is no parallel. In synoptic parallel passages it sometimes happens that the parallel text, for example, in Samuel or Kings, did not follow exactly the same order of clauses, sometimes of verses, as the lead text in Chronicles. Whenever that happens, the order of materials always follows the Chronicles text and the clauses or verses in the parallel text are rearranged; however, any verses that are out of the normal order are enclosed in brackets.

5.1c   *Difficult Hebrew Expressions*

Since the usefulness of our translation depends on whether or not we are accurately reflecting the Hebrew text, we usually marked English words added to smooth out the translation of a difficult Hebrew passage in brackets [ ].

5.1d   *Translation of Gender and Anachronistic Terms*

We have translated gender as it seems to be required by the Hebrew, but have endeavored not to create a gender-biased text where it does not exist in the Hebrew, especially by assuming that English words such as "man" and "mankind" and "sons" automatically include females in their meaning (as has occurred in many standard English translations in the past). Similarly, we have not intentionally translated away all social, cosmological or other ancient aspects of world view or expression because some might term them archaic. At the same time, we have tried to avoid translating anachronisms into the text.

5.1e   *Text and Variant Readings*

The Hebrew manuscript being translated in this volume is the Leningrad Codex B 19ᴬ published in *Biblica Hebraica Stuttgartensia* (Stuttgart: Deutsche Bibelstiftung, 1967/77). This decision means that we have not weighed variant readings in other Hebrew texts (not even in the Hebrew variants from the Qumran texts) or in the Greek translation, the Septuagint (LXX). While such readings are extremely important for scholars, and for scholarly translations, the rendering of the Hebrew text without comparisons such as these occasionally highlights some of the difficulties which invite the

Qere: Aramaic, signals the way the Massoretes required a word in Hebrew Massoretic Text to be read (aloud)

Kethib: Aramaic, denotes the way a word is written in the Hebrew Massoretic Text

efforts of text-critics, who attempt to discern the most probable early reading of a text. There are some indications of different Hebrew readings in the Hebrew text; these were supplied by the Massoretes, Jewish scholars of the Hebrew Bible. A marginal note might read (in Aramaic) Qere, which signifies: "read (**Qere**) instead of what is written (**Kethib**)"; one might call these textual variants within the standard Hebrew text of the Bible. We considered these marginal notations as we translated the Hebrew text, and often we indicate when we have followed the **Qere** reading in the margin.

5.2   *Literary Integrity of Chronicles and its Parallels*

We present a complete translation of Chronicles and also of the synoptic portions of Samuel–Kings, that is, 1 Samuel 31–2 Kings 25. Chronicles appears as the lead or control text: that is, Chronicles appears whole and entire, in its own narrative sequence. As far as we know, this is the only synoptic parallels that includes the entire book of Chronicles, in its own sequence. Once the texts from the Deuteronomistic History begin, that is, 1 Samuel 31, then they are completely represented in the book, though occasionally not in their narrative sequence.

5.3   *Format and Technical Aspects*

5.3a   *Sections/Pericopes*

This synopsis presents the biblical books in sections or pericopes that reflect content divisions. The list of sections included in this volume is found in the Appendix (at the conclusion of the book).

5.3b   *Column format*

We use a flexible format that facilitates viewing of several kinds of information. The pages can be divided into three vertical columns. Throughout the book the only text which will appear in column one (at the left margin of a page) is Chronicles, the lead text or the control text. In many places the page will divide into two columns, but occasionally a third column is introduced whenever it is useful to present additional parallels. Some of these parallels might be "synoptic" while others are generally of two kinds: a related text with similar content and expression from another book of the Bible, or occasionally a vertical parallel from another location within the same book. The related texts are usually parallels not as close as synoptic parallels, including some from the Pentateuch or from Psalms or a prophetic text.

There are many texts in both Chronicles and Samuel–Kings which have no synoptic parallel, and it is very useful to read and study those texts as reflective of the peculiar vision or concern of the text in which it appears; these are often called "nonsynoptic sections." When a nonsynoptic section of Chronicles appears, that text is spread horizontally across the entire (three column) page. If the nonsynoptic section is in Samuel–Kings, then that text spreads horizontally across two columns of the page, beginning one-third of the space from the left margin.

5.3c   *Horizontal Parallels*

Horizontal parallels allow different versions of the same text to be observed and studied side by side. In this work, primary (or lead) texts appear in the left column, with parallels in the two columns to the right.

5.3d   *Vertical Parallels*

Vertical parallels are those which occur within the same book, when a text or motif reappears. Such parallels provide extremely useful data for describing the narrative genius in a text; these prove especially helpful for study of the composition and tradition history of Samuel and Kings. Occasionally they are provided either in a second or third column entry; one can easily identify them, because they will come from a different location (chapter and verse) within the same text; where possible, they appear synoptically.

6. *Using the Synoptic Parallels*

When dealing with a specific passage within the Chronicler's History or the Deuteronomistic History the reader should first consult the appropriate Index of Parallel Passages to learn its assigned number, title, and location. Note that chapter and verse numeration in this book always accords with the Hebrew Massoretic Text, and not according to the standard English versions in use today. In passages where the verse and/or chapter numbers differ, both sets of numbers will be indicated in the content title. For example: 296 **The Descendants of Levi** 1 Chr 5:27–6:15H (6:1-30E) shows that the first set of numbers refer to the Hebrew verse numbers, while the numbers in parentheses refer to the verse numbers in many English Bibles.

> **H**: Hebrew verse numbers
>
> **E**: English verse numbers

7. *Synoptic Parallels and Old Testament Studies*

Studying similar passages together leads one to ask various questions. Why does the text appear more than once? What are the differences in wording or tone or context? Did the author copy another source? Did each author hear the same (or similar) oral tradition of a narrative or poem? Should we ignore the differences? Could these variations in texts teach us something important about the authors, their writing styles and theologies?

Biblical scholars ask many of these synoptic questions about texts, eventually transforming them into particular methods of investigating biblical texts. The following review suggests a number of ways in which study of synoptic parallels assists biblical study and research.

7.1 *Source Criticism*

Source criticism grew out of attempts to appreciate the literary qualities of biblical texts. Early biblical interpreters often studied the elements and structure of texts to discern the author's intentions and artistry. Beginning with Richard Simon in the seventeenth century and continuing through Julius Wellhausen's works in the nineteenth century, Old Testament scholars gradually joined together their literary observations with hypotheses about the historical location and setting of various biblical sources in the Pentateuch. Their literary observations were used to demonstrate how our present biblical texts reflect underlying traditions or sources, which could hypothetically be dated (according to century) or localized (Israel or Judah).

> **Source criticism**: study of a text or document to discover what sources its author utilized

By comparing two versions of a similar passage within the same book (e.g., Gen 1:1–2:4a/2:4b-24) one can observe shifts or differences in content, vocabulary, tone, and structure. In turn, the patterns in which these variations occur might be explained by the hypothesis of different sources/traditions which have been brought together in the composition of this text. Synoptic viewing of parallel texts by students facilitates a process which often seemed arcane and reserved to specialists.

7.2 *Historical Criticism*

Historical critics attempt either to describe how and whether events and situations narrated in the biblical text "really happened" and the historical setting and circumstances of the document itself. Different versions of the "same" event may raise questions about the point of view of an author or redactor. When multiple versions of a story exist, one could compare the different parallel versions in order to observe more historical details than any single version contains. For example, many nineteenth-century

> **Historical criticism**: study of document to determine its historical setting, the time and place of persons and events mentioned in a text

scholars combed the accounts in 1–2 Chronicles in order to supplement their knowledge of the history of pre-exilic Israel.

7.3 *Redaction Criticism*

> **Redaction criticism**: attempt to learn how an author used and/or rewrote an earlier tradition or source, and what ideology or theology can be revealed by the process of redaction

Redaction criticism relies on parallel passages in at least two ways. First, observing recurring parallels throughout a single document might reveal aspects of the editor's framework or outline of the text; such observations led to Martin Noth's hypothesis of the Deuteronomistic History and also help to characterize the peculiar ideology and theology of the Chronicler's History. Second, by comparing two or more versions of a passage one can discern differences in their points of view, whether socio-political, ideological, or theological. If one judges that one version is older than the other, it is possible then to suggest how the "authors" of each version differed in their outlooks. In the case of Chronicles, which was probably written after the completion of Samuel–Kings, students can discuss the peculiar ideology, theology and historical viewpoint of the Chronicler by undertaking a careful examination of both the continuities within Chronicles and also the similarities and differences that emerge in comparison with its synoptic parallels in the Deuteronomistic History.

7.4 *Form Criticism*

> **Form criticism**: study of literary genres or forms in a document to learn their function and setting in life

Comparing parallel passages through the lens of form criticism seems to help identify the elements usually found in a form or genre and to learn how Israel's literary genres or forms differ, develop and change; such variations could be regional or social differences, or they might represent change and development over a span of generations (e.g., a speech form in Kings compared with its parallel in Chronicles).

7.5 *Linguistic Scholarship*

> **Linguistic study**: study of the patterns of language in a text; can help to give relative dates and settings for some texts

Comparison of parallel texts occasionally manifests linguistic variations such as morphology, vocabulary, and syntax; many such differences can be observed when comparing passages in Chronicles with their counterparts in Samuel and Kings. Such observations help scholars to trace the development of the Hebrew language, a study which may contribute to the relative dating of various texts.

7.6 *Literary Criticism*

> **Literary criticism**: a study which focuses on the form, structure, rhetoric and artistry of a text in its present state

Synchronic study of biblical texts can benefit from use of synoptic parallels, for comparison of texts could manifest many aspects of the artistry of each text and its "author." In this type of study one studies carefully the internal parallels within the text, e.g., a rhetorical study of Chronicles.

7.7 *Text Criticism*

> **Text criticism**: study of texts or manuscripts to discern their history of change and development, and to reconstruct the most likely early wording of the text

Synoptic viewing of different versions of a text (e.g., Hebrew texts in the MT compared with the Greek and Latin versions) provides an elementary approach to the essential task of noticing differences; such variations in turn raise important questions, e.g., "What version retains the original or the earliest wording of the text? At what point can you describe a text as fixed and/or final?"

7.8 *Inner Biblical Exegesis*

> **Inner-biblical exegesis**: study of the reuse and interpretation of earlier biblical texts by later writings in the Bible

This approach to biblical studies focuses on exegetical developments discovered within the biblical text as we have received it, that is, within the canon of the Hebrew Bible. In this approach, some scholars have described Chronicles as a type of midrash on the books of Samuel and Kings. Others might view the different formulations of the covenant with David as it appears in 2 Samuel 7 and it is recalled in 1 Kings 11. An example of this approach to study appears in: Michael Fishbane, *Biblical Inter-*

pretation in Ancient Israel.[7] Fishbane discusses this phenomenon under the rubric of inner-biblical parallels, showing how Deuteronomic redactors reworked an older tradition.

8. *Abbreviations and Definitions*

Chronicler:

> The designation for the person who utilized sources close if not identical to those of the Deuteronomistic history, to update and modify Israel's historic traditions to meet the needs of the postexilic Jewish community.

Chronicler's History:

> The historical narrative as told only in 1–2 Chronicles. For a few scholars the title refers to the broader historical report given in Ezra and Nehemiah as well.

Chronistic History:

> The historical narrative contained in the books of 1–2 Chronicles, Ezra, and Nehemiah. The use of this term does not prejudge the separate question of the individual authorship of 1–2 Chronicles and Ezra/Nehemiah. Some scholars speak of three editorial levels to this history: CH 1 (ca. 520 B.C.E.); CH 2 (450 B.C.E.); and CH 3 (400 B.C.E.).

Deuteronomistic Historian:

> The person who collected Israel's historic traditions and who produced the historical narrative now contained in Deuteronomy, Joshua, Judges, Samuel, and Kings.

Deuteronomic:

> Term used to refer to the core stratum of the book of Deuteronomy, as opposed to the term "Deuteronomistic."

Deuteronomistic History:

> Term reserved for the larger history comprising the books Deuteronomy, Joshua, Judges, Samuel, and Kings. Many scholars use the sigla Dtr[1] and Dtr[2] to refer to a seventh-century B.C.E. and a later exilic edition of the Deuteronomistic history respectively.

Harmony:

> An arrangement of synoptic materials that smooths out the inconsistencies and contradictions between parallel text materials. The result is a more unified, consistent narrative stream of events; often the goal is to provide a far more comprehensive "historical" portrait of characters or events.

Kethib:

> An Aramaic notation which means "written," as in the MT. Occasionally, one might decide to follow (to read) the Kethib even though the Massoretes had suggested reading an alternative word or phrase (Qere).

LXX*:*

> Designation for the Greek version of the Old Testament/Hebrew Bible called the Septuagint.

MS/MSS:

> Abbreviation for manuscript/manuscripts, that is, a handwritten document or documents.

MT:

> Abbreviation for the Massoretic text, the primary text tradition of the Hebrew Bible upon which contemporary translations of the Old Testament are based.

Pericope:

> Literally, something cut out; a discrete unit of discourse, comparable to a paragraph or stanza.

Qere:

> A marginal note in a rabbinic (Massoretic) Bible which indicates that a word written (Kethib) in the Hebrew text should be read (Qere) in this way.

Synopsis:

> An arrangement of parallel text material that exhibits all parts or divisions of the subject from a comprehensive point of view, e.g., the text of 1–2 Chronicles can be viewed together with all its parallels, mostly from 2 Samuel and 1–2 Kings. Example: Vannutelli, *Libri Synoptici Veteris Testamenti* (1934). This synopsis attempts to respect the literary integrity of each book/text.

Synopticist:

> A person who prepares a volume of synoptic parallels.

---

[1] The United Bible Society has provided for its translators of the Old Testament a listing of section units. Cf. The United Bible Societies' *Helps for Translators.* Vol. IV. *Section Headings and Reference System for the Bible,* ed. Robert G. Bratcher. *Part I. Section Headings for the Old Testament* (London: United Bible Societies, 1961).

[2] Otto Eissfeldt's position represents this approach (*The Old Testament: An Introduction,* trans. P. R. Ackroyd; New York: Harper & Row Publishers, 1965, pp. 241–301).

[3] Martin Noth, *The Deuteronomistic History,* Journal for the Study of the Old Testament Supplement Series, 15 (Sheffield, England: JSOT Press, 1981).

[4] Vannutelli reproduces the Hebrew text of: R. Kittel, *Biblia Hebraica* (Lipsiae: 1905–06); the Greek text is taken from: Swete, *The Old Testament in Greek* (Cambridge, 1905–09).

[5] Pauline Viviano, in a report for the Hebrew Bible Seminar, detected the following inconsistencies in Vannutelli's schema:

> Though he follows the text of Chr in sequence, he deviates from this procedure at no. 49, David's genealogy found in 1 Chr 3:4. This is inserted between 1 Chr 11:1-3, David being declared king (no. 48), and 1 Chr 11:4-9, the taking of Jerusalem (no. 50). Again nos. 55 and 56 interrupt the sequence of Chr, here 1 Chr 14:1-2. No. 55 is from 1 Chr 3:1-4, the children born to David in Hebron. No. 56 is a parallel of three texts, 2 Sam 5:13-16, 1 Chr 14:3-7, and 1 Chr 3:5-9, the children born to David in Jerusalem. In both these instances Vannutelli abandons the order of the Chronicles text, and follows instead the order of 2 Samuel. At 2 Chronicles 12 Vannutelli puts vv. 13-14 first, then follows with vv. 1-14. At no. 207, Sennacherib's invasion of Judah, he parallels 2 Chr 32:1-12 in order, but then inserts v. 18, then later inserts v. 15. When he presents 2 Chr 13 he will skip vv. 18 and 15. 2 Chr 34:1-2 is followed by vv. 18-21. Vv. 3-7 have been relocated and are found after vv. 29-33. 2 Chr 36:18 appears after vv. 20-21. In each case it seems that Vannutelli wants to coordinate these texts with the sequence of Kings and so the sequence of Chr has been abandoned in favor of another text.

[6] The following texts are not printed in Vannutelli's edition: 1 Chr 1:1–9:44; 27:24–34; 23:1-26, 28. 1 Samuel 1–30; 2 Sam 11:6–12:25; 13:1–22:10. 1 Kgs 13:1-34; 15:25–16:34; 17:1–21:29. 2 Kgs 1:1-18; 2:1-25; 4:1-8, 15; 9:1-13; 9:30–10:11; 10:15-36; 13:1-25; 15:8-31; 18:9-31. (Cf. Kegler and Augustin, *Synopse,* pp. 1–2).

[7] Michael Fishbane, *Biblical Interpretation in Ancient Israel* (Oxford: Clarendon Press, 1985).

Genealogies

282 The Descendants of Adam
1 Chron 1:1-4 // Gen 5:1-32

1 Chronicles 1

1 Adam,

Seth,

Enosh;

2 Kenan,

Mahalalel,

Jared;

Genesis 5

1 This is the list of the descendants of Adam. When God created humankind, he made them in the likeness of God.

2 Male and female he created them, and he blessed them and named them "Humankind" when they were created.

3 When Adam had lived one hundred thirty years, he became the father of a son in his likeness, according to his image, and named him Seth.

4 The days of Adam after he became the father of Seth were eight hundred years; and he had other sons and daughters.

5 Thus all the days that Adam lived were nine hundred thirty years; and he died.

6 When Seth had lived one hundred five years, he became the father of Enosh.

7 Seth lived after the birth of Enosh eight hundred seven years, and had other sons and daughters.

8 Thus all the days of Seth were nine hundred twelve years; and he died.

9 When Enosh had lived ninety years, he became the father of Kenan.

10 Enosh lived after the birth of Kenan eight hundred fifteen years, and had other sons and daughters.

11 Thus all the days of Enosh were nine hundred five years; and he died.

12 When Kenan had lived seventy years, he became the father of Mahalalel.

13 Kenan lived after the birth of Mahalalel eight hundred and forty years, and had other sons and daughters.

14 Thus all the days of Kenan were nine hundred and ten years; and he died.

15 When Mahalalel had lived sixty-five years, he became the father of Jared.

16 Mahalalel lived after the birth of Jared eight hundred thirty years, and had other sons and daughters.

17 Thus all the days of Mahalalel were eight hundred ninety-five years; and he died.

18 When Jared had lived one hundred sixty-two years he became the father of Enoch.

19 Jared lived after the birth of Enoch eight hundred years, and had other sons and daughters.

20 Thus all the days of Jared were nine hundred sixty-two years; and he died.

3 Enoch,

21 When Enoch had lived sixty-five years, he became the father of Methuselah.

22 Enoch walked with God after the birth of Methuselah three hundred years, and had other sons and daughters.

23 Thus all the days of Enoch were three hundred sixty-five years.

24 Enoch walked with God; then he was no more, because God took him.

Methuselah,

25 When Methuselah had lived one hundred eighty-seven years, he became the father of Lamech.

26 Methuselah lived after the birth of Lamech seven hundred eighty-two years, and had other sons and daughters.

27 Thus all the days of Methuselah were nine hundred sixty-nine years; and he died.

Lamech;

28 When Lamech had lived one hundred eighty-two years, he became the father of a son;

4 Noah,

29 he named him Noah, saying, "Out of the ground that YHWH has cursed this one shall bring us relief from our work and from the toil of our hands."

30 Lamech lived after the birth of Noah five hundred ninety-five years, and had other sons and daughters.

31 Thus all the days of Lamech were seven hundred seventy-seven years; and he died.

Shem, Ham, and Japheth.

32 After Noah was five hundred years old, Noah became the father of Shem, Ham, and Japheth.

283 The Descendants of the Sons of Noah
1 Chron 1:5-23 // Gen 10:1-32

1 Chronicles 1

Genesis 10

1 These are the descendants of Noah's sons, Shem, Ham, and Japheth; children were born to them after the flood.

5 The descendants of Japheth: Gomer, Magog, Madai, Javan, Tubal, Meshech, and Tiras.

6 The descendants of Gomer: Ashkenaz, Diphath, and Togarmah.

7 The descendants of Javan: Elishah, Tarshish, Kittim, and Rodanim.

8 The descendants of Ham: Cush, Egypt, Put, and Canaan.

9 The descendants of Cush: Seba, Havilah, Sabta, Raama, and Sabteca. The descendants of Raamah: Sheba and Dedan.

10 Cush became the father of Nimrod; he was the first to be a mighty one on the earth.

11 Egypt became the father of Ludim, Anamim, Lehabim, Naphtuhim,

12 Pathrusim, Casluhim, and Caphtorim, from whom the Philistines come.

13 Canaan became the father of Sidon his firstborn, and Heth,

14 and the Jebusites, the Amorites, the Girgashites,

15 the Hivites, the Arkites, the Sinites,

16 the Arvadites, the Zemarites, and the Hamathites.

---

2 The descendants of Japheth: Gomer, Magog, Madai, Javan, Tubal, Meshech, and Tiras.

3 The descendants of Gomer: Ashkenaz, Riphath, and Togarmah.

4 The descendants of Javan: Elishah, Tarshish, Kittim, and Rodanim.

5 From these the coastland peoples spread. These are the descendants of Japheth in their lands, with their own language, by their families, in their nations.

6 The descendants of Ham: Cush, Egypt, Put, and Canaan.

7 The descendants of Cush: Seba, Havilah, Sabtah, Raamah, and Sabteca. The descendants of Raamah: Sheba and Dedan.

8 Cush became the father of Nimrod; he was the first on earth to become a mighty warrior.

9 He was a mighty hunter before YHWH; therefore it is said, "Like Nimrod a mighty hunter before YHWH."

10 The beginning of his kingdom was Babel, Erech, and Accad, all of them in the land of Shinar.

11 From that land he went into Assyria, and built Nineveh, Rehoboth-Ir, Calah, and

12 Resen between Nineveh and Calah; that is the great city.

13 Egypt became the father of Ludim, Anamim, Lehabim, Naphtuhim,

14 Pathrusim, Casluhim, and Caphtorim, from *whom* the Philistines come.

15 Canaan became the father of Sidon his firstborn, and Heth,

16 and the Jebusites, the Amorites, the Girgashites,

17 the Hivites, the Arkites, the Sinites,

18 the Arvadites, the Zemarites, and the Hamathites. Afterward the families of the Canaanites spread abroad.

19 And the territory of the Canaanites extended from Sidon, in the direction of Gerar, as far as Gaza, and in

the direction of Sodom, Gomorrah, Admah, and Zeboiim, as far as Lasha.

20 These are the descendants of Ham, by their families, their languages, their lands, and their nations.

21 To Shem also, the father of all the children of Eber, the elder brother of Japheth, children were born.

17 The descendants of Shem: Elam, Asshur, Arpachshad, Lud, Aram, Uz, Hul, Gether, and Meshech.

22 The descendants of Shem: Elam, Asshur, Arpachshad, Lud, and Aram.

23 The descendants of Aram: Uz, Hul, Gether, and Mash.

18 Arpachshad became the father of Shelah; and Shelah became the father of Eber.

24 Arpachshad became the father of Shelah; and Shelah became the father of Eber.

19 To Eber were born two sons: the name of the one was Peleg, for in his days the earth was divided, and *his brother's name was Joktan.*

25 To Eber were born two sons: the name of the one was Peleg, for in his days the earth was divided, and his brother's name was Joktan.

20 Joktan became the father of Almodad, Sheleph, Hazarmaveth, Jerah,

26 Joktan became the father of Almodad, Sheleph, Hazarmaveth, Jerah,

21 Hadoram, Uzal, Diklah,

27 Hadoram, Uzal, Diklah,

22 Ebal, Abimael, Sheba,

28 Obal, Abimael, Sheba,

23 Ophir, Havilah, and Jobab; all these were the descendants of Joktan.

29 Ophir, Havilah, and Jobab; all these were the descendants of Joktan.

30 The territory in which they lived extended from Mesha in the direction of Sephar, the hill country of the east.

31 These are the descendants of Shem, by their families, their languages, their lands, and their nations.

32 These are the families of Noah's sons, according to their genealogies, in their nations; and from these the nations spread abroad on the earth after the flood.

284 The Descendants of Shem
1 Chron 1:24-27 // Gen 11:10-32

1 Chronicles 1	*Genesis 11:10-32*
24 Shem,	10 These are the descendants of Shem. When Shem was one hundred years old, he became the father of Arpachshad two years after the flood;
	11 and Shem lived after the birth of Arpachshad five hundred years, and had other sons and daughters.
Arpachshad,	12 When Arpachshad had lived thirty-five years, he became the father of Shelah;
	13 and Arpachshad lived after the birth of Shelah four hundred three years, and had other sons and daughters.
Shelah;	14 When Shelah had lived thirty years, he became the father of Eber;
	15 and Shelah lived after the birth of Eber four hundred three years, and had other sons and daughters.
25 Eber,	16 When Eber had lived thirty-four years, he became the father of Peleg;
	17 and Eber lived after the birth of Peleg four hundred thirty years, and had other sons and daughters.
Peleg,	18 When Peleg had lived thirty years, he became the father of Reu;
	19 and Peleg lived after the birth of Reu two hundred nine years, and had other sons and daughters.
Reu;	20 When Reu had lived thirty-two years, he became the father of Serug;
	21 and Reu lived after the birth of Serug two hundred seven years, and had other sons and daughters.
26 Serug,	22 When Serug had lived thirty years, he became the father of Nahor;
	23 and Serug lived after the birth of Nahor two hundred years, and had other sons and daughters.
Nahor,	24 When Nahor had lived twenty-nine years, he became the father of Terah;
	25 and Nahor lived after the birth of Terah one hundred nineteen years, and had other sons and daughters.
Terah;	26 When Terah had lived seventy years, he became the father of Abram, Nahor, and Haran.
27 Abram, that is, Abraham.	27 Now these are the descendants of Terah. Terah was the father of Abram, Nahor, and Haran; and Haran was the father of Lot.

28 Haran died before his father Terah in the land of his birth, in Ur of the Chaldeans.

29 Abram and Nahor took wives; the name of Abram's wife was Sarai, and the name of Nahor's wife was Milcah. She was the daughter of Haran the father of Milcah and Iscah.

30 Now Sarai was barren; she had no child.

31 Terah took his son Abram and his grandson Lot son of Haran, and his daughter-in-law Sarai, his son Abram's wife, and they went out together from Ur of the Chaldeans to go into the land of Canaan; but when they came to Haran, they settled there.

32 The days of Terah were two hundred five years; and Terah died in Haran.

285 The Descendants of Ishmael and Keturah
1 Chron 1:28-33 // Gen 25:1-6, 12-18

1 Chronicles 1

28 The sons of Abraham: Isaac and Ishmael.

29 These are their genealogies: the firstborn of Ishmael, Nebaioth; and Kedar, Adbeel, Mibsam,

30 Mishma, Dumah, Massa, Hadad, Tema,

31 Jetur, Naphish, and Kedemah.

These are the sons of Ishmael.

32 The sons of Keturah, Abraham's concubine:

she bore Zimran, Jokshan, Medan, Midian, Ishbak, and Shuah.

The sons of Jokshan: Sheba and Dedan.

33 The sons of Midian: Ephah, Epher, Hanoch, Abida, and Eldaah. All these were the *children* of Keturah.

Genesis 25

12 These are the descendants of Ishmael, Abraham's son, whom Hagar the Egyptian, Sarah's slave-girl, bore to Abraham.

13 These are the names of the sons of Ishmael, named in the order of their birth: Nebaioth, the firstborn of Ishmael; and Kedar, Adbeel, Mibsam,

14 Mishma, Dumah, Massa,

15 Hadad, Tema, Jetur, Naphish, and Kedemah.

16 These are the sons of Ishmael and these are their names, by their villages and by their encampments, twelve princes according to their tribes.

[1 Abraham took another wife, whose name was Keturah.

2 She bore him Zimran, Jokshan, Medan, Midian, Ishbak, and Shuah.

3 Jokshan was the father of Sheba and Dedan. The sons of Dedan were Asshurim, Letushim, and Leummim.

4 The sons of Midian were Ephah, Epher, Hanoch, Abida, and Eldaah. All these were the children of Keturah.

5 Abraham gave all he had to Isaac.

6 But to the sons of his concubines Abraham gave gifts, while he was still living, and he sent them away from his son Isaac, eastward to the east country.]

17 (This is the length of the life of Ishmael, one hundred thirty-seven years; he breathed his last and died, and was gathered to his people.)

18 They settled from Havilah to Shur, which is opposite Egypt in the direction of Assyria; he settled down alongside of all his people.

286 The Descendants of Esau
1 Chron 1:34-54 // Gen 36:1-43

1 Chronicles 1

34 Abraham became the father of Isaac. The sons of Isaac: Esau and Israel.

35 The sons of Esau: Eliphaz, Reuel, Jeush, Jalam, and Korah.

Genesis 36

1 These are the descendants of Esau (that is, Edom).

2 Esau took his wives from the Canaanites: Adah daughter of Elon the Hittite, Oholibamah daughter of Anah son of Zibeon the Hivite,

3 and Basemath, Ishmael's daughter, sister of Nebaioth.

4 Adah bore Eliphaz to Esau; Basemath bore Reuel;

5 and Oholibamah bore Jeush, Jalam, and Korah. These are the sons of Esau who were born to him in the land of Canaan.

6 Then Esau took his wives, his sons, his daughters, and all the members of his household, his cattle, all his livestock, and all the property he had acquired in the land of Canaan; and he moved to a land *away* from his brother Jacob.

7 For their possessions were too great for them to live together; the land where they were staying could not support them because of their livestock.

8 So Esau settled in the hill country of Seir; Esau is Edom.

9 These are the descendants of Esau, *father of Edom,* in the hill country of Seir.

10 These are the names of Esau's sons: Eliphaz son of Adah the wife of Esau; Reuel, the son of Esau's wife Basemath.

36 The sons of Eliphaz: Teman, Omar, Zephi, Gatam, Kenaz, Timna, and Amalek.

37 The sons of Reuel: Nahath, Zerah, Shammah, and Mizzah.

38 The sons of Seir: Lotan, Shobal, Zibeon, Anah,

Dishon, Ezer, and Dishan.

39 The sons of Lotan: Hori and Homam; and Lotan's sister was Timna.

40 The sons of Shobal: Alian, Manahath, Ebal, Shephi, and Onam.

The sons of Zibeon: Aiah and Anah.

41 The sons of Anah: Dishon.

The sons of Dishon: Hamran, Eshban, Ithran, and Cheran.

42 The sons of Ezer: Bilhan, Zaavan, and Jaakan.

11 The sons of Eliphaz were Teman, Omar, Zepho, Gatam, and Kenaz.

12 (Timna was a concubine of Eliphaz, Esau's son; she bore Amalek to Eliphaz.) These were the sons of Adah, Esau's wife.

13 These were the sons of Reuel: Nahath, Zerah, Shammah, and Mizzah. These were the sons of Esau's wife, Basemath.

14 These were the sons of Esau's wife Oholibamah, daughter of Anah son of Zibeon: she bore to Esau Jeush, Jalam, and Korah.

15 These are the clans of the sons of Esau. The sons of Eliphaz the firstborn of Esau: the clans Teman, Omar, Zepho, Kenaz,

16 Korah, Gatam, and Amalek; these are the clans of Eliphaz in the land of Edom; they are the sons of Adah.

17 These are the sons of Esau's son Reuel: the clans Nahath, Zerah, Shammah, and Mizzah; these are the clans of Reuel in the land of Edom; they are the sons of Esau's wife Basemath.

18 These are the sons of Esau's wife Oholibamah: the clans Jeush, Jalam, and Korah; these are the clans born of Esau's wife Oholibamah, the daughter of Anah.

19 These are the sons of Esau (that is, Edom), and these are their clans.

20 These are the sons of Seir the Horite, the inhabitants of the land: Lotan, Shobal, Zibeon, Anah,

21 Dishon, Ezer, and Dishan; these are the clans of the Horites, the sons of Seir in the land of Edom.

22 The sons of Lotan were Hori and Heman; and Lotan's sister was Timna.

23 These are the sons of Shobal: Alvan, Manahath, Ebal, Shepho, and Onam.

24 These are the sons of Zibeon: Aiah and Anah; he is the Anah who found the springs in the wilderness, as he pastured the donkeys of his father Zibeon.

25 These are the *sons* of Anah: Dishon and Oholibamah daughter of Anah.

26 These are the sons of Dishon: Hemdan, Eshban, Ithran, and Cheran.

27 These are the sons of Ezer: Bilhan, Zaavan, and Akan.

The sons of Dishan: Uz and Aran.

28 These are the sons of Dishan: Uz and Aran.

29 These are the clans of the Horites: the clans Lotan, Shobal, Zibeon, Anah,

30 Dishon, Ezer, and Dishan; these are the clans of the Horites, clan by clan in the land of Seir.

43 These are the kings who reigned in the land of Edom before any king reigned over the Israelites:

31 These are the kings who reigned in the land of Edom, before any king reigned over the Israelites.

Bela son of Beor, whose city was called Dinhabah.

32 Bela son of Beor reigned in Edom, the name of his city being Dinhabah.

44 When Bela died, Jobab son of Zerah of Bozrah succeeded him *as king.*

33 *When* Bela died, Jobab son of Zerah of Bozrah succeeded him as king.

45 When Jobab died, Husham of the land of the Temanites succeeded him as king.

34 *When* Jobab died, Husham of the land of the Temanites succeeded him as king.

46 When Husham died, Hadad son of Bedad, who defeated Midian in the country of Moab, succeeded him *as king;* the name of his city was Avith.

35 *When* Husham died, Hadad son of Bedad, who defeated Midian in the country of Moab, succeeded him as king; the name of his city *was* Avith.

47 When Hadad died, Samlah of Masrekah succeeded him *as king.*

36 *When* Hadad died, Samlah of Masrekah succeeded him as king.

48 When Samlah died, Shaul of Rehoboth on the Euphrates succeeded him *as king.*

37 *When* Samlah died, Shaul of Rehoboth on the Euphrates succeeded him as king.

49 When Shaul died, Baal-hanan son of Achbor succeeded him *as king.*

38 *When* Shaul died, Baal-hanan son of Achbor succeeded him as king.

50 When Baal-hanan died, Hadad succeeded him *as king;* the name of his city was Pai, and his wife's name Mehetabel daughter of Matred, daughter of Me-zahab.

39 *When* Baal-hanan son of Achbor died, Hadar succeeded him as king; the name of his city *was* Pau; his wife's name was Mehetabel, the daughter of Matred, daughter of Me-zahab.

51 And Hadad died. The clans of Edom were: clans Timna, Aliah, Jetheth,

40 These are the names of the clans of Esau, according to their families and their localities by their names: the clans Timna, Alvah, Jetheth,

52 Oholibamah, Elah, Pinon,

41 Oholibamah, Elah, Pinon,

53 Kenaz, Teman, Mibzar,

42 Kenaz, Teman, Mibzar,

54 Magdiel, and Iram; these are the clans of Edom.

43 Magdiel, and Iram; these are the clans of Edom (that is, Esau, the father of Edom), according to their settlements in the land that they *possessed.*

287 The Descendants of Israel
1 Chron 2:1-2 // Gen 35:22b-26; Exod 1:1-6

1 Chronicles	*Genesis 35*	*Exodus 1*
1 These are the sons of Israel:	22 While Israel lived in that land, Reuben went and lay with Bilhah his father's concubine; and Israel heard of it. Now the sons of Jacob were twelve.	1 These are the names of the sons of Israel who came to Egypt with Jacob, each with his household:
Reuben, Simeon, Levi, Judah, Issachar, Zebulun,	23 The sons of Leah: Reuben (Jacob's firstborn), Simeon, Levi, Judah, Issachar, and Zebulun.	2 Reuben, Simeon, Levi and Judah,
		3 Issachar, Zebulun, and Benjamin,
2 Dan, Joseph, Benjamin,	24 The sons of Rachel: Joseph and Benjamin.	
Naphtali,	25 The sons of Bilhah, Rachel's maid: Dan and Naphtali.	4 Dan and Naphtali, Gad and Asher.
Gad, and Asher.	26 The sons of Zilpah, Leah's maid: Gad and Asher. These were the sons of Jacob who were born to him in Paddan-aram.	
		5 The total number of people born to Jacob was seventy. Joseph was already in Egypt.
		6 Then Joseph died, and all his brothers, and that whole generation.

288 The Descendants of Judah
1 Chron 2:3-55 // Gen 38:1-7, 29b-30 // Gen 46:12 // Num 26:19-22; Jos 7:1
// 1 Kings 4:31E // 1 Sam 16:1-13 // 2 Sam 2:18a; 17:25 // Ruth 4:18-22

1 Chronicles 2	*Genesis 38*	*Genesis 46*
3 The sons of Judah:	1 It happened at that time that Judah went down from his brothers and *pitched his tent and made camp* near a certain Adullamite *man* whose name was Hirah.	12a The children of Judah: Er, Onan, Shelah, Perez, and Zerah (but Er and Onan died in the land of Canaan);
	2 There Judah saw the daughter of a Canaanite *man* whose name was Shua; he married her and went in to her.	

Er,

Onan,

and Shelah; these three the Canaanite woman Bath-shua bore to him.

Now Er, Judah's firstborn, was wicked in the sight of YHWH, and he put him to death.

4 His daughter-in-law Tamar also bore him Perez and Zerah. Judah had five sons in all.

5 The sons of Perez: Hezron and Hamul.

6 The sons of Zerah: Zimri, Ethan, Heman, Calcol, and Dara, five in all.

7 The sons of Carmi: Achar, the troubler of Israel, who transgressed in the matter of the devoted thing;

---

3 She conceived and bore a son; and he named him Er.

4 Again she conceived and bore a son whom she named Onan.

5 Yet again she bore a son, and she named him Shelah. She was in Chezib when she bore him.

6 Judah took a wife for Er his first-born; her name was Tamar.

7 But Er, Judah's firstborn, was wicked in the sight of YHWH, and YHWH put him to death.

Genesis 38
29 But just then he drew back his hand, and out came his brother; and she said, "What a breach you have made for yourself!" Therefore he was named Perez.

30 Afterward his brother came out with the crimson thread on his hand; and he was named Zerah.

Genesis 46
12b and the *sons* of Perez were Hezron and Hamul

1 Kings 5 [4:31 English]
11 For he was wiser than all humankind, [wiser] than Ethan the Ezrahite, and Heman, Calcol, and Darda, the sons of Mahol; and his name was in all the nations round about.

Joshua 7
1 But the Israelites broke faith in regard to the devoted things: Achan son of Carmi son of Zabdi son of Zerah, of the tribe of Judah, took some of the devoted things; and the anger of YHWH burned against the Israelites.

Numbers 26
19 The sons of Judah: Er

and Onan; Er and Onan died in the land of Canaan.

20 The descendants of Judah by their clans were: of Shelah, the clan of the Shelanites;

of Perez, the clan of the Perezites; of Zerah, the clan of the Zerahites.

21 The *sons* of Perez were: of Hezron, the clan of the Hezronites; of Hamul, the clan of the Hamulites.

22 These are the clans of Judah: the number of those enrolled was seventy-six thousand five hundred.

8 and Ethan's son was Azariah.

Ruth 4
18 Now these are the descendants of Perez: Perez became the father of Hezron,

9 The sons of Hezron, who were born to him: Jerahmeel, Ram, and Chelubai.

19 Hezron of Ram, Ram of Amminadab,

10 Ram became the father of Amminadab, and Amminadab became the father of Nahshon, prince of the sons of Judah.

20 Amminadab of Nahshon, Nahshon of Salmon,

Extended material about Jesse

11 Nahshon became the father of Salma, Salma of Boaz,

21 Salmon of Boaz, Boaz of Obed,

1 Samuel 16
1 YHWH said to Samuel, "How long will you lament for Saul, while I myself have rejected him from reigning over Israel? Fill your horn with oil and go. I will send you to Jesse of Bethlehem, for I have seen a king for me among his sons."

12 Boaz of Obed, Obed of Jesse.

22 Obed of Jesse, and Jesse of David.

13 Jesse became the father of Eliab his firstborn, Abinadab the second, Shimea the third,

14 Nethanel the fourth, Raddai the fifth,

2 Samuel said, "How can I go? Saul will hear and kill me." YHWH said, "Take in your possession a calf of the herd and say, 'I am going to sacrifice to YHWH.'

15 Ozem the sixth, David the seventh;

3 You will invite Jesse at the sacrifice, and I myself will make known to you what you should do. You will anoint for me the one about whom I have been telling you."

2 Samuel 2
18 Now the three sons of Zeruiah were there, Joab, Abishai, and Asahel, with Asahel as swift of foot as one of the gazelles that are in the open field.

16 and their sisters were Zeruiah and Abigail. The sons of Zeruiah: Abishai, Joab, and Asahel, three.

4 Samuel did what YHWH had spoken and went to Bethlehem. The elders of the city trembled to meet him, and they said, "Peace at your coming."

2 Samuel 17
25 Now Absalom had set Amasa over the army in the place of Joab. Amasa was the son of a man named Ithra the Ishmaelite, who had gone into Abigal daughter of Nahash, sister of Zeruiah, mother of Joab.

17 Abigail bore Amasa, and the father of Amasa was Jether the Ishmaelite.

5 He said, "Peace! I have come to sacrifice to YHWH. Sanctify yourselves and come with me for the sacrifice." He sanctified Jesse and his sons and he invited them to the sacrifice.

18 Caleb son of Hezron had children by his wife Azubah, and by Jerioth; these were her sons: Jesher, Shobab, and Ardon.

6 When they came, he saw Eliab. He said, "YHWH's anointed is indeed before him."

19 When Azubah died, Caleb married Ephrath, who bore him Hur.

20 Hur became the father of Uri, and Uri became the father of Bezalel.

21 Afterward Hezron went in to the daughter of Machir father of Gilead, whom he married when he was sixty years old; and she bore him Segub;

22 and Segub became the father of Jair, who had twenty-three towns in the land of Gilead.

23 But Geshur and Aram took from them Havvoth-jair, Kenath and its villages, sixty towns. All these were descendants of Machir, father of Gilead.

24 After the death of Hezron, in Caleb-ephrathah, Abijah wife of Hezron bore him Ashhur, father of Tekoa.

25 The sons of Jerahmeel, the first-born of Hezron: Ram his firstborn, Bunah, Oren, Ozem, and Ahijah.

26 Jerahmeel also had another wife, whose name was Atarah; she was the mother of Onam.

27 The sons of Ram, the firstborn of Jerahmeel: Maaz, Jamin, and Eker.

28 The sons of Onam: Shammai and Jada. The sons of Shammai: Nadab and Abishur.

29 The name of Abishur's wife was Abihail, and she bore him Ahban and Molid.

30 The sons of Nadab: Seled and Appaim; and Seled died childless.

31 The son of Appaim: Ishi. The son of Ishi: Sheshan. The son of Sheshan: Ahlai.

32 The sons of Jada, Shammai's brother: Jether and Jonathan; and Jether died childless.

7 YHWH said to Samuel, "Do not look at his appearance or at the height of his stature, for I have rejected him. For it is not the one whom a person sees, since a person sees according to the eyes, but YHWH sees according to the heart."

8 Jesse called to Abinadab and had him pass in front of Samuel. He said, "YHWH has not chosen this one either."

9 Jesse had Shammah pass by, and he said, "YHWH has not chosen this one either."

10 Jesse had seven of his sons pass before Samuel, but Samuel said to Jesse, "YHWH has not chosen these."

11 Samuel said to Jesse, "Have you finished (showing me) the boys?" and he said, "Only the youngest remains, but, see, he is tending the flock." Samuel said to Jesse, "Send and take him, for we will not turn aside until he comes here."

12 He sent and brought him: he was ruddy, with beautiful eyes and a good appearance. YHWH said, "Arise, anoint him, for this is he."

13 Samuel took the horn of oil and anointed him in the midst of his brothers, and the spirit of YHWH fell upon David from that day forward. Then Samuel arose and went to Ramah.

33 The sons of Jonathan: Peleth and Zaza. These were the descendants of Jerahmeel.

34 Now Sheshan had no sons, only daughters; but Sheshan had an Egyptian slave, whose name was Jarha.

35 So Sheshan gave his daughter in marriage to his slave Jarha; and she bore him Attai.

36 Attai became the father of Nathan, and Nathan of Zabad.

37 Zabad became the father of Ephlal, and Ephlal of Obed.

38 Obed became the father of Jehu, and Jehu of Azariah.

39 Azariah became the father of Helez, and Helez of Eleasah.

40 Eleasah became the father of Sismai, and Sismai of Shallum.

41 Shallum became the father of Jekamiah, and Jekamiah of Elishama.

42 The sons of Caleb brother of Jerahmeel: Mesha his firstborn, who was father of Ziph. The sons of Mareshah father of Hebron.

43 The sons of Hebron: Korah, Tappuah, Rekem, and Shema.

44 Shema became father of Raham, father of Jorkeam; and Rekem became the father of Shammai.

45 The son of Shammai: Maon; and Maon was the father of Beth-zur.

46 Ephah also, Caleb's concubine, bore Haran, Moza, and Gazez; and Haran became the father of Gazez.

47 The sons of Jahdai: Regem, Jotham, Geshan, Pelet, Ephah, and Shaaph.

48 Maacah, Caleb's concubine,
bore Sheber and Tirhanah.

49 She also bore Shaaph father of
Madmannah, Sheva father of
Machbenah and father of Gibea; and
the daughter of Caleb was Achsah.

50 These were the descendants of
Caleb. The sons of Hur the firstborn
of Ephrathah: Shobal father of
Kiriath-jearim,

51 Salma father of Bethlehem, and
Hareph father of Beth-gader.

52 Shobal father of Kiriath-jearim
had other sons: Haroeh, half of the
Menuhoth.

53 And the families of Kiriath-
jearim: the Ithrites, the Puthites, the
Shumathites, and the Mishraites;
from these came the Zorathites and
the Eshtaolites.

54 The sons of Salma: Bethlehem,
the Netophathites, Atroth-beth-joab,
and half of the Manahathites, the
Zorites.

55 The families also of the scribes
that lived at Jabez: the Tirathites,
the Shimeathites, and the Sucathites.
These are the Kenites who came
from Hammath, father of the house
of Rechab.

289 The Descendants of David
1 Chron 3:1-9 // 2 Sam 3:2-5; 5:5; 5:13-16; 13:1; 1 Chron 14:3-7

1 Chronicles 3

1 These are the sons of David who were born to him in
Hebron: the firstborn Amnon, by Ahinoam the Jezreelite;

the second Daniel, by Abigail the Carmelite;

2 Samuel 3

2 Sons were born to David at Hebron: his firstborn was
Amnon, of Ahinoam the Jezreelitess;

3 his second, Chileab, of Abigail[1] the wife of Nabal the
Carmelite;

2 the third Absalom, son of Maacah, daughter of King Talmai of Geshur;

the fourth Adonijah, son of Haggith;

3 the fifth Shephatiah, by Abital;

the sixth Ithream, by his wife Eglah;

4 six were born to him in Hebron, where he reigned for seven years and six months. And he reigned thirty-three years in Jerusalem.

5 These were born to him in Jerusalem: Shimea, Shobab, Nathan, and Solomon, four by Bath-shua, daughter of Ammiel;

6 then Ibhar, Elishama, Eliphelet,

7 Nogah, Nepheg, Japhia,

8 Elishama, Eliada, and Eliphelet, nine.

9 All these were David's sons, besides the sons of the concubines; and Tamar was their sister.

and the third, Absalom son of Maacah, daughter of Talmai, king of Geshur;

4 and the fourth, Adonijah son of Haggith;

and the fifth, Shephatiah son of Abital;

5 and the sixth, Ithream *by* Eglah, wife of David. These were born to David in Hebron.

2 Samuel 5
5 At Hebron he reigned over Judah seven years and six months; and at Jerusalem he reigned over all Israel and Judah thirty-three years.

2 Samuel 5
13 David took more concubines and wives from Jerusalem, after he had come from Hebron; and more sons and daughters were born to David.

14 These are the names of those born to him in Jerusalem: Shammua, Shobab, Nathan, Solomon,

15 Ibhar, Elishua, Nepheg, Japhia,

16 Elishama, Eliada, and Eliphelet.

Other Parallels to David's Children
2 Samuel 13
1 Sometime afterward this happened: Absalom son of David had a beautiful sister and her name was Tamar; and Amnon son of David was in love with her.

1 Chronicles 14
3 David took more wives in Jerusalem, and David fathered more sons and daughters.

4 These are the names of the children which he had in Jerusalem: Shammua, Shobab, and Nathan; Solomon,

5 Ibhar, Elishua, and Elpelet;

6 Nogah, Nepheg, and Japhia;

7 Elishama, Beeliada, and Eliphelet.

---

[1] Reading the Qere.

290 The Descendants of Solomon
1 Chron 3:10-24 // Ezra 3:2; Hag 1:1

1 Chronicles 3

10 The descendants of Solomon: Rehoboam, Abijah his son, Asa his son, Jehoshaphat his son,

11 Joram his son, Ahaziah his son, Joash his son,

12 Amaziah his son, Azariah his son, Jotham his son,

13 Ahaz his son, Hezekiah his son, Manasseh his son,

14 Amon his son, Josiah his son.

15 The sons of Josiah: Johanan the firstborn, the second Jehoiakim, the third Zedekiah, the fourth Shallum.

16 The descendants of Jehoiakim: Jeconiah his son, Zedekiah his son;

17 and the sons of Jeconiah, the captive: Shealtiel his son,

18 Malchiram, Pedaiah, Shenazzar, Jekamiah, Hoshama, and Nedabiah;

19 The sons of Pedaiah: Zerubbabel and Shimei; and the sons of Zerubbabel: Meshullam and Hananiah, and Shelomith was their sister;

20 and Hashubah, Ohel, Berechiah, Hasadiah, and Jushab-hesed, five.

21 The sons of Hananiah: Pelatiah and Jeshaiah, his son Rephaiah, his son Arnan, his son Obadiah, his son Shecaniah.

22 The son of Shecaniah: Shemaiah. And the sons of Shemaiah: Hattush, Igal, Bariah, Neariah, and Shaphat, six.

23 The sons of Neariah: Elioenai, Hizkiah, and Azrikam, three.

24 The sons of Elioenai: Hodaviah, Eliashib, Pelaiah, Akkub, Johanan, Delaiah, and Anani, seven.

Parallels to Shealtiel

Ezra 3
2 *Then Jeshua son of Jozadak rose up with his brother priests and Zerubbabel son of Shealtiel and his brothers, and they built the altar of the God of Israel, to offer upon it burnt offerings, as written in the Torah of Moses the man of God.*

Haggai 1
1 In the second year of King Darius, in the sixth month, on the first day of the month, the word of YHWH came by the prophet Haggai to Zerubbabel son of Shealtiel, governor of Judah, and to Joshua son of Jehozadak, the high priest:

291 The Descendants of Judah
1 Chron 4:1-23 // Josh 15:17; Judg 1:13; Num 13:6

1 Chronicles 4

1 The sons of Judah: Perez, Hezron, Carmi, Hur, and Shobal.

2 Reaiah son of Shobal became the father of Jahath, and Jahath became the father of Ahumai and Lahad. These were the families of the Zorathites.

3 These were the sons of Etam: Jezreel, Ishma, and Idbash; and the name of their sister was Hazzelelponi,

4 and Penuel was the father of Gedor, and Ezer the father of Hushah. These were the sons of Hur, the first-born of Ephrathah, the father of Bethlehem.

5 Ashhur father of Tekoa had two wives, Helah and Naarah;

6 Naarah bore him Ahuzzam, Hepher, Temeni, and Haahashtari. These were the sons of Naarah.

7 The sons of Helah: Zereth, Izhar, and Ethnan.

8 Koz became the father of Anub, Zobebah, and the families of Aharhel son of Harum.

9 Jabez was honored more than his brothers; and his mother named him Jabez, saying, "Because I bore him in pain."

10 Jabez called on the God of Israel, saying, "Oh that you would bless me and enlarge my border, and that your hand might be with me, and that you would keep me from hurt and harm!" And God granted what he asked.

11 Chelub the brother of Shuhah became the father of Mehir, who was the father of Eshton.

12 Eshton became the father of Beth-rapha, Paseah, and Tehinnah the father of Irnahash. These are the men of Recah.

13 The sons of Kenaz: Othniel and Seraiah; and the sons of Othniel: Hathath and Meonothai.

Joshua 15

17 Othniel son of Kenaz, the brother of Caleb, took it; and he gave him his daughter Achsah as wife.

Judges 1

13 And Othniel son of Kenaz, Caleb's younger brother, took it; and he gave him his daughter Achsah as wife.

14 Meonothai became the father of Ophrah; and Seraiah became the father of Joab father of Ge-harashim,
so-called because they were artisans.

15 The sons of Caleb son of Jephunneh: Iru, Elah, and
Naam; and the son of Elah: Kenaz.

16 The sons of Jehallelel: Ziph, Ziphah, Tiria, and Asarel.

17 The sons of Ezrah: Jether, Mered, Epher, and Jalon.
These are the sons of Bithiah, daughter of Pharaoh,
whom Mered married; and she conceived and bore
Miriam, Shammai, and Ishbah father of Eshtemoa.

18 And his Judean wife bore Jered father of Gedor,
Heber father of Soco, and Jekuthiel father of Zanoah.

19 The sons of the wife of Hodiah, the sister of
Naham, were the fathers of Keilah the Garmite and
Eshtemoa the Maacathite.

20 The sons of Shimon: Amnon, Rinnah, Ben-hanan,
and Tilon. The sons of Ishi: Zoheth and Ben-zoheth.

21 The sons of Shelah son of Judah: Er father of
Lecah, Laadah father of Mareshah, and the families of
the guild of linen workers at Beth-ashbea;

22 and Jokim, and the men of Cozeba, and Joash, and
Saraph, who married into Moab but returned to Lehem
(now the records are ancient).

23 These were the potters and inhabitants of Netaim and
Gederah; they lived there with the king in his service.

Numbers 13

6 from the tribe of Judah, Caleb son of Jephunneh;

292 The Descendants of Simeon
1 Chron 4:24-43 // Jos 15:20-32, 42-44; Neh 11:25-30; Jos 19:1-9; Gen 46:10; Exod 6:15; Num 26:12-14

1 Chronicles 4

24 The sons of Simeon: Nemuel,
Jamin, Jarib, Zerah, Shaul;

25 Shallum was his son, Mibsam
his son, Mishma his son.

26 The sons of Mishma: Hammuel
his son, Zaccur his son, Shimei his
son.

Genesis 46

10 The *sons* of Simeon: Jemuel,
Jamin, Ohad, Jachin, Zohar, and
Shaul, the son of a Canaanite
woman.

Exodus 6

15 The sons of Simeon: Jemuel,
Jamin, Ohad, Jachin, Zohar, and
Shaul, the son of a Canaanite
woman; these are the families of
Simeon.

27 Shimei had sixteen sons and six daughters; but his brothers did not have many children, nor did all their family multiply like the Judeans.

28 They lived in Beer-sheba, Moladah, Hazar-shual,

29 Bilhah, Ezem, Tolad,

30 Bethuel, Hormah, Ziklag,

31 Beth-marcaboth, Hazar-susim, Beth-biri, and Shaaraim. These were their towns until David became king.

32 And their villages were Etam, Ain, Rimmon, Tochen, and Ashan, five towns,

33 along with all their villages that were around these towns as far as Baal. These were their settlements. And they kept a genealogical record.

34 Meshobab, Jamlech, Joshah son of Amaziah,

Joshua 19

1 The second lot came out for Simeon, for the tribe of Simeon, according to its families; its inheritance lay within the inheritance of the tribe of Judah.

2 It had for its inheritance Beer-sheba, Sheba, Moladah,

3 Hazar-shual, Balah, Ezem,

4 Eltolad, Bethul, Hormah,

5 Ziklag, Beth-marcaboth, Hazar-susah,

6 Beth-lebaoth, and Sharuhen—thirteen towns with their villages;

7 Ain, Rimmon, Ether, and Ashan—four towns with their villages;

8 together with all the villages all around these towns as far as Baalath-beer, Ramah of the Negeb. This was the inheritance of the tribe of Simeon according to its families.

9 The inheritance of the tribe of Simeon formed part of the territory of Judah; because the portion of the tribe of Judah was too large for them, the tribe of Simeon obtained an inheritance within their inheritance.

Secondary Parallels

Nehemiah 11

25 And as for the villages, with their fields, some of the people of Judah lived in Kiriath-arba and its villages, and in Dibon and its villages, and in Jekabzeel and its villages,

26 and in Jeshua and in Moladah and Beth-pelet,

27 in Hazar-shual, in Beer-sheba and its villages,

28 in Ziklag, in Meconah and its villages,

29 in En-rimmon, in Zorah, in Jarmuth,

30 Zanoah, Adullam, and their villages, Lachish and its fields, and Azekah and its villages. So they camped from Beer-sheba to the valley of Hinnom.

Joshua 15

20 This is the inheritance of the tribe of the people of Judah according to their families.

21 The towns belonging to the tribe of the people of Judah in the extreme South, toward the boundary of Edom, were Kabzeel, Eder, Jagur,

22 Kinah, Dimonah, Adadah,

23 Kedesh, Hazor, Ithnan,

24 Ziph, Telem, Bealoth,

25 Hazor-hadattah, Kerioth-hezron (that is, Hazor),

35 Joel, Jehu son of Joshibiah son
of Seraiah son of Asiel,

36 Elioenai, Jaakobah, Jeshohaiah,
Asaiah, Adiel, Jesimiel, Benaiah,

37 Ziza son of Shiphi son of Allon
son of Jedaiah son of Shimri son of
Shemaiah—

38 these mentioned by name were
leaders in their families, and their
clans increased greatly.

39 They journeyed to the entrance
of Gedor, to the east side of the valley, to seek pasture for their flocks,

40 where they found rich, good pasture, and the land was very broad,
quiet, and peaceful; for the former
inhabitants there belonged to Ham.

41 These, registered by name, came
in the days of King Hezekiah of
Judah, and attacked their tents and
the Meunim who were found there,
and exterminated them to this day,
and settled in their place, because
there was pasture there for their
flocks.

42 And some of them, five hundred
men of the Simeonites, went to
Mount Seir, having as their leaders
Pelatiah, Neariah, Rephaiah, and
Uzziel, sons of Ishi;

43 they destroyed the remnant of
the Amalekites that had escaped,
and they have lived there to this day.

26 Amam, Shema, Moladah,

27 Hazar-gaddah, Heshmon, Beth-
pelet,

28 Hazar-shual, Beer-sheba,
Biziothiah,

29 Baalah, Iim, Ezem,

30 Eltolad, Chesil, Hormah,

31 Ziklag, Madmannah, Sansannah,

32 Lebaoth, Shilhim, Ain, and
Rimmon: in all, twenty-nine towns,
with their villages.

33 And in the Lowland, Eshtaol,
Zorah, Ashnah,

34 Zanoah, En-gannim, Tappuah,
Enam,

35 Jarmuth, Adullam, Socoh,
Azekah,

36 Shaaraim, Adithaim, Gederah,
Gederothaim: fourteen towns with
their villages.

37 Zenan, Hadashah, Migdal-gad,

38 Dilan, Mizpeh, Jokthe-el,

39 Lachish, Bozkath, Eglon,

40 Cabbon, Lahmam, Chitlish,

41 Gederoth, Beth-dagon, Naamah,
and Makkedah: sixteen towns with
their villages.

42 Libnah, Ether, Ashan,

43 Iphtah, Ashnah, Nezib,

44 Keilah, Achzib, and Mareshah:
nine towns with their villages.

Numbers 26
12 The descendants of Simeon by
their clans: of Nemuel, the clan of

the Nemuelites; of Jamin, the clan of the Jaminites; of Jachin, the clan of the Jachinites;

13 of Zerah, the clan of the Zerahites; of Shaul, the clan of the Shaulites.

14 These are the clans of the Simeonites, twenty-two thousand two hundred.

293 The Descendants of Reuben
1 Chron 5:1-10 // Gen 35:22; 46:8b-9; Exod 6:14; Num 26:5-11

1 Chronicles 5

1 The sons of Reuben the firstborn of Israel. (He was the firstborn, but because he defiled his father's bed his birthright was given to the sons of Joseph son of Israel, so that he is not enrolled in the genealogy according to the birthright;

2 though Judah became prominent among his brothers and a ruler came from him, yet the birthright belonged to Joseph.)

3 The sons of Reuben, the firstborn of Israel: Hanoch, Pallu, Hezron, and Carmi.

4 The sons of Joel: Shemaiah his son, Gog his son, Shimei his son,

5 Micah his son, Reaiah his son, Baal his son,

6 Beerah his son, whom King Tilgath-pilneser of Assyria carried away into exile; he was a chieftain of the Reubenites.

7 And his kindred by their families, when the genealogy of their generations was reckoned: the chief, Jeiel, and Zechariah,

Genesis 35

22 While Israel lived in that land, Reuben went and lay with Bilhah his father's concubine; and Israel heard of it. Now the sons of Jacob were twelve.

Genesis 46
8 Now these are the names of the Israelites, Jacob and his offspring, who came to Egypt. Reuben, Jacob's firstborn,

9 and the children of Reuben: Hanoch, Pallu, Hezron, and Carmi.

Exodus 6

14 The following are the heads of their ancestral houses: the sons of Reuben, the firstborn of Israel: Hanoch, Pallu, Hezron, and Carmi; these are the families of Reuben.

Numbers 26
5 Reuben, the firstborn of Israel.

The descendants of Reuben: of Hanoch, the clan of the Hanochites; of Pallu, the clan of the Palluites;

6 of Hezron, the clan of the Hezronites; of Carmi, the clan of the Carmites.

7 These are the clans of the Reubenites; the number of those enrolled was forty-three thousand seven hundred thirty.

8 And the descendants of Pallu: Eliab.

9 The descendants of Eliab: Nemuel, Dathan, and Abiram. These are the same Dathan and Abiram,

8 and Bela son of Azaz, son of Shema, son of Joel, who lived in Aroer, as far as Nebo and Baal-meon.

9 He also lived to the east as far as the beginning of the desert this side of the Euphrates, because their cattle had multiplied in the land of Gilead.

10 And in the days of Saul they made war on the Hagrites, who fell by their hand; and they lived in their tents throughout all the region east of Gilead.

chosen from the congregation, who rebelled against Moses and Aaron in the company of Korah, when they rebelled against YHWH.

10 *The* earth opened its mouth and swallowed them up along with Korah, when that company died, when the fire devoured two hundred *and* fifty men; and they became a warning.

11 *But* the sons of Korah did not die.

294 The Descendants of Gad
1 Chron 5:11-17 // Gen 46:16; Num 26:15-18

1 Chronicles 5

11 The sons of Gad lived beside them in the land of Bashan as far as Salecah:

12 Joel the chief, Shapham the second, Janai, and Shaphat in Bashan.

13 And their kindred according to their clans: Michael, Meshullam, Sheba, Jorai, Jacan, Zia, and Eber, seven.

14 These were the sons of Abihail son of Huri, son of Jaroah, son of Gilead, son of Michael, son of Jeshishai, son of Jahdo, son of Buz;

15 Ahi son of Abdiel, son of Guni, was chief in their clan;

16 and they lived in Gilead, in Bashan and in its towns, and in all the pasture lands of Sharon to their limits.

17 All of these were enrolled by genealogies in the days of King Jotham of Judah, and in the days of King Jeroboam of Israel.

Genesis 46

16 The *sons* of Gad: Ziphion, Haggi, Shuni, Ezbon, Eri, Arodi, and Areli.

Numbers 26
15 The *sons* of Gad by their clans: of Zephon, the clan of the Zephonites; of Haggi, the clan of the Haggites; of Shuni, the clan of the Shunites;

16 of Ozni, the clan of the Oznites; of Eri, the clan of the Erites;

17 of Arod, the clan of the Arodites; of Areli, the clan of the Arelites.

18 These are the clans of the Gadites: the number of those enrolled was forty thousand five hundred.

295 History of the Two and a Half Tribes
1 Chron 5:18-26 // 2 Kings 15:19-20; 17:6; 18:11-12

1 Chronicles 5

18 The Reubenites, the Gadites, and the half-tribe of Manasseh had valiant warriors, who carried shield and sword, and drew the bow, expert in war, forty-four thousand seven hundred sixty, ready for service.

19 They made war on the Hagrites, Jetur, Naphish, and Nodab;

20 and when they received help against them, the Hagrites and all who were with them were given into their hands, for they cried to God in the battle, and he granted their entreaty because they trusted in him.

21 They captured their livestock: fifty thousand of their camels, two hundred fifty thousand sheep, two thousand donkeys, and one hundred thousand captives.

22 Many fell slain, because the war was of God. And they lived in their territory until the exile.

23 The members of the half-tribe of Manasseh lived in the land; they were very numerous from Bashan to Baal-hermon, Senir, and Mount Hermon.

24 These were the heads of their clans: Epher, Ishi, Eliel, Azriel, Jeremiah, Hodaviah, and Jahdiel, mighty warriors, famous men, heads of their clans.

25 But they transgressed against the God of their ancestors, and prostituted themselves to the gods of the peoples of the land, whom God had destroyed before them.

26 So the God of Israel stirred up the spirit of King Pul of Assyria, the spirit of King Tilgath-pilneser of Assyria, and he carried them away, namely, the Reubenites, the Gadites, and the half-tribe of Manasseh, and brought them to Halah, Habor, Hara, and the river Gozan, to this day.

Parallels to 1 Chron 5:26, King Pul of Assyria

2 Kings 15
19 Pul king of Assyria came against the land; and Menahem gave to Pul one thousand talents of silver that his hand might be with him to strengthen his hold on the kingdom.

20 So Menahem laid the silver-[tax] on Israel, on all the men of substance, [who had] to give to the king of Assyria fifty shekels of silver for each man. Then the king of Assyria turned back and did not stay there in the land.

2 Kings 17
6 In the ninth year of Hoshea the king of Assyria took Samaria and exiled Israel to Assyria. He settled them in Halah, on the Habor, the river of Gozan, and [in] the cities of the Medes.

2 Kings 18
11 The king of Assyria exiled Israel to Assyria, resettled them down in Halah, and on the Habor, the river of Gozan and [in] the cities of the Medes,

12 because they had not listened to the voice of YHWH their God, but had transgressed his covenant; all that Moses the servant of YHWH had commanded they did not listen to and they did not do.

296 The Descendants of Levi
1 Chron 5:27–6:15H (6:1-30E) // Gen 46:11; Exod 6:16-25; Num 3:17-20; 26:57-62; 1 Sam 8:1-2

1 Chronicles 5 [H] 1 Chron 5:27-41=[1 Chron 6:1-15E]

27/6:1 The sons of Levi: Gershom, Kohath, and Merari.

28/6:2 The sons of Kohath: Amram, Izhar, Hebron, and Uzziel.

29/6:3 The children of Amram: Aaron, Moses, and Miriam.

The sons of Aaron: Nadab, Abihu, Eleazar, and Ithamar.
30/6:4 Eleazar became the father of Phinehas, Phinehas of Abishua,

31/6:5 Abishua of Bukki, Bukki of Uzzi,

32/6:6 Uzzi of Zerahiah, Zerahiah of Meraioth,

33/6:7 Meraioth of Amariah, Amariah of Ahitub,

34/6:8 Ahitub of Zadok, Zadok of Ahimaaz,

35/6:9 Ahimaaz of Azariah, Azariah of Johanan,

Genesis 46

11 The *sons* of Levi: Gershon, Kohath, and Merari.

Exodus 6
16 The following are the names of the sons of Levi according to their genealogies: Gershon, Kohath, and Merari, and the length of Levi's life was one hundred thirty-seven years.

17 The sons of Gershon: Libni and Shimei, by their families.

18 The sons of Kohath: Amram, Izhar, Hebron, and Uzziel, and the length of Kohath's life was one hundred thirty-three years.

19 The sons of Merari: Mahli and Mushi. These are the families of the Levites according to their genealogies.

20 Amram married Jochebed his father's sister and she bore him Aaron and Moses, and the length of Amram's life was one hundred thirty-seven years.

21 The sons of Izhar: Korah, Nepheg, and Zichri.

22 The sons of Uzziel: Mishael, Elzaphan, and Sithri.

23 Aaron married Elisheba, daughter of Amminadab and sister of Nahshon, and she bore him Nadab, Abihu, Eleazar, and Ithamar.

24 The sons of Korah: Assir, Elkanah, and Abiasaph; these are the families of the Korahites.

25 Aaron's son Eleazar married one of the daughters of Putiel, and she bore him Phinehas.

36/6:10 and Johanan of Azariah (it was he who served as priest in the house that Solomon built in Jerusalem).

37/6:11 Azariah became the father of Amariah, Amariah of Ahitub,

38/6:12 Ahitub of Zadok, Zadok of Shallum,

39/6:13 Shallum of Hilkiah, Hilkiah of Azariah,

40/6:14 Azariah of Seraiah, Seraiah of Jehozadak;

41/6:15 and Jehozadak went into exile when YHWH sent Judah and Jerusalem into exile by the hand of Nebuchadnezzar.

1 Chronicles 6

1 The sons of Levi: Gershom, Kohath, and Merari.

2 These are the names of the sons of Gershom: Libni and Shimei.

3 The sons of Kohath: Amram, Izhar, Hebron, and Uzziel.

4 The sons of Merari: Mahli and Mushi. These are the clans of the Levites according to their ancestry.

5 Of Gershom: Libni his son, Jahath his son, Zimmah his son,

6 Joah his son, Iddo his son, Zerah his son, Jeatherai his son.

7 The sons of Kohath: Amminadab his son, Korah his son, Assir his son,

8 Elkanah his son, Ebiasaph his son, Assir his son,

9 Tahath his son, Uriel his son, Uzziah his son, and Shaul his son.

10 The sons of Elkanah: Amasai and Ahimoth,

11 Elkanah his son, Zophai his son, Nahath his son,

12 Eliab his son, Jeroham his son, Elkanah his son.

13 The sons of Samuel: Joel his firstborn, the second Abijah.

14 The sons of Merari: Mahli, Libni his son, Shimei his son, Uzzah his son,

Numbers 3

17 The following were the sons of Levi, by their names: Gershon, Kohath, and Merari.

18 These are the names of the sons of Gershon by their clans: Libni and Shimei.

19 The sons of Kohath by their clans: Amram, Izhar, Hebron, and Uzziel.

20 The sons of Merari by their clans: Mahli and Mushi. These are the clans of the Levites, by their ancestral houses.

1 Samuel 8

1 When Samuel grew old, he set his sons as judges in Israel.

2 The name of his eldest son was Joel and the name of his second son was Abijah. They were judges in Beer-sheba.

15 Shimea his son, Haggiah his son, and Asaiah his son.

Numbers 26

57 This is the enrollment of the Levites by their clans: of Gershon, the clan of the Gershonites; of Kohath, the clan of the Kohathites; of Merari, the clan of the Merarites.

58 These are the clans of Levi: the clan of the Libnites, the clan of the Hebronites, the clan of the Mahlites, the clan of the Mushites, the clan of the Korahites. Now Kohath was the father of Amram.

59 The name of Amram's wife was Jochebed daughter of Levi, who was born to Levi in Egypt; and she bore to Amram: Aaron, Moses, and their sister Miriam.

60 To Aaron were born Nadab, Abihu, Eleazar, and Ithamar.

61 But Nadab and Abihu died when they offered illicit fire before YHWH.

62 The number of those enrolled was twenty-three thousand, every male one month old and up; for they were not enrolled among the Israelites because there was no allotment given to them among the Israelites.

297 The Temple Singers Appointed by David
1 Chron 6:16-33H (31-48E)

1 Chronicles 6

16/31 These are the men whom David put in charge of the service of song in the house of YHWH, after the ark came to rest there.

17/32 They ministered with song before the tabernacle of the tent of meeting, until Solomon had built the house of YHWH in Jerusalem; and they performed their service in due order.

18/33 These are the men who served; and their sons were: Of the Kohathites: Heman, the singer, son of Joel, son of Samuel,

19/34 son of Elkanah, son of Jeroham, son of Eliel, son of Toah,

20/35 son of Zuph, son of Elkanah, son of Mahath, son of Amasai,

21/36 son of Elkanah, son of Joel, son of Azariah, son of Zephaniah,

22/37 son of Tahath, son of Assir, son of Ebiasaph, son of Korah,

23/38   son of Izhar, son of Kohath, son of Levi, son of Israel;

24/39   and his brother Asaph, who stood on his right, namely, Asaph son of Berechiah, son of Shimea,

25/40   son of Michael, son of Baaseiah, son of Malchijah,

26/41   son of Ethni, son of Zerah, son of Adaiah,

27/42   son of Ethan, son of Zimmah, son of Shimei,

28/43   son of Jahath, son of Gershom, son of Levi.

29/44   On the left were their kindred the sons of Merari: Ethan son of Kishi, son of Abdi, son of Malluch,

30/45   son of Hashabiah, son of Amaziah, son of Hilkiah,

31/46   son of Amzi, son of Bani, son of Shemer,

32/47   son of Mahli, son of Mushi, son of Merari, son of Levi;

33/48   and their kindred the Levites were appointed for all the service of the tabernacle of the house of God.

298 The Descendants of Aaron
1 Chron 6:34-38H (6:49-53E) // 1 Chron 5:29; Num 3:2-4, 17-20

1 Chronicles 6

34/49   But Aaron and his sons made offerings on the altar of burnt offering and on the altar of incense, doing all the work of the most holy place, to make atonement for Israel, according to all that Moses the servant of God had commanded.

35/50   These are the sons of Aaron: Eleazar his son, Phinehas his son, Abishua his son,

36/51   Bukki his son, Uzzi his son, Zerahiah his son,

37/52   Meraioth his son, Amariah his son, Ahitub his son,

38/53   Zadok his son, Ahimaaz his son.

1 Chronicles 5

29   The children of Amram: Aaron, Moses, and Miriam. The sons of Aaron: Nadab, Abihu, Eleazar, and Ithamar.

Numbers 3

2   These are the names of the sons of Aaron: Nadab the firstborn, and Abihu, Eleazar, and Ithamar;

3   These are the names of the sons of Aaron, the anointed priests, whom he ordained to minister as priests.

4   Nadab and Abihu died before YHWH when they offered illicit fire before YHWH in the *desert* of Sinai, and they had no children. Eleazar and Ithamar served as priests *before Aaron their father.* . . .

17   The following were the sons of Levi, by their names: Gershon, Kohath, and Merari.

18 These are the names of the sons of Gershon by their clans: Libni and Shimei.

19 The sons of Kohath by their clans: Amram, Izhar, Hebron, and Uzziel.

20 The sons of Merari by their clans: Mahli and Mushi. These are the clans of the Levites, by their ancestral houses.

299 The Cities of the Levites
1 Chron 6:39-66 (54-80E) // Josh 21:1-42

1 Chronicles 6

39/54 These are their dwelling places according to their settlements within their borders:

to the sons of Aaron of the families of Kohathites—for the lot fell to them first—

40/55 to them they gave Hebron in the land of Judah and its surrounding pasture lands,

41/56 but the fields of the city and its villages they gave to Caleb son of Jephunneh.

Joshua 21

1 Then the heads of the families of the Levites came to the priest Eleazar and to Joshua son of Nun and to the heads of the families of the tribes of the Israelites;

2 they said to them at Shiloh in the land of Canaan, "YHWH commanded through Moses that we be given towns to live in, along with their pasture lands for our livestock."

3 So by command of YHWH the Israelites gave to the Levites the following towns and pasture lands out of their inheritance.

4 The lot came out for the families of the Kohathites. So those Levites who were descendants of Aaron the priest received by lot thirteen towns from the tribes of Judah, Simeon, and Benjamin.

[10 which went to the descendants of Aaron, one of the families of the Kohathites who belonged to the Levites, since the lot fell to them first.

11 They gave them Kiriath-arba (Arba being the father of Anak), that is Hebron, in the hill country of Judah, along with the pasture lands around it.

12 But the fields of the town and its villages had been given to Caleb son of Jephunneh as his holding.

13 To the descendants of Aaron the priest they gave Hebron, the city of refuge for the slayer, with its pasture lands, Libnah with its pasture lands,

42/57 To the sons of Aaron they gave the cities of refuge: Hebron, Libnah with its pasture lands, Jattir, Eshtemoa with its pasture lands,

43/58 Hilen with its pasture lands, Debir with its pasture lands,

44/59 Ashan with its pasture lands, and Beth-shemesh with its pasture lands.

45/60 From the tribe of Benjamin, Geba with its pasture lands, Alemeth with its pasture lands, and Anathoth with its pasture lands. All their towns throughout their families were thirteen.

46/61 To the rest of the Kohathites were given by lot out of the family of the tribe, out of the half-tribe, the half of Manasseh, ten towns.

47/62 To the Gershomites according to their families were allotted thirteen towns out of the tribes of Issachar, Asher, Naphtali, and Manasseh in Bashan.

48/63 To the Merarites according to their families were allotted twelve towns out of the tribes of Reuben, Gad, and Zebulun.

49/64 So the people of Israel gave the Levites the towns with their pasture lands.

50/65 They also gave them by lot out of the tribes of Judah, Simeon, and Benjamin these towns that are mentioned by name.

51/66 And some of the families of the sons of Kohath had towns of their territory out of the tribe of Ephraim.

52/67 They were given the cities of refuge: Shechem with its pasture lands in the hill country of Ephraim, Gezer with its pasture lands,

53/68 Jokmeam with its pasture lands, Beth-horon with its pasture lands,

14 Jattir with its pasture lands, Eshtemoa with its pasture lands,

15 Holon with its pasture lands, Debir with its pasture lands,

16 Ain with its pasture lands, Juttah with its pasture lands, and Beth-shemesh with its pasture lands—nine towns out of these two tribes.

17 Out of the tribe of Benjamin: Gibeon with its pasture lands, Geba with its pasture lands,

18 Anathoth with its pasture lands, and Almon with its pasture lands—four towns.

19 The towns of the descendants of Aaron—the priests—were thirteen in all, with their pasture lands.]

5 The rest of the Kohathites received by lot ten towns from the families of the tribe of Ephraim, from the tribe of Dan, and the half-tribe of Manasseh.

6 The Gershonites received by lot thirteen towns from the families of the tribe of Issachar, from the tribe of Asher, from the tribe of Naphtali, and from the half-tribe of Manasseh in Bashan.

7 The Merarites according to their families received twelve towns from the tribe of Reuben, the tribe of Gad, and the tribe of Zebulun.

8 These towns and their pasture lands the Israelites gave by lot to the Levites, as YHWH had commanded through Moses.

9 Out of the tribe of Judah and the tribe of Simeon they gave the following towns mentioned by name,

20 As to the rest of the Kohathites belonging to the Kohathite families of the Levites, the towns allotted to them were out of the tribe of Ephraim.

21 To them were given Shechem, the city of refuge for the slayer, with its pasture lands in the hill country of Ephraim, Gezer with its pasture lands,

22 Kibzaim with its pasture lands, and Beth-horon with its pasture lands—four towns.

54/69 Aijalon with its pasture lands, Gath-rimmon with its pasture lands;

55/70 and out of the half-tribe of Manasseh, Aner with its pasture lands, and Bileam with its pasture lands, for the rest of the families of the Kohathites.

56/71 To the Gershomites: out of the half-tribe of Manasseh: Golan in Bashan with its pasture lands and Ashtaroth with its pasture lands;

57/72 and out of the tribe of Issachar: Kedesh with its pasture lands, Daberath with its pasture lands,

58/73 Ramoth with its pasture lands, and Anem with its pasture lands;

59/74 out of the tribe of Asher: Mashal with its pasture lands, Abdon with its pasture lands,

60/75 Hukok with its pasture lands, and Rehob with its pasture lands;

61/76 and out of the tribe of Naphtali: Kedesh in Galilee with its pasture lands, Hammon with its pasture lands, and Kiriathaim with its pasture lands.

62/77 To the rest of the Merarites out of the tribe of Zebulun: Rimmono with its pasture lands, Tabor with its pasture lands,

63/78 and across the Jordan from Jericho, on the east side of the Jordan, out of the tribe of Reuben: Bezer in the steppe with its pasture lands, Jahzah with its pasture lands,

64/79 Kedemoth with its pasture lands, and Mephaath with its pasture lands;

23 Out of the tribe of Dan: Elteke with its pasture lands, Gibbethon with its pasture lands,

24 Aijalon with its pasture lands, Gath-rimmon with its pasture lands—four towns.

25 Out of the half-tribe of Manasseh: Taanach with its pasture lands, and Gath-rimmon with its pasture lands—two towns.

26 The towns of the families of the rest of the Kohathites were ten in all, with their pasture lands.

27 To the Gershonites, one of the families of the Levites, were given out of the half-tribe of Manasseh, Golan in Bashan with its pasture lands, the city of refuge for the slayer, and Beeshterah with its pasture lands—two towns.

28 Out of the tribe of Issachar: Kishion with its pasture lands, Daberath with its pasture lands,

29 Jarmuth with its pasture lands, En-gannim with its pasture lands—four towns;

30 Out of the tribe of Asher: Mishal with its pasture lands, Abdon with its pasture lands,

31 Helkath with its pasture lands, and Rehob with its pasture lands—four towns.

32 Out of the tribe of Naphtali: Kedesh in Galilee with its pasture lands, the city of refuge for the slayer, Hammoth-dor with its pasture lands, and Kartan with its pasture lands—three towns.

33 The towns of the several families of the Gershonites were in all thirteen, with their pasture lands.

34 To the rest of the Levites—the Merarite families—were given out of the tribe of Zebulun: Jokneam with its pasture lands, Kartah with its pasture lands,

35 Dimnah with its pasture lands, Nahalal with its pasture lands—four towns.

36 Out of the tribe of Reuben: Bezer with its pasture lands, Jahzah with its pasture lands,

37 Kedemoth with its pasture lands, and Mephaath with its pasture lands—four towns.

65/80 and out of the tribe of Gad: Ramoth in Gilead with its pasture lands, Mahanaim with its pasture lands,

66/81 Heshbon with its pasture lands, and Jazer with its pasture lands.

38 Out of the tribe of Gad: Ramoth in Gilead with its pasture lands, the city of refuge for the slayer, Mahanaim with its pasture lands,

39 Heshbon with its pasture lands, Jazer with its pasture lands—four towns in all.

40 As for the towns of the several Merarite families, that is, the remainder of the families of the Levites, those allotted to them were twelve in all.

41 The towns of the Levites within the holdings of the Israelites were in all forty-eight towns with their pasture lands.

42 Each of these towns had its pasture lands around it; so it was with all these towns.

300 The Descendants of Issachar
1 Chron 7:1-5 // Gen 46:13; Num 26:23-25

1 Chronicles 7

1 The sons of Issachar: Tola, Puah, Jashub, and Shimron, four.

2 The sons of Tola: Uzzi, Rephaiah, Jeriel, Jahmai, Ibsam, and Shemuel, heads of their ancestral houses, namely of Tola, mighty warriors of their generations, their number in the days of David being twenty-two thousand six hundred.

3 The son of Uzzi: Izrahiah. And the sons of Izrahiah: Michael, Obadiah, Joel, and Isshiah, five, all of them chiefs;

4 and along with them, by their generations, according to their ancestral houses, were units of the fighting force, thirty-six thousand, for they had many wives and sons.

5 Their kindred belonging to all the families of Issachar were in all eighty-seven thousand mighty warriors, enrolled by genealogy.

Genesis 46

13 The *sons* of Issachar: Tola, Puvah, Jashub, and Shimron.

Numbers 26

23 The *sons* of Issachar by their clans: of Tola, the clan of the Tolaites; of Puvah, the clan of the Punites;

24 of Jashub, the clan of the Jashubites; of Shimron, the clan of the Shimronites.

25 These are the clans of Issachar: sixty-four thousand three hundred enrolled.

301 The Descendants of Benjamin
1 Chron 7:6-12 // 1 Chron 8:1-28; Gen 46:21; Num 26:38-41

1 Chronicles 7

6 The sons of Benjamin: Bela, Becher, and Jediael, three.

7 The sons of Bela: Ezbon, Uzzi, Uzziel, Jerimoth, and Iri, five, heads of ancestral houses, mighty warriors; and their enrollment by genealogies was twenty-two thousand thirty-four.

8 The sons of Becher: Zemirah, Joash, Eliezer, Elioenai, Omri, Jeremoth, Abijah, Anathoth, and Alemeth. All these were the sons of Becher;

9 and their enrollment by genealogies, according to their generations, as heads of their ancestral houses, mighty warriors, was twenty thousand two hundred.

10 The sons of Jediael: Bilhan. And the sons of Bilhan: Jeush, Benjamin, Ehud, Chenaanah, Zethan, Tarshish, and Ahishahar.

11 All these were the sons of Jediael according to the heads of their ancestral houses, mighty warriors, seventeen thousand two hundred, ready for service in war.

12 And Shuppim and Huppim were the sons of Ir, Hushim the son of Aher.

Genesis 46

21 The *sons* of Benjamin: Bela, Becher, Ashbel, Gera, Naaman, Ehi, Rosh, Muppim, Huppim, and Ard.

Numbers 26

38 The *sons* of Benjamin by their clans: of Bela, the clan of the Belaites; of Ashbel, the clan of the Ashbelites; of Ahiram, the clan of the Ahiramites;

39 of Shephupham, the clan of the Shuphamites; of Hupham, the clan of the Huphamites.

40 And the sons of Bela were Ard and Naaman: of Ard, the clan of the Ardites; of Naaman, the clan of the Naamites.

41 These are the *sons* of Benjamin by their clans; the number of those enrolled was forty-five thousand six hundred.

1 Chronicles 8

1 Benjamin became the father of Bela his firstborn, Ashbel the second, Aharah the third,

2 Nohah the fourth, and Rapha the fifth.

3 And Bela had sons: Addar, Gera, Abihud,

4 Abishua, Naaman, Ahoah,

5 Gera, Shephuphan, and Huram.

6 These are the sons of Ehud (they were heads of ancestral houses of the inhabitants of Geba, and they were carried into exile to Manahath):

7 Naaman, Ahijah, and Gera, that is, Heglam, who became the father of Uzza and Ahihud.

8 And Shaharaim had sons in the country of Moab after he had sent away his wives Hushim and Baara.

9 He had sons by his wife Hodesh: Jobab, Zibia, Mesha, Malcam,

10 Jeuz, Sachia, and Mirmah. These were his sons, heads of ancestral houses.

11 He also had sons by Hushim: Abitub and Elpaal.

12 The sons of Elpaal: Eber, Misham, and Shemed, who built Ono and Lod with its towns,

13 and Beriah and Shema (they were heads of ancestral houses of the inhabitants of Aijalon, who put to flight the inhabitants of Gath);

14 and Ahio, Shashak, and Jeremoth.

15 Zebadiah, Arad, Eder,

16 Michael, Ishpah, and Joha were sons of Beriah.

17 Zebadiah, Meshullam, Hizki, Heber,

18 Ishmerai, Izliah, and Jobab were the sons of Elpaal.

19 Jakim, Zichri, Zabdi,

20 Elienai, Zillethai, Eliel,

21 Adaiah, Beraiah, and Shimrath were the sons of Shimei.

22 Ishpan, Eber, Eliel,

23 Abdon, Zichri, Hanan,

24 Hananiah, Elam, Anthothijah,

25 Iphdeiah, and Penuel were the sons of Shashak.

26 Shamsherai, Shehariah, Athaliah,

27 Jaareshiah, Elijah, and Zichri were the sons of Jeroham.

28 These were the heads of ancestral houses, according to their generations, chiefs. These lived in Jerusalem.

302 The Descendants of Naphtali
1 Chron 7:13 // Gen 46:24; Num 26:48-50

1 Chronicles 7

13 The *sons* of Naphtali: Jahziel, Guni, Jezer, and Shallum, the descendants of Bilhah.

Genesis 46

24 The *sons* of Naphtali: Jahzeel, Guni, Jezer, and Shillem.

Numbers 26

48 The *sons* of Naphtali by their clans: of Jahzeel, the clan of the Jahzeelites; of Guni, the clan of the Gunites;

49 of Jezer, the clan of the Jezerites; of Shillem, the clan of the Shillemites.

50 These are the Naphtalites by their clans: the number of those enrolled was forty-five thousand four hundred.

303 The Descendants of Manasseh
1 Chron 7:14-19 // Num 26:29-34

1 Chronicles 7

14 The sons of Manasseh: Asriel, whom his Aramean concubine bore; she bore Machir the father of Gilead.

15 And Machir took a wife for Huppim and for Shuppim. The name of his sister was Maacah. And the name of the second was Zelophehad; and Zelophehad had daughters.

16 Maacah the wife of Machir bore a son, and she named him Peresh; the name of his brother was Sheresh; and his sons were Ulam and Rekem.

17 The son of Ulam: Bedan. These were the sons of Gilead son of Machir, son of Manasseh.

Numbers 26

29 The *sons* of Manasseh: of Machir, the clan of the Machirites; and Machir was the father of Gilead; of Gilead, the clan of the Gileadites.

[33 Now Zelophehad son of Hepher had no sons, but daughters: and the names of the daughters of Zelophehad were Mahlah, Noah, Hoglah, Milcah, and Tirzah.]

30 These are the *sons* of Gilead: of Iezer, the clan of the Iezerites; of Helek, the clan of the Helekites;

31 and of Asriel, the clan of the Asrielites; and of Shechem, the clan of the Shechemites;

32 and of Shemida, the clan of the Shemidaites; and of Hepher, the clan of the Hepherites.

18 And his sister Hammolecheth bore Ishhod, Abiezer, and Mahlah.

19 The sons of Shemida were Ahian, Shechem, Likhi, and Aniam.

34 These are the clans of Manasseh; the number of those enrolled was fifty-two thousand seven hundred.

304 The Descendants of Ephraim
1 Chron 7:20-29 // Num 26:35-37

1 Chronicles 7

20 The sons of Ephraim: Shuthelah, and Bered his son, Tahath his son, Eleadah his son, Tahath his son,

21 Zabad his son, Shuthelah his son, and Ezer and Elead. Now the people of Gath, who were born in the land, killed them, because they came down to raid their cattle.

22 And their father Ephraim mourned many days, and his brothers came to comfort him.

23 Ephraim went in to his wife, and she conceived and bore a son; and he named him Beriah, because disaster had befallen his house.

24 His daughter was Sheerah, who built both Lower and Upper Beth-horon, and Uzzen-sheerah.

25 Rephah was his son, Resheph his son, Telah his son, Tahan his son,

26 Ladan his son, Ammihud his son, Elishama his son,

27 Nun his son, Joshua his son.

28 Their possessions and settlements were Bethel and its towns, and eastward Naaran, and westward Gezer and its towns, Shechem and its towns, as far as Ayyah and its towns;

29 also along the borders of the Manassites, Beth-shean and its towns, Taanach and its towns, Megiddo and its towns, Dor and its towns. In these lived the sons of Joseph son of Israel.

Numbers 26

35 These are the *sons* of Ephraim according to their clans: of Shuthelah, the clan of the Shuthelahites; of Becher, the clan of the Becherites; of Tahan, the clan of the Tahanites.

36 And these are the *sons* of Shuthelah: of Eran, the clan of the Eranites.

37 These are the clans of the Ephraimites: the number of those enrolled was thirty-two thousand five hundred.

These are the *sons* of Joseph by their clans.

305 The Descendants of Asher
1 Chron 7:30-40 // Gen 46:17; Num 26:44-47

1 Chronicles 7

Numbers 26

Genesis 46

30 The sons of Asher: Imnah, Ishvah, Ishvi, Beriah, and their sister Serah.

44 The *sons* of Asher by their families: of Imnah, the clan of the Imnites; of Ishvi, the clan of the Ishvites; of Beriah, the clan of the Beriites.

[46 And the name of the daughter of Asher was Serah.]

17 The *sons* of Asher: Imnah, Ishvah, Ishvi, Beriah, and their sister Serah. The children of Beriah: Heber and Malchiel.

31 The sons of Beriah: Heber and Malchiel, who was the father of Birzaith.

45 Of the *sons* of Beriah: of Heber, the clan of the Heberites; of Malchiel, the clan of the Malchielites.

32 Heber became the father of Japhlet, Shomer, Hotham, and their sister Shua.

33 The sons of Japhlet: Pasach, Bimhal, and Ashvath. These are the sons of Japhlet.

34 The sons of Shemer: Ahi, Rohgah, Hubbah, and Aram.

35 The sons of Helem his brother: Zophah, Imna, Shelesh, and Amal.

36 The sons of Zophah: Suah, Harnepher, Shual, Beri, Imrah,

37 Bezer, Hod, Shamma, Shilshah, Ithran, and Beera.

38 The sons of Jether: Jephunneh, Pispa, and Ara.

39 The sons of Ulla: Arah, Hanniel, and Rizia.

40 All of these were *Asherites,* heads of ancestral houses, select mighty warriors, chief of the princes. Their number enrolled by genealogies, for service in war, was twenty-six thousand men.

47 These are the clans of the Asherites: the number of those enrolled was fifty-three thousand four hundred.

306 The Descendants of Benjamin
1 Chron 8:1-28 // 1 Chron 7:6-12; Gen 46:21; Num 26:38-41

1 Chronicles 8

1 Benjamin became the father of Bela his firstborn, Ashbel the second, Aharah the third,

2 Nohah the fourth, and Rapha the fifth.

3 And Bela had sons: Addar, Gera, Abihud,

4 Abishua, Naaman, Ahoah,

5 Gera, Shephuphan, and Huram.

6 These are the sons of Ehud (they were heads of ancestral houses of the inhabitants of Geba, and they were carried into exile to Manahath):

7 Naaman, Ahijah, and Gera, that is, Heglam, who became the father of Uzza and Ahihud.

8 And Shaharaim had sons in the country of Moab after he had sent away his wives Hushim and Baara.

9 He had sons by his wife Hodesh: Jobab, Zibia, Mesha, Malcam,

10 Jeuz, Sachia, and Mirmah. These were his sons, heads of ancestral houses.

11 He also had sons by Hushim: Abitub and Elpaal.

12 The sons of Elpaal: Eber, Misham, and Shemed, who built Ono and Lod with its towns,

13 and Beriah and Shema (they were heads of ancestral houses of the inhabitants of Aijalon, who put to flight the inhabitants of Gath);

Genesis 46

21 The *sons* of Benjamin: Bela, Becher, Ashbel, Gera, Naaman, Ehi, Rosh, Muppim, Huppim, and Ard.

Numbers 26

38 The *sons* of Benjamin by their clans: of Bela, the clan of the Belaites; of Ashbel, the clan of the Ashbelites; of Ahiram, the clan of the Ahiramites;

39 of Shephupham, the clan of the Shuphamites; of Hupham, the clan of the Huphamites.

40 And the sons of Bela were Ard and Naaman: of Ard, the clan of the Ardites; of Naaman, the clan of the Naamites.

41 These are the *sons* of Benjamin by their clans; the number of those enrolled was forty-five thousand six hundred.

1 Chronicles 7

6 The sons of Benjamin: Bela, Becher, and Jediael, three.

7 The sons of Bela: Ezbon, Uzzi, Uzziel, Jerimoth, and Iri, five, heads of ancestral houses, mighty warriors; and their enrollment by genealogies was twenty-two thousand thirty-four.

8 The sons of Becher: Zemirah, Joash, Eliezer, Elioenai, Omri, Jeremoth, Abijah, Anathoth, and Alemeth. All these were the sons of Becher;

9 and their enrollment by genealogies, according to their generations, as heads of their ancestral houses, mighty warriors, was twenty thousand two hundred.

10 The sons of Jediael: Bilhan. And the sons of Bilhan: Jeush, Benjamin, Ehud, Chenaanah, Zethan, Tarshish, and Ahishahar.

11 All these were the sons of Jediael according to the heads of their ancestral houses, mighty warriors, seventeen thousand two hundred, ready for service in war.

12 And Shuppim and Huppim were the sons of Ir, Hushim the son of Aher.

14 and Ahio, Shashak, and Jeremoth.

15 Zebadiah, Arad, Eder,

16 Michael, Ishpah, and Joha were sons of Beriah.

17 Zebadiah, Meshullam, Hizki, Heber,

18 Ishmerai, Izliah, and Jobab were the sons of Elpaal.

19 Jakim, Zichri, Zabdi,

20 Elienai, Zillethai, Eliel,

21 Adaiah, Beraiah, and Shimrath were the sons of Shimei.

22 Ishpan, Eber, Eliel,

23 Abdon, Zichri, Hanan,

24 Hananiah, Elam, Anthothijah,

25 Iphdeiah, and Penuel were the sons of Shashak.

26 Shamsherai, Shehariah, Athaliah,

27 Jaareshiah, Elijah, and Zichri were the sons of Jeroham.

28 These were the heads of ancestral houses, according to their generations, chiefs. These lived in Jerusalem.

307 The Genealogy of Saul
1 Chron 8:29-40 // 1 Chron 9:35-44; 1 Sam 9:1-2; 1 Sam 14:49

1 Chronicles 8

29 In Gibeon lived the father of Gibeon, Jeiel, and the name of his wife was Maacah.

30 His firstborn son was Abdon, then Zur, Kish, Baal, Nadab,

31 Gedor, Ahio, Zecher,

32 and Mikloth became the father of Shimeah. Now these also lived opposite their kindred in Jerusalem, with their kindred.

33 Ner became the father of Kish, Kish of Saul, Saul of Jonathan, Malchishua, Abinadab, and Esh-baal;

34 and the son of Jonathan was Merib-baal; and Merib-baal became the father of Micah.

35 The sons of Micah: Pithon, Melech, Tarea, and Ahaz.

36 Ahaz became the father of Jehoaddah; and Jehoaddah became the father of Alemeth, Azmaveth, and Zimri; Zimri became the father of Moza.

37 Moza became the father of Binea; Raphah was his son, Eleasah his son, Azel his son.

38 Azel had six sons, and these are their names: Azrikam, Bocheru, Ishmael, Sheariah, Obadiah, and Hanan; all these were the sons of Azel.

39 The sons of his brother Eshek: Ulam his firstborn, Jeush the second, and Eliphelet the third.

1 Samuel 9

1 There was a man of Benjamin whose name was Kish son of Abiel son of Zeror son of Becorath son of Aphiah, a Benjaminite, a man of valor.

2a He had a son whose name was Saul.

1 Samuel 14

49 Now the sons of Saul were Jonathan, Ishvi, and Malchishua; and the names of his two daughters were these: the name of the firstborn was Merab, and the name of the younger, Michal.

1 Chronicles 9

35 In Gibeon lived the father of Gibeon, Jeiel, and the name of his wife was Maacah.

36 His firstborn son was Abdon, then Zur, Kish, Baal, Ner, Nadab,

37 Gedor, Ahio, Zechariah, and Mikloth;

38 and Mikloth became the father of Shimeam; and these also lived opposite their kindred in Jerusalem, with their kindred.

39 Ner became the father of Kish, Kish of Saul, Saul of Jonathan, Malchishua, Abinadab, and Esh-baal;

40 and the son of Jonathan was Merib-baal; and Merib-baal became the father of Micah.

41 The sons of Micah: Pithon, Melech, Tahrea, and Ahaz;

42 Ahaz became the father of Jarah, and Jarah became the father of Alemeth, Azmaveth, and Zimri; Zimri became the father of Moza.

43 Moza became the father of Binea; and Rephaiah was his son, Eleasah his son, Azel his son.

44 Azel had six sons, and these are their names: Azrikam, Bocheru, Ishmael, Sheariah, Obadiah, and Hanan; these were the sons of Azel.

40 The sons of Ulam were mighty
warriors, archers, having many children and grandchildren, one hundred fifty. All these were
Benjaminites.

308 Those Who Returned from Babylon
1 Chron 9:1-34 // Neh 11:3-19

1 Chronicles 9

1 So all Israel was enrolled by genealogies; and these
are written in the Book of the Kings of Israel. And
Judah was taken into exile in Babylon because of their
unfaithfulness.

2 Now the first to live again in their possessions in
their towns were Israelites, priests, Levites, and temple
servants.

3 And in Jerusalem lived some of the people of Judah,
Benjamin, Ephraim, and Manasseh:

4 Uthai son of Ammihud, son of Omri, son of Imri,
son of Bani, from the sons of Perez son of Judah.

5 And of the Shilonites: Asaiah the firstborn, and his
sons.

6 Of the sons of Zerah: Jeuel and their kin, six hundred
ninety.

7 Of the Benjaminites: Sallu son of Meshullam, son of
Hodaviah, son of Hassenuah,

8 Ibneiah son of Jeroham, Elah son of Uzzi, son of
Michri, and Meshullam son of Shephatiah, son of
Reuel, son of Ibnijah;

9 and their kindred according to their generations, nine
hundred fifty-six. All these were heads of families
according to their ancestral houses.

Nehemiah 11

3 These are the leaders of the province who lived in
Jerusalem; but in the towns of Judah all lived on their
property in their towns: Israel, the priests, the Levites,
the temple servants, and the descendants of Solomon's
servants.

4 And in Jerusalem lived some of the Judahites and of
the Benjaminites. Of the Judahites: Athaiah son of
Uzziah son of Zechariah son of Amariah son of
Shephatiah son of Mahalalel, of the descendants of
Perez;

5 and Maaseiah son of Baruch son of Col-hozeh son of
Hazaiah son of Adaiah son of Joiarib son of Zechariah
son of the Shilonite.

6 All the descendants of Perez who lived in Jerusalem
were four hundred sixty-eight valiant warriors.

7 And these are the Benjaminites: Sallu son of
Meshullam son of Joed son of Pedaiah son of Kolaiah
son of Maaseiah son of Ithiel son of Jeshaiah.

8 And his brothers Gabbai, Sallai: nine hundred
twenty-eight.

9 Joel son of Zichri was their overseer; and Judah son
of Hassenuah was second in charge of the city.

10 Of the priests: Jedaiah, Jehoiarib, Jachin,

11 and Azariah son of Hilkiah, son of Meshullam, son of Zadok, son of Meraioth, son of Ahitub, the chief officer of the house of God;

12 and Adaiah son of Jeroham, son of Pashhur, son of Malchijah, and Maasai son of Adiel, son of Jahzerah, son of Meshullam, son of Meshillemith, son of Immer;

13 and their kindred, heads of their ancestral houses, one thousand seven hundred sixty, qualified for the work of the service of the house of God.

14 Of the Levites: Shemaiah son of Hasshub, son of Azrikam, son of Hashabiah, of the sons of Merari;

15 and Bakbakkar, Heresh, Galal, and Mattaniah son of Mica, son of Zichri, son of Asaph;

16 and Obadiah son of Shemaiah son of Galal son of Jeduthun, and Berechiah son of Asa, son of Elkanah, who lived in the villages of the Netophathites.

17 The gatekeepers were: Shallum, Akkub, Talmon, Ahiman; and their kindred Shallum was the chief,

18 stationed previously in the king's gate on the east side. These were the gatekeepers of the camp of the Levites.

19 Shallum son of Kore son of Ebiasaph son of Korah and his kindred of his ancestral house, the Korahites, were in charge of the work of the service, guardians of the thresholds of the tent, as their ancestors had been in charge of the camp of YHWH, guardians of the entrance.

20 And Phinehas son of Eleazar was chief over them in former times; YHWH was with him.

21 Zechariah son of Meshelemiah was gatekeeper at the entrance of the tent of meeting.

10 Of the priests: Jedaiah son of Joiarib, Jachin,

11 Seraiah son of Hilkiah son of Meshullam son of Zadok son of Meraioth son of Ahitub, officer of the house of God,

12 and their associates who did the work of the house, eight hundred twenty-two; and Adaiah son of Jeroham son of Pelaliah son of Amzi son of Zechariah son of Pashhur son of Malchijah,

13 and his associates, heads of ancestral houses, two hundred forty-two; and Amashsai son of Azarel son of Ahzai son of Meshillemoth son of Immer,

14 and their kindred, valiant warriors, one hundred twenty-eight; their overseer was Zabdiel son of Haggedolim.

15 Of the Levites: Shemaiah son of Hasshub son of Azrikam son of Hashabiah son of Bunni;

16 and Shabbethai and Jozabad, of the leaders of the Levites, who were over the outside work of the house of God;

17 and Mattaniah son of Mica son of Zabdi son of Asaph, who was the leader to begin the thanksgiving in prayer, and Bakbukiah, the second among his associates; and Abda son of Shammua son of Galal son of Jeduthun.

18 All the Levites in the holy city were two hundred eighty-four.

19 The gatekeepers were: Akkub, Talmon and their kindred, who kept watch at the gates, were one hundred seventy-two.

22 All these who were chosen as gatekeepers at the thresholds were two hundred twelve. They were enrolled by genealogies in their villages. David and the seer Samuel established them in their office of trust.

23 So they and their descendants were in charge of the gates of the house of YHWH, that is, the house of the tent, as guards.

24 The gatekeepers were on the four sides, east, west, north, and south;

25 and their kindred who were in their villages were obliged to come in every seven days in turn to be with them;

26 for the four chief gatekeepers, who were Levites, were in charge of the chambers and the treasures of the house of God.

27 And they would spend the night near the house of God; for on them lay the duty of watching, and they had charge of opening it every morning.

28 Some of them had charge of the utensils of service, for they were required to count them when they were brought in and taken out.

29 Others of them were appointed over the furniture, and over all the holy utensils, also over the choice flour, the wine, the oil, the incense, and the spices.

30 Others, of the sons of the priests, prepared the mixing of the spices,

31 and Mattithiah, one of the Levites, the firstborn of Shallum the Korahite, was in charge of making the flat cakes.

32 Also some of their kindred of the Kohathites had charge of the rows of bread, to prepare them for each sabbath.

33 Now these are the singers, the heads of ancestral houses of the Levites, living in the chambers of the temple free from other service, for they were on duty day and night.

34 These were heads of ancestral houses of the Levites, according to their generations; these leaders lived in Jerusalem.

309 The Genealogy of Saul
1 Chron 9:35-44 // 1 Chron 8:29-40; 1 Sam 9:1-2; 1 Sam 14:49

1 Chronicles 9

35 In Gibeon lived the father of Gibeon, Jeiel, and the name of his wife was Maacah.

36 His firstborn son was Abdon, then Zur, Kish, Baal, Ner, Nadab,

37 Gedor, Ahio, Zechariah, and Mikloth;

38 and Mikloth became the father of Shimeam; and these also lived opposite their kindred in Jerusalem, with their kindred.

39 Ner became the father of Kish, Kish of Saul, Saul of Jonathan, Malchishua, Abinadab, and Esh-baal;

40 and the son of Jonathan was Merib-baal; and Merib-baal became the father of Micah.

41 The sons of Micah: Pithon, Melech, Tahrea, and Ahaz;

42 Ahaz became the father of Jarah, and Jarah became the father of Alemeth, Azmaveth, and Zimri; Zimri became the father of Moza.

43 Moza became the father of Binea; and Rephaiah was his son, Eleasah his son, Azel his son.

44 Azel had six sons, and these are their names: Azrikam, Bocheru, Ishmael, Sheariah, Obadiah, and Hanan; these were the sons of Azel.

1 Samuel 9

1 There was a man of Benjamin whose name was Kish son of Abiel son of Zeror son of Becorath son of Aphiah, a Benjaminite, a man of valor.

2a He had a son whose name was Saul.

1 Samuel 14

49 Now the sons of Saul were Jonathan, Ishvi, and Malchishua; and the names of his two daughters were these: the name of the firstborn was Merab, and the name of the younger, Michal.

1 Chronicles 8

29 In Gibeon lived the father of Gibeon, Jeiel, and the name of his wife was Maacah.

30 His firstborn son was Abdon, then Zur, Kish, Baal, Nadab,

31 Gedor, Ahio, Zecher,

32 and Mikloth became the father of Shimeah. Now these also lived opposite their kindred in Jerusalem, with their kindred.

33 Ner became the father of Kish, Kish of Saul, Saul of Jonathan, Malchishua, Abinadab, and Esh-baal;

34 and the son of Jonathan was Merib-baal; and Merib-baal became the father of Micah.

35 The sons of Micah: Pithon, Melech, Tarea, and Ahaz.

36 Ahaz became the father of Jehoaddah; and Jehoaddah became the father of Alemeth, Azmaveth, and Zimri; Zimri became the father of Moza.

37 Moza became the father of Binea; Raphah was his son, Eleasah his son, Azel his son.

38 Azel had six sons, and these are their names: Azrikam, Bocheru, Ishmael, Sheariah, Obadiah, and Hanan; all these were the sons of Azel.

39 The sons of his brother Eshek: Ulam his firstborn, Jeush the second, and Eliphelet the third.

40 The sons of Ulam were mighty warriors, archers, having many children and grandchildren, one hundred fifty. All these were Benjaminites.

David

David-1
Sections 494–513

Number	Title	1 Chronicles	1 Samuel
494	The Death of Saul and His Sons	10:1-14	31:1-13
495	David Learns of Saul's Death		2 Sam 1:1-16
496	David's Lament over Saul and Jonathan		1:17-27
497	David Made King over Judah		2:1-7
498	David Fights the House of Saul		2:8-3:1
499	David's Sons Born at Hebron	[3:1-4a]	3:2-5
500	Abner Plans a Covenant with David		3:6-21
501	Joab Murders Abner		3:22-39
502	The Assassination of Ish-bosheth		4:1-12
503	David Made King in Israel	11:1-3	5:1-5
504	David Captures Zion	11:4-9	5:6-10
[535]	David's Mighty Men	11:10-47	[23:8-39]
[536]	David's Helpers at Ziklag	12:1-23	
[537]	David's Army at Hebron	12:24-41	
[508]	David Proposes to Bring Ark to Jerusalem	13:1-4	
[509]	David Goes to Bring the Ark	13:5-14	[6:1-11]
505	Hiram's Recognition of David	14:1-2	5:11-12
506	David's Children Born at Jerusalem	14:3-7	5:13-16
507	David Defeats the Philistines	14:8-17	5:17-25
508	David Proposes to Bring Ark to Jerusalem	[13:1-4]	
509	David Goes to Bring the Ark	[13:5-14]	6:1-11
510	The Ark Brought to Jerusalem	15:1-16:6	6:12-19a
511	David's Psalm of Thanksgiving	16:7-36	
512	The Levites Appointed for the Ark	16:37-43	6:19b-23
513	God's Covenant with David	17:1-27	7:1-29

494 The Death of Saul and His Sons
1 Chron 10:1-14 // 1 Sam 31:1-13

1 Chronicles 10	*1 Samuel 31*
1 Now the Philistines fought against Israel; and the men of Israel fled from the Philistines and they fell slain on Mount Gilboa.	1 Now the Philistines were fighting against Israel; and the men of Israel fled from the Philistines and they fell slain on Mount Gilboa.
2 The Philistines pursued after Saul and his sons: and the Philistines struck down Jonathan and Abinadab and Malchishua, sons of Saul.	2 The Philistines overtook Saul and his sons: and the Philistines struck down Jonathan and Abinadab and Malchishua, sons of Saul.
3 The battle went heavily against Saul, and the archers found him with [their] bow and he was badly wounded by the archers.	3 The battle went heavily against Saul, and the archers found him with [their] bow and he was badly wounded by the archers.
4 Then Saul spoke to his armor-bearer, "Draw out your sword and pierce me with it so that these uncircumcised ones cannot come and abuse me." But his armor-bearer did not consent because he was very much afraid, so Saul took the sword and fell upon it.	4 Then Saul spoke to his armor-bearer, "Draw out your sword and pierce me with it so that these uncircumcised ones cannot come and pierce me and abuse me." But his armor-bearer did not consent because he was very much afraid, so Saul took the sword and fell upon it.
5 When his armor-bearer saw that Saul was dead, he also fell upon the sword and died.	5 When his armor-bearer saw that Saul was dead, he also fell upon his sword and died with him.
6 So Saul died; and his three sons and his whole household, they all died together.	6 So Saul died; and his three sons and his armor-bearer, also all his men, together on that same day.
7 When all the men of Israel who were in the valley saw that they had fled and that Saul and his sons had died, they abandoned their cities and fled; so the Philistines came and dwelt in them.	7 When the men of Israel who were across the valley and those across the Jordan saw that the men of Israel had fled and that Saul and his sons had died, they abandoned their cities and fled; so the Philistines came and dwelt in them.
8 Now it happened on the next day when the Philistines came to strip the slain, they found Saul and his sons fallen on Mount Gilboa.	8 Now it happened on the next day when the Philistines came to strip the slain, they found Saul and his three sons fallen on Mount Gilboa.
9 They stripped him and they carried his head and his armor and they sent around in the land of the Philistines to proclaim the good news to their idols and to the people.	9 They cut off his head and stripped his armor, and they sent around in the land of the Philistines to proclaim the good news to the house of their idols and to the people.
10 They installed his armor in the temple of their gods, and they displayed his skull in the temple of Dagon.	10 They installed his armor in the temple of Astarte, and they displayed his corpse on the wall of Beth-shan.
11 When all of Jabesh-gilead heard everything that the Philistines had done to Saul,	11 When the inhabitants of Jabesh-gilead heard what the Philistines had done to Saul,

12 all the valiant men arose and they carried the body of Saul and the body of his sons and they brought them to Jabesh.

Then they buried their bones under the terebinth tree in Jabesh, and they fasted for seven days.

13 Thus Saul died because of his unfaithfulness in which he was unfaithful to YHWH, since he had not kept the word of YHWH and had even gone to consult a medium.

14 He had not consulted YHWH so he put him to death and turned the kingship over to David son of Jesse.

12 all the valiant men arose and they walked all night and they took the corpse of Saul and the corpses of his sons from the wall of Beth-shan and they came to Jabesh and they burned them there.

13 Then they took their bones and buried them under the terebinth tree in Jabesh, and they fasted for seven days.

495 David Learns of Saul's Death
2 Sam 1:1-16

2 Samuel

1 After the death of Saul, when David had returned from defeating the Amalekites, David stayed in Ziklag for two days.

2 On the third day a man came from the camp of Saul—his clothes were torn and there was dirt on his head. When he came to David, he fell to the ground and prostrated himself.

3 David said to him, "Where have you come from?" He said to him, "I have escaped from the camp of Israel."

4 David said to him, "What was the situation? Tell me!" He said, "The people have fled from the battle, and a great many of the people have fallen and died. Also Saul and Jonathan his son are dead."

5 Then David said to the young man who was reporting to him, "How do you know that Saul and Jonathan his son are dead?"

6 The young man reporting to him said, "I happened to be on Mount Gilboa, and there was Saul leaning on his spear while chariot and horsemen were closing in on him.

7 When he looked behind himself he saw me and summoned me; and I said, 'Here I am.'

8 He said to me, 'Who are you?' I said to him, 'I am an Amalekite.'

9 Then he said to me, 'Stand by me and kill me for death-throes have gripped me, and yet my life is still in me.'

10 So I stood by him and I killed him for I knew that he could not live after he had fallen. I took the crown that was on his head and the armlet that was on his arm, and I have brought them here to my lord."

11 At this David took hold of his clothes and tore them; and so did all the men who were with him.

12 They mourned and wept and fasted until evening for Saul and Jonathan his son, and for the people of YHWH and for the house of Israel, because they had fallen by the sword.

13 David said to the young man who reported to him, "Where are you from?" He said, "I am the son of a resident alien, an Amalekite."

14 David said to him, "Were you not afraid to stretch out your hand to destroy the anointed of YHWH?"

15 Then David summoned one of the young men and said, "Come here and strike him." So he struck him down and he died.

16 David said to him, "Your blood be on your head, for your mouth has testified against you, saying, "I have killed the anointed of YHWH."

496 David's Lament over Saul and Jonathan
2 Sam 1:17-27

2 Samuel

17 David recited this lamentation over Saul and Jonathan his son.

18 He ordered the sons of Judah to teach "[The] Bow." It is written in the Book of Jashar.

19 "[Your] glory O Israel on your high places lies slain. How the valiant have fallen!

20 Tell [it] not in Gath; proclaim it not in the streets of Ashkelon, lest the daughters of the Philistines rejoice, lest the daughters of the uncircumcised exult.

21 O mountains in Gilboa let there not be dew nor rain on you, nor fields for offerings. For there was defiled the shield of the valiant, the shield of Saul; no more anointed with oil.

22 From the blood of the slain, from the fat of the valiant, the bow of Jonathan did not retreat nor the sword of Saul return empty.

23 Saul and Jonathan, beloved and dear—in their life and in their death they were not apart. They were swifter than eagles; they were stronger than lions.

24 O daughters of Israel, weep over Saul who clothed you in style with crimson, who had embroidery of gold put on your attire.

25 How the valiant have fallen in the midst of the battle! Upon your heights Jonathan lies slain.

26 I am grief-stricken over you my brother Jonathan. Especially dear you were to me; your love was more wonderful to me than the love of women.

27 How the valiant have fallen and the weapons of war perished!"

497 David Made King over Judah
2 Sam 2:1-7

2 Samuel

1 Sometime afterwards David inquired of YHWH, saying "Shall I go up into one of the cities of Judah?" YHWH said to him, "Go up." David said, "To which one shall I go up?" He said, "To Hebron."

2 So David went up there and also his two wives, Ahinoam the Jezreelite, and Abigail wife of Nabal the Carmelite.

3 David brought up his men who were with him, each one with his household, and they settled in the towns of Hebron.

4 Then the men of Judah came, and there they anointed David king over the house of Judah. When they told David, saying, "It was the men of Jabesh-gilead who buried Saul,"

5 David sent messengers to the men of Jabesh-gilead and said to them, "May you be blessed by YHWH because you did this kindness to your lord Saul, that you buried him.

6 Now may YHWH show kindness and faithfulness to you, and I too will do good to you because you have done this thing."

7 So now let your hands be strong, and be valiant; for your lord Saul is dead, and the house of Judah has anointed me king over them."

498 David Fights the House of Saul
2 Sam 2:8–3:1

2 Samuel

8 Now Abner son of Ner, commander of Saul's army, had taken Ish-bosheth son of Saul, and had brought him over to Mahanaim.

9 He had made him king for Gilead, the Ashurites, and Jezreel, and over Ephraim, Benjamin, and all Israel.

10 Ish-bosheth son of Saul was forty years old when he became king over Israel, and he was king for two years. However the house of Judah followed David.

11 The number of days that David was king in Hebron over the house of Judah was seven years and six months.

12 Abner son of Ner, and the servants of Ish-bosheth son of Saul, went out from Mahanaim to Gibeon.

13 Joab son of Zeruiah and the servants of David went out and met them at the pool of Gibeon at the same time. One contingent sat on one side of the pool, and the other contingent on the opposite side of the pool.

14 Abner said to Joab, "Come now let the young men arise and have some competition before us." Joab said, "Let them arise."

15 So they arose and passed over in [equal] number, twelve represented Benjamin and Ish-bosheth son of Saul, and twelve from the servants of David.

16 Each one grabbed his opponent by the head and [thrust] his sword into the side of his opponent, and so they fell down together. So that place, which is at Gibeon, was called Helkath-hazzurim.

17 Now the battle was so very fierce that day; and Abner and the men of Israel were routed before the servants of David.

18 Now the three sons of Zeruiah were there: Joab, Abishai, and Asahel; with Asahel as swift of foot as one of the gazelles that are in the open field.

19 Asahel chased after Abner, and did not veer to the right or to the left from following Abner.

20 Abner looked behind him and said, "Is that you, Asahel?" He said, "It is I."

21 Then Abner said to him, "Veer off to your right or to your left and seize for yourself one of the young men, and take for yourself his equipment." But Asahel would not turn away from following him.

22 So Abner once again said to Asahel, "Turn away from following me! Why must I strike you down to the ground? How could I show my face to Joab your brother?"

23 When he refused to turn away, Abner struck him in the belly with the end of his spear, so that the spear came out behind him and he fell there, and died there beneath him. And all who came to the place where Asahel had fallen and died, stood there.

24 But Joab and Abishai chased after Abner. As the sun was setting, they came up to the hill of Ammah, which is opposite Giah on the way to the wilderness of Gibeon.

25 The Benjaminites rallied themselves behind Abner and became one unified band; and they stood [there] as one on the top of a hill.

26 Then Abner called out to Joab and said, "Must the sword keep on devouring forever? Do you not know that it will be bitter in the end? How long will it be before you order your people to turn from following after their brothers?"

27 Joab said, "As God lives, if you had not spoken, then the people would have given up following after his brother in the morning."

28 So Joab sounded the horn and all the people stood still and pursued Israel no longer nor continued to do battle anymore.

29 Yet Abner and his men kept on going through the Arabah all that night and crossed the Jordan; they kept on going along the entire ravine until they came to Mahanaim.

30 When Joab returned from following Abner, he gathered together all the people; and there were missing from the servants of David nineteen men as well as Asahel.

31 However, the servants of David had struck down from the Benjaminites and from Abner's men, and three hundred and sixty of them died.

32 They carried Asahel away and buried him in the tomb of his father, which was at Bethlehem. Then Joab and his men kept going all night; and day broke upon them at Hebron.

3:1 The war was prolonged between the house of Saul and the house of David; but David went on growing stronger while the house of Saul grew weaker.

499 David's Sons Born at Hebron
2 Sam 3:2-5 // 1 Chron 3:1-4a (see also 289)

2 Samuel 3	*1 Chronicles 3*
2 Sons were born to David at Hebron: his firstborn was Amnon of Ahinoam the Jezreelitess;	1 These were the sons of David who were born to him at Hebron: the firstborn Amnon of Ahinoam the Jezreelitess;
3 his second, Chileab of Abigail,[1] the wife of Nabal the Carmelite;	the second, Daniel of Abigail the Carmelitess;
and the third, Absalom son of Maacah, daughter of Talmai king of Geshur;	2 the third Absalom, son of Maacah, daughter of Talmai king of Geshur;
4 and the fourth, Adonijah son of Haggith;	the fourth, Adonijah son of Haggith;
and the fifth, Shepahtiah son of Abital;	3 the fifth, Shephatiah of Abital;
5 and the sixth, Ithream of Eglah wife of David. These were born to David in Hebron.	4 the sixth, Ithream of Eglah his wife. Six were born to him at Hebron.

---

[1] Reading the Qere.

500 Abner Plans a Covenant with David
2 Sam 3:6-21

2 Samuel

6 While there was war between the house of Saul and the house of David, Abner was making himself strong within the house of Saul.

7 Now Saul had a concubine and her name was Rizpah daughter of Aiah. He [Ish-bosheth] said to Abner, "Why have you gone into my father's concubine?"

8 Abner became very angry at the words of Ish-bosheth, and said, "Am I some dog's head for Judah? Today I am doing a kindness to the house of Saul your father, to his brothers, and his friends, and have not delivered you into the hands of David; and yet you charge me with wrongdoing over this woman today.

9 So may God do to Abner and even more so to him, for just what YHWH swore to David that I will do for him:

10 to transfer the kingdom from the house of Saul, and set up the throne of David over Israel and Judah from Dan to Beersheba."

11 At that [Ish-bosheth] could not answer Abner another word because of his fear of him.

12 Then Abner sent messengers to David in his place, saying, "Whose land is it," saying also, "Make a covenant with me, and see my hand is with you, to bring over to you all Israel."

13 He said, "Good, I will make a covenant with you. Only one thing I ask of you: you shall not see my face unless you first bring Michal daughter of Saul, when you come to see me."

14 Then David sent messengers to Ish-bosheth son of Saul, saying, "Give me my wife Michal to whom I became betrothed at the cost of one hundred foreskins of the Philistines."

15 So Ish-bosheth sent and took her from [her] husband, from Paltiel son of Laish.

16 But her husband went with her, weeping after her right up to Bahurim. Abner said to him, "Go, go back!" And back he went.

17 Now a message from Abner came to the elders of Israel, saying, "For some time now, as formerly, you have been seeking to have David as king over you.

18 Now do it, for YHWH has promised David, 'By the hand of David my servant he has saved my people Israel from the hand of the Philistines and from the hand of all their enemies.'"

19 Abner likewise spoke into the ears of Benjamin; and Abner also went to speak into the ears of David at Hebron all that was good in the eyes of Israel and in the eyes of all the house of Benjamin.

20 When Abner came to David at Hebron, there were twenty men with him; so David made a feast for Abner and the men who were with him.

21 Abner said to David, "Let me get up and go and rally to my lord the king all Israel, that they may make a covenant with you, and that you may become king over all that you yourself desire." So David dismissed Abner and he went away in peace.

501 Joab Murders Abner
2 Sam 3:22-39

2 Samuel

22 Just then the servants of David and Joab arrived from a raid, and they brought with them much plunder. But Abner was no longer with David at Hebron because he had sent him away and he had gone in peace.

23 When Joab and all the army that was with him came, they told Joab, saying, "Abner son of Ner came to the king, but he has sent him away and he has gone in peace."

24 Then Joab went to the king and said, "What have you done? Look, Abner came to you; why did you send him away? Now he has certainly gone.

25 You know that Abner son of Ner came to deceive you, and to discover your goings and your comings and to discover everything you are doing."

26 When Joab went out from David, he sent messengers after Abner, and they brought him back from the cistern of Sirah. But David did not know [anything] of it.

27 When Abner returned to Hebron, Joab took him aside into the middle of the gateway to speak with him in private, and he struck him there in the belly so that he died, [in retaliation] for the blood of Asahel his brother.

28 When David heard about it, afterward he said, "I and my kingdom are innocent forever before YHWH of the blood of Abner son of Ner.

29 Let it fall upon the head of Joab and to all his father's house; and let there not be lacking from the house of Joab one who has a bloody discharge, or one who is leprous, or one who holds a spindle, or who falls by the sword, or who wants for bread."

30 Thus Joab and Abishai his brother murdered Abner because he had killed Asahel their brother in the battle at Gibeon.

31 Then David said to Joab and to all the people who were with him, "Tear your garments, and put on sackcloth, and mourn for Abner." And King David walked behind the bier.

32 They buried Abner at Hebron; and the king lifted up his voice and wept at the tomb of Abner and all the people wept.

33 The king lamented for Abner and said, "As a fool dies, should Abner die?

34 Your hand[s] were not bound and your feet were not placed in fetters; as one fallen before perverse men you have fallen." Then all the people resumed weeping over him.

35 Then all the people came to urge David to eat bread while it was still day, but David swore, saying, "May God do so to me and even more if I taste bread or anything else before the going down of the sun."

36 And all the people took note, and it was good in their eyes; indeed everything the king did was good in the eyes of all the people.

37 So all the people and all Israel understood that day that it had not originated with the king to kill Abner son of Ner.

38 The king said to his servants, "Do you not realize that a prince and a great [man] has fallen this day in Israel?

39 Today I am powerless though anointed king, and these men sons of Zeruiah, are too forceful for me. May YHWH requite the one who does wickedness according to his wickedness!"

502 The Assassination of Ish-bosheth
2 Sam 4:1-12

2 Samuel

1 When the son of Saul heard that Abner had died at Hebron, he became despondent[1] and all Israel was dismayed.

2 Now two men, captains of raiding bands were [with] Saul's son: the name of the first one was Baanah, and the name of the second was Rechab, sons of Rimmon the Beerothite from the Benjaminites.

3 The Beerothites had fled to Gittaim where they are resident aliens to this day.

4 Jonathan son of Saul had a son crippled in [his] feet. He was five years old when the news about Saul and Jonathan came from Jezreel. His nurse picked him up and fled, but it happened in her hurry to flee that he fell and became lame. His name was Mephibosheth.

5 Now the sons of Rimmon the Beerothite, Rechab and Baanah, set out, and about the heat of the day they came to the house of Ish-bosheth, while he was lying down for his noontime nap.

6 They came right inside the house as [supposed] fetchers of wheat, and struck him in the belly. Rechab and Baanah his brother then escaped.

7 Now when they had come right into the house while he was lying on his couch in his bedchamber, they struck him and killed him, and cut off his head. Then they took his head and went by way of the Arabah all night long.

8 They brought the head of Ish-bosheth to David at Hebron and they said to the king, "Here now is the head of Ish-bosheth son of Saul your enemy who sought your life; thus, YHWH has granted to my lord the king vengeance this day on Saul and on his seed."

9 David answered Rechab and Baanah his brother, sons of Rimmon the Beerothite, and said to them, "As YHWH lives who has redeemed my life from every adversity,

10 when the one who informed me, saying, 'See, Saul is dead,' and he had thought himself a bearer of good news, I seized him and I killed him at Ziklag, that I might give him a reward [for such good news]!

11 How much more, when wicked men have killed a righteous man in his house on his bed. Should I not now require his blood from your hand and exterminate you from the earth!"

12 So David commanded the young men and they killed them and cut off their hands and their feet; and hung them up beside the pool at Hebron. But the head of Ish-bosheth they took and buried in the tomb of Abner at Hebron.

---

[1] Literally, "his hands drooped."

503 David Made King in Israel
1 Chron 11:1-3 // 2 Sam 5:1-5

1 Chronicles 11	*2 Samuel 5*
1 Then all Israel gathered to David at Hebron saying, "See, we are of your bone and your flesh."	1 Then all the tribes of Israel came to David at Hebron, and they said, "See, we are of your bone and your flesh."
2 Even in times past when Saul was king, you were the one leading Israel out and in; and YHWH your God said to you, "You shall shepherd my people Israel, and you shall become prince over my people Israel."	2 Even in times past when Saul was king over us, it was you who led Israel out and in; and YHWH said to you, "You shall shepherd my people Israel, and you shall become prince over Israel."
3 All the elders of Israel came to the king at Hebron, and David made a covenant with them at Hebron in the presence of YHWH; so they anointed David as king over Israel according to the word of YHWH through Samuel.	3 All the elders of Israel came to the king at Hebron, and King David made a covenant with them at Hebron in the presence of YHWH; so they anointed David as king over Israel.
	4 David was thirty years old when he became king; he was king for forty years.
	5 In Hebron he was king over Judah for seven years and six months, and in Jerusalem he was king for thirty-three years over all Israel and Judah.

504 David Captures Zion
1 Chron 11:4-9 // 2 Sam 5:6-10

1 Chronicles 11

4 David and all Israel went to Jerusalem, that is Jebus, for there the Jebusites were inhabiting the land.

5 But the inhabitants of Jebus said to David, "You will not come in here!" Then David seized the citadel of Zion; it is now the city of David.

6 David said, "Whoever strikes down Jebusites first will be the chief and commander." Then Joab son of Zeruiah went up first and he became the chief.

7 So David dwelt in the citadel; therefore they call it the City of David.

8 He built the city on all sides from the Millo all around, and Joab rebuilt the rest of the city.

9 David kept growing stronger for YHWH Sabaoth was with him.

2 Samuel 5

6 The king and his men went to Jerusalem, to the Jebusites inhabiting the land; but they said to David, "You will not come in here!" For even the blind and the lame could turn you away, saying, 'David shall not come in here.'"

7 Then David seized the citadel of Zion; it is now the city of David.

8 That day David said, "Everyone who would strike down the Jebusites let him reach the water shaft [and strike down] the lame and the blind, those hated by David's soul." Therefore they say, "The blind and the lame shall not come into the house."

9 So David dwelt in the citadel and he called it the City of David;

then David built [it] around from the Millo to the house.

10 David kept growing stronger for YHWH God of Sabaoth was with him.

535 David's Mighty Men
1 Chron 11:10-47 // 2 Sam 23:8-39

1 Chronicles 11

10 Now these are the chiefs of the mighty men who belonged to David, who used their strength with him in his kingdom together with all Israel to make him king, according to the word of YHWH concerning Israel.

11 These are the number of the mighty men who belonged to David: Jashobeam son of Hachmoni, chief of the officers; he laid bare his spear against three hundred slain at one time.

2 Samuel 23

8 These are the names of the mighty men who belonged to David: Josheb-basshebeth, a Tahchemonite, chief of the officers; he is Adino the Eznite against eight hundred slain at one time.

12 After him was Eleazar son of Dodo, the Ahohite. He was one of the three mighty men.

13 He was with David at Pas-dammim when the Philistines gathered there for battle; and there was a plot of the field full of barley; and the people fled before the Philistines.

14 But they stood in the middle of the plot and defended it, and they slew the Philistines. So YHWH saved them by a great victory.

15 Then three of the thirty chief[s] went down to the rock to David at the Cave of Adullam, while the camp of the Philistines was encamping in the valley of Rephaim.

16 David was then in the stronghold; and the post of the Philistines was then in Bethlehem.

17 Then David had a craving, so he said, "If only someone will give me a drink of water from the well which is at Bethlehem by the gate."

18 So the Three broke into the Philistine camp, and they drew water from the well which was in Bethlehem by the gate, and they carried it and brought it to David, but he was unwilling to drink it so he poured it out as a libation to YHWH.

19 Then he said, "May I be cursed by my God if I do this. Shall I drink the blood of these men at the risk of their lives since they brought it at the risk of their lives?" So he was unwilling to drink it. The three mighty men did these kinds of things.

20 Now Abishai brother of Joab was chief of the Three; he laid bare his spear against three hundred slain, but he had no name among the Three.

21 Among the Three he was honored against the other two so he became their commander; but he did not attain to the Three.

9 After him was Eleazar son of Dodo son of Ahohi. [He was] one of the three mighty men with David when they taunted the Philistines who had gathered there for battle. Then the men of Israel withdrew,

10 [but] he stood his ground and struck down Philistines until his hand grew weary and his hand stuck to the sword. So YHWH brought about a great victory on that day. Then the people returned to him, only to strip [the slain].

11 After him was Shammah son of Agee, the Hararite. The Philistines gathered as a band, and there was a plot of the field there full of lentils; and the people fled before the Philistines.

12 But he stood in the middle of the plot and defended it, and he slew the Philistines. So YHWH brought about a great victory.

13 Then three of the thirty chief[s] went down, and they came to David near the harvest time at the Cave of Adullam, while a band of Philistines were encamping in the valley of Rephaim.

14 David was then in the stronghold; and the garrison of the Philistines was then in Bethlehem.

15 Then David had a craving, so he said, "If only someone will give me a drink of water from the well which is at Bethlehem by the gate."

16 So three of the mighty men broke into the Philistine camp, and they drew water from the well which was in Bethlehem by the gate, and they carried it and brought it to David, but he was unwilling to drink it so he poured it out as a libation to YHWH.

17 Then he said, "May I be cursed O YHWH, if I do this. Is it the blood of the men who went at the risk of their lives?" So he was unwilling to drink it. The three mighty men did these kinds of things.

18 Now Abishai brother of Joab, son of Zeruiah, was chief of the Three; he laid bare his spear against three hundred slain; so he had a name among the Three.

19 Among the Three is he not honored? So he became their commander; but he did not attain to the Three.

22 Benaiah son of Jehoiada was the son of a brave soldier, from Kabzeel, mighty in deeds. He slew two [sons] of Ariel of Moab. He also went down and slew the lion in the middle of the pit on a snowy day.

23 Then he slew the Egyptian man, a man of stature, five cubits [tall]. In the Egyptian's hand there was a spear like a weaver's beam, but he went down against him with a staff; he seized the spear from the Egyptian's hand and he killed him with his spear.

24 These things did Benaiah son of Jehoiada; and he had a name among the three mighty men.

25 Among the Thirty he was indeed honored, but he did not attain to the Three; however David appointed him over his bodyguard.

26 The mighty men of valor were: Asahel brother of Joab; Elhanan son of Dodo, from Bethlehem;

27 Shammoth the Harorite; Helez the Pelonite;

28 Ira son of Ikkesh, the Tekoite; Abiezer of Anathoth;

29 Sibbecai the Hushathite; Ilai the Ahohite;

30 Maharai of Netophah; Heled son of Baanah of Netophah;

31 Ithai son of Ribai, of Gibeah of the Benjaminites; Benaiah of Pirathon;

32 Hurai, from the torrents of Gaash. Abiel the Arbathite;

33 Azmaveth the Baharumite; Eliahba the Shaalbonite;

34 the sons of Hashem the Gizonite: Jonathan, son of Shagee the Hararite;

35 Ahiam son of Sachar the Hararite; Eliphal son of Ur;

36 Hepher the Mecherathite, Ahijah the Pelonite;

37 Hezro the Carmelite; Naarai son of Ezbai;

38 Joel brother of Nathan; Mibhar son of Hagri;

39 Zelek the Ammonite; Naharai of Beeroth, the armor-bearer of Joab son of Zeruiah;

20 Now Benaiah son of Jehoiada was the son of Ish-hai, from Kabzeel, mighty in deeds. He slew two [sons] of Ariel of Moab. He also went down and slew the lion in the middle of the pit on a snowy day.

21 Then he slew an Egyptian man, of [imposing] appearance. In the Egyptian's hand there was a spear, but he went down against him with a staff; he seized the spear from the Egyptian's hand and he killed him with his spear.

22 These things did Benaiah son of Jehoiada; and he had a name among the three mighty men.

23 Among the Thirty he was honored, but he did not attain to the Three; however, David appointed him to his bodyguard.

24 Asahel brother of Joab was among the Thirty, Elhanan son of Dodo, of Bethlehem;

25 Shammah the Harodite; Elika the Harodite;

26 Helez the Paltite; Ira son of Ikkesh, the Tekoite;

27 Abiezer of Anathoth; Mebunnai the Hushathite;

28 Zalmon the Ahohite; Maharai of Netophah;

29 Heleb son of Baanah of Netophah; Ittai son of Ribai of Gibeah of the Benjaminites.

30 Benaihu of Pirathon; Hiddai, from the torrents of Gaash.

31 Abi-albon the Arbathite; Azmaveth of Bahurim;

32 Eliahba the Shaalbonite; the sons of Jashen: Jonathan,

33 Shammah the Hararite; Ahiam son of Sharar the Hararite;

34 Eliphelet son of Ahasbai, son of the Maacathite; Eliam son of Ahithophel the Gilonite;

35 Hezro the Carmelite; Paarai the Arbite;

36 Igal son of Nathan of Zobah; Bani the Gadite;

37 Zelek the Ammonite; Naharai of Beeroth, the armor-bearer of Joab son of Zeruiah;

40 Ira the Ithrite; Gareb the Ithrite;

41 Uriah the Hittite; Zabad son of Ahlai;

42 Adina son of Shiza the Reubenite, a chief of the Reubenites, and thirty with him;

43 Hanan son of Maacah, and Joshaphat the Mithnite;

44 Uzzia the Ashterathite; Shama and Jeiel, sons of Hotham the Aroerite;

45 Jediael son of Shimri, and Joha his brother, the Tizite;

46 Eliel the Mahavite; and Jeribai and Joshaviah, sons of Elnaam; Ithmah the Moabite;

47 Eliel and Obed, and Jaasiel the Mezobaite.

38 Ira the Ithrite; Gareb the Ithrite;

39 Uriah the Hittite.

All [told there were] thirty-seven.

536 David's Helpers at Ziklag
1 Chron 12:1-23

1 Chronicles 12

1 These are the ones who came to David at Ziklag while he still kept a way from Saul son of Kish: they were among the mighty warriors who helped him in war.

2 They were archers, either right-handed or left-handed, who could sling stones or [shoot] arrows with a bow, and from Saul's kindred from Benjamin.

3 The chief was Ahiezer, then Joash, sons of Shemaah of Gibeah; also Jeziel and Pelet, sons of Azmaveth; also Beracah, Jehu of Anathoth;

4 Ishmaiah of Gibeon, a mighty warrior among the Thirty and over the Thirty;

5 Jeremiah, Jahaziel, Johanan, Jozabad of Gederah;

6 Eluzai, Jerimoth, Bealiah, Shemariah, Shephatiah the Haruphite;

7 Elkanah, Isshiah, Azarel, Joezer, Jashobeam the Korahites;

8 Joelah and Zebadiah, sons of Jeroham from Gedor.

9 Also from the Gadites these went over to David at the stronghold in the desert; the mighty men, warriors who could handle shield and lance: their faces [like] the face of a lion, and they were as swift as gazelles on the mountains.

10 Ezer was the head, Obadiah the second, and Eliab the third [in command],

11 Mishmannah the fourth, Jeremiah the fifth,

12 Attai the sixth, Eliel the seventh;

13 Johanan the eighth, Elzabad the ninth;

14 Jeremiah the tenth, Machbannai the eleventh;

15 these were Gadites, leaders of the army; the least one [equal to] a hundred, the greatest to a thousand.

16 These are the ones who crossed the Jordan in the first month when it was overflowing all its banks and put to flight all in the valleys, to the east and to the west.

17 There also came Benjaminites and Judahites to the stronghold, for David.

18 Then David went out before them and replying said to them, "If you have come peacefully to me, to help me, my heart will be as one with yours. But if [you have come] to betray me to my enemies, even though there is no violence on my hands, may the God of our ancestors see it and judge."

19 Then the spirit clothed Amasai, the chief of the Thirty, "[We are] yours O David, and [we are] with you son of Jesse! Peace, peace be yours, and peace to anyone who helps you; for the one who helps you is your God." So David received them and appointed them as leaders of the troop.

20 Some from Manasseh also deserted to David when he came with the Philistines for battle against Saul, but they did not help them because the lords of the Philistines in counsel sent him away, saying, "He will desert to his master Saul at the cost of our heads."

21 As he went to Ziklag there deserted to him from Manasseh: Adnah, Jozabad, Jediael, Michael, Jozabad, Elihu and Zillethai, chiefs of the thousands in Manasseh.

22 They helped David against the bands of raiders for they were all mighty men of valor; and they were officers over the army.

23 Indeed day by day they kept coming to David to help him until there was a great encampment, like the encampment of God.

537 David's Army at Hebron
1 Chron 12:24-41

1 Chronicles 12

24 These are the numbers of the chiefs of those equipped for war [who] came to David at Hebron, to turn over the kingdom of Saul to him according to the command of YHWH:

25 Judahites bearing shield and lance, six thousand eight hundred equipped for war;

26 from the Simeonites, valiant men for the army, seven thousand one hundred;

27 from the Levites, four thousand six hundred;

28 and Jehoiada was prince of [the house of] Aaron and with him three thousand seven hundred;

29 and Zadok, a valiant young warrior; and from his ancestral house twenty-two officers;

30 from the Benjaminites, the kinsfolk of Saul, three thousand—up to this point the majority of them had been keeping guard of the house of Saul.

31 Of the Ephraimites, twenty thousand eight hundred, valiant warriors, men of renown in their ancestral houses;

32 from the half-tribe of Manasseh, eighteen thousand who were designated by [their] names to come to make David king;

33 of the sons of Issachar—who knew discernment of times, to know what Israel should do—two hundred of their chiefs and all their kindred at their command;

34 of Zebulun, those set out for military service equipped for battle with all the weapons for war, fifty thousand, gathered together without division of heart;

35 of Naphtali, a thousand officers, and with them, with shield and spear, thirty-seven thousand;

36 from Dan, equipped for battle, twenty-eight thousand six hundred;

37 from Asher, those set out for military service equipped for battle, forty thousand;

38 from Across-the-Jordan, from the Reubenites and the Gadites and the half-tribe of Manasseh, with all the weapons for war, one hundred twenty thousand.

39 All these warriors drawn up in battle array with a perfect heart, came to Hebron to make David king over all Israel; and also all the rest of Israel were of one mind to make David the king.

40 They were there eating and drinking with David for thirty days since their kindred had made provision for them.

41 Also their neighbors, as far as Issachar and Zebulun and Naphtali, were bringing food [for them] on donkeys and on camels, on mules and on oxen: food—flour, fig cakes, raisin cakes, wine, oil, cattle and sheep—in great quantity, for there was rejoicing in Israel.

508 David Proposes to Bring the Ark to Jerusalem
1 Chron 13:1-4

1 Chronicles 13

1 Then David consulted with the commanders of the thousands and hundreds, with every leader.

2 David said to all the assembly of Israel, "If it seems good to you and to YHWH our God, let us spread out and send to our kinsfolk who are left in all the territories of Israel, including the priests and the Levites in the cities of their pasture lands, that they may gather to us.

3 Then let us lead the ark of our God back to us since we did not seek it out in the days of Saul."

4 Then the entire assembly said to do so, for the matter seemed right in the eyes of all the people.

509 David Goes to Bring the Ark
1 Chron 13:5-14 // 2 Sam 6:1-11

1 Chronicles 13	*2 Samuel 6*
5 So David assembled all Israel from Shihor of Egypt to Lebo-hamath, to bring the ark of God from Kiriath-jearim.	1 David again gathered all the picked men of Israel, thirty thousand.
6 Then David and all Israel went up to Baalah, to Kiriath-jearim which belongs to Judah, to bring up from there the ark of God YHWH Enthroned on the Cherubim, which is called by [his] name.	2 Then David and all the people who were with him arose and set out from Baale-judah, to bring up from there the ark of God which is called by the name, name YHWH Sabaoth Enthroned on the Cherubim.
7 They carried the ark of God upon a new cart from the house of Abinadab; Uzza and Ahio were driving on the cart.	3 They carried the ark of God to a new cart, and conveyed it from the house of Abinadab which was on the hill. Uzzah and Ahio, Abinadab's sons, were driving the new cart.
	4 They conveyed it from the house of Abinadab which was on the hill, with the ark of God; Ahio was walking in front of the ark.
8 Now David and all Israel were dancing before God with all their strength, with songs and with lyres and harps and timbrels, cymbals and trumpets.	5 Then David and the entire house of Israel were dancing before YHWH with all [their] instruments of cypress wood, and with lyres and harps and timbrels, sistrums and cymbals.
9 When they came to the threshing-floor of Chidon, Uzzah reached out his hand to steady the ark, for the oxen had stumbled.	6 When they came to the threshing-floor of Nacon, Uzzah reached out to the ark of God and steadied it, for the oxen had stumbled.
10 YHWH's anger was kindled against Uzzah and he struck him down because he had put out his hand against the ark; so he died there before God.	7 YHWH's anger was kindled against Uzzah and God struck him down there because of his error; so he died there beside the ark of God.
11 David was angry because YHWH had burst out against Uzzah, so he called that place Perez-uzzah, [that is, Breaking out against Uzzah] to this day.	8 David was angry because YHWH had burst out against Uzzah, so he called that place Perez-uzzah, [that is, Breaking out against Uzzah] to this day.
12 David was afraid of God that day saying, "How can I bring the ark of God to me?"	9 David was afraid of YHWH that day and he said, "How can the ark of YHWH come to me?"
13 So David did not bring the ark to himself into the city of David; rather he took it aside to the house of Obed-edom the Gittite.	10 So David was not willing to bring the ark of YHWH to himself into the city of David; rather David took it aside to the house of Obed-edom the Gittite.
14 The ark of God remained with the house of Obed-edom in his house for three months; so YHWH blessed the household of Obed-edom and all he had.	11 The ark of YHWH remained in the house of Obed-edom the Gittite for three months; so YHWH blessed Obed-edom and his whole house.

505 Hiram's Recognition of David
1 Chron 14:1-2 // 2 Sam 5:11-12

1 Chronicles 14

1 Hiram king of Tyre sent messengers to David, as well as cedar wood and builders and carpenters to build a house for him.

2 Then David knew that YHWH had established him as king over Israel, since his kingdom had been highly exalted for the sake of his people Israel.

2 Samuel 5

11 Hiram king of Tyre sent messengers to David, as well as cedar wood and carpenters and stone masons, and they built a house for David.

12 Then David knew that YHWH had established him as king over Israel, and that he had exalted his kingship for the sake of his people Israel.

506 David's Children Born at Jerusalem
1 Chron 14:3-7 // 2 Sam 5:13-16 // 1 Chron 3:5-9

1 Chronicles 14

3 David took more wives in Jerusalem, and David fathered more sons and daughters.

4 These are the names of the children that he had in Jerusalem: Shammua, Shobab, Nathan and Solomon;

5 Ibhar, Elishua, and Elpelet;

6 Nogah, Nepheg, and Japhia;

7 Elishama, Beeliada, and Eliphelet.

2 Samuel 5

13 David took more concubines and wives from Jerusalem after he had come from Hebron, so more sons and daughters were born to David.

14 These are the names of those born to him in Jerusalem: Shammua, Shobab, Nathan and Solomon;

15 Ibhar, Elishua, Nepheg, and Japhia;

16 Elishama, Eliada, and Eliphelet.

1 Chronicles 3

5 These were born to him in Jerusalem: Shimea, Shobab, Nathan and Solomon; four by Bath-shua, daughter of Ammiel.

6 Ibhar, Elishama, and Eliphelet;

7 Nogah, Nepheg, and Japhia;

8 Elishama, Eliada, and Eliphelet—nine in all.

507 David Defeats the Philistines
1 Chron 14:8-17 // 2 Sam 5:17-25

1 Chronicles 14

8 When the Philistines heard that David had been anointed as king over all Israel, all the Philistines went up to search for David. David heard [of it] and went out before them.

9 Now the Philistines had come and were raiding in the valley of Rephaim.

10 David asked God, "Shall I go up against the Philistines, and will you give them into my hands?" YHWH said to him, "Go up, and I will give them into your hands."

11 So they went up to Baal-perazim and David struck them down there and David said, "God has broken my enemies in pieces in my hands like the breaking of water." Therefore they called the name of that place Baal-perazim.

12 The Philistines left their gods there, and David ordered that they be burned in the fire.

13 Still the Philistines kept on raiding in the valley.

14 So David again asked God and God said to him, "You shall not go up after them, but go around them and come upon them opposite the balsam trees.

15 As soon as you hear the sound of marching in the tops of the balsam trees then you shall go out to battle, for God goes out before you to strike down the Philistine camp.

16 David did as God had commanded him, and they struck down the Philistine camp from Gibeon to Gezer.

17 So David's fame went out through all the lands as YHWH put fear of him upon all the nations.

2 Samuel 5

17 When the Philistines heard that they had anointed David as king over Israel, all the Philistines went up to search for David. David heard [of it] and went down to the stronghold.

18 Now the Philistines had come and spread out in the valley of Rephaim.

19 David asked YHWH, "Shall I go up against the Philistines? Will you give them into my hands?" YHWH said to David, "Go up, for I will surely give the Philistines into your hands."

20 So David came to Baal-perazim and David struck them down there and he said, "YHWH has broken my enemies in pieces before me like the breaking of water." Therefore the name of that place is called Baal-perazim.

21 The Philistines left their idols there, and David and his men carried them off.

22 Still the Philistines kept coming up, and they spread out in the Valley of Rephaim.

23 So David asked YHWH who said, "You shall not go up, but go around after them and come to them opposite the balsam trees.

24 As soon as you hear the sound of marching in the tops of the balsam trees then you shall be alert, for then YHWH goes out before you to strike down Philistines in [their] battle camp.

25 David did just as YHWH had commanded him, and he slew the Philistines from Geba as far as the approach to Gezer.

508 David Proposes to Bring the Ark to Jerusalem
1 Chron 13:1-4

1 Chronicles 13

1 Then David consulted with the commanders of the thousands and hundreds, with every leader.

2 David said to all the assembly of Israel, "If it seems good to you and to YHWH our God, let us spread out and send to our kinsfolk who are left in all the territories of Israel, including the priests and the Levites in the cities of their pasture lands, that they may gather to us.

3 Then let us lead the ark of our God back to us since we did not seek it out in the days of Saul."

4 Then the entire assembly said to do so for the matter seemed right in the eyes of all the people.

509 David Goes to Bring the Ark
2 Sam 6:1-11 // 1 Chron 13:5-14

2 Samuel 6	*1 Chronicles 13*
1 David again gathered all the picked men of Israel, thirty thousand.	5 So David assembled all Israel from Shihor of Egypt to Lebo-hamath, to bring the ark of God from Kiriath-jearim.
2 Then David and all the people who were with him arose and set out from Baale-judah, to bring up from there the ark of God which is called by the name, name YHWH Sabaoth Enthroned on the Cherubim.	6 Then David and all Israel went up to Baalah, to Kiriath-jearim which belongs to Judah, to bring up from there the ark of God YHWH Enthroned on the Cherubim, which is called by [his] name.

3 They carried the ark of God to a new cart, and conveyed it from the house of Abinadab which was on the hill. Uzzah and Ahio, Abinadab's sons, were driving the new cart.

4 They conveyed it from the house of Abinadab which was on the hill, with the ark of God; Ahio was walking in front of the ark.

5 Then David and the entire house of Israel were dancing before YHWH with all [their] instruments of cypress wood, and with lyres and harps and timbrels, sistrums and cymbals.

6 When they came to the threshing-floor of Nacon, Uzzah reached out to the ark of God and steadied it, for the oxen had stumbled.

7 YHWH's anger was kindled against Uzzah and God struck him down there because of his error; so he died there beside the ark of God.

8 David was angry because YHWH had burst out against Uzzah, so he called that place Perez-uzzah, [that is, Breaking out against Uzzah] to this day.

9 David was afraid of YHWH that day and he said, "How can the ark of YHWH come to me?"

10 So David was not willing to bring the ark of YHWH to himself into the city of David; rather David took it aside to the house of Obed-edom the Gittite.

11 The ark of YHWH remained in the house of Obed-edom the Gittite for three months; so YHWH blessed Obed-edom and his whole house.

7 They carried the ark of God upon a new cart from the house of Abinadab; Uzza and Ahio were driving on the cart.

8 Now David and all Israel were dancing before God with all their strength, with songs and with lyres and harps and timbrels, cymbals and trumpets.

9 When they came to the threshing-floor of Chidon, Uzzah reached out his hand to steady the ark for the oxen had stumbled.

10 YHWH's anger was kindled against Uzzah and he struck him down because he had put out his hand against the ark; so he died there before God.

11 David was angry because YHWH had burst out against Uzzah, so he called that place Perez-uzzah, [that is, Breaking out against Uzzah] to this day.

12 David was afraid of God that day saying, "How can I bring the ark of God to me?"

13 So David did not bring the ark to himself into the city of David; rather he took it aside to the house of Obed-edom the Gittite.

14 The ark of God remained with the house of Obed-edom in his house for three months; so YHWH blessed the household of Obed-edom and all he had.

510 The Ark Brought to Jerusalem
1 Chron 15:1–16:6 // 2 Sam 6:12-19a

1 Chronicles 15

1 He [David] built for himself houses in the city of David; and established a place for the ark of God and pitched a tent for it.

2 David said that no one except the Levites should carry the ark of God; for YHWH had chosen them to carry the ark of YHWH and to minister to him forever.

3 David assembled all Israel to Jerusalem to bring up the ark of YHWH into its place, which he had established for it.

4 Then David gathered the sons of Aaron and the Levites;

5 of the sons of Kohath: Uriel the chief with one hundred and twenty of his kindred;

6 of the sons of Merari: Asaiah the chief with two hundred and twenty of his kindred;

7 of the sons of Gershom: Joel the chief with one hundred and thirty of his kindred;

8 of the sons of Elizaphan: Shemaiah the chief and two hundred of his kindred;

9 of the sons of Hebron: Eliel the chief and eighty of his kindred;

10 of the sons of Uzziel: Amminadab the chief and one hundred and twelve of his kindred.

11 Then David summoned Zadok and Abiathar the priests; and the Levites: Uriel, Asaiah and Joel, Shemaiah, and Eliel and Amminadab.

12 He said to them, "You are the heads of the fathers of the Levites. Consecrate yourselves, you and your brothers, that you may bring up the ark of YHWH God of Israel to [the place] I have established for it.

13 Since you did not [do it] the first time, YHWH our God has broken out against us because you did not inquire of him according to custom.

14 So the priests and the Levites consecrated themselves to bring up the ark of YHWH God of Israel,

15 and the sons of the Levites carried the ark of God just as Moses had commanded; according to the word of YHWH, on their shoulders with poles upon them.

16 David also said to the chiefs of the Levites to appoint their kindred as singers on musical instruments (harps and lyres and cymbals) playing to raise up a sound of joy.

17 So the Levites appointed Heman son of Joel, and of his brother Asaph son of Berechiah; and of the sons of Merari their kindred, Ethan son of Kushaiah;

18 with them their kindred of second rank: Zechariah son, Jaaziel, Shemiramoth, Jehiel, Unni, Eliab, Benaiah, Maaseiah, Mattithiah, Eliphelehu, Mikneiah; and Obed-edom and Jeiel were doorkeepers.

19 The singers: Heman, Asaph and Ethan were to play on bronze cymbals;

20 and Zechariah, Aziel, Shemiramoth, Jehiel, Unni, Eliab, Maaseiah, and Benaiah on harps according to Alamoth;

21 but Mattithiah, Eliphelehu, Mikniah, Obed-edom, Jeiel, Azaziah with lyres to lead "upon the Sheminith."

22 Chenaniah, chief of the Levites in music should direct it, since he had understanding [of it].

23 Berachiah and Elkanah were to be doorkeepers for the ark.

24 Shebanaiah, Joshaphat, Nethanel, Amasai, Zechariah, Benaiah, Eliezer the priests were blowing the trumpets before the ark of God, while Obed-edom and Jehiah were to be doorkeepers for the ark.

1 Chronicles 15	*2 Samuel 6*
25 So David and the elders of Israel and the officers of the thousands were going to bring up the ark of the covenant of YHWH from the house of Obed-edom with rejoicing.	12 It was reported to king David, "YHWH has blessed the household of Obed-edom and everything he has because of the ark of God." Then David went and brought up the ark of God from the house of Obed-edom [to] the city of David with rejoicing.
26 Since God helped the Levites who were bearing the ark of the covenant of YHWH, they sacrificed seven bulls and seven rams.	13 Whenever the bearers of the ark of YHWH had stepped six steps he sacrificed an ox and a fatling.
27 David also was clothed with a robe of fine linen, as were the Levites who were bearing the ark, and the singers and Chenaniah leader of the melody of the singers; on David [was] a linen ephod.	14 David was dancing with all his strength before YHWH; David was girded with a linen ephod.
28 So all Israel were bringing up the ark of the covenant of YHWH with shouting and the sound of the shofar, with trumpets and cymbals, making sounds on harps and lyres.	15 So David and all the house of Israel were bringing up the ark of YHWH with shouting and with the sound of the shofar.
29 When the ark of the covenant of YHWH came to the city of David, Michal daughter of Saul, looked out through the window and she saw king David leaping and dancing before YHWH, and she despised him in her heart.	16 As the ark of YHWH came into the city of David, Michal daughter of Saul, looked out through the window and she saw king David leaping and dancing before YHWH, and she despised him in her heart.
16:1 They brought the ark of God and set it inside the tent that David had pitched for it; and they presented burnt offerings and peace offerings before God.	17 Then they brought the ark of YHWH and put it in its place within the tent that David had pitched for it; then David offered burnt offerings and peace offerings before YHWH.
2 When David had finished offering up the burnt offering and peace offerings, he blessed the people in the name of YHWH.	18 When David had finished offering up the burnt offering and peace offerings, he blessed the people in the name of YHWH Sabaoth.
3 Then he distributed to every person in Israel, both man and woman, to each a circle of bread and a date-cake and a raisin-cake.	19 Then he distributed to all the people, to all the multitude of Israel, both man and woman, to each one loaf of bread and one date-cake and one raisin-cake.

4 He appointed before the ark of YHWH some of the Levites to serve, to invoke, to give thanks and to praise YHWH God of Israel.

5 Asaph was the chief and his second was Zechariah, Jeiel, Shemiramoth, Jehiel, Mattithiah, Eliab, Benaiah, Obed-edom, and Jeiel, with harps and lyres; Asaph was to make music on the cymbals.

6 Benaiah and Jahaziel were priests on the trumpets continually before the ark of the covenant of God.

511 David's Psalm of Thanksgiving
1 Chron 16:7-36 // Pss 105:1-15; 96:1-13; Isa 42:10; Pss 29:2; 48:1; 98:7-9; 106:1,47-8; 107:1

1 Chronicles 16

Psalm 105

7 On that day, then, David first ordained the praising of YHWH by Asaph and his brothers.

8 Praise YHWH; call on his name; make known among the peoples his deeds.

1 Praise YHWH; call on his name; make known among the peoples his deeds.

9 Sing to him; play to him; tell of all his wonders.

2 Sing to him; play to him; tell of all his wonders.

10 Glory in his holy name; let those who seek YHWH be joyful in heart.

3 Glory in his holy name; let those who seek YHWH be joyful in heart.

11 Turn to YHWH and his strength; seek his face always.

4 Turn to YHWH and his strength; seek his face always.

12 Remember his wonders that he has done, his signs and the judgments of his mouth,

5 Remember his wonders that he has done, his signs and the judgments of his mouth,

13 [O] seed of Israel his servant, sons of Jacob, his chosen ones.

6 [O] seed of Abraham his servant, sons of Jacob, his chosen ones.

14 He is YHWH our God; his judgments are in all the earth.

7 He is YHWH our God; his judgments are in all the earth.

15 Remember his covenant forever; the word he commanded for a thousand generations

8 Remember his covenant forever; the word he commanded for a thousand generations

16 which he made with Abraham, also his oath to Isaac.

17 Then he confirmed it to Jacob as a statute; to Israel, a covenant forever,

18 saying, "To you I will give the land of Canaan, the portion of your inheritance."

19 When you were few in number, insignificant and strangers in it,

20 they wandered up and down, from nation to nation, from one kingdom to another people;

21 he did not let any man oppress them, and he rebuked kings on their behalf,

22 "Do not touch my anointed ones, and do my prophets no harm."

23 Sing to YHWH all the earth; proclaim his salvation from day to day.

24 Declare his glory among the nations, his wonders among all the peoples.

25 For great is YHWH and most worthy of praise;
he is to be feared above all gods.

26 For all the gods of the nations are godlings,
but YHWH made the heavens.

27 Splendor and majesty are before him; strength and joy are in his place.

28 Ascribe to YHWH, families of the peoples;
ascribe to YHWH glory and power.

9 which he made with Abraham, also his oath to Isaac.

10 Then he confirmed it to Jacob as a statute; to Israel, a covenant forever,

11 saying, "To you I will give the land of Canaan, the portion of your inheritance."

12 When they were few in number, insignificant and strangers in it,

13 they wandered up and down from nation to nation, from one kingdom to another people;

14 he did not let any human oppress them, and he rebuked kings on their behalf,

15 "Do not touch my anointed ones, and do my prophets no harm."

Psalm 96
1 Sing to YHWH a new song;
sing to YHWH all the earth.

2 Sing to YHWH; bless his name;
proclaim his salvation from day to day.

3 Declare his glory among the nations, his wonders among all the peoples.

4 For great is YHWH and most worthy of praise;
he is to be feared above all gods.

5 For all the gods of the nations are godlings,
but YHWH made the heavens.

6 Splendor and majesty are before him; strength and beauty are in his sanctuary.

7 Ascribe to YHWH, families of the peoples;
ascribe to YHWH glory and power.

Isaiah 42
10 Sing to YHWH a new song,
his praise from the end of the earth. . . .

Psalm 48
2 Great is YHWH and most worthy of praise
in the city of our God, his holy mountain.

29 Ascribe to YHWH the glory of his name;
bear an offering and come before him.

Bow down to YHWH in holy adornment;
30 tremble before him all the earth.

Also, the world is firmly established;
it shall not be moved.

31 Let the heavens rejoice and let the earth be glad;
let them say among the nations, "YHWH is king!"

32 Let the sea thunder and what fills it;
let the field make merry and all that is in it.

33 Then shall the trees of the forest shout for joy

before YHWH, for he comes to judge the earth.

34 Give thanks to YHWH, for he is good; for his grace is for ever.

35 Say also, "Save us, God of our salvation;
gather us and deliver us from the nations;
to give thanks to your holy name,
to take pride in your praise.

8 Ascribe to YHWH the glory of his name;
bear an offering and come into his courts.

9 Bow down to YHWH in holy adornment;
tremble before him all the earth.

10 Say among the nations, "YHWH is king!"

Also, the world is firmly established;
it shall not be moved.

He will judge the peoples with integrity, his praise from the end of the earth.

11 Let the heavens rejoice and let the earth be glad;

let the sea thunder and what fills it;

12 let the field make merry and all that is in it.

Then shall all the trees of the forest shout for joy

13 before YHWH, for he comes; for he comes to judge the earth.

He will judge the world with righteousness and the peoples with integrity.

Psalm 106
1 Praise YHWH! Give thanks to YHWH, for he is good; for his grace is for ever.

47 Save us, YHWH our God,

gather us from the nations;

to give thanks to your holy name,
to take pride in your praise.

Psalm 29
2 Ascribe to YHWH the glory of his name;

bow down to YHWH in holy adornment.

Psalm 98
7 Let the sea thunder and what fills it;
the world and those who dwell in it.

8 Let the rivers clap their hands; let the mountains shout for joy

9 before YHWH, for he comes to judge the earth.

He will judge the world with righteousness and the peoples with integrity.

Psalm 107
1 Give thanks to YHWH, for he is good; for his grace is for ever.

36 Blessed be YHWH God of Israel, from everlasting to everlasting. Then all the people said, "Amen!" and praised YHWH.	48 Blessed be YHWH God of Israel, from everlasting to everlasting. Then all the people said, "Amen! Praise YHWH!"

512 The Levites Appointed for the Ark: Michal Chides David
1 Chron 16:37-43 // 2 Sam 6:19b-23

1 Chronicles 16	*2 Samuel 6*
37 Then David left Asaph and his kinsfolk there before the ark of the covenant of YHWH to minister on a daily basis before the ark, as each day required,	
38 and Obed-edom and their sixty-eight kinsfolk; and Obed-edom son of Jeduthun and Hosah as doorkeepers.	
39 He also left Zadok the priest and his kindred the priests before the tabernacle of YHWH in the high place which was at Gibeon,	
40 to offer up burnt offerings to YHWH on the altar of burnt offering, continually in the morning and in the evening, according to all that was written in the Torah of YHWH that he commanded Israel.	
41 With them were Heman, Jeduthun and the rest of those chosen—who were specified by [their] names to give thanks to YHWH "for his steadfast love lasts forever."	
42 With them, Heman and Jeduthun, were trumpets and cymbals for playing, and instruments for the sacred song, and the sons of Jeduthun were in charge of the door.	
43 All the people went to their own homes.	19 All the people went to their own homes.
Then David turned around to bless his household.	20 Then David returned to bless his household. But Michal daughter of Saul, went out to meet David and she said, "How the king of Israel has honored himself today: who exposed himself today before the eyes of his servants' maids, as one of the worthless fellows might expose himself!"
	21 David said to Michal, "Before YHWH who chose me over your father and all his house to appoint me prince over the people of YHWH, over Israel, I will make merry before YHWH;

22 and I will make myself even more contemptible than this and I will be humiliated in my own eyes, but among the maids of whom you spoke, among them I will be honored."

23 Now Michal daughter of Saul had no child of her own up to the day of her death.

513 God's Covenant with David
1 Chron 17:1-27 // 2 Sam 7:1-29

1 Chronicles 17

1 Now when David was residing in his house, David said to Nathan the prophet, "Here I am residing in a house of cedar, while the ark of the covenant of YHWH is under tent curtains!"

2 Then Nathan said to David, "Everything that you have in your heart, do it, for God is with you."

3 But when that night came, the word of God [came] to Nathan,

4 "Go and say to David my servant, 'Thus says YHWH: You are not the one who shall build me a house to reside [in].

5 For I have not resided in a house from the day that I brought up Israel even to this day; rather I have been from tent to tent and from tabernacle [to tabernacle].

6 In all my moving about among all Israel, have I ever uttered a word with one of the judges of Israel whom I commanded to shepherd my people saying: Why have you not built me a house of cedar?

7 But now, thus you shall speak to my servant David, 'Thus says YHWH of Sabaoth: I took you from the pasture, from following the flock, to be prince over my people Israel.

2 Samuel 7

1 Now when the king was residing in his house and YHWH had given him rest from all his enemies around him,

2 the king said to Nathan the prophet, "See now I am residing in a house of cedar, while the ark of God resides inside tent curtains!"

3 Then Nathan said to the king, "Everything that is in your heart, go do it, for YHWH is with you."

4 But when that night came the word of YHWH [came] to Nathan,

5 "Go and say to my servant, to David, 'Thus says YHWH: Will you build me a house for me to reside [in]?

6 Surely I have not resided in a house since the day I brought up the Israelites from Egypt even to this day; rather I have been moving about in a tent and in a tabernacle.

7 In all my moving about among all the people of Israel, have I ever uttered a word with one of the tribal chiefs of Israel whom I commanded to shepherd my people Israel, saying: Why have you not built me a house of cedar?

8 But now, thus you shall speak to my servant, to David, 'Thus says YHWH Sabaoth, I took you from the pasture, from following the flock, to be prince over my people, over Israel.

8 I have been with you everywhere you have gone and have cut off all your enemies from before you; and I will make for you a name like the name of the greatest ones of the earth.

9 I will establish a place for my people Israel and I will plant them so that they may settle down in their place and be disturbed no more nor shall wicked ones continue to consume them as in the former [times],

10 as from the days that I appointed judges over my people Israel. I will humble all your enemies. Also I have told you that YHWH will build a house [dynasty] for you.

11 When your days are fulfilled to go with your ancestors, then I will raise up your offspring after you, one of your own sons, and I will establish his kingship.

12 He will build a house for me and I will establish his throne forever.

13 I will be a father to him and he will be a son to me.

But my steadfast love I will not take from him as I withdrew [it] from him who was before you,

14 but I will confirm him in my house and in my kingship forever and his throne shall be established forever.'"

15 According to all these words and all this vision, Nathan spoke to David.

16 King David went in and sat before YHWH and said, "Who am I, YHWH God, and what is my house that you have brought me thus far?

17 Yet this was a small thing in your eyes, O God; you have spoken about the house of your servant for a long time to come, and you have seen me as a type of man on the way up, YHWH God.

18 What more can David say to you about the honor of your servant? For you know your servant.

19 YHWH, for the sake of your servant and according to your heart you have done all this great thing to make known all [your] great deeds.

9 I have been with you everywhere you have gone and have cut off all your enemies from before you; and I will make for you a great name like the name of the greatest ones of the earth.

10 I will establish a place for my people, for Israel, and I will plant them so that they may settle down in their place and be disturbed no more nor shall wicked ones continue to oppress them as in the former [times],

11 as from the day that I appointed judges over my people Israel. I will give you rest from all your enemies. Also, YHWH has said to you that YHWH will make a house [dynasty] for you.

12 When your days are fulfilled and you lie down with your ancestors, then I will raise up your offspring after you, who shall come forth from your loins, and I will establish the throne of his kingdom forever.

13 He will build a house for my name and I will establish his royal throne forever.

14 I will be a father to him and he will be a son to me. When he acts perversely I will punish him with a rod of men and with blows of humans.

15 But my steadfast love will not depart from him as I withdrew [it] from Saul whom I withdrew from before you.

16 Your house and your kingdom shall be secure before you; your throne shall be established forever.'"

17 According to all these words and all this vision, Nathan spoke to David.

18 King David went in and sat before YHWH and said, "Who am I, my lord YHWH, and what is my house that you have brought me thus far?

19 Yet this was still a small thing in your eyes, my lord YHWH; you have spoken also about the house of your servant for a long time to come, and this is the Torah of Adam, my lord YHWH.

20 What more can David still say to you? For you know your servant, my lord YHWH.

21 For the sake of your word and according to your heart you have done all this great thing to make your servant known.

20 YHWH, there is none like you and there is no god besides you, according to everything we have heard with our ears.

21 Who is like your people Israel: one nation on the earth whom God went to redeem for himself [as] a people, and to establish a name for you for great and wonderful things, to drive out nations from before your people whom you have redeemed from Egypt.

22 You have appointed your people Israel as your people forever, and you YHWH have become their God.

23 But now YHWH, the word which you uttered concerning your servant and concerning his house, let it stand forever; and do just as you said.

24 Then your name will stand and grow great forever, in the saying, 'YHWH Sabaoth, God of Israel, God for Israel,' and the house of David your servant: may it be established before you.

25 For you, my God, have revealed to the ear of your servant that you will build for him a house, therefore your servant has found [it] to pray before you.

26 And now YHWH, you are he who is God and you have spoken this good thing to your servant.

27 Now, may you go on to bless the house of your servant so that it may be forever before you, since you YHWH, have blessed it, it shall be blessed forever."

22 Because of this you are great, my lord YHWH, for there is none like you and there is no god besides you, according to everything we have heard with our ears.

23 Who is like your people, like Israel: one nation on the earth whom God went to redeem for himself for a people, and to establish for himself a name and to do for you this great and amazing thing for your land before your people, whom you have redeemed for yourself from Egypt, a nation and its gods.

24 You have established for yourself your people Israel as your people forever, and you YHWH have become their God.

25 But now YHWH God, the word which you uttered concerning your servant and concerning his house, establish it forever; and do just as you said.

26 Then your name will grow great forever in the saying, 'YHWH Sabaoth, God over Israel' and the house of your servant David: let it be established before you.

27 For you, YHWH Sabaoth, God of Israel, have revealed to the ear of your servant, saying, 'I shall build a house for you.' Therefore your servant has found [it in] his heart to pray to you this prayer:

28 And now my lord YHWH, you are he who is God, and your words shall be truth and you promised this good thing to your servant.

29 Now, go on and bless the house of your servant so that it may be forever before you, for you my lord YHWH, have spoken and from your covenant the house of your servant shall be blessed forever."

David-2
Sections 514–532

Number	Title	1 Chronicles	2 Samuel
514	David Extends His Kingdom	18:1-13	8:1-14
515	David's Officers	18:14-17	8:15-18
516	David's Loyalty to Jonathan's Son		9:1-13
517	The Defeat of Ammonites and Arameans	19:1-19	10:1-19
518a	Joab Besieges Rabbah	20:1a	11:1
518b	David and Bathsheba		11:2-27
519	Nathan Reproves David		12:1-25
520	David Captures Rabbah	20:1b-3	12:26-31
521	Amnon and Tamar		13:1-22
522	Absalom's Revenge and Flight		13:23-39
523	Joab's Scheme for Absalom's Return		14:1-33
524	Absalom's Rebellion		15:1–16:23
525	Ahithophel's Advice Undermined		17:1-23
526	David at Mahanaim	[2:17]	17:24-29
527	The Death of Absalom		18:1–19:9b
528	David's Return to Jerusalem		19:9c-44
529a	The Revolt of Sheba		20:1-22
529b	David's Officers	[18:15-17]	20:23-26
530	The Avenging of the Gibeonites		21:1-14
531	Abishai Rescues David from the Giant		21:15-17
532	The Giants Slain by David's Men	20:4-8	21:18-22

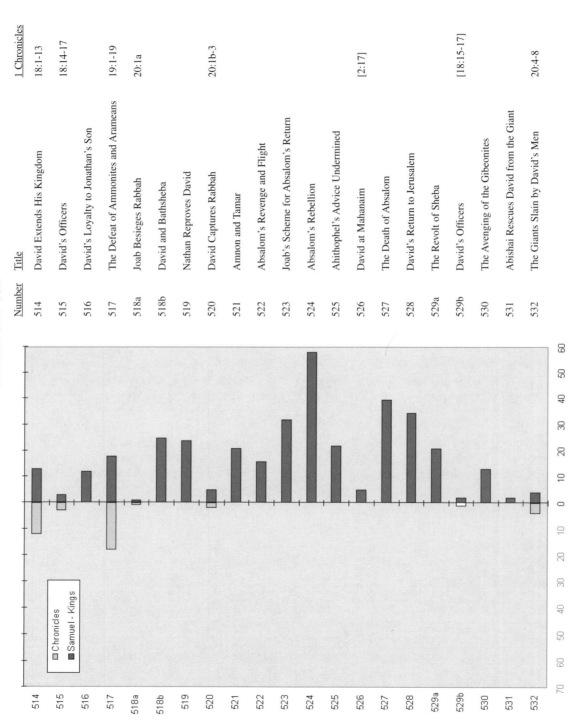

Number of Verses

Section Number

514 David Extends His Kingdom
1 Chron 18:1-13 // 2 Sam 8:1-14; Ps 60:2

1 Chronicles 18	*2 Samuel 8*
1 After this David defeated the Philistines and subdued them, and he took Gath and its daughters [villages] from the hand of the Philistines.	1 After this David defeated the Philistines and subdued them, and David took Metheg-ammah from the hand of the Philistines.
2 Then he defeated Moab and Moab became servants for David, bearing tribute.	2 Then he defeated Moab and he measured them with a cord, making them lie down on the ground; he measured off two cord-lengths to be put to death and a full cord-length to be kept alive. So Moab became servants for David, bearing tribute.
3 Then David defeated Hadadezer king of Zobah at Hamath, as he was going to set up his monument at the Euphrates River.	3 Then David defeated Hadadezer son of Rehob, king of Zobah, as he was going to restore his monument at the River.
4 David captured from him a thousand chariots and seven thousand charioteers and twenty thousand foot soldiers; and David hamstrung all the chariot horses but he spared a hundred chariot horses.	4 David captured from him a thousand seven hundred charioteers and twenty thousand foot soldiers; and David hamstrung all the chariot horses but he spared a hundred chariot horses.
5 When the Arameans of Damascus came to assist Hadadezer king of Zobah, David struck down twenty-two thousand men of the Arameans.	5 When the Arameans of Damascus came to assist Hadadezer king of Zobah, David struck down twenty-two thousand men of the Arameans.
6 Then David placed [garrisons] among the Arameans of Damascus, and the Arameans became servants to David, bearing tribute. So YHWH made David victorious wherever he went.	6 Then David placed garrisons among the Arameans of Damascus, and the Arameans became servants to David, bearing tribute. So YHWH made David victorious wherever he went.
7 Then David took the shields of gold which were upon the servants of Hadadezer and he brought them to Jerusalem.	7 Then David took the shields of gold which had belonged to the servants of Hadadezer and he brought them to Jerusalem.
8 From Tibhath and from Cun, cities of Hadadezer, David took a vast amount of bronze; and with it Solomon made the bronze Sea and the pillars and the bronze vessels.	8 From Betah and from Berothai, cities of Hadadezer, King David took a vast amount of bronze.

9 When Tou king of Hamath, heard that David had struck down all the forces of Hadadezer king of Zobah,

10 he sent Hadoram his son to King David to salute him and to congratulate him, since he had fought against Hadadezer and defeated him, for Tou had been at war with Hadadezer. [He sent] all vessels of silver and gold and bronze.

11 Also King David consecrated them to YHWH, along with the silver and the gold which he carried away from all the nations, from Edom and from Moab and from the Ammonites and from the Philistines and from Amalek.

12 Abishai son of Zeruiah struck down the Edomites in the Valley of Salt, eighteen thousand of them.

13 Then he placed garrisons in Edom; in all Edom he placed garrisons, and all the Edomites became subjects to David. Thus YHWH made David victorious wherever he went.

9 When Toi king of Hamath heard that David had struck down all the forces of Hadadezer,

10 Toi sent his son Joram to King David to salute him and to congratulate him, since he had fought against Hadadezer and defeated him, for Toi had been at war with Hadadezer; and in his hand were vessels of silver and vessels of gold and vessels of bronze.

11 Also King David consecrated them to YHWH, along with the silver and the gold which he had consecrated from all the nations which he had subdued:

12 from Aram and from Moab and from the Ammonites and from the Philistines and from Amalek, and from the booty of Hadadezer son of Rehob king of Zobah.

13 David made a name for himself when he returned from his striking down Aram in the Valley of Salt, eighteen thousand of them.

14 Then he placed garrisons in Edom; in all Edom he placed garrisons, and all the Edomites became subjects to David. Thus YHWH made David victorious wherever he went.

Psalm 60

2 When he struggled with Aram Naharaim and with Aram Zobah, Joab returned and struck down the Edomites in the Valley of Salt, twelve thousand of them.

515 David's Officers
1 Chron 18:14-17 // 2 Sam 8:15-18 // 2 Sam 20:23-26

1 Chronicles 18	*2 Samuel 8*	*2 Samuel 20*
14 When David became king over all Israel, he acted justly and righteously to all his people.	15 When David became king over all Israel, David acted justly and righteously to all his people.	
15 Joab son of Zeruiah was over the army, and Jehoshaphat son of Ahilud was recorder;	16 Joab son of Zeruiah was over the army, and Jehoshaphat son of Ahilud was recorder;	23a Joab was in charge of all the army of Israel; 24b Jehoshaphat son of Ahilud was the recorder;
16 Zadok son of Ahitub and Abimelech son of Abiathar were priests; and Shavsha was scribe;	17 Zadok son of Ahitub and Ahimelech son of Abiathar were priests; and Seraiah was scribe;	25b Zadok and Abiathar were priests; 25a and Sheya was scribe;
17 Benaiah son of Jehoiada was over the Cherethites and the Pelethites, and the sons of David were the chief officials of the king.	18 Benaiah son of Jehoiada and Cherethites and Pelethites and the sons of David were priests.	23b and Benaiah son of Jehoiada was over the Cherethites and over the Pelethites
		24a And Adoram was over the corvée,
		26 also Ira the Jairite was David's priest.

516 David's Loyalty to Jonathan's Son
2 Sam 9:1-13

2 Samuel 9

1 David said, "Is there anyone still remaining to the house of Saul with whom I may deal kindly for the sake of Jonathan?"

2 Now there was a servant belonging to the house of Saul and his name was Ziba; so they summoned him to David.

3 The king said to him, "Are you Ziba?" and he said, "Your servant." Then the king said, "Is there no one still left to the house of Saul, with whom I may share the grace of God?" Ziba said to the king, "[There remains] yet a son to Jonathan, crippled in [his] feet."

4 The king said to him, "Where is he?" Ziba said to the king, "Look, he is [at] the house of Machir son of Ammiel, in Lo-debar."

5 So king David sent and took him from the house of Machir son of Ammiel, from Lo-debar.

6 Mephibosheth son of Jonathan son of Saul came to David, and fell on his face and prostrated himself. David said, "Mephibosheth!" He said, "Your servant."

7 David said to him, "Do not be afraid for I will surely deal with you kindly for the sake of Jonathan your father: I will restore to you all the land of Saul your [grand]father; and you yourself shall eat bread at my table always."

8 Then he bowed himself down and said, "What is your servant that you would look on a dead dog like me?"

9 Then the king summoned Ziba servant of Saul, and said to him, "All that belonged to Saul and to all his house I have given to the son of your master.

10 You will work the land for him, you and your sons and your servants, that you may bring in [the harvest] that there may be bread for the son of your master to eat; for Mephibosheth son of your master will always eat bread at my table." Now Ziba had fifteen sons and twenty servants.

11 Then Ziba said to the king, "According to all that my lord the king has commanded his servant, so shall your servant do." So Mephibosheth was eating at my table like one of the sons of the king.

12 Mephibosheth had a young son and his name was Mica; and all who lived in the house of Ziba [were] servants to Mephibosheth.

13 Mephibosheth lived in Jerusalem, for he ate at the king's table always. Now he was crippled in both his feet.

517 The Defeat of the Ammonites and Arameans
1 Chron 19:1-19 // 2 Sam 10:1-19

1 Chronicles 19	2 Samuel 10
1 When sometime afterward Nahash king of the Ammonites died, his son became king in his place,	1 When sometime afterward the king of the Ammonites died, Hanun his son became king in his place,
2 David said, "I will render loyalty to Hanun son of Nahash, for his father rendered loyalty to me." So David sent messengers to console him on account of his father. When the servants of David entered into the land of the Ammonites, to Hanun, to console him,	2 David said, "I will render loyalty to Hanun son of Nahash, as his father rendered loyalty to me." So David sent to console him through his servants concerning his father. When the servants of David entered the land of the Ammonites,
3 the officials of the Ammonites said to Hanun, "Is David honoring your father in your view, that he has sent consolers to you? Is it not in order to search out, to destroy, and to spy out the land that his servants have come to you?"	3 the officials of the Ammonites said to Hanun their lord, "Is David honoring your father in your view, that he has sent consolers to you? Is it not in order to search out the city, to spy it out and to destroy it that David has sent his servants to you?"

4 So Hanun seized the servants of David, shaved them, cut off their garments halfway up to the crotch and sent them off,

5 and they went. When they told David about the men, he sent to meet them, for the men were very ashamed; and the king said, "Stay in Jericho until your beard[s] have grown back, and then return."

6 When the Ammonites saw that they had rendered themselves odious with David, Hanun and the Ammonites sent a thousand talents of silver to hire for themselves from Aram Naharaim and from Aram Maacah and from Zobah, chariots and horsemen.

7 They hired for themselves thirty-two thousand chariot[s] and the king of Maacah and his people, and they came and camped before Medeba. When the Ammonites were assembled from their cities, they also came out for battle.

8 When David heard, he sent Joab and all the army of warriors.

9 The Ammonites came forth and arrayed [themselves] for battle at the entrance of the city while the kings who had come were by themselves in the field.

10 When Joab saw that a battleline was against him, before and behind, he chose some of all the best picked [men] of Israel and drew them up to confront the Arameans,

11 but the remainder of the people he put into the command of Abishai, his brother, and they drew [themselves] to confront the Ammonites.

12 Then he said, "If the Arameans are too strong for me, you will be my back-up; but if the Ammonites are too strong for you, I will back you up.

13 Be strong and let us indeed be strong for the sake of our people and for the sake of the cities of our God; and whatever is right in his eyes YHWH will do.

14 When Joab and the people who were with him approached the Arameans for battle, they fled before him.

15 When the Ammonites saw that the Arameans were fleeing, they themselves also fled before Abishai, his brother, and went to the city; but Joab went to Jerusalem.

4 So Hanun seized the servants of David, shaved off half of their beard[s], cut off their garments halfway up to their buttocks and sent them off.

5 When they told David, he sent to meet them, for the men were very ashamed; and the king said, "Stay in Jericho till your beard[s] have grown back, and then return."

6 When the Ammonites saw that they had become odious to David, the Ammonites sent and hired the Arameans of Beth-rehob and the Arameans of Zobah [with] twenty thousand infantry and the king of Maacah [with] one thousand men and the men of Tob [with] twelve thousand men.

7 When David heard, he sent Joab and all the army, the warriors.

The Ammonites came forth and arrayed [themselves] for battle at the entrance of the gate while the Arameans of Zobah and Rehob and the men of Tob and Maacah [were] by themselves in the field.

9 When Joab saw that the battleline was against him, before and behind, he chose some of the best picked [men] of Israel and drew them up to confront the Arameans,

10 but the remainder of the people he put into the command of Abishai, his brother, and he drew [them] up to confront the Ammonites.

11 Then he said, "If the Arameans are too strong for me, you will be my back-up; but if the Ammonites are too strong for you, I will come to back you up.

12 Be strong and let us be strong for the sake of our people and for the sake of the cities of our God; and YHWH will do whatever is right in his eyes.

13 When Joab and the people who were with him approached for battle against the Arameans, they fled before him.

14 When the Ammonites saw that the Arameans were fleeing they fled before Abishai, and went [into] the city; but Joab turned back from the Ammonites and went to Jerusalem.

16 When the Arameans saw that they had been routed before Israel, they sent messengers and brought out the Arameans who were beyond the River, and Shophach, commander of the army of Hadadezer, was in front of them.

17 When it was told to David, he assembled all Israel, crossed the Jordan, came to them and drew up his forces against them. When David drew up the battle to meet the Arameans, they fought with him.

18 The Arameans fled before Israel, and David killed some seven thousand Aramean charioteers and forty thousand foot-soldiers; he also put to death Shobach, the commander of their army.

19 When the servants of Hadadezer, saw that they had been routed before Israel, they made peace with David and became subject to him. Thus, the Arameans were unwilling to support the Ammonites any more.

15 When the Arameans saw that they had been routed before Israel, they assembled themselves together,

16 and Hadadezer sent for and brought the Arameans who were beyond the River and they entered Helam, and Shobach, the commander of the army of Hadadezer, was in front of them.

17 When it was told to David, he assembled all Israel, crossed the Jordan, and came to Helam. The Arameans drew themselves up to meet David and they fought with him.

18 The Arameans fled before Israel, and David killed some seven hundred Aramean charioteers and forty thousand horsemen; and he struck down Shobach, the commander of their army, so that he died there.

19 When all the kings, the servants of Hadadezer, saw that they had been routed before Israel, they made peace with Israel and became subject to them. Thus, the Arameans were afraid to support the Ammonites any more.

518a Joab Besieges Rabbah
1 Chron 20:1a // 2 Sam 11:1

1 Chronicles 20

1a At the time of the turn of the year, at the time when kings go forth [to battle], Joab led out the army force and ravaged the land of the Ammonites and went and besieged Rabbah. David, however, remained behind in Jerusalem.

2 Samuel 11

1 At the turn of the year, at the time when messengers go forth, David sent Joab and with him his servants and all Israel, and they ravaged the Ammonites and laid siege to Rabbah. David, however, remained behind in Jerusalem.

518b David and Bathsheba
2 Sam 11:2-27

2 It happened in the late afternoon, when David rose from his couch and was walking about on the roof of the king's house, that he saw from the roof a woman bathing; and the woman was very beautiful.

3 So David sent and inquired about the woman, and [someone] said, "Is this not Bathsheba daughter of Eliam, the wife of Uriah the Hittite?"

4 So David sent messengers and took her and she came to him and he lay with her—now she was purifying herself after her menstrual period; then she returned to her house.

5 The woman conceived; and she sent and informed David and said, "I am pregnant."

6 So David sent word to Joab, "Send me Uriah the Hittite." So Joab sent Uriah to David.

7 When Uriah came to him David asked about the welfare of Joab and the people, and about the progress of the war.

8 Then David said to Uriah, "Go down to your house and wash your feet." So Uriah went out from the house of the king, and a gift from the king followed him.

9 However Uriah slept at the entrance of the king's house with all the servants of his lord, and did not go down to his house.

10 When they informed David, "Uriah did not go down to his house," David said to Uriah, "Have you not come from a journey? Why have you not gone down to your house?"

11 Uriah said to David, "The ark, Israel, and Judah remain in booths; and my lord Joab and the servants of my lord are camped out in the open field. Should I go to my house to eat and drink and lie with my wife? As you live and by your life I will not do such a thing!"

12 Then David said to Uriah, "Stay here also today, but tomorrow I shall send you [back]." So Uriah stayed in Jerusalem that day, and on the morrow.

13 David summoned him and he ate before him and he drank and he got him drunk; and in the evening he went to lie down on his own couch with the servants of his lord and did not go down to his house.

14 Therefore in the morning David wrote a letter to Joab and sent [it] by the hand of Uriah.

15 He wrote in the letter as follows: "Put Uriah in the forefront of the heaviest fighting and then pull back from him that he may be struck down and die."

16 Since Joab kept siege watch over the city, he put Uriah at the place where he knew the valiant warriors would be.

17 When the men of the city came out and fought with Joab, some of the people from David's servants fell, and Uriah the Hittite also died.

18 Then Joab sent and informed David of all the circumstances of the battle;

19 he commanded the messenger, "When you have finished telling the king all the circumstances of the battle,

20 then if the rage of the king mounts up and he says to you, 'Why did you draw so near to the city to fight? Did you not know that they would shoot [arrows] from the top of the wall?

21 Who struck down Abimelech son of Jerubbesheth? Did not a woman throw an upper millstone on him from the top of the wall when he died at Thebez? Why did you go so near to the wall?' Then you shall say, 'Your servant Uriah the Hittite also died.'"

22 So the messenger went and came and told David all that Joab had sent him [to say].

23 The messenger said to David, "Though the men prevailed over us and came out against us into the open field, we drove them back up to the entrance of the gate.

24 Then the archers shot at your servants from the top of the wall, and some of the servants of the king died, and your servant Uriah the Hittite also died."

25 Then David said to the messenger, "Thus you shall say to Joab: 'Let not this matter be troublesome in your eyes, for the sword devours now this one and now that one. Renew your attack on the city and conquer it. So encourage him!'"

26 Now when the wife of Uriah heard that Uriah her husband was dead, she mourned for her spouse.

27 When the mourning was past, David sent for and received her into his house, and she became his wife and bore him a son; but the thing that David had done was troubling in the eyes of YHWH.

519 Nathan Reproves David
2 Sam 12:1-25

2 Samuel 12

1 And YHWH sent Nathan to David. He came to him and said to him, "There were two men in a certain city, one rich and one poor.

2 The rich man had very many flocks and herds,

3 but the poor man had nothing, except one little ewe lamb which he had bought; and he brought it up and it grew up together with him and with his children; and it was accustomed to eat from his morsel and drink from his cup, and lie in his lap, and it was like a daughter to him.

4 Now there came a traveller to the rich man, and he refrained from taking from his own flock and from his own herd to make [something] for the wayfarer who had come to him, but he took the ewe lamb of the poor man and made that for the man who had come to him."

5 Then David's wrath burned greatly against the man, and he said to Nathan, "As YHWH lives, surely the man who has done this is as good as dead,

6 and he shall compensate for the ewe lamb fourfold, because he has done this thing; and since he did not refrain [from taking what belonged to another].

7 Then Nathan said to David, "You are the man! Thus says YHWH the God of Israel, 'I anointed you as king over Israel and I delivered you from the hand of Saul,

8 and I gave you the house of your master and the wives of your master, into your lap, and I gave to you the house of Israel and Judah, and if that were too little, I would have added the same again.

9 Why did you despise the word of YHWH, to do what is wrong in my eyes, that you struck down Uriah the Hittite with the sword, that you took his wife for yourself as your wife and killed him with the sword of the Ammonites?

10 Therefore the sword shall never depart from your house, because you despised me and took the wife of Uriah the Hittite to be your wife.

11 Thus says YHWH, 'See, I am about to raise up disaster upon you from within your own house, and I will take your wives right before your eyes and give them to your neighbor, and he shall lie with your wives in the sight of this sun.

12 For you acted in secret, but I will do this thing before all Israel and before the sun.'"

13 Then David said to Nathan, "I have sinned against YHWH." Nathan said to David, "YHWH has now put away your sin. You shall not die.

14 Yet because you have utterly spurned the enemies of YHWH in this matter, the child that is born to you shall surely die."

15 Then Nathan went to his house and YHWH struck the child that the wife of Uriah had borne to David, it became very sick.

16 Therefore David pleaded with God on behalf of the boy, and David fasted and went in and spent the night lying on the ground.

17 The elders of his house stood over him to urge him to rise up from the ground but he would not, nor would he eat bread with them.

18 Then on the seventh day the child died, and the servants of David were afraid to tell him that the child was dead for they said, "While the child was alive we spoke to him but he would not listen to our voice; how shall we tell him the child is dead? He may do himself harm."

19 But David noted that his servants were whispering and David understood that the child was dead. David said to his servants, "Is the child dead?" They responded, "Dead."

20 Then David arose from the ground, washed, anointed himself, changed his clothes and went to the house of YHWH, and bowed himself down. Then he went to his house, and when he asked they set down bread before him and he ate.

21 His servants said to him, "What is this thing that you have done? You fasted and wept on behalf of the child while [it was] alive, but now when the child is dead you have risen up and eaten bread?"

22 He replied, "While the child was still alive I fasted and wept because I thought, 'Who knows? YHWH may be gracious to me and the child may live.'

23 But now he is dead—why should I fast? Am I able to bring him back again? I shall go to him but he shall not return to me."

24 Then David comforted Bathsheba his wife, and he went to her and lay with her; and she bore a son and she[1] called his name Solomon. YHWH loved him,

25 so he sent [word] through Nathan the prophet; and he called his name Jedidiah because of YHWH.

---

[1] Reading the Qere.

520 David Captures Rabbah
1 Chron 20:1b-3 // 2 Sam 12:26-31

1 Chronicles 20	*2 Samuel 12*
1b When Joab attacked Rabbah, he overthrew it.	26 When Joab fought with Rabbah of the Ammonites, he captured the royal city.
	27 Then Joab sent messengers to David and said, "I have fought against Rabbah; also I have captured the city water [supply].
	28 So now, assemble the rest of the people and encamp against the city and capture it, lest I myself capture the city and my name will be proclaimed over it."
	29 So David assembled all the people and went to Rabbah and fought with it and captured it.

2 David took the crown of their king from off his head; and he found it [in] weight a talent of gold, and upon it a precious stone, and it was set upon David's head. He also brought out the spoil of the city, a vast quantity.

3 Also he brought out the people who were in it and he cut up [the city] with the saw, picks of iron, and saws. Thus David did to all the cities of the Ammonites. Then David and all the people returned to Jerusalem.

30 He took the crown of their king from off his head; and its weight was a talent of gold, and [upon it] a precious stone, and it was set upon David's head. He also brought out the spoil of the city, a vast quantity.

31 Also he brought out the people who were in it and imposed on them saws, picks of iron, and axes of iron, and required them to demolish the brick-works. Thus he did to all the cities of the Ammonites. Then David and all the people returned to Jerusalem.

521 Amnon and Tamar
2 Sam 13:1-22

2 Samuel 13

1 Sometime afterward this happened: Absalom son of David had a beautiful sister and her name was Tamar; and Amnon son of David was in love with her.

2 Now Amnon was so besotted that he made himself sick over Tamar his sister, for she was a virgin and it seemed impossible for Amnon to do anything to her.

3 But Amnon had a friend and his name was Jonadab son of Shimeah, a brother of David: now Jonadab was a very shrewd man,

4 and he said to him, "Why are you so despondent, son of the king, morning after morning? Will you not tell me?" Amnon said to him, "I am in love with Tamar, sister of Absalom my brother."

5 Jonadab said to him, "Lie down on your couch and [pretend to] be sick; and when your father comes to see you, you say to him, 'Please let Tamar my sister come, and let her prepare bread for me and make food in my sight, that I may see [her] and eat from her hand.'"

6 So Amnon lay down and [pretended to] be sick. When the king came to see him, Amnon said to the king, "Please let Tamar my sister come and let her make two pancakes in my sight, that I may be fed from her hand."

7 Then David sent to Tamar at the house, saying, "Go, please, to the house of Amnon your brother, and make food for him."

8 So Tamar went to the house of Amnon her brother, and he was lying down. She took the dough, kneaded [it] and shaped pancakes in his sight and baked the pancakes.

9 Then she took the pan and held it out in front of him, but he refused to eat. Amnon said, "Send everyone away from me!" So everyone went away from him.

10 Then Amnon said to Tamar, "Bring the food [to my] chamber, that I may be fed from your hand." So Tamar took the pancakes that she had made and brought them to Amnon her brother, into the chamber.

11 But when she brought them near to him to eat he overpowered her and said to her, "Come, lie with me, my sister!"

12 She said to him, "No, my brother, do not force me, for such a thing is not done in Israel. Do not do this despicable thing!

13 And I, where could I go with my shame? And you, you would be like one of the depraved men in Israel. Now, please speak to the king, for he will not withhold me from you."

14 But he refused to listen to her voice, but overpowered her and forced her and lay with her.

15 Then Amnon hated her with such very great hatred that the hatred with which he hated her was greater than the love with which he had loved her. Amnon said to her, "Get up! Get out!"

16 But she said to him, "Do not make this evil greater than the one you have just done to me, by sending me away." But he refused to listen to her.

17 Instead, he summoned his servant who waited on him and said, "Put this woman outside, away from me, and bolt the door behind her."

18 Now there was a long gown with sleeves on her, for so the virgin daughters of the king would clothe themselves as to their dresses. So the servant who waited upon him put her out and bolted the door behind her.

19 Then Tamar put ashes on her head, and tore the long gown with sleeves that was on her, and placed her hand on her head and went away, crying out as she went.

20 Absalom her brother said to her, "Has Amnon your brother been with you? Keep quiet for now, my sister, he is your brother. Do not trouble your heart over this matter." So Tamar remained as one forlorn in the house of Absalom her brother.

21 When King David heard of all these things, he became very angry.

22 Absalom, however, did not speak to Amnon, neither bad nor good, although Absalom hated Amnon on account of the fact that he had forced Tamar his sister.

522 Absalom's Revenge and Flight
2 Sam 13:23-39

2 Samuel 13

23 Now it came about two whole years later that Absalom had sheep shearers at Baal-Hazor which is within Ephraim; and Absalom invited all the sons of the king.

24 Absalom came to the king and said, "Look, your servant now has sheep shearers; will the king and his servants please go with your servant?"

25 But the king said to Absalom, "No, my son, let us not all go and be a burden on you." He pressed him, but he was unwilling to go; however, he did bless him.

26 Then Absalom said, "If not, please let my brother Amnon go with us." The king said to him, "Why should he go with you?"

27 When Absalom pressed him, he sent Amnon with him as well as all the sons of the king.

28 Now Absalom had commanded his servants, saying, "Mark when Amnon is mellow with wine, and when I say to you, 'Strike Amnon down,' you will kill him. Do not be afraid; have I myself not commanded you? Be strong and be valiant men."

29 So the servants of Absalom did to Amnon as Absalom had commanded. Then all the sons of the king rose up, each mounted on his mule and fled.

30 While they were on the way, the report reached David: 'Absalom has struck down all the sons of the king and not one of them is left!'

31 The king rose up, tore his garments, and lay down on the ground; and all his servants were standing by with torn garments.

32 Then Jonadab son of Shimeah, brother of David, spoke up and said, "Let not my lord think that they have killed all the young men, the sons of the king, for Amnon alone is dead. This was on the authority of Absalom from the day that he forced Tamar his sister.

33 Now do not let my lord the king take the matter to heart, thinking that all the sons of the king are dead, for Amnon alone is dead."

34 Now Absalom had fled. When the young man keeping watch looked up, he saw many people coming from the road behind him, from the side of the mountain.

35 Then Jonadab said to the king, "See, the sons of the king have come back; as was the word of your servant, so it has happened."

36 As soon as he had finished speaking, the sons of the king came back, and raised their voices and wept; and the king and all his servants also wept most bitterly.

37 Although Absalom had fled and gone to Talmai son of Ammihud king of Geshur, he grieved for his son every day.

38 But Absalom had fled and gone to Geshur, and was there for three years.

39 And [the spirit] of David the king pined to go out to Absalom; for he was comforted over Amnon, that he was dead.

523 Joab's Scheme for Absalom's Return
2 Sam 14:1-33

2 Samuel 14

1 Now Joab son of Zeruiah understood that the heart of the king was [fixed] on Absalom.

2 So Joab sent to Tekoa and took from there a wise woman. He said to her, "Act the [part of] a mourner and dress in the garments of mourning and do not anoint yourself with oil but be like a woman who has been mourning many days for the dead.

3 Then go to the king and say to him this very thing." So Joab put words in her mouth.

4 When the woman from Tekoa spoke to the king, she fell on her face to the ground and prostrated herself and said, "Help [me], O king."

5 The king said to her, "What is your concern?" She said, "Sadly, I am a widow woman and my husband is dead.

6 Your maidservant had two sons and the two of them were fighting in an open field, and there was no one to pull them apart and the one struck down the other and killed him.

7 Now all the family has risen up against your maidservant, and they are saying, 'Give up the one who struck down his brother that we may put him to death for the life of his brother whom he murdered, even though we may be doing away with the heir also.' Thus they would put out my [sole] remaining ember, not leaving to my husband name or progeny on the face of the earth."

8 Then the king said to the woman, "Go to your house, and I myself will give an order concerning you."

9 The woman from Tekoa said to the king, "On me, my lord the king, be the guilt and on the house of my father, but let the king and his throne be innocent."

10 The king said, "If anyone harasses you, then bring him to me, and he will no longer touch you."

11 Then she said, "Let the king now remember YHWH your God that the avenger of blood may destroy no more and that they not do away with my son." He said, "As YHWH lives, not one hair of your son shall fall to the ground."

12 Then the woman said, "Please let your maidservant speak a word to my lord the king." He said, "Speak!"

13 So the woman said, "Why then have you devised thus against the people of God? In speaking this word the king is as one guilty insofar as the king does not bring back his banished one.

14 For we must surely die and [we are] like water poured out on the ground that cannot be gathered up again. But God would not take away a life but would devise plans so that he might not banish from himself one [already] banished.

15 Now I have come to speak to the king my lord about this matter because the people have made me afraid. So your maidservant thought, 'I will speak to the king; perhaps the king can act on the matter of his handmaid,

16 because the king will listen to deliver his handmaid free from the grasp of the man [seeking] to oust both me and my son from the inheritance of God.'

17 Your maidservant thought, 'A word from my lord the king will lay the matter to rest; for my lord the king is like the messenger of God, discerning good and bad. May YHWH your God be with you!'"

18 Then the king answered the woman, "Do not hold back from me anything I am about to ask you." The woman said, "Let my lord the king speak."

19 Then the king said, "Is the hand of Joab with you in all of this?" The woman answered and said, "As surely as you live, my lord the king, one cannot turn to the right or to the left from anything that my lord the king has spoken: for it was your servant Joab who commanded me, and it was he who put all these words in the mouth of your maidservant.

20 In order to change the appearance of the matter your servant Joab did this thing; but my lord is wise like the wisdom of the messenger of God, knowing everything that is on the earth."

21 The king said to Joab, "Look, now I have acted in this matter; go, bring back the young man Absalom!"

22 Joab fell on his face to the ground, prostrated himself, and blessed the king; then Joab said, "Today your servant knows that I have found favor in your sight, my lord the king, since the king has acted in the matter of your servant."

23 Then Joab rose up, went to Geshur, and brought Absalom back to Jerusalem.

24 However, the king said, "Let him return to his house, but he shall not see my face!" So Absalom returned to his house and he did not see the face of the king.

25 Now there was no man in all Israel like Absalom whose good looks were to be so greatly praised, from the sole of his foot to the crown; there was not a blemish on him.

26 Whenever he cut the hair of his head—it was at the end of every year that he used to cut it; for it became too heavy on him and he cut it—he would weigh the hair from his head, two hundred shekels by the stone-weight of the king.

27 Three sons were born to Absalom as well as one daughter, and her name was Tamar; she was a woman very beautiful to behold.

28 So Absalom lived for two whole years in Jerusalem but did not see the face of the king.

29 Then Absalom sent for Joab to send him to the king; but he was unwilling to come to him; he sent yet a second time, but he still was unwilling to come.

30 Then he said to his servants, "See, Joab's plot of land is at my hand, and he has barley there. Go and set it on fire." So the servants of Absalom set the plot of land on fire.

31 Then Joab arose and came to Absalom at his house and said to him, "Why have your servants set the plot of land belonging to me on fire?"

32 Absalom said to Joab, "Look here, I sent to you, saying: Come here that I may send you to the king to say, 'Why have I come back from Geshur?' It would be better for me were I still there. Now let me see the face of the king! If there is blame in me, let him put me to death!"

33 When Joab came to the king and told him, he summoned Absalom and he came to the king and prostrated himself to him with his face to the ground before the king; and the king kissed Absalom.

524 Absalom's Rebellion
2 Sam 15:1–16:23

2 Samuel 15

1 Sometime afterward, Absalom got for himself a chariot and horses and fifty men to be runners in front of him.

2 Absalom used to rise early and stand at the side of the road to the gate; whenever there was anybody who had a lawsuit to bring to the king for judgment, Absalom would call to him and say, "From which city are you?" When he would say, "From such and such a tribe of Israel is your servant,"

3 Absalom would say to him, "Look, your claims are good and right, but there is no one authorized by the king to hear you."

4 Then Absalom would say, "If only he would appoint me a judge in the land, then any person who had a lawsuit could come to me and I would grant him justice."

5 Whenever a person drew near to bow himself down to him, he would extend his hand and take hold of him and kiss him.

6 Absalom acted in this manner to all the Israelites who came for judgment to the king; and thus Absalom stole the hearts of the men of Israel.

7 At the end of forty years Absalom said to the king, "Please let me go that I may fulfill the vow that I vowed to YHWH in Hebron.

8 For your servant made a vow while I was living at Geshur in Aram, saying, 'If YHWH should indeed return me to Jerusalem, then I would serve YHWH.'"

9 The king said to him, "Go in peace!" So he got up and went to Hebron.

10 Then Absalom sent secret agents throughout all the tribes of Israel, saying, "As soon as you hear the sound of the ram's horn, you shall say: Absalom has become king at Hebron!"

11 Also with Absalom there went two hundred men from Jerusalem, invited guests, and they went in their innocence for they knew nothing.

12 Then Absalom sent for Ahithophel the Gilonite, the counselor of David, from his city Giloh while he was offering sacrifices. Thus the conspiracy firmed up and the people going with Absalom kept growing.

13 When an informer came to David, saying, "The hearts of the men of Israel have gone over to Absalom,"

14 David said to all his servants who were with him in Jerusalem, "Get up and let us flee, for there will be no escape for us from Absalom. Hurry up and go lest he hurries and overtakes us, brings down disaster upon us, and strikes the city with the edge of the sword."

15 Then the servants of the king said to the king, "Whatever my lord the king should decide, we are indeed your servants!"

16 So the king went out and all his household followed him; however the king left behind ten women, concubines, to look after the house.

17 So the king went out and all the people followed him; and they stopped at the farthest house.

18 All his servants passed by at his side, all the Cherethites and all the Pelethites, and all the Gittites, six hundred men who had followed him from Gath, passed by before the king.

19 Then the king said to Ittai the Gittite, "Why do you also come with us? Return and stay with the king, for you are a foreigner and you are also an exile from your place.

20 Your coming was only yesterday and today shall I make you wander about with us, while I myself go wherever I can go? Return and take your kinsfolk back with you [in] loyalty and faithfulness."

21 But Ittai answered the king and said, "As YHWH lives, and as my lord the king lives, in whatever place my lord the king must be, whether for death or for life, surely there will be your servant!"

22 David said to Ittai, "Go, then, pass on." So Ittai the Gittite passed on as well as all his men and all the little ones who were with him.

23 The whole country was weeping loudly as all the people were passing by. Then the king crossed over the Wadi Kidron; and all the people passed by upon the highway [to] the wilderness.

24 Then Zadok also came up and all the Levites with him bearing the ark of the covenant of God; and they set down the ark of God—and Abiathar came up—until all the people had finished passing out of the city.

25 The king said to Zadok, "Take the ark of God back to the city. If I find favor in the eyes of YHWH, he will bring me back and let me see both it and its abode.

26 But if he says thus: 'I take no delight in you,' here I am, let him do to me whatever seems good in his eyes."

27 The king said to Zadok the priest, "Are you a seer? Go back to the city in peace [with] Ahimaaz your son and Jonathan son of Abiathar, your two sons with you.

28 See, I will be waiting at the fords of the wilderness until word comes from you to keep me informed.

29 So Zadok and Abiathar took the ark of God back to Jerusalem; and they stayed there.

30 Meanwhile David went up the ascent of the Mount of Olives, weeping as he went up, with his head covered and walking barefoot; and all the people who were with him covered their heads and went up, weeping as they went.

31 David [was told], "Ahithophel is among the conspirators with Absalom." And David said, "Thwart the counsel of Ahithophel, O YHWH!"

32 As David came to the summit where he usually bowed himself down to God, there was Hushai the Archite coming to meet him with his robe torn and earth on his head.

33 David said to him, "If you go along with me, you will become a burden to me.

34 But if you go back to the city and say to Absalom, 'I am your servant, O king. I have been a servant of your father in the past, but from now on I will be your servant'; so you can undermine the counsel of Ahithophel for me.

35 Will not Zadok and Abiathar the priests be with you there, that everything which you hear from the house of the king you can tell to Zadok and to Abiathar the priests.

36 Look, their two sons are with them there, Ahimaaz son of Zadok and Jonathan son of Abiathar, and by their hand you can send to me everything that you hear."

37 So Hushai, the friend of David, came into the city just as Absalom entered Jerusalem.

16:1 When David had passed a bit beyond the summit, there was Ziba the servant of Mephibosheth, to meet him with a pair of asses saddled; and on them two hundred loaves of bread, one hundred clusters of raisins, one hundred of summer fruit, and a skin of wine.

2 The king said to Ziba, "Why are these things with you?" And Ziba said, "The asses are for the household of the king to ride on and the bread and the summer fruit for the young men to eat, and the wine to drink for anyone fainting in the wilderness."

3 The king said, "And where is the son of your master?" Ziba said to the king, "See, he is staying in Jerusalem, for he said, 'Today the house of Israel will give back to me the kingdom of my grandfather.'"

4 The king said to Ziba, "All that belonged to Mephibosheth now is yours!" Ziba said, "I bow myself down; let me find favor in your eyes, my lord the king."

5 When David the king came to Bahurim, there came out from there a man from the family of the house of Saul, and his name was Shimei son of Gera; he came out cursing.

6 He pelted David and all the servants of King David with stones as well as all the people and all the warriors who were on his right and on his left.

7 Shimei said this as he cursed, "Get out, get out, man of blood and worthless fellow.

8 YHWH is turning back on you all the blood of the house of Saul in whose place you became king; and YHWH is giving the kingship into the hand of Absalom, your son. Look at you in your ill fortune, because you have been a man of blood!"

9 Then Abishai son of Zeruiah said to the king, "Why should this dead dog curse my lord the king? Let me go over and take off his head."

10 But the king said, "What is there between me and you, O sons of Zeruiah? Let him curse, for if YHWH has said to him, 'Curse David,' who then can say, 'Why are you doing so?'"

11 David said to Abishai and to all his servants, "Look, my own son who came forth from my loins is seeking my life; how much more now a Benjaminite! Let him be; and let him curse, for YHWH has told him to.

12 Perhaps YHWH will look on my iniquity and YHWH will restore to me good on account of his cursing this day."

13 So David and his men went on the way while Shimei went on the side of the hill alongside him, going on and cursing and pelting him with stones alongside him and throwing dust at him.

14 The king and all the people who were with him arrived exhausted; and he was refreshed there.

15 Now Absalom and all the people, the men of Israel, had come to Jerusalem; and Ahithophel was with him.

16 When Hushai the Archite, the friend of David, came to Absalom, Hushai said to Absalom, "Let the king live! Let the king live!"

17 But Absalom said to Hushai, "Is this your loyalty to your friend? Why did you not go with your friend?"

18 Hushai said to Absalom, "No, for whomever YHWH and this people and every Israelite have chosen, to him[1] I will belong and with him I will remain!"

19 Furthermore, whom should I serve? Should it not be before his son? As I have served before your father, so I will be before you."

20 Then Absalom said to Ahithophel, "Give counsel as to what we should do."

21 So Ahithophel said to Absalom, "Go in to the concubines of your father, whom he has left to look after the house; and all Israel will hear that you have made yourself offensive to your father, and so strengthen the hands of all those with you."

22 So they pitched a tent for Absalom upon the roof and Absalom went in to the concubines of his father in the sight of all Israel.

23 Now in those days the counsel of Ahithophel that he gave was as if one had sought a word from God; so was valued all the counsel of Ahithophel, both by David and by Absalom.

---

[1] Reading the Qere.

525 Ahithophel's Advice Undermined by Hushai
2 Sam 17:1-23

2 Samuel 17

1 Furthermore, Ahithophel said to Absalom, "Let me now choose twelve thousand men and I will rise up and pursue David tonight.

2 I will come upon him while he is exhausted and vulnerable and make him panic; when all the people who are with him flee, I will strike down the king alone.

3 Then I will bring all the people back to you; like the return of the whole [people] is the man whom you are seeking[1]—then all the people will be at peace."

4 The plan seemed to be right in the eyes of Absalom and in the eyes of all the elders of Israel.

5 Nevertheless Absalom said, "Summon also Hushai the Archite, and let us hear what he too has to say."

6 When Hushai came to Absalom, Absalom said to him, "The plan of Ahithophel is like this; shall we carry out his plan? If not, you speak [to us]."

7 So Hushai said to Absalom, "This time the counsel that Ahithophel has given is not good."

8 Hushai continued, "You yourself know your father and his men, that they are warriors, and that when enraged they are like a bear bereft [of her cubs] in the open country. Anyway, your father is a man of war, and he will not spend the night with the people.

9 Even now he is hiding himself in one of the pits in some other place, and if it happens that some of them [our troops] fall at the start of any fighting, anyone who hears of it will say, "There has been a massacre among the people who were following Absalom."

10 Then even he the valiant warrior, whose heart is like the heart of a lion, will utterly melt [with fear]; for all Israel knows that your father is a warrior and valiant warriors are with him.

11 Instead, I advise that all Israel definitely be gathered to you from Dan to Beersheba, like the sand which is by the sea for multitude, and that you in person go on to battle.

12 When we come upon him in whatever of the places where he may be found, we shall come down upon him as dew falls upon the ground, and nothing will be left of him or of all the men who are with him, not a one.

13 If he withdraws to a city, all Israel will bring ropes to that city and we will pull it down into the wadi until not even a pebble can be found there."

14 Then Absalom and all the men of Israel said, "The counsel of Hushai the Archite is better than the counsel of Ahithophel." YHWH had given orders to frustrate the good counsel of Ahithophel in order that YHWH might bring disaster upon Absalom.

15 Then Hushai said to Zadok and Abiathar, the priests, "Such and such did Ahithophel counsel Absalom and the elders of Israel; but such and such did I myself counsel.

16 Therefore now send quickly and tell David, saying, 'Do not spend the night in the wastes of the wastelands, but rather cross over right away, lest the king and all the people who are with him be swallowed up.'"

17 Now Jonathan and Ahimaaz were standing by at En-rogel; and a maid-servant was to go and report to them, and they were to go and report to King David, for they could not be seen entering the city.

18 Nevertheless, a boy did see them and told Absalom; so the two of them went quickly and came to the house of a man in Bahurim; now he had a well in his courtyard, so they went down into it,

19 and the wife took and spread a covering over the mouth of the well, and scattered grain on top of it; and nothing was known about it.

20 When the servants of Absalom came to the woman at the house, they said, "Where are Ahimaaz and Jonathan?" The woman said to them, "They have crossed over Mikal Hammayim."[1] After they had searched and did not find them, they returned to Jerusalem.

21 After they had gone away, they came up from the well and went on and told King David; and they said to David, "Rise up and cross the water quickly for such has Ahithophel counseled against you."

22 So David and the people who were with him rose up and crossed over the Jordan; [they did so] until daybreak, until there was no one who had not crossed the Jordan.

23 When Ahithophel saw that his counsel was not acted upon, he saddled the ass, rose up and went to his house, to his city: he issued orders to his house-hold, and hanged himself. Thus he died, and he was buried in the tomb of his father.

---

[1] Hebrew difficult.

526 David at Mahanaim
2 Sam 17:24-29 // 1 Chron 2:17

2 Samuel 17	*1 Chronicles 2*
24 Meanwhile David came to Mahanaim while Absalom crossed over the Jordan; he and all the men of Israel with him.	
25 Now Absalom had set Amasa over the army in place of Joab. Amasa was the son of a man named Ithra the Israelite who had gone in to Abigal daughter of Nahash, sister of Zeruiah, mother of Joab.	17 Abigail gave birth to Amasa; and the father of Amasa was Jether the Ishmaelite.

26 Israel and Absalom set up camp
in the land of Gilead.

27 When David had come to
Mahanaim, Shobi son of Nahash
from Rabbah of the Ammonites,
Machir son of Ammiel from
Lo-debar, and Barzillai the Gileadite
from Rogelim,

28 brought a couch, bowls, vessels,
wheat, barley, flour, roasted grain,
beans, lentils,

29 honey, curds, sheep, and cheese
from the herd; they brought such
near for David and for the people
who were with him to eat, because
they said, "The people must be hun-
gry, faint, and thirsty in the wilderness."

527 The Death of Absalom
2 Sam 18:1–19:9b

2 Samuel 18

1 Then David mustered the people who were with him and he set over them
commanders of thousands and commanders of hundreds.

2 Then David sent out the people: a third under the command of Joab, a third
under the command of Abishai son of Zeruiah, brother of Joab, and a third
under the command of Ittai the Gittite. The king said to the people, "I myself
will also go out with you."

3 But the people said, "You should not go out; for if we have to flee, they will
not mind about us, even if half of us die they will not mind about us, for there
are now ten thousand like us. So now it is better that you be [ready] to help us
from the city."

4 The king said to them, "Whatever is best in your eyes I will do." So the king
stood by the side of the gate as all the people went out by hundreds and by
thousands.

5 The king had commanded Joab, Abishai, and Ittai, saying, "For my sake, go
easy on the young man Absalom." And all the people heard as the king commanded all the commanders about the matter of Absalom.

6 So the people went out to the field to meet Israel, and the battle took place in the forest of Ephraim.

7 There the people of Israel were routed before the servants of David; and the rout was great there on that day, twenty thousand men.

8 The battle there was spread over the face of all the land, but the forest devoured more of the people than the sword devoured on that day.

9 Absalom happened to encounter the servants of David: Absalom was riding on a mule and as the mule went under the entwined branches of a large oak, his head got caught firmly in the oak, and he ended up hanging between heaven and earth, when the mule which was under him moved on.

10 A certain man saw and he told Joab and said, "Just now I saw Absalom hanging in an oak."

11 Joab said to the man who had told him, "You really saw him? Why did you not strike him down there to the ground? I would have felt obliged to give you ten pieces of silver and one belt."

12 But the man said to Joab, "Even if I were weighing on my palm a thousand pieces of silver I would not put out my hand against the son of the king; for in our hearing the king commanded you and Abishai and Ittai, saying, 'Be very careful with the young man Absalom!'

13 Otherwise, if I had committed treachery against his life—and nothing can be hidden from the king—you yourself would have stood apart."

14 Then Joab said, "I will not waste time like this on you." He took three spears into his hand and drove them into the heart of Absalom while he was still alive in the heart of the oak.

15 The ten young men, bearers of Joab's weapons, surrounded and struck Absalom and they killed him.

16 Then Joab sounded the horn; and the people returned from pursuing Israel, for Joab restrained the people.

17 They took Absalom, cast him into a large pit in the forest, and erected over him a very large cairn of stones while all Israel fled, each to their own homes.

18 Now Absalom while he was alive, had taken and had erected the pillar that is in the Valley of the King, for he said, "I have no son to make my name remembered." So he called the pillar by his own name, and it is called Absalom's Monument to this day.

19 Then Ahimaaz son of Zadok said, "Let me run now and bear the news to the king that YHWH has spared him from the hand of his enemies."

20 However, Joab said to him, "You are not to be a bearer of news this day—you may bear news another day—but this day you shall not bear news since the son of the king is dead!"

21 Then Joab said to the Cushite, "You go, tell the king what you have seen." So the Cushite bowed himself down to Joab, and ran.

22 Then Ahimaaz son of Zadok again said to Joab, "In spite of what has happened, please let me also run after the Cushite." Joab said, "For what reason would you run, my son, since there will be no good news forthcoming for you?"

23 "Come what may let me run." So he said to him, "Run!" Then Ahimaaz ran along the Way of the Oval and outran the Cushite.

24 Now David was sitting between the two gates. As the watchman went to the roof of the gateway over to the city wall, he looked up and saw that there was a man running by himself.

25 So the watchman called out and told it to the king, and the king said, "If he is by himself, there is news in his mouth." As he kept coming nearer,

26 the watchman observed another man running; so the watchman called out to the gatekeeper, and said, "There is another man running by himself, and the king said, "This one too is a bearer of news."

27 Then the watchman said, "I see that the running of the first one is like the running of Ahimaaz son of Zadok." And the king said, "He is a good man and he comes with good news."

28 Ahimaaz called out and said to the king, "All is well" and he bowed himself down before the king with his nose to the ground, and he said, "Blessed be YHWH your God, who has delivered up the men who raised up their hand against my lord the king."

29 The king said, "Is it well with the young man Absalom?" Ahimaaz said, "I saw a great commotion while Joab servant of the king, was sending off your servant, but I do not know what [it was]."

30 And the king said, "Turn aside and stand here." So he turned aside and stood by.

31 Then the Cushite arrived, and the Cushite said, "Let my lord the king receive the news, for YHWH has spared you today from the hand of those who have risen up against you."

32 The king said to the Cushite, "Is it well with the young man Absalom?" And the Cushite said, "May the enemies of my lord the king be like [that] young man, and all who rise up against you for evil."

19:1 Then the king was convulsed with grief and went up to the room over the gate and wept. As he went this is what he said, "O my son Absalom, my son, my son Absalom. Would that I had died instead of you, O Absalom, my son, my son."

2 Now it was reported to Joab, "Look, the king is weeping and mourning for Absalom."

3 So the victory on that day was turned into mourning for all the people because the people heard on the day, "The king is grieving for his son."

4 Thus the people came stealthily that day into the city, as a people steals in who are ashamed of their flight in battle.

5 The king covered his face, and the king cried out [with] a loud voice, "O my son Absalom, Absalom my son."

6 Soon Joab came to the king into the house and said, "You have brought shame today to the faces of all your servants who saved your life today and the life of your sons and your daughters and the life of your wives and the life of your concubines,

7 by loving those who hate you and hating those who love you, since you have made it obvious today that officers and servants are nothing to you, for I know today that were Absalom still alive and all of us today dead, then it would be fine in your eyes.

8 Now get up, go out, and speak to your servants, for I swear by YHWH, that if you do not go out, not a man will remain with you for the night, and this will be more disastrous for you than any disaster that has come upon you from your youth until now."

9 So the king rose up and sat down in the gate. They told all the people, "See, the king is sitting down in the gate," and all the people came before the king.

528 David's Return to Jerusalem
2 Sam 19:9c-44

2 Samuel 19

9 Meanwhile Israel had fled, each one to their own homes.

10 Moreover, all the people were arguing throughout all the tribes of Israel, saying, "The king delivered us from the grasp of our enemies and he saved us from the grasp of the Philistines; but now he has fled from the country because of Absalom.

11 But Absalom whom we anointed over us is dead in battle; so now why are you so silent about bringing back the king?"

12 King David sent to Zadok and Abiathar the priests, saying, "Speak to the elders of Judah, saying, "Why should you be the last ones to bring back the king to his house?" The talk of all Israel had reached the king, to his house.

13 "You are my brothers, you are my bone and my flesh, so why should you be the last ones to bring back the king?"

14 And say to Amasa, "Are you not my bone and my flesh? May God do so to me and more so if you do not become the commander of the army before me for all time in place of Joab!"

15 He touched the heart of all the men of Judah as one; and they sent [word] to the king, "Come back, you and all your servants."

16 So the king turned back and came to the Jordan; Judah came to Gilgal, to go to meet the king, to bring the king across the Jordan.

17 Then Shimei son of Gera, the Benjaminite who was from Bahurim, hurried and came down with the men of Judah to meet King David.

18 With him were a thousand men from Benjamin, and Ziba the servant from the house of Saul and his fifteen sons and his twenty servants; and they plunged into the Jordan in front of the king

19 while at the crossing of the ford to bring over the household of the king, and to do whatever was good in his sight. Now Shimei son of Gera fell down before the king as he was about to cross over the Jordan,

20 and he said to the king, "Let not my lord deem me guilty, nor remember how your servant acted wrongly on the day that my lord the king went forth from Jerusalem, that the king set [it] in his heart.

21 For your servant knows that I myself have sinned; see, I have come today, the first of all the house of Joseph to come down here to meet my lord the king."

22 But Abishai son of Zeruiah answered, "Should not Shimei be put to death because he has cursed the anointed of YHWH?"

23 But David said, "What is there between me and you, sons of Zeruiah, that you should become today my adversary? Shall anyone in Israel be put to death today? For do I not know that today I am king over Israel?"

24 Then the king said to Shimei, "You shall not die!" And the king swore an oath to him.

25 Mephibosheth grandson of Saul came down to meet the king. Now he had not attended to his feet, nor attended to his beard, nor had he washed his clothes from the day that the king left until the day he came back in peace.

26 So when he came from Jerusalem to meet the king, the king said to him, "Why did you not go with me, Mephibosheth?"

27 He said, "My lord the king, my servant deceived me for your servant did say, 'I will saddle up the ass for myself, that I may ride upon it and go with the king, since your servant is lame.'

28 But he vilified your servant to my lord the king; now my lord the king is like a messenger of God; so do what is right in your eyes.

29 Although all the house of my father were only men [worthy] of death to my lord the king, still you set your servant alongside those eating at your table, so what right do I still have to appeal to the king?"

30 The king said to him, "Why speak of your affairs further? I have decided: You and Ziba shall divide the land."

31 Mephibosheth said to the king, "Indeed, let him take it all since my lord the king has come in peace to his house."

32 Now Barzillai the Gileadite had come down from Rogelim, and he passed on with the king to the Jordan, to escort him across the Jordan.

33 Barzillai was a very old man, eighty years old, and he had provisioned the king during his stay at Mahanaim, for he was a very prominent man.

34 The king said to Barzillai, "You cross over with me and I will provide for you in Jerusalem."

35 But Barzillai said to the king, "How many days are the years of my life, that I should go up with the king to Jerusalem?

36 I am eighty years old today? Can I discern between good and bad? Can your servant taste what I eat and what I drink? Can I hear still the sound of singing men and singing women? Why then should your servant become yet another a burden to my lord the king?

37 Your servant will cross over the Jordan but a little way with the king, so why should the king compensate me with such a reward?

38 Please let your servant turn back that I may die in my own city beside the tomb of my father and mother. But here is your servant Chimham; let him cross over with my lord the king; and do for him whatever is good in your sight."

39 So the king said, "Chimham shall cross over with me; and I will do for him whatever is right in your sight—and all that you require of me I will do for you."

40 Then all the people crossed over the Jordan and the king crossed over; the king kissed Barzillai and blessed him, and he returned to his own place.

41 When the king crossed over to Gilgal, Chimham crossed over with him; and all the people of Judah, and also half the people of Israel brought the king along.

42 Then all the men of Israel coming to the king said to the king, "Why have our brothers, the men of Judah, whisked you away and brought the king and his household over the Jordan and all the men of David with him?"

43 Each Judean replied to each Israelite, "Because the king is my own close relative. Why should you be angry over this matter? Have we eaten food from the king? Or has he been too favorable to us?"

44 But each Israelite answered each Judean and said, "I have ten shares in the king, and therefore I have more of a claim on David than you do. So why do you treat me with such contempt? Was I not first to speak of bringing back my king to me?" But the word of each Judean was more fierce than the word of each Israelite.

529a The Revolt of Sheba
2 Sam 20:1-22

2 Samuel 20

1 Now there appeared there a scoundrel whose name was Sheba son of Bichri, a Benjaminite. He sounded the horn and said, "We have no portion in David; we have no stake in the son of Jesse. Everyone to their tents, O Israel!"

2 So all the men of Israel deserted David to follow Sheba son of Bichri, but the men of Judah kept to their king from the Jordan as far as Jerusalem.

3 When David came to his house at Jerusalem, the king took the ten women concubines whom he had left to keep the house and put them in a house of detention and provided for them but did not go in to them. Thus they were confined to the day of their dying, living in widowhood.

4 Then the king said to Amasa, "Call up for me the men of Judah within three days, and you be here yourself."

5 So Amasa went to call up Judah but he tarried beyond the set time that he had appointed for him.

6 David said to Abishai, "Now Sheba son of Bichri will do us even more harm than Absalom. Take the servants of your master yourself and pursue him lest he find for himself fortified cities and escape our surveillance."

7 So the men of Joab went out after him as well as the Cherethites, the Pelethites, and all the warriors; and they went out from Jerusalem to pursue Sheba son of Bichri.

8 When they were by the great stone that is in Gibeon, Amasa came to face them. Now Joab was dressed in his tunic but over it there was a belt with a sword in its scabbard bound at his waist. As he went forward, it fell out.

9 Joab said to Amasa, "Is it well with you, my brother?" And Joab's right hand grasped the beard of Amasa to kiss him.

10 But Amasa did not notice the sword that was in Joab's hand, and he struck him with it in the belly so that he spilled his guts to the ground; and he did not have to strike him twice, for he died. Then Joab and Abishai his brother pursued after Sheba son of Bichri;

11 and one of the servants of Joab stood beside him and said, "Whoever favors Joab, and whoever is for David [follow] after Joab!"

12 Now Amasa was wallowing in his blood in the middle of the roadway, and the man saw that all the people were stopping; and he removed Amasa from the roadway to the field and threw a garment over him, as he saw that all who came by him stopped.

13 Once he had been removed from the roadway, everyone went on after Joab to pursue after Sheba son of Bichri.

14 Meanwhile [Sheba] had passed through all the tribes of Israel up to Abel, namely of Beth-maachah; and all the Berites assembled themselves and likewise followed him inside.

15 They came and besieged him in Abel Beth-maacah and they raised a siege ramp against the city. It stood up against the outer palisade, and all the people who were with Joab kept ramming the wall to topple [it].

16 Then a wise woman called from the city, "Listen, listen. Please tell Joab. Come closer over here, that I may speak with you."

17 So he came closer to her, and the woman said, "Are you Joab?" and he said, "I am." Then she said to him, "Listen to the words of your handmaid." And he said, "I am listening."

18 Then she said, "They used to say long ago, 'Let them but inquire in Abel,' and thus they settled it.

19 I [represent] the peacemaking and the faithful of Israel; you are seeking to destroy a city that is a mother in Israel. Why would you swallow up the heritage of YHWH?"

20 Joab answered and said, "Far be it, far be it from me, that I should swallow up or destroy [anything].

21 Such is not the case; rather a man from the hill country of Ephraim, Sheba son of Bichri is his name, has raised his hand against King David. Give him up alone and I will withdraw from the city." The woman said to Joab, "His head will be thrown over the wall to you."

22 So the woman went to all the people with her solution, and they cut off the head of Sheba son of Bichri, and threw it to Joab, and he sounded the trumpet and they scattered from the city, each one to their own tents. And Joab returned to Jerusalem, to the king.

529b David's Officers
2 Sam 20:23-26 // 1 Chron 18:15-17 [See 515]

2 Samuel 20	*1 Chronicles 18*
23 Joab was in charge of all the army of Israel; and Benaiah son of Jehoiada was over the Cherethites and over the Pelethites	15 Joab son of Zeruiah was over the army,
24 And Adoram was over the corvée, Jehoshaphat son of Ahilud was the recorder;	and Jehoshaphat son of Ahilud was recorder;

25 and Sheya was scribe; Zadok and Abiathar were priests;

26 also Ira the Jairite was David's priest.

16 Zadok son of Ahitub and Abimelech son of Abiathar were priests; and Shavsha was scribe;

17 Benaiah son of Jehoiada was over the Cherethites and the Pelethites, and the sons of David were the chief officials of the king.

530 The Avenging of the Gibeonites
2 Sam 21:1-14

2 Samuel 21

1 Now in the days of David there was a famine for three years, year after year, and David sought the presence of YHWH. YHWH said, "On Saul and on [his] house there is bloodguilt because he put the Gibeonites to death.

2 So the king summoned the Gibeonites and spoke to them. (Now the Gibeonites were not from among the Israelites but were from the remnant of the Amorites; the Israelites had sworn an oath to them, but Saul sought to slay them in his zeal for the Israelites and Judah).

3 Then David said to the Gibeonites, "What shall I do for you? How shall I make atonement that you may bless the inheritance of YHWH?"

4 Then the Gibeonites said to him, "It is not a [question of] silver and gold between us and Saul and his house, and it is not for us to put anyone to death in Israel." So he said, "What are you saying that I should do for you?"

5 They said to the king, "The man who made an end of us and who schemed against us, intending that we should be annihilated within the territory of Israel—

6 let seven men from his sons be handed over to us and we will dismember them before YHWH in Gibeah of Saul, the chosen of YHWH." Then the king said, "I will hand [them] over."

7 However, the king spared Mephibosheth son of Jonathan son of Saul, because of the oath of YHWH that was between them, between David and Jonathan son of Saul.

8 The king took the two sons of Rizpah daughter of Aiah, whom she had borne to Saul, Armoni and Mephibosheth, and the five sons of Michal daughter of Saul, whom she had borne to Adriel, son of Barzillai the Meholathite.

9 He gave them into the hands of the Gibeonites and they dismembered them on the mountain before YHWH, and the seven of them fell together; and they were put to death in the first days of the harvest, at the beginning of the barley harvest.

10 Then Rizpah the daughter of Aiah took sackcloth and spread it out for herself on a rock, from the beginning of the harvest until water was poured forth upon them from the heavens; she did not allow any bird from the heavens to settle upon them by day, nor any beast of the field by night.

11 It was reported to David what Rizpah daughter of Aiah the concubine of Saul had done.

12 Then David went and took the bones of Saul and the bones of Jonathan his son, from the citizens of Jabesh-gilead who had stolen them from the square of Beth-shan where the Philistines had hung them up on the day that the Philistines slew Saul at Gilboa.

13 He took up from there the bones of Saul and the bones of his son Jonathan, and they collected the bones of those who had been dismembered.

14 Then they buried the bones of Saul and of Jonathan his son in the land of Benjamin, in Zela, in the grave of Kish his father; they did all that the king had commanded. God heeded the supplication of the land after that.

531 Abishai Rescues David from the Giant
2 Sam 21:15-17

2 Samuel 21

15 There was war once again by the Philistines with Israel, so David went down and his servants with him: they battled against the Philistines, and David grew weary.

16 Ishbi-benob, who was from the descendants of the Raphah—the weight of his spear was three hundred shekels of bronze, and he was equipped with new [armor]—said he would slay David.

17 But Abishai son of Zeruiah came to aid him and he struck down the Philistine and killed him. Then David's men swore an oath to him, "You shall not go out with us to battle, so that you do not extinguish the lamp of Israel."

532 The Giants Slain by David's Men
1 Chron 20:4-8 // 2 Sam 21:18-22

1 Chronicles 20

4 After this a battle took place at Gezer with the Philistines; then Sibbecai the Hushathite struck down Sippai, one of the descendants of the Rephaim, and they were subdued.

5 There was another battle with the Philistines, and Elhanan son of Jair[1] struck down Lahmi, brother of Goliath the Gittite; and the shaft of his spear was like a weaver's beam.

6 Then there was another battle at Gath, and there was a man of [great] stature, and his fingers were six and six, twenty-four; and he also was born to the Raphah.

7 He taunted Israel, so Jonathan son of Shimei, the brother of David, slew him.

8 These[2] were born to the Raphah at Gath; and they fell by the hand of David and by the hand of his servants.

2 Samuel 21

18 After this there was again a battle at Gob with the Philistines; then Sibbecai the Hushathite struck down Saph, who was one of the descendants of the Raphah.

19 There was another battle at Gob with the Philistines, and Elhanan son of Jaare-oregim, the Bethlehemite, struck down Goliath the Gittite; and the shaft of his spear was like a weaver's beam.

20 Then there was another battle at Gath, and there was a man of Midian and he had six fingers on his hand and six toes on his feet, twenty-four in number; he also was descended from the Raphah.

21 He taunted Israel, so Jonathan son of Shimei, the brother of David, slew him.

22 These four were descended from the Raphah in Gath; and they fell by the hand of David and by the hand of his servants.

---

[1] Reading the Qere.
[2] Literally, "to."

533 David's Song of Deliverance
2 Sam 22:1-51 // Ps 18:1-51

2 Samuel 22

1 David spoke to YHWH the words of this song on the day when YHWH delivered him from the grasp of all his enemies and from the grasp of Saul.

2 He said:

YHWH is my rocky height and my stronghold, my deliverer;

Psalm 18

1 For the leader: of David, the servant of YHWH, who spoke to YHWH the words of this song on the day when YHWH delivered him from the grasp of his enemies and from the grasp of Saul.

2 He said:

I yearn for you, YHWH, my strength; YHWH my rocky height and my stronghold, my deliverer;

3 the God of my rock, in whom I take shelter; my shield and the horn of my salvation, my citadel and my refuge;
from violence you save me.

4 I call upon YHWH, worthy of praise; and I am saved from my enemies.

5 For the breakers of Death hemmed me in and the torrents of Perdition terrified me;

6 the cords of Sheol were round about me; the snares of Death confronted me.

7 In my distress I called on YHWH; to my God I called. From his temple he heard my voice; and my cry [reached] his ears.

8 Then the earth shook and quaked; the foundations of the heavens trembled and shook because he was enraged.

9 Smoke went up from his nostrils, and a consuming fire from his mouth; fiery coals blazed out from him.

10 He bent the heavens and came down, with thick darkness under his feet.

11 He rode upon a cherub and flew; and he was seen on the wings of the wind.

12 He made darkness around him coverings, a massing of clouds, heavy with water.

13 From the brightness before him coals of fire blazed out.

14 YHWH thundered from the heavens; and Elyon gave [forth] his voice.

---

3 my God, my rock, in whom I take shelter; my shield and the horn of my salvation, my citadel.

4 I call upon YHWH, worthy of praise; and I am saved from my enemies.

5 The breakers of Death hemmed me in, and the torrents of Perdition terrified me;

6 the cords of Sheol were round about me; the snares of Death confronted me.

7 In my distress I called on YHWH; and to my God I cried. From his temple he heard my voice; and my cry before him came to his ears.

8 Then the earth shook and quaked; the foundations of the mountains trembled and shook because he was enraged.

9 Smoke went up from his nostrils, and a consuming fire from his mouth; fiery coals blazed out from him.

10 He bent the heavens and came down, with thick darkness under his feet.

11 He rode upon a cherub and flew; and he sped on the wings of the wind.

12 He made darkness his hiding-place, his cover around him, a massing of clouds, dark with water.

13 From the brightness before him his clouds burst through, hail and coals of fire.

14 YHWH thundered in the heavens; and Elyon gave [forth] his voice, hail and coals of fire.

15 He sent out arrows and scattered them, lightning and routed them.[1]

16 Then the channels of the sea were seen; the foundations of the world laid bare at the rebuke of YHWH, at the blast of the breath of his nostrils.

17 He reached [down] from on high and took me; he drew me out of mighty waters.

18 He delivered me from my powerful enemy, from those who hated me; for they were too strong for me.

19 They confronted me in the day of my distress; but YHWH was a support for me.

20 He brought me out to an open space; he delivered me because he was pleased with me.

21 YHWH rewarded me according to my righteousness, according to the cleanness of my hands he requited me.

22 For I have kept the ways of YHWH, and I have not acted wickedly [in turning] from my God.

23 For all his judgments [were] before me; and from his statutes I have not turned aside.

24 I was blameless before him; and I have kept myself from wrongdoing.

25 YHWH has rewarded me according to my righteousness, according to my cleanness before his eyes.

26 With grace you deal graciously; with a valiant one you act perfectly.

27 With the pure you act purely; with the perverse you show yourself cunning.

15 He sent out his arrows and scattered them, great lightnings and routed them.

16 Then the channels of the waters were seen; and the foundations of the world were laid bare at your rebuke, YHWH, at the blast of the breath of your nostrils.

17 He reached [down] from on high and took me; he drew me out of mighty waters.

18 He delivered me from my powerful enemy, and from those who hated me; for they were too strong for me.

19 They confronted me in the day of my distress; but YHWH was like a support for me.

20 He brought me out to an open space; he delivered me because he was pleased with me.

21 YHWH rewarded me according to my righteousness, according to the cleanness of my hands he requited me.

22 For I have kept the ways of YHWH, and I have not acted wickedly [in turning] from my God.

23 For all his judgments [were] before me; and his statutes I did not turn away from me.

24 I was blameless toward him; and I have kept myself from wrongdoing.

25 YHWH has rewarded me according to my rightness, according to the cleanness of my hands before his eyes.

26 With grace you deal graciously; with a perfect man you act perfectly.

27 With the pure you act purely; with the perverse you show yourself cunning.

28 You save an afflicted people; but your eyes look down upon the arrogant.

28 For you indeed save an afflicted people; but you bring arrogant eyes low.

29 For you are my lamp, YHWH; YHWH lightens my darkness.

29 For you light my lamp, YHWH; my God lightens my darkness.

30 For by you I rush a troop; by my God I leap a wall.

30 For by you I rush a troop; by my God I leap a wall.

31 The God, his way is perfect; the word of YHWH is refined. He is a shield to all taking refuge in him.

31 The God, his way is perfect; the word of YHWH is refined. He is a shield to all taking refuge in him.

32 For who is a god except YHWH? Who is a rock except our God?

32 For who is God except YHWH? Who is a rock besides our God?

33 The God is my strong fortress; he opens up my perfect way.

33 The God is girding me with strength; he gives my perfect way.

34 He sets my feet like a stag; upon my high places he makes me stand.

34 He sets my feet like a stag; upon my high places he makes me stand.

35 He teaches my hands to fight; my arms stretch a bronze bow.

35 He teaches my hands to fight; my arms stretch a bronze bow.

36 You have given to me your shield of salvation; your care has made me great.

36 You have given me your shield of salvation, your right arm supports me; your care has made me great.

37 You stretch out my steps beneath me. My ankles do not buckle.

37 You stretch out my steps beneath me. My ankles do not buckle.

38 Let me pursue my enemies and I will destroy them. I will not turn back until they are finished off.

38 I will pursue my enemies and I will overtake them. I will not turn back until they are finished off.

39 I will devour them; I will crush them and they will not arise. They will fall beneath my feet.

39 I will crush them; and they will not be able to arise. They will fall beneath my feet.

40 You girded me with strength for the battle; you laid low my adversaries beneath me.

40 You gird me with strength for the battle; you laid low my adversaries beneath me.

41 You made my enemies turn [their] back to me. I will exterminate those who hate me.

41 You have made my enemies turn their backs to me. Those who hate me, I will exterminate them.

42 They looked but there was no one to save; to YHWH but he did not answer them.

42 They looked but there was no one to save; to YHWH, but he did not answer them.

43 I will pulverize them like the dust of the earth, like the mud of the streets I will pound them, I will stamp [on] them.

43 I will pulverize them like the dust upon the face of the wind, like the mud of the streets I will pour them out.

44 You have let me escape from the contentions of my people; you kept me as the head of the nations; a people I had not known served me.

44 You let me escape from the contentions of the people. You set me as the head of the nations; a people I had not known served me.

45 Foreigners have flattered me; with a listening ear they heeded me.

45 With a listening ear they heeded me; foreigners flatter me.

46 Foreigners acted foolishly; and they emerged terror-stricken from their strongholds.

46 Foreigners acted foolishly; and they emerged terror-stricken from their strongholds.

47 YHWH lives! Blessed be my rock! Exalted is the God of the rock of my salvation.

47 YHWH lives! Blessed be my rock! Exalted is the God of the rock of my salvation.

48 The God who gives vindication to me, bringing down the people beneath me,

48 The God who gives vindication to me, bringing down the people beneath me,

49 who brought me out from my enemies, and lifted me up [away] from my adversaries and delivered me from the man of violent deeds.

49 who made me escape from my enemies, and lifted me up from my adversaries and delivered me from the man of violent deeds.

50 Therefore I praise you, YHWH, among the nations, and I hymn your name.

50 Therefore I praise you among the nations, YHWH, and sing hymns to your name.

51 He is a tower of salvation [for] his king; acting graciously for his anointed, for David and for his seed forever.

51 He is a tower of salvation [for] his king; acting graciously for his anointed, for David and for his seed forever.

---

¹ Reading the Qere.

534 The Last Words of David
2 Sam 23:1-7

2 Samuel 23

1 Now these are the last words of David: saying of David son of Jesse, and a saying of the man who was raised on high, the anointed of the God of Jacob, the delight of the songs of Israel.

2 The spirit of YHWH is speaking through me, and his speech is upon my tongue.

3 The God of Israel said; to me the Rock of Israel has spoken, "One who rules over humans justly, who rules [in] the fear of God,

4 is like the light of morning [when] the sun rises, a morning without clouds from brightness, from rain grass springs from the earth.

5 Is not my house established with God, for he has made an everlasting covenant with me, arranged in everything and preserved. Will he not make all my success and [my] every desire blossom forth?

6 But the one of Belial is like a thorn thrown away; all of them for they are not taken up by hand.

7 Anyone who touches them should be armed with iron and the shaft of a spear and they must surely be burned in fire on the spot.

535 David's Mighty Men
2 Sam 23:8-39 // 1 Chron 11:10-47

2 Samuel 23

1 Chronicles 11

10 Now these are the chiefs of the mighty men who belonged to David, who used their strength with him in his kingdom together with all Israel to make him king, according to the word of YHWH concerning Israel.

8 These are the names of the mighty men who belonged to David: Josheb-basshebeth, a Tahchemonite, chief of the officers; he is Adino the Eznite against eight hundred slain at one time.

11 These are the number of the mighty men who belonged to David: Jashobeam son of Hachmoni, chief of the officers; he laid bare his spear against three hundred slain at one time.

9 After him was Eleazar son of Dodo son of Ahohi. [He was] one of the three mighty men with David when they taunted the Philistines who had gathered there for battle. Then the men of Israel withdrew,

12 After him was Eleazar son of Dodo, the Ahohite. He was one of the three mighty men.

10 [but] he stood his ground and struck down Philistines until his hand grew weary and his hand stuck to the sword. So YHWH brought about a great victory on that day. Then the people returned to him, only to strip [the slain].

11 After him was Shammah son of Agee, the Hararite. The Philistines gathered as a band, and there was a plot of the field there full of lentils; and the people fled before the Philistines.

13 He was with David at Pas-dammim when the Philistines gathered there for battle; and there was a plot of the field full of barley; and the people fled before the Philistines.

12 But he stood in the middle of the plot and defended it, and he slew the Philistines. So YHWH brought about a great victory.

14 But they stood in the middle of the plot and defended it, and they slew the Philistines. So YHWH saved them by a great victory.

13 Then three of the thirty chief[s] went down, and they came to David near the harvest time at the Cave of Adullam, while a band of Philistines were encamping in the valley of Rephaim.

15 Then three of the thirty chief[s] went down to the rock to David at the Cave of Adullam, while the camp of the Philistines was encamping in the valley of Rephaim.

14 David was then in the stronghold; and the garrison of the Philistines was then in Bethlehem.

16 David was then in the stronghold; and the post of the Philistines was then in Bethlehem.

15 Then David had a craving, so he said, "If only someone will give me a drink of water from the well which is at Bethlehem by the gate."

17 Then David had a craving, so he said, "If only someone will give me a drink of water from the well which is at Bethlehem by the gate."

16 So three of the mighty men broke into the Philistine camp, and they drew water from the well which was in Bethlehem by the gate, and they carried it and brought it to David, but he was unwilling to drink it so he poured it out as a libation to YHWH.

18 So the Three broke into the Philistine camp, and they drew water from the well which was in Bethlehem by the gate, and they carried it and brought it to David, but he was unwilling to drink it so he poured it out as a libation to YHWH.

17 Then he said, "May I be cursed O YHWH, if I do this. Is it [not] the blood of the men who went at the risk of their lives?" So he was unwilling to drink it. The three mighty men did these kinds of things.

19 Then he said, "May I be cursed by my God if I do this. Shall I drink the blood of these men at the risk of their lives since they brought it at the risk of their lives?" So he was unwilling to drink it. The three mighty men did these kinds of things.

18 Now Abishai brother of Joab, son of Zeruiah, was chief of the Three; he laid bare his spear against three hundred slain; so he had a name among the Three.

20 Now Abishai brother of Joab was chief of the Three; he laid bare his spear against three hundred slain, but he had no name among the Three.

19 Among the Three is he not honored? So he became their commander; but he did not attain to the Three.

20 Now Benaiah son of Jehoiada was the son of Ish-hai, from Kabzeel, mighty in deeds. He slew two [sons of] of Ariel of Moab. He also went down and slew the lion in the middle of the pit on a snowy day.

21 Then he slew an Egyptian man, of [imposing] appearance. In the Egyptian's hand there was a spear, but he went down against him with a staff; he seized the spear from the Egyptian's hand and he killed him with his spear.

22 These things did Benaiah son of Jehoiada; and he had a name among the three mighty men.

23 Among the Thirty he was honored, but he did not attain to the Three; however, David appointed him to his bodyguard.

24 Asahel brother of Joab was among the Thirty, Elhanan son of Dodo, of Bethlehem;

25 Shammah the Harodite; Elika the Harodite;

26 Helez the Paltite; Ira son of Ikkesh, the Tekoite;

27 Abiezer of Anathoth; Mebunnai the Hushathite;

28 Zalmon the Ahohite; Maharai of Netophah;

29 Heleb son of Baanah of Netophah; Ittai son of Ribai of Gibeah of the Benjaminites.

30 Benaihu of Pirathon; Hiddai, from the torrents of Gaash.

21 Among the Three he was honored against the other two so he became their commander; but he did not attain to the Three.

22 Benaiah son of Jehoiada was the son of a brave soldier, from Kabzeel, mighty in deeds. He slew two [sons of] of Ariel of Moab. He also went down and slew the lion in the middle of the pit on a snowy day.

23 Then he slew the Egyptian man, a man of stature, five cubits [tall]. In the Egyptian's hand there was a spear like a weaver's beam, but he went down against him with a staff; he seized the spear from the Egyptian's hand and he killed him with his spear.

24 These things did Benaiah son of Jehoiada; and he had a name among the three mighty men.

25 Among the Thirty he was indeed honored, but he did not attain to the Three; however David appointed him over his bodyguard.

26 The mighty men of valor were: Asahel brother of Joab; Elhanan son of Dodo, from Bethlehem;

27 Shammoth the Harodite; Helez the Pelonite;

28 Ira son of Ikkesh, the Tekoite; Abiezer of Anathoth;

29 Sibbecai the Hushathite; Ilai the Ahohite;

30 Maharai of Netophah; Heled son of Baanah of Netophah;

31 Ithai son of Ribai, of Gibeah of the Benjaminites; Benaiah of Pirathon;

32 Hurai, from the torrents of Gaash. Abiel the Arbathite;

31 Abi-albon the Arbathite;
Azmaveth of Bahurim;

32 Eliahba the Shaalbonite; the
sons of Jashen: Jonathan,

33 Shammah the Hararite; Ahiam
son of Sharar the Hararite;

34 Eliphelet son of Ahasbai, son of
the Maacathite; Eliam son of
Ahithophel the Gilonite;

35 Hezro the Carmelite; Paarai the
Arbite;

36 Igal son of Nathan of Zobah;
Bani the Gadite;

37 Zelek the Ammonite; Naharai of
Beeroth, the armor-bearer of Joab
son of Zeruiah;

38 Ira the Ithrite; Gareb the Ithrite;

39 Uriah the Hittite.

33 Azmaveth the Baharumite;
Eliahba the Shaalbonite;

34 the sons of Hashem the
Gizonite: Jonathan, son of Shagee
the Hararite;

35 Ahiam son of Sachar the
Hararite; Eliphal son of Ur;

36 Hepher the Mecherathite, Ahijah
the Pelonite;

37 Hezro the Carmelite; Naarai son
of Ezbai;

38 Joel brother of Nathan; Mibhar
son of Hagri;

39 Zelek the Ammonite; Naharai of
Beeroth, the armor-bearer of Joab
son of Zeruiah;

40 Ira the Ithrite; Gareb the Ithrite;

41 Uriah the Hittite; Zabad son of
Ahlai;

42 Adina son of Shiza the Reubenite, a chief of the Reubenites, and
thirty with him;

43 Hanan son of Maacah, and
Joshaphat the Mithnite;

44 Uzzia the Ashterathite; Shama
and Jeiel, sons of Hotham the
Aroerite;

45 Jediael son of Shimri, and Joha
his brother, the Tizite;

46 Eliel the Mahavite; and Jeribai
and Joshaviah, sons of Elnaam;
Ithmah the Moabite;

47 Eliel and Obed, and Jaasiel the
Mezobaite.

All [told there were] thirty-seven.

David-3
Sections 533–551

Number	Title	1 Chronicles	2 Samuel
533	David's Song of Deliverance		22:1-51
534	The Last Words of David		23:1-7
535	David's Mighty Men	[11:10-47]	23:8-39
536	David's Helpers at Ziklag	[12:1-23]	
537	David's Army at Hebron	[12:24-41]	
538	David Numbers Israel and Judah	21:1-27	24:1-25
539	The Site for the Temple	21:28–22:1	
540	David's Preparations for the Temple	22:2–23:1	
541	The Division & Duties of Levites & Priests	23:2–24:31	
542	The Divisions of the Musicians	25:1-31	
543	The Gatekeepers and Overseers	26:1-32	
544	The Officers of the Kingdom	27:1-34	
545	David Commits the Building of the Temple	28:1–29:9	
546	David Blesses YHWH	29:10-19	
547	Abishag Ministers to David		1 Kings 1:1-4
548	Adonijah Usurps the Throne		1:5-27
549	Solomon Is Made King	29:20-22	1:28-53
550	David's Charge to Solomon		2:1-9
551	The Death of David	29:20-30	2:10-12

Number of Verses

Section Number

Chronicles
Samuel - Kings

536 David's Helpers at Ziklag
1 Chron 12:1-23

1 Chronicles 12

1 These are the ones who came to David at Ziklag while he still kept away from Saul son of Kish: they were among the mighty warriors who helped him in war.

2 They were archers, either right-handed or left-handed, who could sling stones or [shoot] arrows with a bow, and from Saul's kindred from Benjamin.

3 The chief was Ahiezer, then Joash, sons of Shemaah of Gibeah; also Jeziel and Pelet, sons of Azmaveth; also Beracah, Jehu of Anathoth;

4 Ishmaiah of Gibeon, a mighty warrior among the Thirty and over the Thirty;

5 Jeremiah, Jahaziel, Johanan, Jozabad of Gederah;

6 Eluzai, Jerimoth, Bealiah, She-mariah, Shephatiah the Haruphite;

7 Elkanah, Isshiah, Azarel, Joezer, Jashobeam the Korahites;

8 Joelah and Zebadiah, sons of Jeroham from Gedor.

9 Also from the Gadites these went over to David at the stronghold in the desert; the mighty men, warriors who could handle shield and lance: their faces [like] the face of a lion, and they were as swift as gazelles on the mountains.

10 Ezer was the head, Obadiah the second, and Eliab the third [in command],

11 Mishmannah the fourth, Jeremiah the fifth,

12 Attai the sixth, Eliel the seventh;

13 Johanan the eighth, Elzabad the ninth;

14 Jeremiah the tenth, Machbannai the eleventh;

15 these were Gadites, leaders of the army; the least one [equal to] a hundred, the greatest to a thousand.

16 These are the ones who crossed the Jordan in the first month when it was overflowing all its banks and put to flight all in the valleys, to the east and to the west.

17 There also came Benjaminites and Judahites to the stronghold, for David.

18 Then David went out before them and replying said to them, "If you have come peacefully to me, to help me, my heart will be as one with yours. But if [you have come] to betray me to my enemies, even though there is no violence on my hands, may the God of our ancestors see it and judge."

19 Then the spirit clothed Amasai, the chief of the Thirty, "[We are] yours O David, and [we are] with you son of Jesse! Peace, peace be yours, and peace to anyone who helps you; for the one who helps you is your God." So David received them and appointed them as leaders of the troop.

20 Some from Manasseh also deserted to David when he came with the Philistines for battle against Saul, but they did not help them because the lords of the Philistines in counsel sent him away, saying, "He will desert to his master Saul at the cost of our heads."

21 As he went to Ziklag there deserted to him from Manasseh: Adnah, Jozabad, Jediael, Michael, Jozabad, Elihu and Zillethai, chiefs of the thousands in Manasseh.

22 They helped David against the bands of raiders for they were all mighty men of valor; and they were officers over the army.

23 Indeed day by day they kept coming to David to help him until there was a great encampment, like the encampment of God.

**537 David's Army at Hebron
1 Chron 12:24-41**

1 Chronicles 12

24 These are the numbers of the chiefs of those equipped for war [who] came to David at Hebron, to turn over the kingdom of Saul to him according to the command of YHWH:

25 Judahites bearing shield and lance, six thousand eight hundred equipped for war;

26 from the Simeonites, valiant men for the army, seven thousand one hundred;

27 from the Levites, four thousand six hundred;

28 and Jehoiada was prince of [the house of] Aaron and with him three thousand seven hundred;

29 and Zadok, a valiant young warrior; and from his ancestral house twenty-two officers;

30 from the Benjaminites, the kins- folk of Saul, three thousand—up to this point the majority of them had been keeping guard of the house of Saul.

31 Of the Ephraimites, twenty thou- sand eight hundred, valiant warriors, men of renown in their ancestral houses;

32 from the half-tribe of Manasseh, eighteen thousand who were designated by [their] names to come to make David king;

33 of the sons of Issachar—who knew discernment of times, to know what Israel should do—two hundred of their chiefs and all their kindred at their command;

34 of Zebulun, those set out for military service equipped for battle with all the weapons for war, fifty thousand, gathered together without division of heart;

35 of Naphtali, a thousand officers, and with them, with shield and spear, thirty seven thousand;

36 from Dan, equipped for battle, twenty eight thousand six hundred;

37 from Asher, those set out for military service equipped for battle, forty thousand;

38 from Across-the-Jordan, from the Reubenites and the Gadites and the half-tribe of Manasseh, with all the weapons for war, one hundred twenty thousand.

39 All these warriors drawn up in battle array with a perfect heart, came to Hebron to make David king over all Israel; and also all the rest of Israel were of one mind to make David the king.

40 They were there eating and drinking with David for thirty days since their kindred had made provision for them.

41 Also their neighbors, as far as Issachar and Zebulun and Naphtali, were bringing food [for them] on donkeys and on camels, on mules and on oxen: food—flour, fig cakes, raisin cakes, wine, oil, cattle and sheep—in great quantity, for there was rejoicing in Israel.

538 David Numbers Israel and Judah
1 Chron 21:1-27 // 2 Sam 24:1-25

1 Chronicles 21

1 Satan stood up against Israel, and he incited David to number Israel.

2 So David said to Joab and to the commanders of the people, "Go count Israel from Beersheba to Dan, and bring me [a report] so that I may know their number."

3 Then Joab said, "May YHWH add to his people a hundred fold. But my lord the king, are they not all my lord's servants? Why does my lord seek this? Why should it become a cause of guilt for Israel?"

4 But the king's word prevailed against Joab, and Joab went out and passed through all of Israel and arrived at Jerusalem.

5 Then Joab gave the numbers of the census of the people to David: all Israel had a million one hundred thousand [ready to] draw the sword; and Judah had four hundred and seventy thousand men ready to draw the sword.

6 And Levi and Benjamin—he did not take the census among them, since the king's word was repugnant to Joab.

7 And there was evil in God's eyes because of this matter; so he struck down Israel.

2 Samuel 24

1 YHWH's wrath again flared up against Israel, and he incited David against them in these words, "Go number Israel and Judah."

2 So the king said to Joab his army commander who was with him, "Travel through all the tribes of Israel from Dan to Beersheba, and take a census of the people that I may know the number of the people."

3 Then Joab said to the king, "May YHWH your God add to the people the like of them a hundred fold, while the eyes of my lord the king see it. But why does my lord the king desire this thing?"

4 But the king's word prevailed against Joab and over the army commanders; Joab and the army commanders went out from the presence of the king to take a census of the people of Israel.

5 They crossed over the Jordan and encamped in Aroer south of the city, which was in the middle of the Wadi Gad, towards Jazer.

6 Then they came to Gilead and to the land of Tahtim-hodshi; next they came to Dan-jaan and around [it] to Sidon,

7 and they came to the fortress of Tyre and all the cities of the Hivites and Canaanites; then they went out to the Negeb of Judah, to Beersheba.

8 They traveled through all the land; at the end of nine months and twenty days they came back to Jerusalem.

9 Then Joab gave the numbers of the census of the people to the king: Israel had eight hundred thousand warriors [ready to] draw the sword; and the men of Judah were five hundred thousand men.

8 David said to God, "I have sinned grievously in what I have done in this matter. But now, please take away the guilt of your servant, for I have acted very foolishly."

9 YHWH spoke to Gad, David's seer,

10 "Go and speak to David, 'Thus says YHWH: I am holding three options up to you; choose one of them for yourself and I will do it to you.'"

11 Gad came to David and said to him, "Take for yourself

12 either three years of famine; or three months being swept away before your adversaries with your enemies' sword overtaking you; or for three days the sword of YHWH, a pestilence in the land, and the divine messenger of YHWH spreading destruction throughout all the territory of Israel? Now consider what answer I shall return to the one who sent me."

13 Then David said to Gad, "I am in great distress. Let me fall into the hand of YHWH, for his compassion is great; but I will not fall into human hands.

14 So YHWH sent a pestilence on Israel and there fell of Israel seventy thousand men.

15 Then God sent a divine messenger to Jerusalem to destroy it, but when he was about to destroy it, YHWH saw and repented of the evil, and he said to the divine messenger, the destroyer, "Enough now; let your hand fall." The messenger of YHWH was standing at the threshing floor of Ornan the Jebusite.

16 Then David raised his eyes and he saw the messenger of YHWH standing between the earth and heaven, his drawn sword in his hand stretched over Jerusalem: David and the elders clothed with sackcloth fell on their faces.

17 David said to God, "Did I not give the order to count the people? I am the one who has sinned and has truly done great evil, but these sheep, what have they done? YHWH my God, let your hand be against me and against my father's house, but let it not become a plague against your people."

10 However, David's conscience struck him after he had numbered the people. David said to YHWH, "I have sinned greatly in what I have done. But now, YHWH, please take away the guilt of your servant, for I have acted very foolishly."

11 When David arose in the morning, the word of YHWH came to Gad the prophet, David's seer,

12 "Go and speak to David, 'Thus says YHWH: I am placing three options up to you; choose one of them for yourself and I will do it to you.'"

13 Gad came to David and told him and said to him, "Shall there come

to you seven years of famine in your land; or three months for you to flee before your adversaries with them pursuing you; or should there be a three-day pestilence in your land? Now consider and see what answer I shall return to the one who sent me."

14 Then David said to Gad, "I am in great distress. Let us fall into the hand of YHWH, for his compassion is great; but do not let me fall into human hands.

15 So YHWH sent a pestilence on Israel from the morning until the appointed time; and from Dan to Beersheba there died of the people seventy thousand men.

16 Then the divine messenger sent forth his hand toward Jerusalem for its destruction, but YHWH repented of evil, and he said to the divine messenger, the destroyer among the people, "Enough now; let your hand fall." The messenger of YHWH was at the threshing floor of Araunah the Jebusite.

17 Then David spoke to YHWH when he saw the divine messenger who was striking down the people,

and he said, "See, I alone have sinned, and I alone have done wrong; but these sheep, what have they done? Let your hand be against me and against my father's house."

18 Then the messenger of YHWH told Gad to say to David that David should go up to erect an altar to YHWH at the threshing floor of Ornan the Jebusite."

19 Then David went up in accord with Gad's word which he had spoken in the name of YHWH.

20 Ornan also turned around and saw the divine messenger and and four of his sons with him hid themselves. Now Ornan had been threshing wheat.

21 So David came to Ornan and Ornan looked and saw David: he went out from the threshing floor and prostrated himself before David with his face to the ground.

22 David said to Ornan, "Give me the place of the threshing floor so I may build on it an altar to YHWH; give it to me at full cost, so that the plague may be turned away from the people."

23 Then Ornan said to David, "Take it for yourself and let my lord the king do whatever seems good in his eyes. Look, I give the oxen for the burnt offerings, and the threshing-sledges for wood, and wheat for a grain offering; I give it all."

24 But King David said to Ornan, "No! For I will surely buy [it] at full cost, that I may not take away for YHWH what is yours, nor offer burnt offerings that cost nothing."

25 So David gave to Ornan for the place six hundred shekels of gold by weight.

26 David built there an altar to YHWH, and he offered up burnt offerings and peace offerings and he called upon YHWH who answered him with fire from heaven on the altar of the burnt offering.

27 Then YHWH spoke to the divine messenger; and he returned his sword to its sheath.

18 Gad came to David that day and said to him, "Go and erect an altar to YHWH at the threshing floor of Araunah the Jebusite."

19 David went up in accord with Gad's word just as YHWH had commanded.

20 Then Araunah looked down and he saw the king and his servants proceeding towards him. Araunah went out and prostrated himself before the king with his face to the ground.

21 Araunah said, "Why has my lord the king come to his servant?" David said, "To purchase the threshing floor from you in order to build an altar to YHWH so that the plague may be turned away from the people."

22 Then Araunah said to David, "Let my lord the king take [it] and offer up whatever seems good in his eyes. Look, here are the oxen for the burnt offering, and the threshing-sledges and the yokes of the oxen for wood.

23 All this, O king, Araunah gives to the king." Araunah also said to the king, "May YHWH your God receive you favorably."

24 But the king said to Araunah, "No! For I will surely buy [it] from you for a price: I shall not offer up to YHWH my God burnt offerings that cost nothing." So David bought the threshing-floor and the oxen for fifty shekels of silver.

25 David built there an altar to YHWH, and he offered up burnt offerings and peace offerings. So YHWH was invoked for the land, and the plague was turned away from Israel.

539 The Site for the Temple
1 Chron 21:28–22:1

1 Chronicles 21

28 At that time, when David saw that YHWH had answered him at the threshing-floor of Ornan the Jebusite, he sacrificed there.

29 For the tabernacle of YHWH that Moses had made in the desert and the altar of burnt offering were at that time in the high place at Gibeon.

30 But David was not able to go before it to inquire of God, since he was terrified of the sword of the angel of YHWH.

22:1 Then David said, "This is the house of YHWH God, and this is the altar of burnt offering for Israel."

540 David's Preparations for the Temple
1 Chron 22:2–23:1

1 Chronicles 22

2 Then David issued an order to gather the resident aliens who were in the land of Israel, and he appointed stonecutters to cut the dressed stones to build the house of God.

3 David provided a large quantity of iron for nails for the doors of the gates and for the clamps, and a large quantity of bronze beyond weighing,

4 and cedar trees beyond numbering; for the Sidonians and the Tyrians had brought a great quantity of cedar trees to David.

5 Then David said, "Solomon my son is young and inexperienced, and the house to be built for YHWH should be very splendid; of fame and glory for all the lands. So I will make preparation for it. Therefore David provided in large quantity before his death.

6 So David called for Solomon his son and he commanded him to build a house for YHWH the God of Israel.

7 David said to Solomon, "My son, I had it in my mind to build a house for the name of YHWH my God,

8 but the word of YHWH came to me, saying, 'You have shed much blood and have fought great battles: you shall not build a house for my name because you have shed much blood upon the ground before me.

9 See, a son shall be born to you. He will be a man of rest, and I will give him rest from all his enemies on every side. Solomon will be his name; and I will give Israel peace and quiet during his days.

10 He will build a house for my name and he will be a son to me and I will be a father to him; and I will establish his royal throne over Israel forever.

11 Now, my son, may YHWH be with you so that you may succeed in building the house of YHWH your God, just as he spoke about you.

12 Surely YHWH will give you intelligence and understanding and command you concerning Israel, to keep the Torah of YHWH your God.

13 Then you shall succeed if you take care to enact the statutes and the ordinances which YHWH commanded Moses for Israel. Be strong and courageous. Do not be afraid and do not be disheartened.

14 See, with great trouble I have provided for the house of YHWH a hundred thousand gold talents and a thousand silver talents, and iron and bronze beyond weighing because of its quantity; and I have provided trees [timbers] and stones and you shall add to them.

15 With you will be an abundance of workers, stonecutters and workers in stone and wood, and every skilled worker for every job;

16 for gold, for silver, for bronze and for iron, [men] beyond counting. Rise and work and may YHWH be with you."

17 David also commanded all the leaders of Israel to aid Solomon his son, saying,

18 "Is not YHWH your God with you and has he not given you rest from every side? For he has given the inhabitants of the land into my hand; and the land is subdued before YHWH and before his people.

19 Now set your heart and your spirit to seek YHWH your God, and rise up and build the sanctuary of YHWH your God; to bring the ark of the covenant of YHWH and the holy vessels of God to the house that has been built for the name of YHWH.

23:1 When David was old and full of days, he made Solomon his son king over Israel.

541 The Division and Duties of Levites and Priests
1 Chron 23:2–24:31

1 Chronicles 23

2 [David] gathered all the leaders of Israel and the priests and the Levites.

3 The Levites from thirty years of age and upwards were numbered, and the number of their head count was thirty-eight thousand men.

4 Of these twenty-four thousand were to be over the work of the house of YHWH, six thousand officers and judges;

5 four thousand gatekeepers; four thousand offering praise to YHWH with instruments that I made for giving praise.

6 Then David divided them up into divisions corresponding to the sons of Levi: Gershon, Kohath and Merari.

7 Of the Gershonites: Ladan and Shimei.

8 The sons of Ladan: the head was Jehiel, Zetham and Joel, three.

9 The sons of Shimei: Shelomoth, Haziel and Haran, three; these were the heads of the fathers of Ladan.

10 The sons of Shimei: Jahath, Zina, Jeush, and Beriah; these four were the sons of Shimei.

11 Jahath was the head and Zizah the second. Since Jeush and Beriah did not have many sons, they became a father's house, enrolled as one.

12 The sons of Kohath: Amram, Izhar, Hebron, and Uzziel, four.

13 The sons of Amram: Aaron and Moses; Aaron was set aside to consecrate the most holy things—he and his sons forever—to offer incense before YHWH, to minister to him and to bless in his name forever;

14 but Moses, the man of God, his sons were to be called according to the tribe of Levi.

15 The sons of Moses: Gershom and Eliezer.

16 The sons of Gershom: Shebuel, the head.

17 Then the sons of Eliezer: Rehabiah, the head, but Eliezer did not have other sons, while the children of Rehabiah multiplied greatly.

18 The sons of Izhar: Shelomith, the head.

19 The sons of Hebron: Jeriah, the head, Amariah the second, Jahaziel the third, and Jekameam the fourth.

20 The sons of Uzziel: Micah the head, and Isshiah the second.

21 The sons of Merari: Mahli and Mushi. The sons of Mahli: Eleazar and Kish.

22 When Eleazar died he had no children except for daughters, so the sons of Kish their kindred married them.

23 The sons of Mushi: Mahli, Eder, and Jeremoth, three.

24 These are the sons of Levi according to the house of their fathers; the heads of the fathers according to their rosters by listing of names of their head poll, whoever does the work for the service of the house of YHWH, from twenty years of age and over.

25 For David said, "YHWH the God of Israel has given rest to his people, that he might reside in Jerusalem forever."

26 Also the Levites are not to carry the tabernacle nor any of the instruments for its service.

27 For according to the last words of David, these were the number of Levites from twenty years of age and over.

28 For their station is [to be] beside the sons of Aaron for the service of the house of YHWH: over the courts and over the chambers and over the purifying of all that is holy, and the work for the service of the house of God,

29 and [to assist with] the showbread and the fine flour for a cereal offering, wafers of unleavened bread or that baked on a pan or that which is mixed, according to every kind of weight and measure.

30 They are to stand every morning to give thanks and to give praise to YHWH and likewise in the evening;

31 and at every offering of burnt offerings to YHWH—at sabbaths and new moons and festivals—by number, according to custom concerning them, continually before YHWH.

32 Also they shall keep charge over the tent of meeting and of the sanctuary and of the sons of Aaron their kinsmen, for the service of the house of YHWH.

24:1 Now the divisions of the sons of Aaron were these. The sons of Aaron: Nadab and Abihu, Eleazar and Ithamar.

2 However, Nadab and Abihu died before their father; and they had no sons, so Eleazar and Ithamar acted as priests.

3 David divided them up [along with] Zadok of the sons of Eleazar and Ahimelech of the sons of Ithamar to their office in their service.

4 Since the sons of Eleazar were found to be more numerous in chief men than the sons of Ithamar, they divided them up [thus]: sixteen heads of the fathers' houses for Eleazar, and eight heads of the fathers' houses for Ithamar.

5 They divided them both up by lots, for they were officials of the sanctuary and officials of God among both the sons of Eleazar and the sons of Ithamar.

6 Shemaiah son of Nethanel the scribe, from the tribe of Levi, wrote them down in the presence of the king, the officials, Zadok the priest, Ahimelek son of Abiathar, the heads of the fathers for the priests and the Levites, one father's house picked out for Eleazar and one[1] picked out for Ithamar.

7 The first lot went to Jehoiarib, the second to Jedaiah,

8 the third to Harim, the fourth to Seorim,

9 the fifth to Malchijah, the sixth to Mijamin,

10 the seventh to Hakkoz, the eighth to Abijah,

11 the ninth to Jeshua, the tenth to Shecaniah,

12 the eleventh to Eliashib, the twelfth to Jakim,

13 the thirteenth to Huppah, the fourteenth to Jeshebeab,

14 the fifteenth to Bilgah, the sixteenth to Immer,

15 the seventeenth to Hezir, the eighteenth to Happizzez,

16 the nineteenth to Pethahiah, the twentieth to Jehezkel,

17 the twenty-first to Jachin, the twenty-second to Gamul,

18 the twenty-third to Delaiah, the twenty-fourth to Maaziah.

19 These were their office[s] for their service to come to the house of YHWH according to their custom at the hand of Aaron their father, as YHWH God of Israel had commanded him.

20 Of the remaining sons of Levi: of the sons of Amram: Shubael; of the sons of Shubael, Jehdeiah.

21 Of Rehabiah: of the sons of Rehabiah: Isshiah, the chief.

22 Of the Izharites: Shelomoth; of the sons of Shelomoth, Jahath.

23 Of the sons of [Hebron²]: Jeriah, Amariah the second, Jahaziel the third, Jekameam the fourth.

24 The sons of Uzziel: Micah; of the sons of Micah, Shamir.

25 The brother of Micah, Isshiah; of the sons of Isshiah, Zechariah.

26 The sons of Merari: Mahli and Mushi. The sons of Jaaziah: Beno.

27 The sons of Merari: of Jaaziah, Beno, Shoham, Zaccur and Ibri.

28 Of Mahli: Eleazar, but he had no sons.

29 Of Kish: the sons of Kish, Jerahmeel.

30 The sons of Mushi: Mahli, Eder, and Jerimoth; these were the sons of the Levites according to the house of their fathers.

31 They also cast lots corresponding to their kinsfolk, the sons of Aaron, in the presence of David the king, Zadok, Ahimelech, the heads of the fathers for the priests and the Levites, the head of the fathers alongside the youngest of his brothers.

---

¹ Literally, "picked out."
² See 1 Chron 23:19.

542 The Divisions of the Musicians
1 Chron 25:1-31

1 Chronicles 25

1 Then David and the officers of the army separated for the service the sons of Asaph, and of Heman, and of Jeduthun, who were prophesying on lyres, harps and cymbals. Their roster of men for the task of their service [was]:

2 of the sons of Asaph: Zaccur, Joseph, Nethaniah, and Asarelah, sons of Asaph, under the direction of Asaph who prophesied at the direction of the king;

3 of Jeduthun, the sons of Jeduthun: Gedaliah, Zeri, Jeshaiah, Hashabiah, and Mattithiah, six under the direction of their father; Jeduthun on the lyre, who prophesied in order to give thanks and to give praise to YHWH;

4 of Heman, the sons of Heman: Bukkiah, Mattaniah, Uzziel, Shebuel, Jerimoth, Hananiah, Hanani, Eliathah, Giddalti, Romamti-ezer, Joshbekashah, Malothi, Hothir, Mahazioth.

5 All these were sons of Heman, the king's seer, by the words of God, to raise up a horn. God gave Heman fourteen sons and three daughters.

6 All these were under the direction of their father in the song in the house of YHWH with cymbals, harps, and lyres for the service of the house of God; under the direction of the king [were] Asaph, Jeduthun and Heman.

7 So their roster, along with their brothers who were trained in singing to YHWH, all who were skilled, was two hundred eighty-eight.

8 And they cast lots for their duty, both small and great, the skilled with the student.

9 The first lot for Asaph fell to Joseph, Gedaliah the second, he and his brothers and his sons, twelve;

10 the third: Zaccur, his sons and brothers, twelve;

11 the fourth to Izri, his sons and brothers, twelve;

12 the fifth: Nethaniah, his sons and brothers, twelve;

13 the sixth: Bukkiah, his sons and brothers, twelve;

14 the seventh: Jesarelah, his sons and brothers, twelve;

15 the eighth: Jeshaiah, his sons and brothers, twelve;

16 the ninth: Mattaniah, his sons and brothers, twelve;

17 the tenth: Shimei, his sons and brothers, twelve;

18 the eleventh: Azarel, his sons and brothers, twelve;

19 the twelfth to Hashabiah, his sons and brothers, twelve;

20 to the thirteenth: Shubael, his sons and brothers, twelve;

21 to the fourteenth: Mattithiah, his sons and brothers, twelve;

22 to the fifteenth, to Jeremoth, his sons and brothers, twelve;

23 to the sixteenth, to Hananiah, his sons and brothers, twelve;

24 to the seventeenth, Joshbekashah, his sons and brothers, twelve;

25 to the eighteenth, to Hanani, his sons and brothers, twelve;

26 to the nineteenth, to Malothi, his sons and brothers, twelve;

27 to the twentieth, to Eliathah, his sons and brothers, twelve.

28 to the twenty-first, to Hothir, his sons and brothers, twelve;

29 to the twenty-second, to Giddalti, his sons and brothers, twelve;

30 to the twenty-third, to Mahazioth, his sons and brothers, twelve;

31 to the twenty-fourth, to Romamti-ezer, his sons and brothers, twelve.

543 The Gatekeepers and Overseers
1 Chron 26:1-32

1 Chronicles 26

1 As for the divisions of the gatekeepers, of the Korahites: Meshelemiah son of Kore of the sons of Asaph.

2 And Mechelemiah had sons: Zechariah the first-born, Jediael the second, Zebadiah the third, Jathniel the fourth,

3 Elam the fifth, Jehohanan the sixth, Eliehoenai the seventh.

4 Obed-edom had sons: Shemaiah the first-born, Jehozabad the second, Joah the third, Sachar the fourth, Nethanel the fifth,

5 Ammiel the sixth, Issachar the seventh, Peullethai the eighth, for God blessed him.

6 To Shemaiah, his son, sons were born who were rulers over the houses of their fathers, since they were warriors.

7 The sons of Shemaiah: Othni, Rephael, Obed and Elzabad, whose brothers were warriors, Elihu and Semachiah.

8 All of these, from the sons of Obed-edom and their sons and brothers, were warriors equipped for the service, sixty-two from Obed-edom.

9 Meshelemiah had sons and brothers, warriors, eighteen.

10 Hosah, from the sons of Merari, had sons: Shimri, the head even though he was not first-born but his father designated him as head,

11 Hilkiah the second, Tebaliah the third, Zechariah the fourth; all the sons and brothers of Hosah, thirteen.

12 These divisions of the gatekeepers, corresponding to their head men, had watches alongside their brothers, to serve in the house of YHWH.

13 They cast lots, small and great alike, by their fathers' houses, for their respective gates.

14 The lot from the east fell to Shelemiah, and [for] Zechariah his son, a prudent counselor; they cast lots and his lot fell to the north.

15 For Obed-edom the south, and to his sons fell the storehouse.

16 For Shuppim and Hosah it fell for the west, with the gate of Shallecheth on the upward road, watch corresponding to watch.

17 On the east there were six Levites, to the north, four each day, to the south, four each day, and for the storehouses, two [each] day.

18 For the "Parbar" to the west: four at the road, two at the Parbar.

19 These were the divisions of the gatekeepers of the sons of Korah and the sons of Merari.

20 As for the Levites: Ahijah [was] over the treasuries of the house of God, and of the treasuries of the dedicated gifts.

21 The sons of Ladan, the sons of the Gershonites belonging to Ladan, heads of the fathers of Ladan the Gershonite: Jehieli.

22 The sons of Jehieli: Zetham and Joel his brother, were in charge of the treasuries of the house of YHWH.

23 With regard to the Amramites, Izharites, Hebronites, and Uzzielites:

24 Shebuel son of Gershom, son of Moses, was in charge of the treasuries.

25 His brothers: to Eliezer [belonged] Rehabiah his son, Jesaiah his son, Joram his son, Zichri his son, and Shelomoth his son.

26 This Shelomoth and his brothers were in charge of all the treasuries of the dedicated gifts which King David and the heads of the fathers in charge of the officers of the thousands and the hundreds and the officers of the army had consecrated.

27 From the battle spoil they had consecrated [gifts] to maintain the house of YHWH.

28 Also all that Samuel the seer and Saul son of Kish and Abner son of Ner and Joab son of Zeruiah had consecrated, all the consecrated [material] was under the direction of Shelomoth and his brothers.

29 Of the Izharites: Chenaniah and his sons [were appointed] to outside tasks for Israel as officials and as judges.

30 Of the Hebronites: Hashabiah and his brothers, warriors, one thousand seven hundred were over the administration of Israel, from across the Jordan westward, for every task of YHWH and for the service of the king.

31 Of the Hebronites: Jerijah was head Hebronite according to the genealogies of the fathers in the fortieth year of the reign of David they searched in the genealogies and there were found renowned warriors in Jazer of Gilead.

32 His brothers, warriors, were two thousand seven hundred heads of the fathers; and David the king appointed them over the Reubenites, the Gadites, the half-tribe of Manasseh, for every matter of God and matter of the king.

544 The Officers of the Kingdom
1 Chron 27:1-34

1 Chronicles 27

1 This is the roster of the Israelite heads of the fathers, officers of the thousands and the hundreds, and the officials who served the king, in every matter of the divisions which entered and which exited month by month for all the months of the year, one division [numbering] twenty-four thousand.

2 Over the first division, for the first month, was Jashobeam son of Zabdiel: in his division were twenty-four thousand.

3 He was from the sons of Perez, head of all the army officers for the first month.

4 Over the division for the second month was Dodai the Ahohite; and Mikloth was the leader of his division; in his division were twenty-four thousand.

5 The third officer of the army, for the third month, was Benaiah son of Jehoiada the chief priest; in his division were twenty-four thousand.

6 This Benaiah was a mighty man of the Thirty and over the Thirty; [over] his division was Ammizabad his son.

7 The fourth, for the fourth month, was Asahel brother of Joab, and Zebadiah his son after him; in his division were twenty-four thousand.

8 The fifth, for the fifth month, was the officer Shamhuth, the Izrahite; in his division were twenty-four thousand.

9 The sixth, for the sixth month, was Irah son of Ikkesh the Tekoite; in his division were twenty-four thousand.

10 The seventh, for the seventh month, was Helez the Pelonite, of the Ephraimites; in his division were twenty-four thousand.

11 The eighth, for the eighth month, was Sibbecai the Hushathite, of the Zerahites; in his division were twenty-four thousand.

12 The ninth, for the ninth month, was Abiezer of Anathoth, of the Benjaminites; in his division were twenty-four thousand.

13 The tenth, for the tenth month, was Maharai of Netophah, of the Zerahites; in his division were twenty-four thousand.

14 The eleventh, for the eleventh month, was Benaiah of Pirathon, of the Ephraimites; in his division were twenty-four thousand.

15 The twelfth, for the twelfth month, was Heldai the Nethophathite of Othniel; in his division were twenty-four thousand.

16 Over the tribes of Israel: for the Reubenites, the leader, Eliezer son of Zichri; for Simeon, Shephatiah son of Maacah;

17 for Levi, Hashabiah son of Kemuel; for Aaron, Zadok;

18 for Judah, Elihu of the brothers of David; for Issachar, Omri son of Michael;

19 for Zebulun, Ishmaiah son of Obadiah; for Naphtali, Jerimoth son of Azriel;

20 for the Ephraimites, Hoshea son of Azaziah; for the half-tribe of Manasseh, Joel son of Pedaiah;

21 for the half of Manasseh at Gilead, Iddo son of Zechariah; for Benjamin, Jaasiel son of Abner;

22 for Dan, Azarel son of Jeroham. These were the officers of the tribes of Israel.

23 David did not number those from twenty years and under, for YHWH had promised to increase Israel like the stars of the heavens.

24 Joab son of Zeruiah began to count but did not finish. So there was wrath upon Israel on account of this, and the number was not entered into the number of the Annals of King David.

25 Over the storehouses of the king was Azmaveth son of Adiel, and over the storehouses in the countryside, in the cities, in the villages, and in the towers, was Jonathan son of Uzziah.

26 Over those who did the work of the field, tilling the soil, was Ezri son of Chelub.

27 Over the vineyards was Shimei the Ramathite; and over that which was in the vineyards, the wine stores, was Zabdi the Shiphmite.

28 Over the olive and the sycamore fig trees, which were in the Shephelah, was Baal-hanan the Gederite; and over the oil stores was Joash.

29 Over the cattle pasturing in Sharon was Shitrai the Sharonite. Over the cattle in the valleys was Shaphat son of Adlai.

30 Over the camels was Obil the Ishmaelite, and over the donkeys was Jehdeiah the Meronothite.

31 Over the flocks was Jaziz the Hagrite. All these were stewards of the property which belonged to King David.

32 Jonathan, the uncle of David, was a counselor, being a man of understanding and a scribe; and Jehiel son of Hachmoni was with the sons of the king.

33 Ahitophel was counselor to the king, and Hushai the Archite was friend of the King.

34 After Ahithophel [was] Jehoiada son of Benaiah, and Abiathar; and the commander of the king's army was Joab.

545 David Commits the Building of the Temple to Solomon
1 Chron 28:1–29:9

1 Chronicles 28

1 David assembled all the officials of Israel and officials of the tribes and officials of the divisions which were serving the king and officials of the thousands and officials of the hundreds and officials of all the property and cattle which belonged to the king and to his descendants, together with the court officials and the mighty men and even every warrior, at Jerusalem.

2 Then King David rose to his feet and said, "Hear me, my brothers and my people! It was my intention to build a house of rest for the ark of the covenant of YHWH, for the footstool of our God, and I made preparations to build.

3 God said to me, 'You shall not build a house for my name, since you are a man of war and you have shed blood.'

4 YHWH God of Israel chose me from the entire house of my father to become king over Israel forever, for he chose Judah as prince and in the house of Judah [he chose] my father's house; and among my father's sons he favored me to make me king over all Israel.

5 And from all my sons, for YHWH has given me many sons, he chose Solomon my son to sit on the throne of the kingdom of YHWH over Israel.

6 Then he said to me, "Solomon your son shall build my house and my courts, since I have chosen him for myself as son and I will be a father to him.

7 I will establish his kingdom forever if only he strengthens himself to do my commandments and my ordinances as this day.

8 Now, in the sight of all Israel, the assembly of YHWH, and in the ears of our God, observe and search out all the commandments of YHWH your God so that you may possess the good land and cause your sons to inherit it after you forever.

9 Therefore you, Solomon my son, know the God of your father with a perfect heart and a willing spirit, for YHWH examines all hearts and understands every inclination of [human] thoughts; if you search for him, he will be found by you, but if you forsake him he will abandon you forever.

10 See now, for YHWH has chosen you to build a house as a sanctuary: be strong and act!"

11 Then David gave Solomon his son the plan of the porch and its rooms and its storerooms and its upper chambers and its inner chambers and the house of the mercy seat,

12 and the plan of everything which was in mind with him for the court of the house of YHWH and all the chambers round about, for the treasuries of the house of God and for the treasuries for the dedicated gifts:

13 for the divisions of the priests and Levites and for all the work of the service of the house of YHWH and for all the vessels of service for the house of YHWH,

14 for [all the vessels of] gold by weight for gold, for all vessels for each service, for all the vessels of silver by weight for all the vessels of each service,

15 the weight of the golden menorahs and their lamps, by the weight of each menorah and its lamps, and for the silver menorahs by the weight of a menorah and its lamps, according to the service of each menorah,

16 and the weight of gold for the tables of showbread, table by table, and silver for the silver table

17 and pure gold for the forks and the basins and the flagons, for the golden bowls by weight of each bowl, for the silver bowls, by weight of each bowl,

18 for the incense altar, refined gold by weight, and for the plan of the golden chariot of the cherubim spreading their wings and covering the ark of the covenant of YHWH.

19 All this in writing from the hand of YHWH he taught me, all the workings of the plan.

20 David said also to his son Solomon, "Be strong, be courageous, and act: do not be afraid and do not be terrified, for YHWH God, my God, is with you. He will neither forsake you nor abandon you until completion of all the work for the service of the house of YHWH.

21 Here are the divisions of the priests and Levites for all the service of the house of God: and with you in all the work will be every skilled, willing worker for all the service, and the officials and all the people will be at your commands.

29:1 Then King David said to all the assembly, "Solomon my son, whom alone God has chosen, is young and inexperienced, and the task is great, for the temple is not for humans but for YHWH God.

2 So, according to all my ability I have prepared for the house of my God gold for the things of gold, silver for the silver, bronze for the bronze, iron for the iron, wood for the wood, stone of onyx, [stones for] setting, stones of antimony, mosaic pebbles, and every precious stone and marble in abundance.

3 Moreover, because of my delight in the house of my God, personal property of gold and silver which belongs to me I have given to the house of my God above all that I have prepared for the holy house:

4 three thousand talents of gold from the gold of Ophir, seven thousand talents of refined silver for covering the walls of the rooms,

5 gold for the things of gold and silver for the things of silver and for all work done by the hand of artisans. Who will volunteer to consecrate themselves today for YHWH?

6 Then the officials of the houses of the fathers and the chiefs of the tribes of Israel and the chiefs of the thousands and of the hundreds and those over all the king's work volunteered.

7 They gave to the service of God's house five thousand talents and ten thousand darics of gold, ten thousand talents of silver, eighteen thousand talents of bronze, and one hundred thousand talents of iron.

8 Whoever was found to have [precious] stones gave them to the treasury of the house of YHWH into the care of Jehiel the Gershonite.

9 Then the people rejoiced over their generous offerings, for they had offered freely to YHWH with a perfect heart, and also King David rejoiced with great rejoicing.

546 David Blesses YHWH
1 Chron 29:10-19

1 Chronicles 29

10 Then David blessed YHWH before all the assembly. David said, "Blessed are you, YHWH God of Israel, our father from eternity to eternity.

11 Yours YHWH, are greatness and power and splendor and victory and the majesty, for everything in heaven and on earth belongs to you, YHWH; yours is the kingdom, and you are raised high as head over all.

12 The wealth and the glory are before you; and you are ruling over all and in your hand are power and strength; and it is in your hand to make everything great and strong.

13 So now, our God, we are giving you thanks and praising your splendid name.

14 But who am I, and what is my people, that we should be able to offer so generously as this, for everything is from you and from your hand we have given to you.

15 For we are aliens before you and pilgrims as all our fathers were; our days are like a shadow upon the earth, and there is no hope.

16 YHWH our God, all this abundance which we have prepared to build you a house for your holy name, it all comes from your hand and it all belongs to you.

17 I know, my God, that you test hearts and that you delight in upright deeds. In the uprightness of my heart I have generously offered all these; and now your people who are found here, I have seen [them] rejoicing to give generously to you.

18 YHWH, God of Abraham, Isaac and Israel our fathers, keep this forever as a frame for the thoughts of the heart of your people and make their heart ready for you.

19 Give to Solomon my son a perfect heart to keep your commandments and your testimonies and your statutes, and to do all these things and to build the temple which I have prepared."

547 Abishag Ministers to David
1 Kings 1:1-4

1 Now King David grew old, up in years, and though they covered him with clothes, he could not keep himself warm.

2 So his servants said to him, "Let them search for a girl, a virgin, for my lord the king and let her attend the king and be his maid-in-waiting; let her lie in your bosom and my lord the king will keep warm."

3 So they searched for a beautiful girl in all the territory of Israel, and they found Abishag the Shunammite and they brought her to the king.

4 The girl was very beautiful and she was maid-in-waiting to the king and attended to him; but the king did not know her.

548 Adonijah Usurps the Throne
1 Kings 1:5-27

1 Kings 1

5 Then Adonijah son of Haggith raised himself up saying, "I will be king" and he made for himself a chariot and horsemen and fifty men to run in front of him.

6 Now his father had never checked him in his life saying, "Why have you acted in this way?" He was also very good-looking and she [his mother] had borne him after Absalom.

7 So he spoke with Joab son of Zeruiah and with Abiathar the priest, and they gave their support to Adonijah;

8 but Zadok the priest and Benaiah son of Jehoiada and Nathan the prophet and Shimei and Rei, along with David's [own] warriors, these were not with Adonijah.

9 Adonijah sacrificed sheep, oxen and fatlings at the stone of Zoheleth which is beside En-Rogel; and he invited all his brothers, sons of the king, and all the men of Judah servants of the king:

10 but Nathan the prophet and Benaiah and the warriors and Solomon his brother he did not invite.

11 Then Nathan said to Bathsheba mother of Solomon, "Have you not heard that Adonijah son of Haggith has become king, and our lord David does not know?

12 Come now, let me give you [this] advice: save your life and the life of your son Solomon.

13 Go in right now to King David and say to him, 'Did not you, my lord the king, swear to your handmaid that "Solomon your son shall become king after me and he shall sit upon my throne?" So why has Adonijah become king?'

14 While you are still speaking there with the king, I will certainly come in after you and confirm your words."

15 So Bathsheba went to the king into his bedchamber; the king was very old and Abishag the Shunnamite was attending the king.

16 Bathsheba bowed and prostrated herself before the king and the king said, "What is your [wish]?"

17 Then she said to him, "My lord, you surely swore by YHWH your God to your handmaid that, 'Solomon your son will become king after me and he will sit upon my throne.'

18 But now here is Adonijah become king and now, my lord the king, you do not know [it].

19 Moreover, he has sacrificed oxen and fatlings and sheep in large quantities and he has invited all the sons of the king, Abiathar the priest and Joab the commander of the army, but Solomon your servant he did not invite.

20 But you, my lord the king, the eyes of all Israel are on you to declare to them who shall sit upon the throne of my lord the king after him:

21 or it will happen when my lord the king lies at rest with his ancestors, that I and my son Solomon will be [considered] wrongdoers."

22 Then indeed while she was still speaking with the king, Nathan the prophet came in.

23 So they announced to the king, "Here is Nathan the prophet," and he came in before the king and prostrated himself before the king with his face to the ground.

24 Then Nathan said, "My lord the king, have you [actually] said, 'Adonijah shall become king after me and he shall sit upon my throne?'

25 For he has gone down today and has sacrificed oxen, fatlings and sheep in large quantities, and he has invited all the sons of the king, the commander of the army and Abiathar the priest: even now they are eating and drinking before him and they are saying 'Let Adonijah the king live!'

26 But he did not invite me, your servant, or Zadok the priest or Benaiah son of Jehoiada or Solomon your son.

27 If this thing has come about through my lord the king, then you have not informed [us] your servants: who is to sit upon the throne of my lord the king after him?"

549 Solomon Is Made King
1 Kings 1:28-53 // 1 Chron 23:1; 29:20-22

1 Kings 1

28 Then King David answered, "Call to me Bathsheba" and she came before the king and stood before the king.

29 The king swore an oath and said, "As YHWH lives who has saved my life from all adversity,

30 as I swore to you, by YHWH God of Israel, that Solomon your son should become king after me and that he should sit on my throne in my place, so will I do this day."

31 Then Bathsheba bowed her face [to] the ground and prostrated herself before the king and said, "let my lord King David live for ever."

32 Thereupon King David said, "Call to me Zadok the priest and Nathan the prophet and Benaiah son of Jehoiada," and they came before the king.

33 The king said to them, "Take with you the servants of your lord and make Solomon my son ride on the mule which belongs to me; and lead him down to Gihon.

34 There Zadok the priest and Nathan the prophet shall anoint him king over Israel; then you shall blow on the shophar and say, 'Let King Solomon live!'

35 You shall come up after him and he shall come in and sit upon my throne and he will become king in my place; for him I have ordained to be prince over Israel and Judah.

36 Then Benaiah son of Jehoiada answered the king, "So be it; let

1 Chronicles 23

1 Now David was old and advanced in years and he made Solomon his son king over Israel.

1 Chronicles 29
20 Then David said to all the congregation, "Now bless YHWH your God"; and all the congregation blessed YHWH the God of their ancestors; and they bowed and prostrated themselves before YHWH and the king.

21 Then they offered sacrifices to YHWH and made offerings to YHWH on the very next morning: a thousand oxen, a thousand rams and a thousand lambs, along with their drink-offering and sacrifices in large quantities for all Israel.

22 So they ate and drank in the presence of YHWH on that day with great joy. Then, for a second time they made Solomon son of David king and they anointed him as prince for YHWH, with Zadok as priest.

YHWH the God of my lord the king
say it so.

37 As YHWH has been with my
lord the king, so may he be with
Solomon and make his throne
greater than the throne of my lord
King David."

38 So Zadok the priest and Nathan
the prophet and Benaiah son of
Jehoiada, with the Kerethites and
the Pelethites, went down and they
made Solomon ride King David's
mule and they walked him down to
Gihon.

39 Then Zadok the priest took the
horn of oil from the tent and he
anointed Solomon; and they blew
the shophar and all the people
shouted, "Let King Solomon live!"

40 And all the people went up after
him, and the people [were] playing
on pipes and rejoicing with great
joy, so that the earth was split by
their clamor.

41 Now Adonijah and all the guests
who were with him heard [the
clamor] as they finished eating.
[When] Joab heard the sound of the
shophar he said, "Why is [there] the
sound of uproar in the city?"

42 While he was still speaking, one
Jonathan son of Abiathar the priest
came. Adonijah said, "Come in, for
you are a man of worth and bring
good news."

43 But Jonathan answered Adonijah,
"No, rather our lord King David has
made Solomon king:

44 and the king has sent with him
Zadok the priest, Nathan the prophet
and Benaiah son of Jehoiada and the
Kerethites and the Pelethites and
they have made him ride on the
king's [own] mule;

45 and Zadok the priest and Nathan the prophet have anointed him king at Gihon, and they have come up from there rejoicing and the city is in uproar. That was the clamor that you heard.

46 Also Solomon sits on the royal throne.

47 Moreover, even the servants of the king have come to congratulate our lord King David thus, 'May your God make the name of Solomon more glorious than your [own] name, and make his throne greater than your throne.' Then the king bowed himself on the couch.

48 The king also spoke thus, 'Blessed be YHWH God of Israel who has given this day one to sit upon my throne and my eyes to see it.'"

49 Then all those invited who belonged to Adonijah panicked, got up and went each his own way.

50 Now Adonijah feared Solomon, so he got up and went and took hold of the horns of the altar.

51 It was told to Solomon, "Adonijah surely fears King Solomon, for he has indeed grasped the horns of the altar saying, 'Let King Solomon swear to me as of today that he will not put his servant to death by the sword.'"

52 So Solomon said, "If he shows himself to be a man of worth, not one hair [of his head] shall fall to the ground; but if wickedness is found in him, he shall die."

53 Then King Solomon sent [orders] that they bring him down from the altar: and he came and prostrated himself before King Solomon and Solomon said to him, "Go to your house!"

550 David's Charge to Solomon
1 Kings 2:1-9 // 1 Kings 8:25; 9:4-5

1 Kings 2	*1 Kings 8*	*1 Kings 9*
1 Now David's time to die drew near and he commanded Solomon his son thus:		
2 "I am going [in] the way of all the earth, so you are to be strong and you are to act like a man.		
3 You are to keep the charge of YHWH your God, to walk in his ways, to keep his statutes, his commandments and his ordinances and his testimonies as written in the Torah of Moses, so that you may prosper in all that you do and wherever you turn:		4 But you, if you will walk before me just as David your father walked, in perfection of heart and in uprightness, acting according to everything which I have commanded you, and keeping my statutes and my ordinances,
4 so that YHWH may confirm his word which he spoke about me, 'If your sons keep their way to walk before me in truth with all their heart and with all their being, there shall not be cut off from you a man [of your line] upon the throne of Israel.	25 But now, YHWH, God of Israel, keep for your servant David my father what you spoke to him, 'There shall not be cut off a man [of your line] from before me sitting on the throne of Israel; but only let your sons keep their way: to walk before me just as you have walked before me.'	5 then I will raise up the throne of your kingdom over Israel forever, just as I spoke to David your father: there shall not be cut off from you a man [of your line] from upon the throne of Israel.
5 Furthermore you also know what Joab son of Zeruiah did to me, what he did to the two commanders of the armies of Israel, to Abner son of Ner and to Amasa son of Jether: how he slaughtered them and shed the blood of war in peace [time] and put the blood of war on his sash which was around his waist and on his sandals which were on his feet.		

6 Therefore, act according
to your wisdom and do not
let his old age go down in
peace to Sheol.

7 However, you are to act
loyally to the sons of
Barzillai the Gileadite and
let them be among those
who eat at your table, for
thus [with loyalty] they
approached me when I
fled from Absalom your
brother.

8 Then there is surely
with you Shimei son of
Gera the Benjaminite from
Bahurim. Now he cursed
me with a baleful curse on
the day when I went out to
Mahanaim: but when he
came down to meet me at
the Jordan, I swore to him
by YHWH thus, 'I will
surely not put you to death
by the sword.'

9 But now, do not exempt
him from punishment, for
you are a wise man and
you know what to do with
him and you will bring
down his old age in blood
[to] Sheol."

551 The Death of David
1 Chron 29:20-30 // 1 Kings 2:10-12

1 Chronicles 29   *1 Kings 2*

20 Then David said to all the congregation, "Now
bless YHWH your God"; and all the congregation
blessed YHWH God of their ancestors; and they bowed
and prostrated themselves before YHWH and the king.

21 They offered sacrifices to YHWH and made burnt
offerings to YHWH on the very next morning; a thousand oxen, a thousand rams and a thousand lambs,

along with their drink-offering and sacrifices in great quantities for all Israel:

22 and they ate and drank before YHWH on that day with great joy. Then, for a second time, they made Solomon son of David king and they anointed him as prince for YHWH, with Zadok as priest.

23 So Solomon sat on the throne of YHWH as king in place of David his father; he prospered and all Israel obeyed him.

[12 So Solomon sat upon the throne of David his father and his royal power was firmly established.

24 All the commanders and the warriors, and also the sons of King David gave their allegiance to King Solomon.

25 Now YHWH magnified Solomon highly in the eyes of all Israel; and he gave him a royal splendor not [bestowed] upon any king before him over Israel.

26 Thus David son of Jesse was king over all Israel.

27 The time that David was king over Israel was forty years: in Hebron he was king for seven years and in Jerusalem he was king for thirty-three years.

11 The time that David was king over Israel was forty years: in Hebron he was king for seven years and in Jerusalem he was king for thirty-three years.

28 So he died in a good old age full of years, riches and honor; and Solomon his son became king in his place.

10 When David lay down to rest with his ancestors, he was buried in the city of David.]

29 Now the acts of King David, [from] the first to the last, they are indeed written in the Chronicles of Samuel the Seer, and in the Chronicles of Nathan the Prophet, and in the Chronicles of Gad the Seer,

30 with [accounts of] all his reign and his power and the times that came upon him and upon all Israel and upon all the kingdoms of the world.

Solomon

Solomon
Sections 552–569

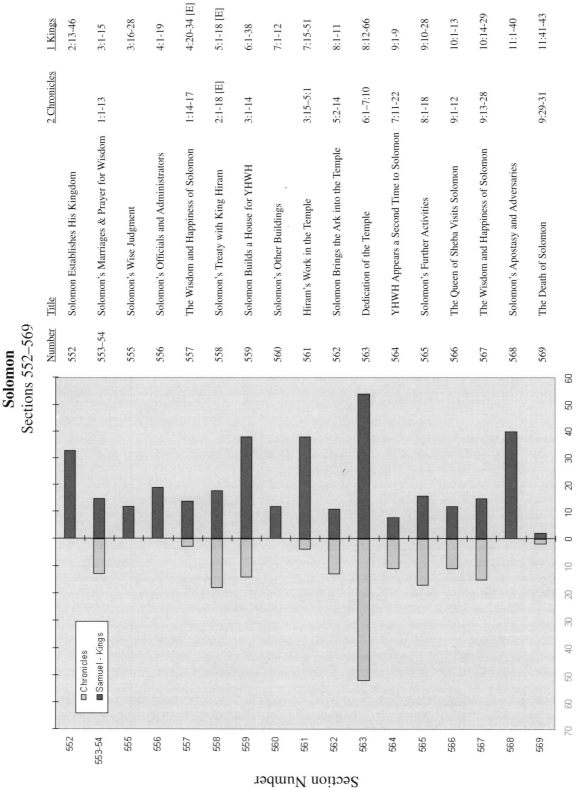

Number	Title	2 Chronicles	1 Kings
552	Solomon Establishes His Kingdom		2:13-46
553–54	Solomon's Marriages & Prayer for Wisdom	1:1-13	3:1-15
555	Solomon's Wise Judgment		3:16-28
556	Solomon's Officials and Administrators		4:1-19
557	The Wisdom and Happiness of Solomon	1:14-17	4:20-34 [E]
558	Solomon's Treaty with King Hiram	2:1-18 [E]	5:1-18 [E]
559	Solomon Builds a House for YHWH	3:1-14	6:1-38
560	Solomon's Other Buildings		7:1-12
561	Hiram's Work in the Temple	3:15–5:1	7:15-51
562	Solomon Brings the Ark into the Temple	5:2-14	8:1-11
563	Dedication of the Temple	6:1–7:10	8:12-66
564	YHWH Appears a Second Time to Solomon	7:11-22	9:1-9
565	Solomon's Further Activities	8:1-18	9:10-28
566	The Queen of Sheba Visits Solomon	9:1-12	10:1-13
567	The Wisdom and Happiness of Solomon	9:13-28	10:14-29
568	Solomon's Apostasy and Adversaries		11:1-40
569	The Death of Solomon	9:29-31	11:41-43

552 Solomon Establishes His Kingdom
1 Kings 2:13-46

1 Kings 2

13 Then Adonijah son of Haggith came to Bathsheba mother of Solomon, and she said, "Do you come peacefully?" He said, "Peacefully."

14 Then he said, "I have a word [to say] to you." She said, "Speak!"

15 So he said, "You know indeed that the royal power was mine and that all Israel looked up to me to become king, but the royal power passed to my brother, for it was his from YHWH:

16 and now I am requesting but one thing from you, do not turn me down." She said to him, "Speak!"

17 Then he said, "Speak, now, to Solomon the king, for he will not turn you down, that he may give to me Abishag the Shunammite for a wife."

18 Bathsheba said, "It is good, I will certainly speak for you to the king."

19 So Bathsheba went into King Solomon to speak to him for Adonijah, and the king rose to meet her and bowed down to her. Then he sat down upon his throne and he had placed a throne for the king's mother and she sat down at his right hand.

20 Thereupon she said, "I am requesting but one small thing from you; do not turn me down." The king said to her, "Make your request, mother, for I will not turn you down."

21 So she said, "Let Abishag the Shunammite be given to Adonijah your brother for a wife."

22 King Solomon answered his mother, "Now why do you request Abishag the Shunammite for Adonijah? Request also the kingship for him, for he is my elder brother, and not just for him, but also for Abiathar the priest and for Joab son of Zeruiah!"

23 Then King Solomon swore by YHWH, "God do so to me and more also, for Adonijah has requested this thing in [peril of] his life.

24 And now, as YHWH lives, who has established me and sat me upon the throne of David my father and who has made me a house as he said, today Adonijah shall be put to death."

25 So King Solomon sent Benaiah son of Jehoiada and he struck him down and he died.

26 To Abiathar the priest the king said, "Go to Anathoth, to your estate, for you are a man [deserving] death. However, on this day I will not put you to death because you carried the Ark of Lord YHWH before David my father and because you suffered in all that my father suffered."

27 Thus Solomon expelled Abiathar from being priest to YHWH to fulfil the word of YHWH that he spoke against the house of Eli in Shiloh.

28 Now the news came to Joab, for Joab had gone after Adonijah—though he had not gone after Absalom—and Joab fled to the tent of YHWH and he took hold of the horns of the altar.

29 It was told to King Solomon that Joab had fled to the tent of YHWH and now he was beside the altar, and Solomon sent Benaiah son of Jehoiada saying, "Go and strike him down!"

30 Benaiah came to the tent of YHWH and said to him [Joab], "Thus says the king, 'Come out!'" But he said, "No, for I will die here." So Benaiah brought word back to the king accordingly, "So spoke Joab and so I answered."

31 Then the king said to him, "Do as he has spoken: strike him down and bury him; and [so] you will remove the blood that Joab shed without cause, from me and from my father's house.

32 For YHWH will bring back his blood upon his [own] head because he struck down two men, more righteous and better than he, and slew them with the sword, and my father David did not know [of it]: Abner son of Ner, commander of the army of Israel and Amasa son of Jether, commander of the army of Judah.

33 Thus their blood shall come back upon the head of Joab and upon the head of his descendants for ever; but to David and to his seed and to his house and to his throne, there shall be peace for ever from YHWH."

34 Then Benaiah son of Jehoiada went up and struck him [Joab] down and killed him; and he was buried in his house in the desert.

35 The king put Benaiah son of Jehoiada in his [Joab's] place over the army; and Zadok the priest, the king put in place of Abiathar.

36 Then the king sent and called Shimei and said to him, "Build for yourself a house in Jerusalem and there you will reside, and not go out from there anywhere at all.

37 For on the day that you go out and cross the Wadi Kidron, know for certain that you will surely die; your blood shall be upon your own head."

38 So Shimei said to the king, "The command is good; as my lord the king has spoken, so will your servant do." So Shimei resided in Jerusalem many days.

39 But it happened at the end of three years two slaves [belonging] to Shimei fled to Achish son of Maacah, king of Gath. So they told Shimei, "Your slaves are definitely in Gath."

40 So Shimei rose up and saddled his ass and went to Gath, to Achish to look for his slaves; Shimei went and brought his slaves from Gath.

41 It was told to Solomon that Shimei had gone out from Jerusalem and returned.

42 So the king sent and called Shimei and said to him, "Did I not swear by YHWH and warn you thus, 'On the day that you go out anywhere at all, know for certain that you will surely die?' And you said to me, 'The command is good; I have heard [it].'

43 Then why did you not keep the oath [made to] YHWH and the command that I commanded you?"

44 Also the king said to Shimei, "You know all the evil that your own heart knows that you did to David my father; and [now] YHWH is bringing back evil upon your [own] head.

45 But king Solomon shall be blessed and the throne of David shall be established before YHWH for ever."

46 Then the king commanded Benaiah son of Jehoiada and he went out and struck him [Shimei] down and he died. So the kingdom was established in the hand of Solomon.

553 & 554 Solomon's Marriages and Prayer for Wisdom
2 Chron 1:1-13 // 1 Kings 2:12b; 2:46b; 3:1-15; 4:1a

2 Chronicles 1

1 Now Solomon son of David grasped his royal power firmly and YHWH his God was with him and made him exceedingly great.

2 Solomon spoke to all Israel, to the officers of thousands and hundreds and to the judges and to every official for the whole of Israel, the heads of families.

3 Then Solomon and all the assembly with him went to the high place which was at Gibeon; for there was the tent of meeting of God that Moses the servant of YHWH had made in the desert.

1 Kings 2

12b . . . and his royal power was firmly established.
46b . . . so the kingdom was established in the hand of Solomon.

1 Kings 3
1 Solomon allied [himself] in marriage with Pharaoh king of Egypt; and he took Pharaoh's daughter and brought her to the city of David until he had finished building his house, and the house of YHWH, and the city-wall around Jerusalem.

2 Only, the people were still sacrificing on the high places, for a house had not been built to the name of YHWH until these [present] days.

3 Now Solomon loved YHWH, walking in the statutes of David his father; only, he still sacrificed and burned incense on the high places.

4 Then the king went to Gibeon to sacrifice there, for it was a great high place,

4 (In fact David had brought up the ark of God from Kiriath-jearim [to the place] David had prepared for it, for he had pitched a tent for it in Jerusalem.)

5 Now the altar of bronze that Bezalel son of Uri, son of Hur, had made [was] there in front of the tabernacle of YHWH, and Solomon and the assembly inquired at it.

6 Then Solomon went up there to the altar of bronze in front of YHWH which was in the tent of meeting; and he offered upon it a thousand burnt offerings.

and he offered up a thousand burnt offerings upon that altar.

5 At Gibeon YHWH appeared to Solomon in a dream at night, and God said, "Ask what I should give you."

7 In that night God appeared to Solomon and said to him, "Ask what I should give you."

6 So Solomon said, "You did great kindness to your servant David my father, because he walked before you in truth and righteousness and in uprightness of heart with you; and you kept for him this great kindness that you gave him a son to sit upon his throne as of this day.

8 So Solomon said to God, "You did great kindness to David my father, and you have made me king in his place.

7 Now, YHWH my God, you have made your servant king in the place of David my father, and I am [but] a little lad; I do not know how to go out or come in.

9 Now, YHWH God, let your word to David my father be confirmed, for you have made me king over a people numerous as the dust of the earth.

8 And your servant is in the midst of your people whom you have chosen, a great people who cannot be numbered nor counted for size.

9 Now may you give me a listening heart to judge your people, to discern between good and evil, for who is able to judge this your worthy people?"

10 Now give me wisdom and knowledge and I shall go out before this people and I shall come in, for who can judge this your great people?"

10 It was good in the eyes of the Lord that Solomon had asked for this thing [that is, wisdom].

11 So God said to Solomon, "Since this was in your heart and you have not asked for wealth, riches and honor, the life of those who hate you, nor even many days, but you have asked for yourself wisdom and knowledge with which to judge my people over whom I have made you king:

11 So God said to him, "Since you have asked for this thing, and you have not asked for yourself many days, nor asked for yourself wealth, nor the life of your enemies, but have asked for yourself understanding to hear judgment:

12 wisdom and knowledge are given to you; riches and wealth and honor will I also give to you, the like of which were not given to the kings who were before you and after you none shall have the like."

12 I am indeed acting according to your word. I will certainly give you a wise and understanding heart, whose like was not before you, nor after you shall arise the like.

13 Also what you have not asked I give you, both riches and honor, that no king shall be like you all your days.

14 Now if you walk in my ways, keeping my statutes and commandments as David your father walked, then I will lengthen your days."

13 Then Solomon came from the high place which was at Gibeon, from before the tent of meeting, to Jerusalem,

15 Then Solomon woke up and indeed it was a dream: he came to Jerusalem and stood before the ark of the covenant of the Lord and offered up burnt-offerings and made peace-offerings, and made a feast for all his servants.

1 Kings 4

and he was king over Israel.

1a Now King Solomon was king over all Israel,

555 Solomon's Wise Judgment
1 Kings 3:16-28

1 Kings 3

16 Then two women, prostitutes, came to the king and stood before him.

17 And the first woman said, "O my lord, I and this woman live in one house and I gave birth while she was in the house.

18 Then it happened on the third day after I gave birth, that this woman also gave birth. And we were together; no stranger was with us in the house, only we two were in the house.

19 Now this woman's son died in the night because she lay upon him:

20 so she got up in the middle of the night and took my son from my side while your maidservant slept, and laid him on her breast; and she laid the dead son on my breast.

21 When I got up in the morning to nurse my son, he was dead! But when I looked at him carefully in the morning, he was not my child which I had borne!"

22 But the other woman said, "No, for my son is the living one and your son the dead." Then this one [the first] said, "No, for your son is the dead one and my son the living." So they spoke before the king.

23 Then the king said, "This one says, 'This is my son, the living one and your son the dead'; but this one says, 'No, for your son is the dead one and mine the living.'"

24 So the king said, "Fetch me a sword"; and they brought the sword before the king.

25 The king said, "Divide the live boy in two and give half to the one and half to the other."

26 Then the woman whose son was alive said to the king, for her womb burned with compassion for her son, and she said, "O my lord, give her the living boy, you must not kill it." But the other said, "Neither mine nor yours shall it be. Divide it!"

27 At this the king answered, "Give her the live boy and certainly do not kill him. She is his mother."

28 All Israel heard of the judgment that the king had judged, and they were in awe of the king, for they saw that the wisdom of God was in him to do justice.

556 Solomon's Officials and Administrators
1 Kings 4:1-19

1 Kings 4

1 Now King Solomon was king over all Israel.

2 These were his officials: Azariah son of Zadok the priest;

3 Elihoreph and Ahijah, sons of Shisha, scribes; Jehoshaphat son of Ahilud, secretary;

4 Benaiah son of Jehoiada, over the army; Zadok and Abiathar, priests;

5 Azariah son of Nathan, over the deputies; Zabud son of Nathan, priest and friend of the king;

6 Ahishar, over the house; Adoniram son of Abda, over the corvée.

7 Further, Solomon had twelve deputies over all Israel and they provisioned the king and his house; for a month in the year it used to fall upon each [deputy] to make provision.

8 These were their names: Ben-hur in the hill-country of Ephraim;

9 Ben-deker in Makats, in Shaalbim and Beth-shemesh and Elon [and] Beth-hanan;

10 Ben-hesed in Aruboth; belonging to him were Soco and all the land of Hepher;

11 Ben-abinadab [in] all Napath-Dor, Tapath daughter of Solomon was his wife;

12 Baaba son of Ahilud, [in] Taanach and Megiddo and all Beth-shean which is beside Zartanah, below Jezreel from Beth-shean as far as Abel-meholah as far as the other side of Jokmeam;

13 Ben-geber in Ramoth-gilead (he had the encampments of Jair son of Manasseh which are in Gilead; he had [also] the region of Argob which is in Bashan: sixty great cities with walls and bars of bronze);

14 Ahinadab son of Iddo, Mahanaim;

15 Ahimaaz in Naphtali, he also took Basemath daughter of Solomon to wife;

16 Baana son of Hushai, in Asher and in Aloth;

17 Jehoshaphat son of Paruah, in Issachar;

18 Shimei son of Ela, in Benjamin;

19 Geber son of Uri, in the land of Gilead, the land of Sihon king of the Amorites and Og king of Bashan; and there was one deputy who was over the land.

557 The Wisdom and Happiness of Solomon
2 Chron 1:14-17 // 1 Kings 4:20–5:14 H 4:20-34 E // 2 Chron 9:25-28 // 1 Kings 10:26-29

2 Chronicles 1	*1 Kings 10*	*2 Chronicles 9*
14 Solomon gathered chariots and horsemen; and he had one thousand four hundred chariots and twelve thousand horsemen; and he put them in chariot cities and with the king in Jerusalem.	26 Also Solomon gathered chariots and horsemen; and he had one thousand four hundred chariots and twelve thousand horsemen; and he put them in chariot cities and with the king in Jerusalem.	25 Solomon had four thousand stalls of horses and chariots and twelve thousand horsemen and he put them in chariot cities and with the king in Jerusalem.
	1 Kings 4 20 Judah and Israel were as numerous as the sand by the sea: eating, drinking and enjoying themselves.	
	1 Kings 5 1/4:21 Solomon ruled over all the kingdoms from the River, the land of the Philistines and as far as the border of Egypt; they brought tribute and served Solomon all the days of his life.	26 He ruled over all the kings from the River to the land of the Philistines and as far as the border of Egypt.
15 The king put silver and gold in Jerusalem like stones; and he put cedars as numerous as the sycamores that were in the Shephelah.	*1 Kings 10* 27 And the king put silver in Jerusalem like stones; and he put cedars as numerous as the sycamores that were in the Shephelah.	27 And the king put silver in Jerusalem like stones; and he put cedars as numerous as the sycamores that were in the Shephelah.

16 The export of horses which was for Solomon was from Egypt and Qewe. The merchants of the king would take them from Qewe at a price.

17 They imported and then exported a chariot from Egypt for six hundred pieces of silver and a horse for one hundred and fifty. Thus they used to export by their hand to all the kings of the Hittites and the kings of Aram.

28 The export of horses which was for Solomon was from Egypt and Qewe. The merchants of the king would take them from Qewe at a price.

29 A chariot which was exported from Egypt went for six hundred pieces of silver and a horse for one hundred and fifty. Thus they used to export by their hand to all the kings of the Hittites and the kings of Aram.

1 Kings 5
2/4:22 The provisions for Solomon for one day were thirty measures of flour and sixty measures of meal,

3/4:23 ten fat oxen and twenty head of pastured cattle and a hundred sheep, besides stags, gazelles, roebucks and fattened fowl.

4/4:24 For he held sway over all West-of-the-River from Tipsah and as far as Gaza, over all the kings of West-of-the-River and he had peace on all sides around him.

5/4:25 So Judah and Israel lived in safety, each person under his vine and under his fig-tree, from Dan as far as Beer-sheba all the days of Solomon.

6/4:26 Now Solomon had forty-thousand stalls of horses for his chariotry and twelve thousand horsemen.

7/4:27 For those deputies provisioned King Solomon and all who came to King Solomon's table, each one in his month; they did not omit anything.

8/4:28 Also they brought barley and straw for the horses and the chariot horses to the place where it should be, each according to his charge.

28 They used to export horses for Solomon from Egypt, and also from all the countries.

9/4:29 God gave wisdom to Solomon and very great discernment and breadth of heart like the sand by the sea shore,

10/4:30 so that the wisdom of Solomon was greater than the wisdom of all the sons of the east, and than all the wisdom of Egypt.

11/4:31 For he was wiser than all humankind, [wiser] than Ethan the Ezrahite, and Heman, Calcol, and Darda, sons of Mahol; and his name was in all the nations round about.

12/4:32 He spoke three thousand proverbs; and his songs were one thousand and five.

13/4:33 Further, he spoke about trees, from the cedar that is in Lebanon to the hyssop that comes out of the wall; and he spoke about beasts and birds, about crawling things and fish.

14/4:34 Thus they came from all peoples to hear the wisdom of Solomon, from all the kings of the earth who had heard of his wisdom.

558 Solomon's Treaty with King Hiram
2 Chron 1:18-2:17 H [2:1-18 E] // 1 Kings 5:15-32 H [5:1-18 E]; 7:13-14; 8:27

2 Chronicles 1

18/2:1 Now Solomon said [that he intended] to build a house for the name of YHWH and a house for his royal power.

2 Chronicles 2

1/2:2 So Solomon mustered seventy thousand laborers and eighty thousand quarrymen; and overseeing them, three thousand six hundred.

2/2:3 Then Solomon sent to Huram king of Tyre this message,

1 Kings 5

15/5:1 Now Hiram king of Tyre sent his servants to Solomon, for he had heard that they had anointed him as king in place of his father; because Hiram had been a friend to David all his days.

16/5:2 Then Solomon sent to Hiram this message,

"Just as you dealt with David my father and sent him cedar-wood to build for himself a house to dwell in:

17/5:3 "You knew David my father that he was not able to build a house for the name of YHWH his God because of the battles with which they [his enemies] surrounded him, until YHWH put them under the soles of his feet.

18/5:4 But now YHWH my God has given me rest on every side, there is no adversary and no evil incident.

3/2:4 I am now about to build a house for the name of YHWH my God, to consecrate it to him for burning before him aromatic incense and for presenting continually the rows of bread and for burnt offerings morning and evening, on the sabbaths and the new moons and the appointed festivals of YHWH our God—this on behalf of Israel forever.

19/5:5 See, I mean to build a house for the name of YHWH my God, just as YHWH said to David my father, 'Your son, whom I shall put in your place upon your throne, he shall build the house for my name.'

4/2:5 The house that I am about to build will be great, for our God is greater than all the gods.

5/2:6 But who is able to build a house for him, for heaven and the highest heavens cannot contain him? And who am I that I should build a house for him except to burn incense before him?

1 Kings 8
[27 "But will God really dwell on the earth? Behold heaven and the highest heavens cannot contain you! How much less this house that I have built!"]

6/2:7 So now send me a man skilled to work in gold and silver, in bronze and iron, and in purple and crimson and violet [yarn], and who knows how to carve engravings; to be with the skilled workers who are with me in Judah and Jerusalem, whom my father David set up.

7/2:8 Also send me trees of cedar, cypress and algum from Lebanon, for I know that your servants know how to cut the trees of Lebanon. And my servants will certainly be with your servants

1 Kings 5
20/5:6 Now, therefore, command that they cut for me cedars from Lebanon: and my servants will be with your servants, and I will give you wages for your servants as you shall determine; for you certainly know that there is no one among us who knows how to cut trees like the Sidonians."

8/2:9 to provide for me trees in abundance; for the house that I am building [will be] great and wonderful.

[24/5:10 So Hirom gave to Solomon cedar trees and cypress trees, all his requirements.

25/5:11 Then Solomon gave to Hiram twenty thousand kor of wheat as food for his house(hold), and twenty thousand kor of refined oil; Solomon used to give this to Hiram year by year.]

9/2:10 As for your servants, for the woodsmen, those who cut the trees, I will give twenty thousand kors of crushed wheat and twenty thousand kors of barley, with twenty thousand baths of wine and twenty thousand baths of oil."

10/2:11 Then Huram king of Tyre said in a letter which he sent to Solomon, "Because of the love of YHWH for his people, he has made you king over them."

11/2:12 Huram also said, "Blessed is YHWH the god of Israel who made the heavens and the earth, who has given to David the king a wise son, knowing prudence and discernment, who will build a house for YHWH and a house for his royal power.

12/2:13 Now I am sending [you] a skilled and discerning man, one Huram-abi,

13/2:14 the son of a woman from the daughters of Dan, and his father a Tyrian man: one who knows how to work in gold and in silver, in bronze, in iron, in stone and in wood, in purple, in violet and in fine linen and crimson fabric, to engrave all kinds of engraving and to complete any design given to him, with your skilled craftsmen and the craftsmen of my lord David your father.

14/2:15 Now, as for the wheat and the barley, the oil and the wine of which my lord spoke, let him send them to his servants.

15/2:16 Now we will cut trees from Lebanon according to all your need, and bring them to you as rafts by sea to Joppa, and you will take them to Jerusalem."

16/2:17 Then Solomon took a count of all the [male] resident aliens who were in the land of Israel following the count that David his father had made; and they were found to be one hundred and fifty-three thousand six hundred.

21/5:7 Now when Hiram heard the words of Solomon, he rejoiced greatly and he said, "Blessed is YHWH today who has given to David a wise son over this great people.

1 Kings 7
13 Then King Solomon sent and took Hiram from Tyre.

14 He was the son of a widowed woman from the tribe of Naphtali, and his father a Tyrian man, an engraver in bronze, and he was filled with skill and understanding and know-how in making every [kind of] bronze work. He came to Solomon and did all his work.

1 Kings 5
22/5:8 Then Hiram sent to Solomon this message, "I have heard what you sent to me. I will fulfill all your requirements concerning cedar trees and cypress trees.

23/5:9 My servants shall bring them down from Lebanon to the sea, and I will make them into rafts [to go] upon the sea to the place that you send to me. I will break them up there and you will take them away. Then you will fulfill my requirement by giving food to my house[hold]."

[24/5:10 and 25/5:11 appear above, following 20/5:6.]

26/5:12 For YHWH had given Solomon wisdom as he had said to him: and there was peace between Hiram and Solomon, and the two of them made a covenant.

27/5:13 King Solomon raised a corvée from all Israel, and the corvée was thirty thousand men.

28/5:14 He sent them to Lebanon, ten thousand in a month in relays; they would be a month in Lebanon and two months at their home. Adoniram was over the corvée.

17/2:18 He made seventy thousand of them laborers and eighty thousand quarrymen; and three thousand six hundred overseers to make the people work.

29/5:15 Solomon also had seventy thousand [forced] laborers and eighty thousand quarrymen;

30/5:16 besides Solomon's three thousand three hundred chief deputies who were over the work, who superintended the people doing the work.

31/5:17 Then the king gave orders and they quarried out huge stones, costly stones, to lay the foundations of the house with dressed stones.

32/5:18 Thus the builders of Solomon and the builders of Hiram and the Giblites cut the stones and prepared the wood and the stones to build the house.

559 Solomon Builds a House for YHWH
2 Chron 3:1-14 // 1 Kings 6:1-38

2 Chronicles 3

1 Then Solomon began to build the house of YHWH in Jerusalem on the mountain of Moriah, where he [YHWH] had appeared to David his father, at the place that David had established on the threshing-floor of Ornan the Jebusite.

2 He began to build on the second [day] in the fourth year of his reign.

3 Now these are Solomon's foundation [measurements] for building the house of God: the length [in] cubits of the old measure, was sixty cubits, and the width twenty cubits.

4 The porch that was in the front: its length in front of the width of the house was twenty cubits, and its height one hundred and twenty; he overlaid it on the inside with pure gold.

1 Kings 6

1 In the four hundred and eightieth year after the coming out of the Israelites from the land of Egypt, in the fourth year, in the month Ziv, that is the second month, of the reign of Solomon over Israel, he began building the house of YHWH.

2 The house that King Solomon built for YHWH: sixty cubits [was] its length, and twenty its width, and thirty cubits its height.

3 The porch in front of the sanctuary of the house: twenty cubits its length in front of the width of the house, and ten cubits its width in front of the house.

4 For the house he made framed, recessed windows.

5 He also built against the wall of the house an aisle all around the walls of the house, the sanctuary and the shrine; and he made tiers all around.

6 The lowest aisle: five cubits [was] its width, and the middle six cubits its width, and the third, seven cubits its width; for he put niches for the house around the outside, so as not to inset the [supporting beams] into the walls of the house.

7 The house, as it was being built, was built with stone finished at the quarry; and neither hammers, nor pickaxe, nor any iron tool was heard in the house when it was being built.

8 The entrance to the middle tier was on the right [south] side of the house, and by winding stairs they would go up to the middle tier, and from the middle to the third.

9 Thus he built the house and finished it: and he roofed the house [with] beams and coffers of cedar wood.

10 He built the aisle against the whole house, five cubits its height, and it held on to the house by beams of cedar.

11 Now the word of YHWH came to Solomon,

12 "[As for] this house that you are building: if you walk in my statutes, and carry out my judgments, and keep my commandments by walking in them, then I will establish my word with you that I spoke to David your father.

13 For I will dwell in the midst of the Israelites, and I will not forsake my people Israel."

14 Thus Solomon built the house and he finished it.

15 He built the walls of the house inside with plank[s] of cedar[s] from the floor of the house right to the rafters; he overlaid them with wood on the inside, and he covered the floor with planks of cypress.

16 Then he built twenty cubits in the innermost part of the house with planks of cedar from the floor right to the rafters, as a shrine for the holy of holies.

17 Now the house was forty cubits long, that is, the sanctuary in front of me.

18 The cedar of the interior of the house was carved with gourds and garlands of flowers; and all was cedar, no stone was seen.

5 He lined the great house with cypress wood and he covered it with good gold, and he mounted upon it palms and chains.

6 He overlaid the house with costly stone for adornment; the gold was gold of Parvaim.

7 So he lined the house: the beams, the thresholds, the
rafters and the doors with gold and he carved cherubim
on the walls.

8 Then he made the most holy house: its length, based
upon the width of the house, was twenty cubits, and its
width was twenty cubits. He lined it with good gold,
six hundred talents.

9 Now the weight of the nails was fifty shekels of gold,
and he lined the roof-chambers with gold.

10 He made in the most holy place two cherubim,
sculpted work, and he overlaid them with gold.

11 Now the wings of the cherubim, [in] their length
were twenty cubits: the wing of the one five cubits,
extended to the wall of the house, and the other wing,
five cubits, reached to the wing of the other cherub,

12 and the wing of this one cherub, five cubits, reached
to the wall of the house, and the other wing, five cubits,
joined to the wing of the other cherub.

13 The wings of these cherubim extended twenty
cubits: and they were standing upon their feet and their
faces [were] towards the house.

19 He set up the inner shrine in the house, in its innermost part, to put there the ark of the covenant of
YHWH.

20 The inner shrine was twenty cubits in length, and
twenty cubits in width and twenty cubits its height; and
he overlaid it with rare gold; also he overlaid the altar
with cedar.

21 Solomon also overlaid the house inside with rare
gold, and he drew across chains of gold in front of the
shrine and overlaid it with gold.

22 He overlaid the entire house with gold so that all
the house was completed: every altar that belonged to
the shrine, he overlaid with gold.

23 He made in the shrine two cherubim of olive wood:
ten cubits was [their] height.

24 Five cubits was the one wing of the cherub, and five
cubits the second wing of the cherub—ten cubits from
the tip of its [one] wing to the tip of its [other] wing.

25 The second cherub also measured ten cubits; the
two cherubim had one measure and one shape.

26 The height of the one cherub was ten cubits, and so
was the second cherub.

27 Then he placed them in the innermost part of the
house; and the wings of the cherubim were extended so
that the one wing [of the first] touched the wall, and the
wing of the second touched the second wall, and their
wings towards the middle of the house were touching
wing[tip] to wing[tip].

28 And he overlaid the cherubim with gold.

29 Then round about all the walls of the house he
carved figures of cherubim and palm-trees and garlands
of flowers, in the inner and outer chambers.

30 The floor of the house he overlaid with gold, in the
inner and outer chambers.

31 At the entrance to the shrine he made a door of olive wood; the lintel and the door posts [were] a pentagon.

32 The two doors were of olive wood, and he carved upon them figures of cherubim and palm-trees and garlands of flowers, and he overlaid them with gold; he plated the cherubim and the palm-trees with gold.

14 Then Solomon made the curtain of violet and crimson fabric and fine linen, and mounted [embroidered] cherubim on it.

33 He also made for the entrance to the sanctuary door posts of olive wood in a rectangular frame,

34 and two doors of cypress wood; two folding panels [on] the one door, and two folding panels [on] the second door.

35 then he carved cherubim and palm-trees and garlands of flowers, and he overlaid [them] with gold plated over the carving.

36 He built the inner court with three courses of hewn stone and one course of cedar beams.

37 In the fourth year the foundation of the house of YHWH was laid, in the month of Ziv;

38 and in the eleventh year, in the month of Bul, that is the eighth month, he completed the house in all its parts and to all its specifications. Now he built it over seven years.

560 Solomon's Other Buildings
1 Kings 7:1-12

1 Kings 7

1 Solomon was building his own house for thirteen years, and he completed all his house.

2 He built the House of the Forest of Lebanon: one hundred cubits was its length, fifty cubits its width, thirty cubits its height; upon four rows of cedar pillars and with cedar beams atop the pillars.

3 It was covered with cedar from above the crossbars that were on top of the pillars, [of which there were] forty-five, fifteen per row.

4 [There were] three rows of window-frames facing each other [repeated] three times.

5 All the doors and doorposts had four-sided door-frames, opposite, facing each [repeated] three times.

6 He made the Porch of Pillars: fifty cubits its length and thirty its width. [There was] a porch in front of them, with pillars and a canopy in front of them.

7 Then he made the Portico of the Throne where he used to pass judgment— the Portico of Judgment covered with cedar from floor to floor.

8 His [own] house where he dwelt, [in] a court behind the House of the Porch, was like this in construction. He also made a house for the daughter of Pharaoh whom Solomon had taken, similar to this porch.

9 All these [were] of rare stones, hewn according to measurement, sawn with the saw, inside and outside, from the foundation to the coping and from the outside to the great court.

10 The foundation was of rare stones, huge stones, stones of ten cubits and stones of eight cubits.

11 There were rare stones above, hewn according to measurement, and cedar [wood].

12 The great court had three courses of hewn stone [all] around, and one row of cedar beams, like the inner court of the house of YHWH and the porch of the house.

561 Hiram's Work in the Temple
2 Chron 3:15–5:1 // 1 Kings 7:15-51 // 2 Kings 25:17; Jer 52:21-23

2 Chronicles 3	*1 Kings 7*	*Jeremiah 52*
15 In front of the house he made two pillars thirty-five cubits long;	15 He formed the two pillars of bronze; eighteen cubits was the height of the one pillar, and a twelve cubit cord would go around the second pillar.	21 The pillars were eighteen cubits high; and a twelve cubit cord would go around it; and its thickness was four fingers, hollowed out.
and the plated capital that was on top of it was five cubits.	16 Then he made two capitals to put on the tops of the pillars, cast of bronze; and the height of one capital was five cubits, and five cubits the height of the second capital.	22 Upon it was a capital of bronze, and the height of the one capital was five cubits; the networking and pomegranates on the capital all around it were all of bronze; and for the second pillar it was like this, with pomegranates.

16 He made chains in the inner sanctuary and he put them on top of the pillars;

17 Nettings were made of networking, festoons made of chains, for the capitals that were on top of the pillars, seven for the one capital, and seven for the second capital.

2 Kings 25

17 Eighteen cubits was the height of one pillar, and it had a bronze capital on it, and the height of the capital was three cubits, and the networking and pomegranates on the capital all around it were all of bronze; and for the second pillar it was like this, with the networking.

18 He made the pillars and two rows around on the one networking, to cover the capitals that were on top of the pomegranates; he did the same to the second capital.

19 The capitals that were on the top of the pillars in the hall had lily work, four cubits high;

20 and the capitals were upon two of the pillars and also above the bulge which was beside the networking; and there were two hundred pomegranates in rows around on top of the second capital.

and he made one hundred pomegranates and put them on the chains.

17 He set up the pillars in front of the temple; one on the right and one on the left; he called the name of the [one on the] right Jachin and the name of the [one on the] left Boaz.

21 He set up the pillars at the portico of the temple; and he set up the right pillar and called its name Jachin; and he set up the left pillar and called its name Boaz.

22 And on top of the pillars [there was] lily work. Then the work of the pillars was finished.

2 Chronicles 4

1 He made a bronze altar: twenty cubits long and twenty cubits wide and twenty cubits high.

1 Kings 7

2 Then he made the Sea of cast metal, ten cubits from rim to rim, round in circuit, and five cubits was its height, and a thirty cubit measuring line surrounded it.

23 Then he made the Sea of cast metal, ten cubits from rim to rim, round in circuit, and five cubits was its height, and a thirty cubit measuring line surrounded it.

3 There was the likeness of oxen under it, surrounding it all around, ten to a cubit, encircling the Sea all around; there were two rows of oxen, cast when it was cast.

24 There were gourds under its rim, surrounding it around, ten to a cubit, encircling the Sea all around; there were two rows of gourds, cast when it was cast.

4 It stood upon twelve oxen, three facing north, three facing the Sea [west], three facing the Negev [south], three facing east; the Sea was upon them, and all their hindparts [faced] inwards.

25 It stood upon twelve oxen, three facing north, three facing the Sea [west], three facing the Negev [south], three facing east; the Sea was upon them, and all their hindparts faced inwards.

5 Its thickness was a hand span; and its rim was like the construction of a cup's rim, like a flower of a lily; it held three thousand baths.

26 Its thickness was a hand span; and its rim was like the construction of a cup's rim, like a flower of a lily; it held two thousand baths.

27 Then he made ten bronze watercarts; each watercart was four cubits long and four cubits wide and three cubits high.

28 This was the construction of the watercarts: they had framing pieces, and there were framing pieces between the cross-rungs;

29 and on the framing pieces that were between the cross-rungs there were lions, oxen and cherubim; and on the cross-rungs a pedestal; above and below the lions and the oxen there were wreaths, a pendant work.

30 Each watercart had four bronze wheels and four bronze axletrees; its four feet had struts—they were below the laver; the struts were cast, with wreaths at the side of each one.

31 Its opening was within the capital and it went up a cubit; its opening was circular like construction of a pedestal; it was a cubit and a half in measure; also at its opening were carvings and their framing-pieces, squared but not circular.

32 There were four wheels under the framing-pieces, and the sockets of the wheels [were fixed] in the watercart; and the height of one wheel was a cubit and a half in measure.

33 The construction of the wheels was like the construction of a chariot wheel, their sockets, their rims, their spokes and their hubs all of cast [metal].

34 Four shoulderpieces ran to the four corners of each watercart; the shoulderpieces were part of the watercart.

35 On top of the watercart was a round band half a cubit high, and on top of the watercart its sockets and its framing-pieces were part of it.

36 On the panels of its sockets and on its framing-pieces he engraved cherubim and lions and palm-figures according to the clear space on each [plate] and with wreaths around it.

37 In this way he made the ten watercarts, cast [alike], with one measure, one form for all of them.

6 Then he made ten lavers, and he put five on the south (right) and five on the north (left), for washing in them the service of the burnt offering; and the Sea for the priests to rinse in it.

7 He made ten gold lampstands, according to their specifications; then he put them in the temple, five on the right (south) and five on the left (north).

8 He made ten tables and placed them in the temple, five on the right (south) and five on the left (north).

9 Then he made the courtyard of the priests and the great court, and doors for the court, and he overlaid their doors with bronze.

10 He put the Sea at the right corner, eastward toward the south.

11 Huram also made the pots, the shovels, and the sprinkling vessels; then Hiram finished doing the work that he had been doing for King Solomon on the house of God:

12 the two pillars, and the bowls of the capitals that were on top of the two pillars; two networks to cover the two bowls of the capitals that were on top of the pillars;

13 the four hundred pomegranates for the two networks, two rows of pomegranates for each network, to cover the two bowls of the capitals that were on the front of the pillars;

14 and he made the watercarts and he made the lavers on the watercarts;

15 the one Sea and the twelve oxen under it;

16 and the pots and the shovels and the sprinkling vessels. All their vessels Huram-abi made for King Solomon for the house of YHWH were of scoured bronze.

17 In the plain of the Jordan the king cast them in the earthen foundries between Succoth and Zeredah.

18 Solomon made all these vessels in great quantity, since the weight of the bronze was not ascertained.

38 Then he made ten bronze lavers; each laver could contain forty baths; each laver measured four cubits, and there was one laver on each of the ten watercarts.

39 And he put five watercarts on the south corner of the house, and five on the north corner of the house; he put the Sea at the south corner of the house, eastward toward the south.

40 Hirom also made the lavers, the shovels, and the sprinkling vessels; then Hiram finished doing all the work that he had been doing for King Solomon on the house of YHWH:

41 the two pillars, and the bowls of the capitals that were on top of the two pillars; two networks to cover the two bowls of the capitals that were on top of the pillars;

42 the four hundred pomegranates for the two networks, two rows of pomegranates for each network, to cover the two bowls of the capitals that were on the front of the pillars;

43 the ten watercarts and ten lavers on the watercarts;

44 the one Sea and the twelve oxen under the Sea;

45 and the pots and the shovels and the sprinkling vessels. All those vessels that Hiram made for King Solomon for the house of YHWH were of polished bronze.

46 In the plain of the Jordan the king cast them in the earthen foundry between Succoth and Zarethan.

47 Solomon left all the vessels [unweighed] because of their very great quantity. The weight of the bronze was not ascertained.

19 So Solomon made all the vessels that were in the house of God: the golden altar and the tables and upon them the Bread of Presence;

20 the lampstands with their lamps to burn in front of the shrine, of refined gold;

21 and the flowers, the lamps and the tongs were of gold, that is, of perfect gold.

22 the snuffers, the bowls, the incense dishes, and the firepans were of refined gold; as for the entrance of the house, the innermost doors to the Holy of Holies, and the doors of the house, the temple, were of gold.

5:1 When Solomon had completed all the work which he did in the house of YHWH, Solomon brought the consecrated articles of David his father, the silver and the gold and all the vessels: and he put them in the treasury rooms of the house of God.

48 So Solomon made all the vessels that were in the house of YHWH: the golden altar and the table that had the Bread of Presence on it, of gold;

49 the lampstands, five on the right and five on the left, in front of the shrine, of refined gold;

and the flowers, the lamps and the tongs were of gold.

50 And the basins, the snuffers, the bowls, the incense dishes, and the firepans were of refined gold; and the hinge sockets for the doors to the inner [part] of the house, the Holy of Holies, [and] for the doors to the house, the temple, were of gold.

51 When King Solomon had completed all the work which he did in the house of YHWH, Solomon brought the consecrated articles of David his father, the silver and the gold and the vessels: and he put them in the treasury rooms of the house of YHWH.

562 Solomon Brings the Ark into the Temple
2 Chron 5:2-14 // 1 Kings 8:1-11

2 Chronicles 5

2 Then Solomon assembled the elders of Israel, all the heads of the tribes, the chiefs of the ancestors of the Israelites to Jerusalem, to bring up the ark of the covenant of YHWH from the city of David, that is, Zion.

3 So every person of Israel was assembled to the king on the festival which is in the seventh month.

4 Then all the elders of Israel came and the Levites lifted up the ark,

5 and they brought up the ark and the tent of meeting, and all the holy vessels which [were] in the tent; and the priests and the Levites brought them up.

6 King Solomon and all the congregation of Israel who had been gathered to him were before the ark, sacrificing sheep and oxen which could not be numbered or counted because of the quantity.

1 Kings 8

1 Then Solomon called together the elders of Israel, all the heads of the tribes, the chiefs of the ancestors of the children of Israel, to King Solomon in Jerusalem, to bring up the ark of the covenant of YHWH from the city of David, that is, Zion.

2 So every person of Israel was assembled to King Solomon in the month of Ethanim, on the festival which is in the seventh month.

3 Then all the elders of Israel came and the priests lifted up the ark,

4 and they brought up the ark of YHWH and the tent of meeting and all the holy vessels which [were] in the tent; and the priests and the Levites brought them up,

5 King Solomon and all the congregation of Israel who had been gathered to him were with him before the ark, sacrificing sheep and oxen which could not be numbered or counted because of the quantity.

7 Then the priests brought the ark [of the covenant of YHWH] to its place, to the shrine of the house, to the Holy of Holies, to [the place] under the wings of the cherubim.

8 And the cherubim were spreading out their wings over the place of the ark so that the cherubim covered the ark and its poles from above.

9 The poles had been lengthened so that the tips of the poles were seen from the ark in front of the shrine but they were not seen outside; and it has been there to this very day.

10 There was nothing in the ark except for the two tablets which Moses placed at Horeb when YHWH made a covenant with the Israelites, when they went out from Egypt.

11 When the priests came out of the holy place, for all the priests who were found [there] had consecrated themselves; there was no keeping to divisions

12 and the Levites who were singers, for all of them, Asaph, Heman, Jeduthun and their sons and their brothers, were clothed in fine linen and with cymbals and with harps and with lyres were standing east of the altar; and with them were the priests, one hundred and twenty of them sounding on the clarions.

13 It happened, when the clarion-players and the singers were as one, they made themselves heard [with] one voice to give praise and to give thanks to YHWH; and when they raised a sound with clarions and with cymbals and with other instruments of music in praise to YHWH: "For [he is] good, for his graciousness [is] forever"; the house was filled with a cloud, the house of YHWH;

14 and the priests were not able to stand to minister in front of the cloud, for the glory of YHWH filled the house of God.

6 Then the priests brought the ark of the covenant of YHWH to its place, to the shrine of the house, to the Holy of Holies, to [the place] under the wings of the cherubim.

7 For the cherubim were spreading out their wings toward the place of the ark so that the cherubim overshadowed the ark and its poles from above.

8 The poles had been lengthened so that the tips of the poles were seen from the holy place in front of the shrine but they were not seen outside; and they have been there to this very day.

9 There was nothing in the ark except for the two tablets of stone which Moses put to rest there at Horeb when YHWH made a covenant with the Israelites, when they went out from the land of Egypt.

10 When the priests came out of the holy place,

the cloud filled the house of YHWH,

11 and the priests were not able to stand to minister in front of the cloud, for the glory of YHWH filled the house of YHWH.

563 Dedication of the Temple
2 Chron 6:1–7:10 // 1 Kings 8:12-66 // 2 Chron 5:13-14 // Ps 132:1, 8-10 // Ps 136:1

2 Chronicles 6

1 Then Solomon said, "YHWH has said [he wishes] to dwell in thick darkness.

2 And I have built a lofty house for you, a place for you to live in forever."

3 Then the king turned around and blessed all the assembly of Israel, and all the whole assembly of Israel was standing.

4 He said, "Blessed be YHWH the God of Israel who spoke by his mouth with David my father, and with his hands has fulfilled it, saying,

5 'Since the day when I brought out my people from the land of Egypt, I did not choose a city from all the tribes of Israel to build a house that my name might be there, and I did not choose a man to be prince over my people Israel;

6 but I chose Jerusalem that my name might be there, and I did choose David to be over my people Israel.'"

7 It was in the heart of David my father to build a house for the name of YHWH the God of Israel,

8 but YHWH said to David my father, "As much as it was in your heart to build a house for my name, you did well that it was in your heart;

9 only, you shall not build the house, but your son who shall go forth from your loins, he shall build the house for my name.

10 Then YHWH upheld his word which he had spoken, for I have arisen in place of David my father and have been enthroned on the throne of Israel just as YHWH spoke; and I built the house for the name of YHWH the God of Israel.

11 And I have set there the ark in which is the covenant of YHWH which he made with the children of Israel.

12 Then he stood before the altar of YHWH in the sight of all the assembly of Israel and spread out the palms of his hands.

1 Kings 8

12 Then Solomon said, "YHWH has said [he wishes] to dwell in thick darkness.

13 I have surely built a lofty house for you, a place for you to live in forever."

14 Then the king turned around and blessed all the assembly of Israel, and all the whole assembly of Israel was standing.

15 He said, "Blessed be YHWH the God of Israel who spoke by his mouth with David my father, and with his hand has fulfilled it, saying,

16 'Since the day when I brought out my people Israel from Egypt, I did not choose a city from all the tribes of Israel to build a house that my name might be there,

but I did choose David to be over my people Israel.'"

17 It was in the heart of David my father to build a house for the name of YHWH the God of Israel,

18 but YHWH said to David my father, "As much as it was in your heart to build a house for my name, you did well that it was in your heart;

19 only, you shall not build the house, but your son who shall go forth from your loins, he shall build the house for my name.

20 Then YHWH upheld his word which he had spoken, for I have arisen in place of David my father and have been enthroned on the throne of Israel just as YHWH spoke; and I built the house for the name of YHWH the God of Israel.

21 And I have set there a place for the ark in which is the covenant of YHWH which he made with our ancestors when he was leading them out of the land of Egypt.

22 Then Solomon stood before the altar of YHWH in the sight of all the assembly of Israel and spread out the palms of his hands to heaven.

13 For Solomon had made a platform of bronze (and he put it in the midst of the assembly) five cubits in its length and five cubits in its breadth and three cubits in its height, and he stood on it and knelt on his knees opposite the entire assembly of Israel, and he spread out the palms of his hands to the heavens.

14 Then he said, "O YHWH, God of Israel, there is no god like you in the heavens or on the earth, keeping covenant loyalty for your servants who are walking before you with all their heart;

23 Then he said, "O YHWH, God of Israel, there is no god like you in heaven above or on earth below, keeping covenant loyalty for your servants who are walking before you with all their heart;

15 who has kept for your servant David my father that which you spoke to him; you spoke it with your mouth and with your hand you fulfilled it this [very] day.

24 who have kept for your servant David my father that which you spoke to him; you spoke with your mouth and with your hand you fulfilled this [very] day.

16 So now, YHWH, God of Israel, keep for your servant David my father that which you spoke to him, 'There shall not be cut off from before me a man of your line who shall sit on the throne of Israel, but only let your posterity guard their way, to walk in my Torah just as you have walked before me.'

25 So now, YHWH, God of Israel, keep for your servant David my father that which you spoke to him, 'There shall not be cut off from before me a man of your line who shall sit on the throne of Israel, but only let your posterity guard their way, to walk before me just as you have walked before me.'

17 Therefore, O God of Israel, let your word be confirmed which you spoke to your servant David.

26 Therefore, O God of Israel, let your word be confirmed which you spoke to your servant David, my father.

18 But will God really dwell with humankind on the earth? Behold, the highest heavens cannot contain you; how much less this house that I have built!

27 But will God really dwell on the earth? Behold, the highest heavens cannot contain you; how much less this house that I have built!

19 Turn toward the prayer of your servant and to his supplication, YHWH my God, to heed the cry and the prayer which your servant is praying before you.

28 Turn toward the prayer of your servant and to his supplication, YHWH my God, to heed the cry and the prayer which your servant is praying before you today.

20 May your eyes be open toward this house day and night, to the place about which you said you would put your name there, to heed the prayer which your servant prays toward this place.

29 May your eyes be open toward this house night and day, to the place about which you said, "My name shall be there"; heed the prayer which your servant prays toward this place.

21 You shall give heed to the supplications of your servant and of your people Israel which they pray continually toward this place; and when you give heed to the place of your dwelling from the heavens, then hear and pardon.

30 You shall give heed to the supplication of your servant and of your people Israel which they pray toward this place; and when you give heed to the place of your dwelling, the heavens, then hear and pardon.

22 If anyone sins against his neighbor and obliges him to take on himself an oath and comes and takes an oath before your altar in this house,

31 If anyone sins against his neighbor and obliges him to take on himself an oath and comes [and] takes an oath before your altar in this house,

23 then give heed from the heavens, and act and judge your servants, requiting the evil one by bringing his conduct upon his head, and vindicating the righteous by giving to him according to his righteousness.

24 And if your people Israel is struck down before an enemy, because they sinned against you, if they return and praise your name and pray and make supplication before you in this house,

25 then give heed from the heavens and pardon the sinning of your people Israel and return them to the land which you gave to their ancestors.

26 When the heavens are closed up and there is no rain because they have sinned against you, if they pray to this place and praise your name and turn back from their sins because you afflict them,

27 then give heed from the heavens and pardon the sinning of your servants and your people Israel, when you teach them toward the good way in which they should walk, then do you give rain upon your land which you have given to your people as an inheritance.

28 Famine, when it occurs in the land, pestilence when it occurs, scorching and mildew, locust and caterpillar, if it occurs; when his enemies press hard on him in the land of their city-gates; every plague, every illness,

29 every prayer, every supplication which belongs to any individual human and to all your people Israel, who knows, each one, the vexation of his heart, and stretches out his hands toward this house,

30 then give heed from the heavens, the place of your dwelling, and pardon and act and give to the man according to his ways, since you know his heart; because you know, you alone, the heart of every human being,

31 so that they might fear you by walking in your paths all the days that they live on the face of the land that you gave to our ancestors.

32 Also concerning the foreigner, who is not from among your people Israel, and he comes from a land far away for the sake of your great name

and your strong hand and your outstretched arm, then if they come and pray toward this house,

32 then give heed in heaven, and act and judge your servants, condemning the wicked as guilty by bringing his conduct upon his head, and vindicating the righteous by giving to him according to his righteousness.

33 Whenever your people Israel is struck down before an enemy, when they sin against you, if they return to you and praise your name and pray and make supplication to you in this house,

34 then give heed in heaven and pardon the sinning of your people Israel and return them to the land which you gave to their ancestors.

35 When heaven is closed up and there is no rain because they have sinned against you, if they pray to this place and praise your name and turn back from their sins because you afflict them,

36 then give heed [in] heaven and pardon the sinning of your servants and your people Israel, when you teach them the good way in which they should walk, then do you give rain upon your land which you have given to your people as an inheritance.

37 Famine, when it occurs in the land, pestilence when it occurs, scorching, mildew, locust or caterpillar, if it occurs; when his enemy presses hard on him in the land of their city-gates; every plague, every illness,

38 every prayer, every supplication which belongs to every individual human among your people Israel, who knows, each one, the affliction in his heart, and stretches out his hands toward this house,

39 then give heed [in] heaven, the place of your dwelling, and pardon and act and give to each according to his ways, since you know his heart; because you alone know the heart of every human being,

40 so that they might fear you all the days that they live on the face of the land that you gave to our ancestors.

41 Also concerning the foreigner, who is not from among your people Israel, and he comes from a land far away for the sake of your name

42 for they shall hear of your great name and your strong hand and your outstretched arm, then if one comes and prays toward this house,

33 then heed from heaven the place of your dwelling and do according to all that the foreigner calls out to you, so that all the peoples of the earth might know your name, to fear you like your people Israel, and to know that your name is called [down] upon this house which I have built.

34 If your people goes out to battle against its enemies, in the way by which you send them, and they pray to you [on] the way to this city which you have chosen and the house which I have built for your name,

35 then heed from the heavens to their prayer and their supplication and act for their cause.

36 If they sin against you—for there is no human being who does not sin—and you are angry at them and hand them over before an enemy, and their captors take them captive to a land far or near,

37 if they bring back to their mind in the land where they were taken captive and turn and implore compassion from you in the land of their captivity, saying, "We have sinned; and we have acted wickedly, [and] we have become guilty,"

38 and they return to you with all their heart and all their soul in the land of their captivity where they led them away captive and pray in the direction of their land which you gave to their ancestors, the city which you chose and toward the house which I built for your name,

39 then heed from the heavens, the place of your dwelling, their prayer and their supplications, and act for their cause and have pardon on your people who have sinned against you.

43 then heed in heaven the place of your dwelling and do according to all that the foreigner calls out to you, so that all the peoples of the earth might know your name, to fear you like your people Israel, and to know that your name is called [down] upon this house which I have built.

44 If your people goes out to battle against its enemy, in the way by which you send them, and they pray to YHWH [on] the way to the city which you have chosen and the house which I have built for your name,

45 then heed in heaven to their prayer and their supplication and act for their cause.

46 If they sin against you—for there is no human being who does not sin—and you are angry at them and hand them over before an enemy, and their captors take them captive to the land of the enemy far or near,

47 if they bring back to their mind in the land where they were taken captive and turn and implore compassion from you in the land of their captors, saying, "We have sinned; we have acted wickedly, [and] we have become guilty,"

48 and they return to you with all their heart and all their soul in the land of their enemies who led them away captive and pray to you in the direction of their land which you gave to their ancestors, the city which you chose and the house which I built for your name,

49 then heed in heaven, the place of your dwelling, their prayer and their supplication, and act for their cause,

50 and have pardon on your people who have sinned against you and on all of their transgressions which they have transgressed against you, and grant them compassion before their captors that they might have compassion on them.

51 For they are your people and your inheritance, whom you brought out of Egypt from the midst of the furnace of iron.

2 Chronicles 6

40 Now, my God, let your eyes be open and your ears inclined to the prayer of this place.

1 Kings 8

52 Now let your eyes be open to the supplication of your servant and to the supplication of your people Israel, to heed them whenever they are calling to you.

53 For you have separated them to yourself as an inheritance from all the peoples of the earth, just as you spoke by the hand of Moses your servant when you were bringing out our ancestors from Egypt, Lord YHWH."

41 Now arise, YHWH God, to your [place of rest], you and the ark of your might.

Your priests, YHWH God, may they be clothed with salvation; and your loyal faithful ones, let them rejoice in good[ness].

42 YHWH God, do not turn away the face of your anointed ones:

remember the faithful deeds of David your servant.

2 Chronicles 7
1 When Solomon finished praying

54 It came about when Solomon finished praying to YHWH all this prayer and this supplication,

the fire came down from the heavens and it consumed the burnt offerings and the sacrifices, and the glory of YHWH filled the house.

2 The priests were not able to come into the house of YHWH, since the glory of YHWH filled the house of YHWH.

3 All the Israelites were looking on as the fire was coming down and the glory of YHWH [was] upon the house; and they bowed their faces to the ground upon the pavement and they worshiped and gave thanks to YHWH, "For [he is] good, for his graciousness [is] forever."

he arose from before the altar of YHWH, from kneeling down on his knees, and then his palms [were] spread out to heaven.

Psalm 132
8 Arise, O YHWH, to your resting place, you and the ark of your might.

9 Your priests, may they be clothed with righteousness; and your loyal faithful ones, let them sing out.

10 For the sake of David your servant, do not turn away the face of your anointed one.

[1 O YHWH remember in David's favor all the hardships he endured.]

2 Chronicles 5
13 It happened, when the clarion-players and the singers were as one, they made themselves heard [with] one voice, to give praise and to give thanks to YHWH; and when they raised a sound with clarions and with cymbals and other instruments of music in praise to YHWH, for [he is] good, for his graciousness [is] forever; the house was filled with a cloud, the house of YHWH,

14 and the priests were not able to stand to minister in front of the cloud, since the glory of YHWH filled the house of God.

Psalm 136
1 "Give thanks to YHWH, for he is good; for his graciousness [is] forever."

55 Then he stood and blessed all the assembly of Israel with a great voice,

56 "Blessed be YHWH who has given rest to his people Israel, in accordance with all that he spoke—not one word has fallen of all his good word which he spoke by the hand of Moses his servant!

57 May YHWH our God be with us just as he was with our ancestors—may he not abandon us or forsake us—

58 to incline our hearts to himself, to walk in all his ways and to keep his commandments and his statutes and his ordinances, which he commanded our ancestors.

59 May these words of mine with which I have made supplication before YHWH be near [to] YHWH our God day and night, to act for the cause of his servant and the cause of his people Israel, the matter of a day on its day,

60 so that all peoples of the earth may know that YHWH is God; there is no other!

61 Let your heart be at peace with YHWH our God, to walk in his statutes and to keep his commandments as on this day."

4 Then the king and all the people were sacrificing a sacrifice before YHWH.

62 Then the king, and all Israel with him, were sacrificing a sacrifice before YHWH.

5 King Solomon sacrificed the peace offering, twenty-two thousand oxen and one hundred and twenty thousand sheep. So the king and all the people dedicated the house of God.

63 Solomon sacrificed the sacrifices which he sacrificed to YHWH, twenty-two thousand oxen and one hundred and twenty thousand sheep. So all the children of Israel dedicated the house of YHWH.

6 The priests were standing according to their offices and the Levites with the instruments of music for

YHWH, that David the king had
made to give thanks to YHWH, for
his steadfast love lasts forever, when
David was praising with their hands.
The priests were sounding the clarions opposite them, and all Israel
were standing there.

7 Solomon consecrated the middle
of the court that was in front of the
house of YHWH, because there he
made the burnt offerings and the fat
parts of the peace offerings, for the
altar of bronze that Solomon made
was not able to hold the burnt offering and the cereal offering and the
fat portions.

8 Solomon made at that time the
festival of seven days, and all Israel
[was] with him, a very great assembly from Lebo Hamath to the Wadi
of Egypt.

9 On the eighth day they made an
assembly, since they consecrated the
altar for seven days and the festival
for seven days.

10 On the twenty-third day of the
seventh month he sent the people to
their tents rejoicing and with good
hearts because of the good that
YHWH had done for David and for
Solomon and for Israel his people.

64 On that same day the king consecrated the middle of the court that
was in front of the house of YHWH,
because there he made the burnt
offering and the cereal offering and
the fat parts of the peace offerings,
for the altar of bronze that is before
YHWH was too small to hold the
burnt offering and the cereal offering and the fat of the peace offerings.

65 Solomon made at that time the
festival and all Israel [was] with
him, a great congregation from
Lebo Hamath to the Wadi of Egypt,
before YHWH our God, seven days
and seven days, fourteen days.

66 On the eighth day he sent forth
the people, and they blessed the
king and they went to their tents
rejoicing and with good hearts because of the good that YHWH had
done for David his servant and
Israel his people.

564 YHWH Appears a Second Time to Solomon
2 Chron 7:11-22 // 1 Kings 9:1-9

2 Chronicles 7

11 Solomon finished the house of YHWH and the
house of the king, and every thing that came into the
heart of Solomon to do in the house of YHWH and in
his house, he brought to success.

1 Kings 9

1 It happened when Solomon had finished building the
house of YHWH and the house of the king and every
desire of Solomon that he wanted to make,

12 Then YHWH appeared to Solomon in the night and said to him, "I have heard your prayer and I have chosen this place for myself as a house for sacrifice.

13 See, if I shut up the heavens so that there will be no rain, and if I command the grasshopper to devour the land, and if I send a pestilence among my people,

14 and if they are humbled, my people upon whom my name is called, and if they pray and seek my face and turn from their evil ways, then I will hear from the heavens and I will pardon their sins and I will heal their land.

15 Now my eyes will be open and my ears attentive to the prayer of this place.

16 For I have chosen and dedicated this house that my name might be there forever; my eyes and my heart will be there for all days.

17 But you, if you will walk before me just as David your father walked, acting according to all that I have commanded you, and if you keep my statutes and my ordinances,

18 then I will raise up the throne of your kingship just as I covenanted with David your father, 'There shall not be cut off a man of your line ruling over Israel.'

19 If you turn aside from me and you forsake my statutes and my commandments that I have given before you, but you go and serve other gods and worship them,

20 then I will pluck them up from my land that I have given them; and this house which I have dedicated for my name, I will fling out of my sight; and I will give it as a proverb and a byword among all the peoples.

21 This house which has been so exalted, for everyone passing by it will be appalled. Then someone will say, 'Why did YHWH do thus to this land and to this house?'

22 Then they will say, 'Because they forsook YHWH the God of their ancestors who brought them out of the land of Egypt, and held fast to other gods, and worshiped them and served them; therefore he brought upon them all this evil.'"

2 that YHWH appeared to Solomon a second time, just as he had appeared to him at Gibeon.

3 Then YHWH said to him, "I have heard your prayer and your supplication, with which you have made supplication before me; I have dedicated this house which you have built, to put my name there forever; my eyes and my heart will be there for all days.

4 But you, if you will walk before me just as David your father walked, in wholeness of heart and uprightness, acting according to all that I have commanded you, and keep my statutes and my ordinances,

5 then I will raise up the throne of your kingdom over Israel forever, as I spoke to David your father, 'There shall not be cut off a man of your line from upon the throne of Israel.'

6 If you surely turn aside from me, you or your descendants, and do not keep my commandments and my statutes which I have put before you, but you go and serve other gods and worship them,

7 then I will cut off Israel from the face of the land that I have given them; and the house which I have dedicated for my name I will cast out of my sight; and Israel will become a proverb and a byword among all the peoples.

8 This house will be exalted; everyone passing by it will be appalled and will hiss; and they will say, 'Why did YHWH do thus to this land and to this house?'

9 Then they will say, 'Because they forsook YHWH their God who brought their ancestors out of the land of Egypt, and held fast to other gods, and worshiped them and served them; therefore YHWH brought upon them all this evil.'"

565 Solomon's Further Activities
2 Chron 8:1-18 // 1 Kings 9:10-28

2 Chronicles 8

1 At the end of twenty years, during which Solomon had built the house of YHWH and his [own] house;

2 the cities which Hiram had given to Solomon, Solomon built anew; and he settled the Israelites there.

3 Then Solomon went to Hamat-Zobah and captured it.

4 He built Tadmor in the wilderness and all the storage cities which he built in Hamath.

5 He also built Beth-horon the Upper and Beth-horon the Lower, fortified cities with walls and gates and bars

6 and Baalath

and all the storage-cities that belonged to Solomon, and all the cities for the chariots, and the cities for the cavalry, and all that Solomon wanted to build in Jerusalem, in Lebanon, and in all the land of his dominion.

7 All the people who remained of the Hittites and the Amorites and the Perizzites and the Hivites and the Jebusites, who were not from Israel,

1 Kings 9

10 At the end of twenty years, during which Solomon had built the two houses, the house of YHWH and the house of the king,

11 Hiram king of Tyre had supplied Solomon with cedar and cypress timber and gold, as much as he desired; then King Solomon gave to Hiram twenty cities in the land of Galilee.

12 So Hiram went out from Tyre to see the cities that Solomon had given him, but they were not satisfactory in his eyes.

13 Therefore, he said, "What are these cities that you have given me, my brother?" So they called them the "land of Cabul" to this day.

14 Hiram had sent to the king one hundred and twenty talents of gold.

15 Now this is the record of the corvée which King Solomon raised, to build the house of YHWH and his [own] house and the Millo and the wall of Jerusalem and Hazor and Megiddo and Gezer.

16 Pharaoh king of Egypt had gone up and captured Gezer and destroyed it with fire, and he slew the Canaanites who lived in the city, then he gave it as dowry for his daughter, a wife of Solomon;

17 so Solomon rebuilt Gezer and Beth-horon the Lower

18 and Baalath and Tamar in the wilderness, in the land,

19 and all the storage-cities that belonged to Solomon, and the cities for the chariots, and the cities for the cavalry, and all that Solomon wanted to build in Jerusalem, in Lebanon, and in all the land of his dominion.

20 All the people who remained of the Amorites, the Hittites, the Perizzites, the Hivites, and the Jebusites, who were not from the children of Israel,

8 from their descendants who remained after them in the land, whom the Israelites did not finish off, Solomon raised them up as forced labor to this day.

9 But from the Israelites Solomon did not hand over [any] as slaves for his project, because they were the men of war and commanders of his captains, commanders of his chariots and his cavalry.

10 These were King Solomon's chief overseers of those in charge: two hundred and fifty, who superintended the people.

11 Solomon brought the daughter of Pharaoh up from the city of David to the house which he had built for her, for he said "No wife of mine shall reside in the house of David, the king of Israel, for holy are the [precincts] to which the ark of YHWH has come;

12 Then Solomon offered up burnt offerings to YHWH upon the altar of YHWH which he had built in front of the porch,

13 in accord with the roster, day by day, to make offerings, according to the commandment of Moses, for the sabbaths and for the new moons and for the festivals three times in a year, for the festival of Mazzot and the festival of Shabuot and the festival of Sukkoth.

14 Moreover, according to the ordinance of David his father he appointed the divisions of the priests for their service, and the Levites for their duties to give praise and to minister before the priests according to the activity day by day, and the gatekeepers in their divisions for each gate, for thus was the commandment of David, the man of God.

15 They did not turn away from the commandment of the king for priests and Levites in any matter, and including the treasuries.

16 Thus all the work of Solomon was established until the day of foundation of the house of YHWH up till its completion; the house of YHWH was finished.

17 Then Solomon went to Ezion-geber, and to Eloth on the shore of Edom.

18 And Huram sent him by the hands of his servants the boats and servants who knew well the sea; they went with the servants of Solomon

21 their descendants who remained after them in the land, whom the Israelites were not able to destroy utterly, Solomon raised them up as a corvée of forced labor to this day.

22 The Israelites, however, Solomon did not hand over as slaves; because they were the men of war and his servants, his commanders, his captains, commanders of his chariots and his cavalry.

23 These were the chief overseers who were over the work of Solomon: five hundred and fifty, who superintended the people doing the work.

24 But the daughter of Pharaoh went up from the city of David to her house which he had built for her; then he built the Millo.

25 Solomon offered up three times in the year burnt offerings and peace offerings upon the altar that he had built for YHWH, and he burned incense offerings before YHWH. So he completed the house.

26 King Solomon also made a fleet at Ezion-geber, which is beside Eloth on the shore of the Sea of Reeds, in the land of Edom.

27 Hiram sent with the fleet his servants, sailors who knew the sea, together with the servants of Solomon.

to Ophir and took from there four hundred and twenty talents of gold, and they brought it to King Solomon.

28 They went to Ophir, and took from there gold, four hundred and twenty talents, and they brought it to King Solomon.

566 The Queen of Sheba Visits Solomon
2 Chron 9:1-12 // 1 Kings 10:1-13

2 Chronicles 9

1 When the Queen of Sheba heard the report of Solomon she came to try Solomon with riddles

in Jerusalem with a very great retinue, camels bearing balsam and very much gold and precious stones; then she came to Solomon and spoke with him all that was in her heart.

2 Then Solomon expounded to her all her words, and not a word was concealed from Solomon which he did not expound to her.

3 So the Queen of Sheba saw the wisdom of Solomon and the house that he had built:

4 the food of his table, the seating of his servants, the attending of his domestics and their clothing, his cup-bearers and their clothing and his ascent by which he went up to the house of YHWH; and there was no more spirit in her.

5 Then she said to the king, "The report was true that I heard in my [own] land about your affairs and about your wisdom;

6 but I did not believe their words until I came and my eyes saw it. In fact, not half of the greatness of your wisdom was told to me; you have added to the report that I had heard.

7 Happy your men! And happy these your servants who stand before you always hearing your wisdom!

8 May YHWH your God be blessed who delighted in you by setting you on his throne as king for YHWH your God. Since your God loves Israel and he established it forever, he has set you over them as king to enact justice and righteousness."

1 Kings 10

1 When the Queen of Sheba was hearing the report of Solomon to the name of YHWH, she went to test him with riddles.

2 She came to Jerusalem with a very great retinue, camels bearing balsam and very much gold and precious stones. Then she went to Solomon and spoke to him all that was in her heart.

3 Then Solomon expounded to her all her words; no word was concealed from the king which he did not expound to her.

4 So the Queen of Sheba saw all the wisdom of Solomon and the house that he had built:

5 the food of his table, the seating of his servants, the attending of his domestics, his cup-bearers and his burnt offerings that he brought up to the house of YHWH; and there was no more spirit in her.

6 Then she said to the king, "The report was true that I heard in my [own] land about your affairs and about your wisdom;

7 but I did not believe th[ese] words until I came and my eyes saw it. In fact, not half of it was told to me; you have added wisdom and goodness to the report that I heard.

8 Happy your men! Happy these your servants who stand before you always, who hear your wisdom!

9 May YHWH your God be blessed who delighted in you by setting you on the throne of Israel. Since YHWH loves Israel forever he has put you as king to enact justice and righteousness."

9 Then she gave to the king one hundred and twenty talents of gold and very much balsam and precious stone; and there was no balsam like that which the Queen of Sheba gave to King Solomon.

10 Also the servants of Hiram and the servants of Solomon who brought gold from Ophir brought almug wood and precious stones.

11 So the king made the algum wood [into] courses for the house of YHWH and the house of the king and [into] lyres and harps for the singers; and such has not been seen like them in the land of Judah.

12 King Solomon gave to the Queen of Sheba all that delighted her, which she had requested, more than what she brought to the king; then she turned and went to her country, she and her servants.

10 Then she gave to the king one hundred and twenty talents of gold and very much balsam and precious stone; not ever again did as much balsam come in such quantity as that which the Queen of Sheba gave to King Solomon.

11 Also the fleet of Hiram that carried gold from Ophir, brought from Ophir very much almug wood and precious stones.

12 So the king made the almug wood [into] supports for the house of YHWH and the house of the king and [into] lyres and harps for the singers; there never came such almug wood, and such has not been seen up till this day.

13 King Solomon gave to the Queen of Sheba all that delighted her [and] which she had requested, in addition to what he had given her by the hand of King Solomon; then she turned and went to her country, she and her servants.

567 The Wisdom and Happiness of Solomon
2 Chron 9:13-28; 1:14-17 // 1 Kings 10:14-29 // 1 Kings 4:26

2 Chronicles 9

13 The weight of the gold which came to Solomon in one year was six hundred and sixty-six talents of gold,

14 apart from what the merchants and the traders were bringing; and all the kings of Arabia and the governors of the land were bringing gold and silver to Solomon.

15 King Solomon made two hundred large shields of beaten gold; six hundred [units] of beaten gold he brought up on one large shield.

16 And three hundred shields of beaten gold: three hundred shekels of gold went into each shield; and the king put them in the house of the forest of Lebanon.

17 The king made a great throne of ivory, and he covered it over with pure gold;

18 and six steps [belonged] to the throne, and a footstool in gold for the throne was fastened to it, with arms from this side and that toward the place of sitting, and two lions standing next to the arms;

1 Kings 10

14 The weight of the gold which came to Solomon in one year was six hundred and sixty-six talents of gold,

15 apart from [what came from] the merchants and from the traffic of the traders, and all the kings of Arabia and the governors of the land.

16 King Solomon made two hundred large shields of beaten gold; six hundred [units] of gold he brought up on one large shield.

17 And three hundred shields of beaten gold: three minas of gold went into each shield; and the king put them in the house of the forest of Lebanon.

18 The king made a great throne of ivory, and he covered it over with refined gold;

19 six steps to the throne, and a rounded top for the throne from behind it, with arms from this side and that toward the place of sitting, and two lions standing next to the arms;

19 and twelve lions standing there on the six steps from this side and that side; not[hing] like this was made in any [other] kingdom.

20 All of King Solomon's drinking vessels were of gold, and all the vessels of the house of the forest of Lebanon were of refined gold. There was no silver; it was considered as nothing in the days of Solomon.

21 For ships belonging to the king were going to Tarshish, along with the servants of Huram. Once each three years the ships of Tarshish came, bearing gold and silver, ivory, apes and peacocks.

22 So King Solomon became greater than all the kings of the earth with regard to riches and wisdom.

23 All the kings of the earth were seeking the presence of Solomon, to hear his wisdom which God had put in his mind.

24 Each one of them were bringing their own present: vessels of silver and vessels of gold and outer garments and armory and balsam, horses and mules: the amount [due] year by year.

20 and twelve lions standing there on the six steps from this side and that side; not[hing] like this was made for any [other] kingdom.

21 All of King Solomon's drinking vessels were of gold, and all the vessels of the house of the forest of Lebanon were of refined gold. There was no silver; it was not considered as [anything] in the days of Solomon.

22 For a fleet of Tarshish belonging to the king was on the sea, together with the fleet of Hiram. Once every three years the fleet of Tarshish came, bearing gold and silver, ivory, apes and peacocks.

23 So King Solomon became greater than all the kings of the earth with regard to riches and wisdom.

24 All the earth were seeking the presence of Solomon, to hear his wisdom which God had put in his mind.

25 Each one of them were bringing their own present: vessels of silver and vessels of gold and outer garments and armory and balsam, horses and mules: the amount [due] year by year.

2 Chronicles 9

25 Solomon had four thousand stalls of horses and chariots and twelve thousand horsemen and he put them in chariot cities and with the king in Jerusalem.

26 He ruled over all the kings from the River to the land of the Philistines, and as far as the border of Egypt.

27 And the king put silver in Jerusalem like stones; and he put cedars as numerous as the sycamores that were in the Shephelah.

28 They used to export horses to Solomon from Egypt, and also from all the countries.

1 Kings 10

26 Solomon gathered chariots and horsemen; and he had one thousand four hundred chariots and twelve thousand horsemen; and he put them in chariot cities and with the king in Jerusalem.

1 Kings 5

1 Solomon ruled over all the kingdoms from the River, the land of the Philistines, and as far as the border of Egypt; they brought tribute and served Solomon all the days of his life.

1 Kings 10

27 And the king put silver in Jerusalem like stones; and he put cedars as numerous as the sycamores that were in the Shephelah.

28 The export of horses which was to Solomon was from Egypt and Qewe. The merchants of the king would take them from Qewe at a price.

2 Chronicles 1

14 Solomon gathered chariots and horsemen; and he had one thousand four hundred chariots and twelve thousand horsemen; and he put them in chariot cities and with the king in Jerusalem.

15 The king put silver and gold in Jerusalem like stones; and he put cedars as numerous as the sycamores that were in the Shephelah.

16 The export of horses which was to Solomon was from Egypt and Qewe. The merchants of the king would take them from Qewe at a price.

29 A chariot which was exported from Egypt went for six hundred pieces of silver and a horse for one hundred and fifty. Thus they used to export by their hand to all the kings of the Hittites and the kings of Aram.

17 They imported and then exported a chariot from Egypt for six hundred pieces of silver and a horse for one hundred and fifty. Thus they used to export by their hand to all the kings of the Hittites and the kings of Aram.

568 Solomon's Apostasy and Adversaries
1 Kings 11:1-40

1 Kings 11

1 King Solomon loved many foreign women: the daughter of Pharaoh, Moabite, Ammonite, Edomite, Sidonian, [and] Hittite women,

2 from the nations about which YHWH had said to the Israelites, "You shall not go into them and they shall not come into you; surely they will turn your heart after their gods." Solomon clung to them in love.

3 He had seven hundred wives, princesses, and three hundred concubines; and his wives turned away his heart.

4 Now it happened during the time of Solomon's old age that his wives turned away his heart after other gods, and his heart was not perfect with YHWH his god, like the heart of David his father.

5 For Solomon went after Ashtoreth, god of the Sidonians, and after Milcom, the filth of the Ammonites,

6 and Solomon did evil in the eyes of YHWH and did not completely follow YHWH like David his father.

7 Then Solomon was building a high place for Chemosh, the filth of Moab, on the mountain which is east of Jerusalem, and for Molech, the filth of the Ammonites.

8 He did thus for all his foreign wives who made incense offerings and offered sacrifices to their gods.

9 Then YHWH was angry with Solomon because his heart had turned away from YHWH the God of Israel who had appeared to him two times,

10 and commanded him concerning this matter: not to go after other gods; but he did not keep that which YHWH had commanded him.

11 Therefore YHWH said to Solomon, "Since it has been this way with you, and you did not keep my covenant and my statutes which I commanded you, I will surely tear the kingdom from you and I will give it to your servant.

12 Yet I will not do it in your days because of David your father; from the hand of your son I will tear it away.

13 Only I will not tear away the whole kingdom; one tribe I will give to your son because of David my servant and because of Jerusalem which I have chosen."

14 So YHWH raised up an adversary against Solomon, Hadad the Edomite; he was from the offspring of the king in Edom.

15 Now while David was in Edom, Joab the commander of the army went up there to bury the slain, and he struck down every male in Edom;

16 for six months Joab and all Israel remained there, until he cut down every male in Edom.

17 But Adad had fled, he and some Edomite men from his father's servants with him, to come to Egypt; and Hadad was a young lad.

18 They set out from Midian and came to Paran, and they took men with them from Paran and came to Egypt, to Pharaoh king of Egypt, and he gave him a house and assigned food for him, and he gave land to him.

19 Then Hadad found much favor in the eyes of Pharaoh, so he gave him as wife the sister of his wife, the sister of Tahpenes, the Great Lady.

20 The sister of Tahpenes bore him Genubath, his son, and Tahpenes weaned him in the midst of the household of Pharaoh; and Genubath was in the house of Pharaoh in the midst of Pharaoh's children.

21 When Hadad heard in Egypt that David lay with his ancestors, and that Joab, commander of the army, was dead, Hadad said to Pharaoh, "Send me, that I might go to my country."

22 But Pharaoh said to him, "Indeed what are you lacking with me that you are seeking to go to your country?" Nevertheless he said, "No, but surely send me away."

23 Then God raised up against him an[other] adversary, Rezon son of Eliada, who had fled from Hadadezer, king of Zobah, his master.

24 He had gathered men around himself and had become chief of a marauding band when David was slaughtering them; and they went to Damascus and they dwelt there and ruled in Damascus.

25 So he became an adversary to Israel all the days of Solomon, and the evil which Hadad [did], and he despised Israel and was king over Aram.

26 Jeroboam son of Nebat, an Ephrathite from Zeredah (the name of his mother was Zeruah, a widow woman) was a servant of Solomon; but he raised his hand against the king.

27 This is the matter in which he raised his hand against the kin. Solomon had built the Millo; he closed the breach of the city of David his father.

28 Now this man Jeroboam was a mighty man of valor, and Solomon saw the young man, that he got a job done, and he made him an overseer over all the forced labor of the house of Joseph.

29 It happened at that time that Jeroboam went out from Jerusalem, and Ahijah the Shilonite prophet found him on the way, and he was wearing a new garment; and the two of them were alone in the open country.

30 Ahijah grasped the new garment which was on him, and he tore it into twelve torn pieces.

31 Then he said to Jeroboam, "Take for yourself ten torn pieces, for thus says YHWH the God of Israel, 'Behold, I am tearing the kingdom from the hand of Solomon, and I will give you the ten tribes.

32 But the one tribe will remain for him on account of my servant David and on account of Jerusalem, the city which I have chosen from all the tribes of Israel,

33 because they have abandoned me and have prostrated themselves in worship to Ashtoreth the god of the Sidonians and to Chemosh the god of Moab and to Milcom the god of the Ammonites; and they did not walk in my ways to do what was right in my eyes, and my statutes and my ordinances, like David his father.

34 I will not take the whole kingdom from his hand, since I will appoint him ruler all the days of his life on account of David my servant, whom I chose [and] who kept my commandments and my statutes;

35 but I will take the kingship from the hand of his son and I will give it to you, the ten tribes.

36 Yet to his son I will give one tribe, in order that there might be a lamp for David my servant all the days before me in Jerusalem, the city which I have chosen for myself to put my name there.

37 But you I will take and you will be king over everything that your soul desires, and you will be king over Israel.

38 Now it will happen, if you heed everything which I command you and you walk in my paths and you do what is right in my eyes, keep my statutes and commandments just as David my servant did, then I will be with you and will build you a lasting house just as I built [one] for David, and I will give Israel to you.

39 And I will punish the offspring of David because of this—only not all the days."

40 Then Solomon sought to kill Jeroboam, but Jeroboam rose and fled to Egypt, to Shishak the king of Egypt. He was in Egypt until Solomon died.

569 The Death of Solomon
2 Chron 9:29-31 // 1 Kings 11:41-43

2 Chronicles 9

29 Now the remainder of the acts of Solomon, from the first to the last, are they not written in the words of Nathan the Prophet and in the prophecy of Ahijah the Shilonite, and in the visions of Iddo the Seer concerning Jeroboam the Son of Nebat?

30 Solomon reigned as king in Jerusalem over all Israel, for forty years.

31 When Solomon lay down to rest with his ancestors, they buried him in the city of David his father; then Rehoboam his son became king in his place.

1 Kings 11

41 Now the rest of the acts of Solomon and everything which he did and his wisdom, are they not written in the Book of the Acts of Solomon?

42 The days that Solomon reigned as king in Jerusalem over all Israel, were forty years.

43 When Solomon lay down to rest with his ancestors, he was buried in the city of David his father; then Rehoboam his son became king in his place.

Divided Monarchy

Divided Monarchy-1
Sections 570–589

Number	Title	2 Chronicles	1 Kings
570	Israel's Revolt	10:1–11:4	12:1-24
571	Jeroboam I Leads Israel into Sin		12:25-33
572	Man of God from Judah Warns		13:1-34
573	Ahijah's Prophecy against Jeroboam I		14:1-20
574	The Prosperity of Rehoboam	11:5-23	
575	Rehoboam's Reign/Shishak's Invasion	12:1-16	14:21-31
576	The Reign of Abijah (Abijam)	13:1-23	15:1-8
577	The Reign of Asa	14:1-14	15:9-12
578	Asa's Reforms	15:1-19	15:13-16
579	Asa's League with Ben-Hadad	16:1–17:1	15:17-24
580	The Reign of Nadab		15:25-32
581	The Reign of Baasha		15:33–16:7
582	The Reign of Elah		16:8-14
583	The Reign of Zimri		16:15-20
584	The Reign of Omri		16:21-28
585	The Reign of Ahab		16:29-34
586	Elijah Predicts Drought		17:1-7
587	Elijah and the Widow of Zarephath		17:8-24
588	Elijah Returns to Ahab		18:1-19
589	The Contest on Mount Carmel		18:20-40

194

570 Israel's Revolt
2 Chron 10:1–11:4 // 1 Kings 12:1-24

2 Chronicles 10

1 Rehoboam went to Shechem since all Israel had come to Shechem to make him king.

why?

2 Now when Jeroboam son of Nebat heard [of it]—as he was in Egypt where he had fled from the presence of King Solomon—Jeroboam returned from Egypt.

3 So they sent and called for him: and Jeroboam and all Israel came and they spoke to Rehoboam,

4 "Your father made our yoke hard, but now, lighten the hard servitude of your father and his heavy yoke that he has put upon us, then we will serve you."

5 But he said to them, "Another three days and [then] return to me." So the people went away.

6 Then King Rehoboam took counsel with the elders who had stood before Solomon his father when he was alive, "How do you counsel [me] to answer to this people?"

7 So they spoke to him, "If you would be kind to this people and please them and speak to them kind words, then they will be your servants all the[ir] days."

8 But he rejected the counsel of the elders who had counselled him, and he took counsel with the young men who had grown up with him standing before him.

9 He said to them, "What do you counsel that we should answer this people who have spoken to me, 'Lighten the yoke that your father put upon us?'"

10 Then the young men who had grown up with him spoke with him, "Thus shall you say to the people who spoke to you: 'Your father made our yoke heavy, but you—lighten our yoke'; thus you shall say to them, 'My little finger is thicker than the loins of my father.

11 Now my father loaded upon you a heavy yoke, but I will add to your yoke; my father controlled you with whips, but I with scorpions.'"

1 Kings 12

1 Rehoboam went to Shechem since all Israel had come to Shechem to make him king.

2 Now when Jeroboam son of Nebat heard [of it]—as he was still in Egypt where he had fled from the presence of King Solomon—Jeroboam remained in Egypt.

3 So they sent and called for him: and Jeroboam and all the assembly of Israel came[1] and they spoke to Rehoboam,

4 "Your father made our yoke hard, but you now, lighten the hard servitude of your father and his heavy yoke that he has put upon us, then we will serve you."

5 But he said to them, "Go away for another three days and [then] return to me." So the people went away.

6 Then King Rehoboam took counsel with the elders who had stood in the presence of Solomon his father when he was alive, "How do you counsel [me] to answer this people?"

7 So they spoke[2] to him, "If today you would be a servant to this people, serve them and answer them and speak to them kind words, then they will be your servants all the[ir] days."

8 But he rejected the counsel of the elders who had counselled him and he took counsel with the young men who had grown up with him who were standing before him.

9 He said to them, "What do you counsel that we should answer this people who have spoken to me, 'Lighten the yoke that your father put upon us?'"

10 Then the young men who had grown up with him spoke to him, "Thus shall you say to this people who spoke to you: 'Your father made our yoke heavy, but you—lighten our yoke'; thus you shall speak to them, 'My little finger is thicker than the loins of my father.

11 Now my father loaded upon you a heavy yoke, but I will add to your yoke; my father controlled you with whips, but I will control you with scorpions.'"

12 So Jeroboam and all the people came to Rehoboam on the third day just as the king had said, "Return to me on the third day."

13 The king answered them harshly, for King Rehoboam had rejected the counsel of the elders,

14 and he spoke to them according to the counsel of the young men, "I will make your yoke heavy, and I will add to it; my father controlled you with whips, but I with scorpions."

15 Thus the king did not listen to the people, for it was a turn of events from God in order that YHWH might fulfill his word which he had spoken through Ahijah the Shilonite to Jeroboam son of Nebat [16[4]] and all Israel.

Because the king had not listened to them, the people answered the king, "What portion is there for us in David? Nor is there an inheritance in the son of Jesse! Each [of you] to your tents O Israel! Now look to your [own] house O David!" Thereupon Israel departed to its tents.

17 As for the Israelites who were dwelling in the cities of Judah, Rehoboam [still] was king over them.

18 When King Rehoboam sent Hadoram who was in charge of the corvée, the Israelites pelted him with stones and he died. Then King Rehoboam hurried to mount a chariot to flee to Jerusalem.

19 So Israel has been in rebellion against the house of David till this day.

11:1 Then Rehoboam came to Jerusalem and he gathered all the house of Judah and Benjamin, one hundred and eighty thousand chosen to do battle with Israel in order to restore the kingdom to Rehoboam.

2 But there was a word of YHWH to Shemaiah the man of God,

3 "Say to Rehoboam son of Solomon, king of Judah, and to all Israel in Judah and Benjamin,

---

12 So Jeroboam and all the people came[3] to Rehoboam on the third day just as the king had said, "Return to me on the third day."

13 The king answered the people harshly, for he had rejected the counsel of the elders that they had counselled him,

14 and he spoke to them according to the counsel of the young men, "My father made your yoke heavy, but I will add to your yoke; my father controlled you with whips, but I will control you with scorpions."

15 Thus the king did not listen to the people, for it was a turn of events from YHWH in order to fulfill his word which YHWH had spoken through Ahijah the Shilonite to Jeroboam son of Nebat.

16 When all Israel saw that the king had not listened to them, the people answered the king, "What portion is there for us in David? Nor is there an inheritance in the son of Jesse! To your tents O Israel! Now look to your [own] house O David!" Thereupon Israel departed to its tents.

17 As for the Israelites who were dwelling in the cities of Judah, Rehoboam [still] was king over them.

18 When King Rehoboam sent Adoram who was in charge of the corvée, all Israel pelted him with stones and he died. Then King Rehoboam hurried to mount a chariot to flee to Jerusalem.

19 So Israel has been in rebellion against the house of David till this day.

20 Now when all Israel heard that Jeroboam had returned, they sent and called him to the assembly and they made him king over all Israel; there was none who followed the house of David except for the tribe of Judah alone.

21 Then Rehoboam came[5] to Jerusalem and he gathered all the house of Judah and the tribe of Benjamin, one hundred and eighty thousand chosen to do battle with the house of Israel in order to restore the kingship to Rehoboam son of Solomon.

22 But there was a word of God to Shemaiah the man of God,

23 "Say to Rehoboam son of Solomon, king of Judah, and to the entire house of Judah and Benjamin and the rest of the people,

4 'Thus says YHWH: You shall not go up nor shall you wage war with your kinfolk. Return, each of you to your home, for this thing is from me.'" So they heeded the words of YHWH and they turned back from going against Jeroboam.

24 'Thus says YHWH: You shall not go up nor shall you wage war with your kinfolk the Israelites. Return, each of you to your home, for this thing is from me.'" So they heeded the word of YHWH and they turned to go [back] according to the word of YHWH.

---

[1] Reading the Qere.
[2] Reading the Qere.
[3] Reading the Qere.
[4] Ignore the Massoretic versification and allow v. 15 to conclude here.
[5] Reading the Qere.

571 Jeroboam I Leads Israel into Sin
1 Kings 12:25-33

1 Kings 12

25 Jeroboam built Shechem in Mount Ephraim and dwelt in it; then he went out from there and built Penuel.

26 Then Jeroboam thought in his heart, "Now the kingdom may return to the house of David.

27 If this people continues to go up to make sacrifices in the house of YHWH in Jerusalem, then the heart of this people may return to their master, to Rehoboam king of Judah, and they will kill me and return to Rehoboam king of Judah."

28 So the king took counsel and made two calves of gold. Then he said to them [the people], "You have been going up to Jerusalem long enough! Here are your gods[1] O Israel, who brought you up from the land of Egypt."

29 He put one in Bethel and the other he placed in Dan.

30 This matter became a sin, for the people went before the one as far as Dan.

31 Next he built a shrine for the high places and he made priests from among the people who were not from the Levites.

32 Also Jeroboam made a festival in the eighth month, on the fifteenth day of the month, like the festival that [was] in Judah and he went up to the altar— thus he did in Bethel—to sacrifice to the calves that he had made; and he established at Bethel the priests of the high places that he had made.

33 Thus he went up to the altar that he had made in Bethel on the fifteenth day of the eighth month, in the month that he had devised from his [own] mind:[2] since he had made a festival for the Israelites, he went up to the altar to burn incense.

---

[1] Alternative translation: "Here is your God. . . ."
[2] Reading the Qere.

572 The Man of God from Judah Warns Jeroboam I
1 Kings 13:1-34

1 Kings 13

1 Now a man of God came from Judah to Bethel by the word of YHWH. While Jeroboam was standing near the altar to burn incense,

2 he [the man of God] cried out against the altar by the word of YHWH, and said, "'Altar, Altar,' thus says YHWH, 'A son will surely be born to the house of David, Josiah [will be] his name. He will sacrifice upon you the priests of [the] high places who burn incense upon you, and human bones they will burn upon you.'"

3 On that day he gave a sign, "This is the sign that YHWH has spoken: 'The altar shall surely be torn down and the ashes that are upon it shall be poured out.'"

4 Now when the king heard the word of the man of God that he had cried out against the altar at Bethel, Jeroboam stretched out his hand from over the altar, saying, "Take him!" But his hand that he stretched out against him, withered, so that he was unable to draw it back to himself.

5 Moreover, the altar was torn down and the ashes were poured out from the altar according to the sign that the man of God had given by the word of YHWH.

6 The king responded, saying to the man of God, "Entreat now the favor of YHWH your God, and pray on my behalf that my hand will be restored to me." So the man of God entreated the favor of YHWH, and the hand of the king was restored to him and it became as it was before.

7 Then the king spoke to the man of God, "Come with me to [my] house and take food and I will give to you a gift."

8 But the man of God said to the king, "If you were to give me half of your house I would not come with you, nor would I eat bread, nor would I drink water in this place.

9 For thus it was commanded to me by the word of YHWH: 'You shall not eat bread, neither shall you drink water, nor shall you return by the road on which you came.'"

10 So he went by another road; he did not return on the road by which he had come to Bethel.

11 Now there was a certain old prophet living in Bethel; and his son came and reported to him all the deeds that the man of God had done that day in Bethel. The words that he had spoken to the king they reported to their father.

12 Then their father spoke to them, "Which road [is] the way that he went?" Now his sons had seen the road that the man of God who had come from Judah had gone.

13 So he said to his sons, "Saddle the ass for me." They saddled the ass for him and he rode on it.

14 He went after the man of God and found him sitting under the terebinth. He said to him, "Are you the man of God who came from Judah?" He said, "I am."

15 Then he said to him, "Come with me to [my] house and eat bread."

16 But he said, "I am unable to return with you nor to come with you, nor will I eat bread nor will I drink water with you in this place,

17 for the message [came] to me by the word of YHWH: 'You shall not eat bread, nor shall you drink water there. You shall not return on the road by which you came.'"

18 But he said to him, "I am also a prophet like you, and a divine messenger spoke to me by the word of YHWH: 'Bring him [back] with you to your house, and let him eat bread and drink water.'" [Thus] he deceived him.

19 So he returned with him and he ate bread in his house and drank water.

20 But while they were sitting at table, the word of YHWH came to the prophet who had brought him back,

21 and he cried out to the man of God who had come from Judah, "Thus says YHWH: because you have rebelled against [the] utterance of YHWH, and you have not kept the command that YHWH your God commanded you,

22 but have returned and eaten bread and drunk water in the place of which he said to you, 'Do not eat bread and do not drink water,' your corpse shall not come to the tomb of your ancestors."

23 After he had eaten bread and after he had drunk, he saddled the ass for him, for the prophet whom he had brought back.

24 As he went, a lion found him on the road and killed him, and his corpse was thrown on the road with the ass standing beside it, and the lion standing beside the corpse.

25 Now [some] men passing by saw the corpse [that had been thrown] on the road with the lion standing near the corpse. When they arrived they spoke [about it] in the city [in which] the old prophet lived.

26 When the prophet, who had brought him back from the road heard [about it], he said, "It is the man of God who rebelled against the utterance of YHWH, therefore YHWH gave him to the lion and it tore him apart and killed him according to the word of YHWH that he had spoken to him."

27 Then he spoke to his sons, "Saddle the ass for me," and they saddled [it].

28 So he went and found his corpse thrown on the road and an ass and the lion standing beside the corpse. The lion had not eaten the corpse and had not torn apart the ass.

29 The prophet lifted up the corpse of the man of God and laid it down upon the ass. Then he brought it back and came to the city of the old prophet to mourn and to bury him.

30 He laid down his corpse in his [own] tomb and they mourned over him, "Alas, my brother."

31 After having buried him, he said to his sons, "When I die, then bury me in the tomb in which the man of God is buried; next to his bones lay my bones down.

32 For surely shall come to pass the word that he proclaimed by the word of YHWH against the altar that is at Bethel, and against all the shrines of the high places that are in the cities of Samaria."

33 Even after this incident Jeroboam did not turn from his evil way, but he went on and made priests for the high places from among the people; anyone who desired, he ordained[1] as priests for the high places.

34 Thus it happened that this practice became sin to the house of Jeroboam thereby cutting [it] off and destroying [it] from the face of the ground.

---

[1] Literally: "filled [their] hands."

573 Ahijah's Prophecy against Jeroboam I
1 Kings 14:1-20

1 Kings 14

1 At that time Abijah son of Jeroboam, became sick.

2 So Jeroboam said to his wife, "Rise up now and disguise yourself so that they will not know that you[1] are the wife of Jeroboam, and go to Shiloh: for Ahijah the prophet is there, he [who] spoke concerning me that I should be king over this people.

3 Take in your hand ten [loaves of] bread and cakes and a flask of honey and go to him; he will tell you what will happen to the boy."

4 The wife of Jeroboam did so. She rose up and went to Shiloh and came to the house of Ahijah. Now Ahijah was unable to see, for his eyes were set due to his old age.

5 However, YHWH had said to Ahijah, "Now the wife of Jeroboam is coming to seek a word from you about her son, for he is sick. Thus and so you shall say to her, though when she comes she will pretend to be a stranger."

6 So when Ahijah heard the sound of her feet [as] she came into the doorway he said, "Come in, wife of Jeroboam. Why do you pretend to be a stranger? Now I have been sent a harsh message for you.

7 Go, say to Jeroboam, 'Thus says YHWH God of Israel: because I have raised you up from among the people and have appointed you a leader over my people Israel,

8 and I have torn the kingdom from the house of David and have given it to you—but you have not been like my servant David who kept my commandments and who followed after me with all his heart, doing only what was right in my eyes—

9 rather you have done evil more than all who were before you: you have gone and made for yourself other gods and molten images to provoke me to anger; and me, you have thrust behind your back.

10 Therefore, I am about to bring disaster upon the house of Jeroboam. I will cut off from Jeroboam every man[2] in Israel, bound or free, and I will burn up the house of Jeroboam as one burns dung until it is consumed.

11 [Anyone belonging] to Jeroboam who dies in the city, the dogs shall eat; anyone who dies in the open field, the birds of the sky shall eat, for YHWH has spoken.'

12 Now get up and go to your house. When your feet enter the city, the child will die:

13 and all Israel will mourn for him and they will bury him for he alone of Jeroboam's line shall enter a tomb, because in him there was found something in the house of Jeroboam pleasing to YHWH God of Israel.

14 Then YHWH shall raise up for himself a king over Israel who shall cut off the house of Jeroboam. This is the day! Even now![3]

15 YHWH shall strike Israel like the reed is tossed about in the waters; he shall uproot Israel from this good ground that he gave to their ancestors and he shall scatter them beyond the River because they made their asherim, provoking YHWH to anger.

16 He will give Israel [up] because of the sins of Jeroboam, those which he sinned and which he caused Israel to sin."

17 Then the wife of Jeroboam got up and came to Tirzah. When she came to the threshold of the house, the child died.

18 All Israel buried him and they mourned him according to the word of YHWH that he had spoken through his servant Ahijah the prophet.

19 Now the rest of the acts of Jeroboam, how he fought and how he was king, indeed they are written in the Book of the Chronicles of the Kings of Israel.

20 The time that Jeroboam was king was twenty-two years. When he lay down to rest with his ancestors, Nadab his son became king in his place.

---

¹ Reading the Qere.
² Literally, "one who urinates against the wall."
³ Meaning of Hebrew in last clause is uncertain.

574 The Prosperity of Rehoboam
2 Chron 11:5-23

2 Chronicles 11

5 Now Rehoboam dwelt in Jerusalem and he built cities for defense in Judah.

6 He built Bethlehem, Etam, Tekoa,

7 Beth-zur, Soco, Adullam,

8 Gath, Mareshah, Ziph,

9 Adoraim, Lachish, Azekah,

10 Zorah, Aijalon, and Hebron, that are in Judah and Benjamin, as fortified cities.

11 He strengthened the fortresses and put in them commanders and stores of food, oil and wine,

12 and in every city, shields and spears. Thus he made them very strong and so Judah and Benjamin were his.

13 Now the priests and the Levites who were in all Israel presented themselves to him from all their territory.

14 The Levites had left their common lands and their possessions and they had come to Judah and Jerusalem, because Jeroboam and his sons had prevented them from being priest[s] to YHWH

15 for he had appointed for himself priests for high places, for the satyrs, and for the calves that he had made.

16 After them, those from all the tribes of Israel, those who set their heart to seek YHWH the God of Israel, [those] came to Jerusalem to sacrifice to YHWH the God of their ancestors.

17 They strengthened the kingdom of Judah and supported Rehoboam son of Solomon for three years, for they walked in the way of David and Solomon for three years.

18 Now Rehoboam took for himself a wife, Mahalath daughter[1] of Jerimoth, son of David [and] of Abihail daughter of Eliab, son of Jesse.

19 She bore him sons: Jeush, Shemariah, and Zaham.

20 After her he took Maacah daughter of Absalom and she bore him Abijah, Attai, Ziza and Shelomith.

21 Now Rehoboam loved Maacah daughter of Absalom more than all his [other] wives and concubines; indeed he took eighteen wives and sixty concubines and fathered twenty-eight sons and sixty daughters.

22 Rehoboam appointed as the head, Abijah son of Maacah as crown prince among his brothers in order to make him king.

23 He [Rehoboam] was discerning and so he distributed some of his sons to every region of Judah and Benjamin, to all the fortified cities, and gave them abundant provisions and obtained [for them] a great number of wives.

---

[1] Reading the Qere.

575 Rehoboam's Reign / Shishak's Invasion of Judah
2 Chron 12:1-16 // 1 Kings 14:21-31

2 Chronicles 12

1 As soon as the kingdom of Rehoboam was established and he had grown strong, he forsook the law of YHWH and all Israel with him.

[13 King Rehoboam established himself in Jerusalem and he became king. Now Rehoboam was forty-one years old when he became king, and he was king seventeen years in Jerusalem, the city where YHWH chose to put his name out of all the tribes of Israel. The name of his mother was Naamah the Ammonite.

14 He did what was evil for he did not set his heart to seek YHWH.]

1 Kings 14

21 Now Rehoboam son of Solomon, became king in Judah. Rehoboam was forty-one years old when he became king, and he was king seventeen years in Jerusalem, the city where YHWH chose to put his name out of all the tribes of Israel. The name of his mother was Naamah the Ammonite.

22 Judah did what was evil in the eyes of YHWH; they provoked him to jealous anger more than all that their ancestors had done by their sins that they had sinned.

23 They even built for themselves high places, pillars and asherim upon every high hill and under every flourishing tree.

24 There were even male votaries in the land. They acted according to all the abominations of the nations that YHWH had dispossessed before the Israelites.

2 Now it happened in the fifth year of King Rehoboam, that Shishak king of Egypt came up against Jerusalem because they had been unfaithful to YHWH,

3 with twelve hundred chariots and sixty thousand horsemen; there were people without number who came with him from Egypt: Libyans, Sukkiim, and Cushites.

4 He captured the fortified cities which belonged to Judah and came as far as Jerusalem.

5 Then Shemaiah the prophet came to Rehoboam and the princes of Judah who were gathered at Jerusalem because of Shishak, and he said to them, "Thus says YHWH, 'You have abandoned me, so I have abandoned you into the hand of Shishak.'"

6 Then the princes of Israel and the king humbled themselves and said, "YHWH is righteous."

7 When YHWH saw that they humbled themselves, the word of YHWH came to Shemaiah, "Since they have humbled themselves, I will not destroy them but I will give them some measure of escape, and my anger shall not pour out against Jerusalem by the hand of Shishak.

8 Nevertheless they shall become his servants that they may distinguish [between] my service and the service of the kingdoms of the [other] countries.

9 So Shishak king of Egypt came up against Jerusalem. He took treasures of the house of YHWH and treasures of the house of the king; he took everything. He also took the shields of gold that Solomon had made.

10 Then King Rehoboam made shields of copper in their place, and entrusted [them] into the hand of the officers of the guard who kept guard at the entrance of the house of the king.

11 Whenever the king entered the house of YHWH the royal guards would come carrying them along, and return them to the chamber of the royal guard.

12 Since he had humbled himself, the wrath of YHWH turned from him so as not to destroy [Judah] completely. In fact there were even good things in Judah.

13 King Rehoboam established himself in Jerusalem and he became king. Now Rehoboam was forty-one years old when he became king and he was king

25 Now it happened in the fifth year of King Rehoboam that Shishak[1] king of Egypt came up against Jerusalem.

26 He took treasures of the house of YHWH and treasures of the house of the king; he took everything. He also took all the shields of gold that Solomon had made.

27 Then King Rehoboam made shields of copper in their place, and entrusted [them] into the hand of the officers of the guard who kept guard at the entrance of the house of the king.

28 Whenever the king entered the house of YHWH, the royal guards would carry them and return them to the chamber of the royal guard.

seventeen years in Jerusalem, the city where YHWH chose to put his name out of all the tribes of Israel. The name of his mother was Naamah the Ammonite.

14 And he did what was evil for he did not set his heart to seek YHWH.

15 Now the acts of Rehoboam, the first and the last, are they not written in the Deeds of Shemaiah the Prophet and of Iddo the Seer for enrollment in a genealogy? [There were] wars [between] Rehoboam and Jeroboam continually.

16 When Rehoboam lay down to rest with his ancestors, he was buried in the city of David, and Abijah his son became king in his place.

29 Now the rest of the acts of Rehoboam and all that he did are they not written in the Book of the Chronicles of the Kings of Judah?
30 There was war between Rehoboam and Jeroboam continually.

31 When Rehoboam lay down to rest with his ancestors, he was buried with his ancestors in the city of David. The name of his mother was Naamah the Ammonite, and Abijam his son became king in his place.

---

[1] Reading the Qere.

576 The Reign of Abijah (Abijam)
2 Chron 13:1-23 // 1 Kings 15:1-8

2 Chronicles 13

1 In the eighteenth year of King Jeroboam, Abijah became king over Judah.

2 He was king for three years in Jerusalem. The name of his mother was Micaiah daughter of Uriel of Gibeah.

And there was war between Abijah and Jeroboam.

1 Kings 15

1 In the eighteenth year of King Jeroboam son of Nebat, Abijam became king over Judah.

2 He was king for three years in Jerusalem. The name of his mother was Maacah daughter of Abishalom.

3 He walked in all the sins of his father that he had done before him; his heart was not whole with YHWH his God, as the heart of David his [fore]father [had been].

4 Nevertheless for the sake of David, YHWH his God made him a lamp in Jerusalem by raising up his son after him and by establishing Jerusalem

5 because David had done what was right in the eyes of YHWH. He had not turned aside from all that he had commanded him all the days of his life except in the matter of Uriah the Hittite.

6 And there was war between Rehoboam and Jeroboam all the days of his life.

3 Abijah joined battle with an army of four hundred thousand mighty warriors, picked men, but Jeroboam arrayed for battle with him eight hundred thousand picked men, mighty warriors.

4 Then Abijah stood up on Mount Zemaraim that is in the hill-country of Ephraim, and said, "Hear me, Jeroboam and all Israel!

5 Is it not known to you that YHWH the God of Israel, has given to David kingship over Israel forever, to him and to his sons, a covenant of salt?

6 Yet Jeroboam son of Nebat, servant of Solomon son of David, rose up and rebelled against his master.

7 Worthless men, scoundrels, gathered about him. They strengthened themselves against Rehoboam son of Solomon when Rehoboam was young and indecisive and could not stand up against them.

8 Now you think you can stand up against the kingdom of YHWH, [that is] in the hand of the sons of David, because you are a great multitude and [have] with you calves of gold which Jeroboam made as gods for you.

9 Have you not banished the priests of YHWH, sons of Aaron and the Levites, and made for yourselves priests like the people of [other] lands? Everyone who comes to be consecrated with a bull from the herd and seven rams, he becomes a priest to [what are] not gods.

10 But as for us, YHWH is our God, and we have not forsaken him; the priests who minister to YHWH, the sons of Aaron and the Levites, are at [their] duties.

11 They make sacrifice to YHWH, burnt offerings every morning and evening, and spicy incense. [They set] rows of bread on the pure table. A gold lampstand and its lamps they light each evening because we are keeping the charge of YHWH our God while you have forsaken it.

12 Look, God is with us at our head and there are his priests and the trumpets to sound the battle-cry against you. O Israelites, do not fight against YHWH God of our ancestors, for you will not succeed."

13 Now Jeroboam had set up an ambush to come from behind them. They [Jeroboam's soldiers] were before Judah but the ambush was behind them.

14 When Judah turned around the battle was there, in front and behind, and they cried out to YHWH with the priests blowing the[ir] horns.

15 The men of Judah raised a shout and when the men of Judah shouted, God routed Jeroboam and all Israel before Abijah and Judah.

16 And the Israelites fled from before Judah but God gave them into their hand.

17 Abijah and his people inflicted upon them a severe defeat: five hundred thousand picked men from Israel fell slain.

18 The Israelites were humbled at that time while the Judahites prevailed because they relied upon YHWH God of their ancestors.

19 Then Abijah pursued after Jeroboam and captured from him [some] cities: Bethel and its villages, Jeshanah and its villages, and Ephron and its villages.

20 And Jeroboam did not regain [his] power in the days of Abijah; YHWH struck him down and he died.

21 But Abijah grew strong and took for himself fourteen wives and fathered twenty-two sons and sixteen daughters.

22 Now the rest of the acts of Abijah, his ways and his words are written in the Commentary of the Prophet Iddo.

7 Now the rest of the acts of Abijam and all that he did, are they not written in the Book of the Chronicles of the Kings of Judah? There was war between Abijam and Jeroboam.

23 When Abijah lay down to rest with his ancestors, they buried him in the city of David, and Asa his son became king in his place. In his days the land was quiet for ten years.

8 When Abijam lay down to rest with his ancestors, they buried him in the city of David, and Asa his son became king in his place.

577 The Reign of Asa
2 Chron 14:1-14 // 1 Kings 15:9-12

2 Chronicles 14

1 Kings 15

9 In the twentieth year of Jeroboam king of Israel, Asa became king of Judah,

10 and he was king for forty-one years in Jerusalem. The name of his mother was Maacah daughter of Abishalom.

1 Now Asa did [what was] good and upright in the eyes of YHWH his God.

11 Now Asa did what was upright in the eyes of YHWH as David his [fore]father [had done].

2 He removed the foreign altars and the high places. He shattered the pillars, and he hewed down the asherim.

12 He took away the male votaries from the land and he removed all the idols that his ancestors had made.

3 He told Judah to inquire of YHWH God of their ancestors and to do the Torah and the commandment.

4 He also removed from all the cities of Judah the high places and the incense stands, and the kingdom had quiet before him.

5 Then he built fortified cities in Judah, for the land was quiet. There was no war with him in those years for YHWH had given him rest.

6 He said to Judah, "Let us build these cities and let us surround them [with] a wall, towers, gates, and bars. The land before us is still ours, for we have sought YHWH our God. We have sought [him] and he has given rest to us on every side." So they built and they prospered.

7 Asa had an army of three hundred thousand from Judah bearing shield and spear, and from Benjamin shield-bearers and drawers of the bow two hundred and eighty thousand; all these were mighty warriors.

8 Zerah, the Cushite, came out against them with an army of a thousand thousands and three hundred chariots; he came as far as Mareshah.

9 So Asa went out before him, and arrayed [his troops for] the battle in the valley of Zephathah at Mareshah.

10 Then Asa cried to YHWH his God and said, "YHWH, there is no difference for you in helping either [those with] much strength or [those with] none. Help us, YHWH our God, for we rely upon you, and in

your name we have come against this horde. YHWH, you are our God, let no mortal restrain you."

11 So YHWH struck the Cushites before Asa and before Judah and the Cushites fled.

12 Then Asa and the people who were with him pursued them as far as Gerar. So many of the Cushites fell that none of them remained alive, for they were routed before YHWH and before his camp. They carried away very much booty.

13 Then they struck down all the cities around Gerar—for the dread of YHWH was upon them—and they plundered all the cities for there was much plunder in them.

14 They even struck [the] tents of herdsmen, and they took captive many sheep and camels. Then they returned to Jerusalem.

578 Asa's Reforms
2 Chron 15:1-19 // 1 Kings 15:13-16

2 Chronicles 15   *1 Kings 15*

1 Now the spirit of God came upon Azariah son of Oded.

2 So he went out before Asa and said to him, "Hear me Asa and all Judah and Benjamin: YHWH is with you when you are with him and if you seek him he will be found by you; but if you abandon him he will abandon you.

3 For a long time Israel had gone without the true God, without a teaching priest, and without Torah,

4 but in their distress they turned to YHWH the God of Israel. They sought him and he was found by them.

5 In those times there was no security for anyone going out or coming in because there was [so] much disturbance among all the inhabitants of the lands.

6 They were crushed, nation against nation, and city against city, for God disturbed them with every [kind of] affliction.

7 But you, be strong and do not weaken your hands for there shall be a reward for your work."

8 When Asa heard these words and the prophecy of Oded the prophet, he strengthened himself; he put away the despicable idols from all the land of Judah and Benjamin, and from the cities which he had captured from the hill-country of Ephraim. Then he repaired the altar of YHWH which was in front of the vestibule of YHWH.

9 He gathered all Judah, Benjamin, and those sojourning with them from Ephraim, Manasseh and Simeon, for many had deserted to him from Israel when they saw that YHWH his God was with him.

10 They gathered [in] Jerusalem in the third month of the fifteenth year of the kingship of Asa.

11 They sacrificed to YHWH on that day from the plunder they had brought, seven hundred oxen, and seven thousand sheep.

12 Then they entered into [a] covenant to seek YHWH the God of their ancestors, with all their heart and with all their being:

13 anyone who did not seek YHWH the God of Israel, would be put to death, whether young or old, or man or woman.

14 They swore to YHWH with a loud voice, with a shout, with trumpets, and with horns.

15 All Judah rejoiced over the oath because they had sworn with all their heart, and sought him with all their desire: he was found by them and YHWH gave them rest on every side.

16 Now Asa the king even removed Maacah [his] mother from [being] queen-mother, because she made for Asherah an abominable image. Asa cut down her abominable image and he pulverized and burned [it] in the Wadi Kidron.

13 Now he even removed Maacah his mother from [being] queen-mother because she made an abominable image for Asherah. Asa cut down her abominable image and burned [it] in the Wadi Kidron.

17 But the high places were not removed from Israel. Nevertheless the heart of Asa was [at] peace all his days.

14 But the high places were not removed. Nevertheless the heart of Asa was [at] peace with YHWH all his days.

18 He brought the sacred objects of his father and his sacred objects [into] the house of God, silver and gold and vessels.

15 He brought the sacred objects of his father and his sacred objects[1] [into] the house of YHWH, silver and gold and vessels.

19 And there was no war until the thirty-fifth year of the kingship of Asa.

16 And there was war between Asa and Baasha king of Israel, all their days.

---

¹ Reading the Qere.

579 Asa's League with Ben-Hadad
2 Chron 16:1–17:1 // 1 Kings 15:17-24

2 Chronicles 16

1 In the thirty-sixth year of the kingship of Asa, Baasha king of Israel came up against Judah, and he built Ramah so as not to allow anyone to go out or to come in to Asa king of Judah.

2 Then Asa brought out silver and gold from the treasuries of the house of YHWH and the house of the king and he sent [them] to Ben-hadad king of Aram who dwelt in Damascus saying,

3 "[Let there be] a covenant between me and you [as] between my father and your father. See I have sent you silver and gold. Go, break your covenant with Baasha king of Israel that he may withdraw from me.

4 Whereupon Ben-hadad listened to King Asa, and he sent the officers of his armies to the cities of Israel. They struck Ijon, Dan, Abel-maim and all the supply cities of Naphtali.

5 When Baasha heard, he stopped building Ramah and put an end to his work.

6 Then Asa the king, took all Judah and they carried away the stones of Ramah and its lumber with which Baasha had been building; and with them he built Geba and Mizpah.

7 At that time Hanani the seer came to Asa king of Judah, and said to him, "Because you relied upon the king of Aram and did not rely on YHWH your God, therefore the army of the king of Aram has escaped from your hand.

1 Kings 15

17 Now Baasha king of Israel came up against Judah, and he built Ramah so as not to allow anyone to go out or to come in to Asa king of Judah.

18 Then Asa took all the silver and the gold that were left in the treasuries of the house of YHWH and the treasuries of the¹ house of the king, and he handed them over to his servants; and King Asa sent them to Ben-hadad son of Tabrimmon son of Hezion, king of Aram, who dwelt in Damascus saying,

19 "[Let there be] a covenant between me and you, [as] between my father and your father. See I have sent you a present of silver and gold. Go, break your covenant with Baasha king of Israel, that he may withdraw from me.

20 Whereupon Ben-hadad listened to King Asa, and he sent officers of his armies against the cities of Israel. He struck Ijon, Dan, Abel-beth-maacah and all Chinneroth, against all the land of Naphtali.

21 When Baasha heard, he stopped building Ramah; and dwelt in Tirzah.

22 King Asa summoned all Judah, there was none exempt; they carried away the stones of Ramah and its lumber with which Baasha had been building; and with them King Asa built Geba of Benjamin and Mizpah.

8 Were not the Cushites and the Libyans an exceedingly large army with chariots and horsemen? Yet because you relied upon YHWH, he gave them into your hand.

9 For the eyes of YHWH range quickly over all the earth to give strength to those whose heart is [at] peace with him. You have acted foolishly in this [matter]; for from now [on] you will have wars."

10 Then Asa was angry with the seer. He put him in confinement, for he was in a rage with him concerning this [matter]. Moreover, Asa oppressed others of the people at that time.

11 Now see, the acts of Asa, the first and the last, indeed they are written in the Book of the Kings of Judah and Israel.

23 Now the rest of all the acts of Asa, all his valor, and everything that he did and the cities that he built, are they not written in the Book of the Chronicles of the Kings of Judah? However, at the time of his old age he was diseased in his feet.

12 And Asa became diseased in his feet in the thirty-ninth year of his kingship; his disease was severe. Yet even with his sickness he did not seek YHWH, but [went] to healers.

13 When Asa lay down to rest with his ancestors, dying in the forty-first year of his kingship,

14 they buried him in his tomb which he had dug for himself in the city of David. They laid him on a bier which was full of spices and skillfully blended ointments[2] and they made a very great fire in his honor.

24 When Asa lay down to rest with his ancestors, he was buried with his ancestors in the city of David, his [fore]father;

17:1 Jehoshaphat his son became king in his place; and he fortified himself against Israel.

and Jehoshaphat his son became king in his place.

---

[1] Reading the Qere.
[2] Hebrew somewhat obscure.

580 The Reign of Nadab
1 Kings 15:25-32

1 Kings 15

25 Nadab son of Jeroboam became king over Israel in the second year of Asa king of Judah, and he was king over Israel for two [years].

26 He did evil in the eyes of YHWH; he walked in the way of his father, in his sin which he caused Israel to sin.

27 Now Baasha son of Ahijah, of the house of Issachar, conspired against him: Baasha struck him down at Gibbethon which belonged to the Philistines, while Nadab and all Israel were besieging Gibbethon.

28 Baasha killed him in the third year of Asa king of Judah, and he became king in his place.

29 As soon as he became king, he struck down the entire house of Jeroboam. He did not leave a living person to Jeroboam until he had annihilated [them] according to the word of YHWH that he had spoken through his servant Ahijah the Shilonite

30 because of the sins of Jeroboam that he sinned and that he had caused Israel to sin, by his provoking YHWH the God of Israel, to anger.

31 Now the rest of the acts of Nadab and all that he did, are they not written in the Book of the Chronicles of the Kings of Israel?

32 There was war between Asa and Baasha king of Israel, all their days.

581 The Reign of Baasha
1 Kings 15:33–16:7

1 Kings 15

33 In the third year of Asa king of Judah, Baasha son of Ahijah became king over all Israel at Tirzah; [he was king] for twenty-four years,

34 and did what was evil in the eyes of YHWH. He walked in the way of Jeroboam, in his sin which he had caused Israel to sin.

16:1 Then the word of YHWH came to Jehu son of Hanani against Baasha,

2 "Because I have lifted you up from the dust and have appointed you a leader over my people Israel, but you walked in the way of Jeroboam and you have made my people Israel to sin so as to provoke me to anger with their sins,

3 now I am about to consume Baasha and his house and I will make your house like the house of Jeroboam son of Nebat.

4 Whoever dies belonging to Baasha in the city, the dogs shall eat, and whoever dies belonging to him in the field, the birds of the sky shall eat."

5 Now the rest of the acts of Baasha what he did and his valor, are they not written in the Book of the Chronicles of the Kings of Israel?

6 When Baasha lay down to rest with his ancestors, he was buried at Tirzah; Elah his son became king in his place.

7 Thus indeed through Jehu son of Hanani, the prophet, the word of YHWH came against Baasha and against his house on account of all the evil that he had done in the eyes of YHWH so as to provoke him to anger with the work of his hands, by being like the house of Jeroboam. On account of that he had struck it down.

582 The Reign of Elah
1 Kings 16:8-14

1 Kings 16

8 In the twenty-sixth year of Asa king of Judah, Elah son of Baasha became king over Israel in Tirzah; [he was king] for two years.

9 However, his servant Zimri commander of half the chariotry, conspired against him. He was in Tirzah getting drunk [at] the house of Arza, who was in charge of the house[1] at Tirzah.

10 Zimri came in, struck him down and killed him in the twenty-seventh year of Asa king of Judah, and he became king in his place.

11 Now when he became king, as soon as he had assumed his throne, he struck down the entire house of Baasha; he did not leave to him a male,[2] neither his kinsmen nor his friend.

12 Zimri annihilated the entire house of Baasha in accord with the word of YHWH that he had spoken against Baasha through Jehu the prophet

13 because of all the sins of Baasha and the sins of Elah his son, that they had sinned and that they had caused Israel to sin so as to provoke YHWH the God of Israel to anger with their idols.

14 Now the rest of the acts of Elah and all that he did, are they not written in the Book of the Chronicles of the Kings of Israel?

---

[1] Literally, "over the house [chamberlain]."
[2] Literally, "[any]one who urinates against the wall."

583 The Reign of Zimri
1 Kings 16:15-20

1 Kings 16

15 In the twenty-seventh year of Asa king of Judah, Zimri was king for seven days in Tirzah. Now the people were encamped against Gibbethon which belonged to the Philistines.

16 When the people who were encamped heard: "Zimri has conspired and also has struck down the king," all Israel made Omri the commander of the host, king over Israel on that day in the camp.

17 So Omri went up and all Israel with him from Gibbethon, and laid siege against Tirzah.

18 Now when Zimri saw that the city had been captured, he went to the citadel of the house of the king, and he burned down the house of the king over himself with fire and he died

19 because of his sins[1] that he had sinned, doing what was evil in the eyes of YHWH, walking in the way of Jeroboam and his sin that he did, causing Israel to sin.

20 Now the rest of the acts of Zimri and his conspiracy that he conspired, are they not written in the Book of the Chronicles of the Kings of Israel?

---

[1] Reading plural with the Qere.

584 The Reign of Omri
1 Kings 16:21-28

1 Kings 16

21 Then the people of Israel were divided into half: half of the people followed Tibni son of Ginath, to make him king; and the [other] half followed Omri.

22 The people who followed Omri overcame the people following Tibni son of Ginath, so Tibni died and Omri became king.

23 In the thirty-first year of Asa king of Judah, Omri became king over Israel and [he was king] for twelve years—at Tirzah he was king for six years.

24 He purchased the hill of Samaria from Shemer for two talents of silver. He built [up] the hill and called the name of the city that he had built Samaria after the name of Shemer, the owner of the hill.

25 Omri did what was evil in the eyes of YHWH; he did more evil than all who had preceded him.

26 He walked in every way of Jeroboam son of Nebat and in his sin[1] that he caused Israel to sin so as to provoke YHWH God of Israel to anger, with their idols.

27 Now the rest of the acts of Omri that he did and his valor which he showed, are they not written in the Book of the Chronicles of the Kings of Israel?

28 When Omri lay down to rest with his ancestors, he was buried in Samaria; Ahab his son became king in his place.

---

[1] Reading the singular with the Qere.

585 The Reign of Ahab
1 Kings 16:29-34

1 Kings 16

29 Ahab son of Omri became king over Israel in the thirty-eighth year of Asa king of Judah. Ahab son of Omri was king over Israel in Samaria for twenty-two years.

30 Ahab son of Omri did what was evil in the eyes of YHWH, more than all who had preceded him.

31 As though it had been a slight thing for him to walk in the sins of Jeroboam son of Nebat, he took a wife, Jezebel daughter of Ethbaal king of the Sidonians. He went and served Baal and he bowed down to him.

32 He set up an altar to Baal [in] the house of Baal that he had built in Samaria;

33 Ahab also made the asherah. Ahab did even more to provoke YHWH the God of Israel to anger than all the kings of Israel who had preceded him.

34 In his days, Hiel the Bethelite built Jericho; with Abiram his first-born he laid the foundation; with Segub[1] his youngest he set up its doors according to the word of YHWH that he spoke through Joshua son of Nun.

---

[1] Reading the Qere.

586 Elijah Predicts Drought
1 Kings 17:1-7

1 Kings 17

1 Now Elijah the Tishbite from Tishbe of Gilead, said to Ahab, "As YHWH the God of Israel lives, before whom I stand, there shall be no dew or rain these years except by my word!"

2 Then the word of YHWH came to him,

3 "Go from this [place] and turn eastward and hide yourself by the Wadi Cherith which is east of the Jordan.

4 You shall drink from the wadi, and I have commanded the ravens to nourish you there."

5 So he went and did according to the word of YHWH: he went and he dwelt by the Wadi Cherith which is east of the Jordan.

6 The ravens brought him bread and meat in the morning, bread and meat in the evening, and he drank from the wadi.

7 Now it happened that after [some] days the wadi dried up since there was no rain on the land.

587 Elijah and the Widow of Zarephath
1 Kings 17:8-24

1 Kings 17

8 Then the word of YHWH came to him,

9 "Rise up, go to Zarephath which belongs to Sidon, and you shall dwell there, for I have commanded a widow-woman there to nourish you."

10 So he rose up and went to Zarephath. He came to the gateway of the city and there indeed [was] a widow-woman gathering twigs. He called to her and said, "Bring me, please, a little water in a vessel so that I may drink."

11 As she went to bring [it] he called to her and said, "Bring me, please, a morsel of bread in your hand."

12 She said, "As YHWH your God lives, I have no cake but only a handful of meal in a jar and a little oil in a jug. Look, I am gathering a couple of twigs so that I may go and prepare it for me and my son that we may eat it and die."

13 Elijah said to her, "Do not fear, go, do according to your word, only make me a small cake from there first and bring [it] to me. And afterwards make [something] for yourself and your son.

14 For thus says YHWH the God of Israel, 'The jar of meal will not come to an end and the jug of oil will not fail until the day YHWH gives rain upon the face of the ground.'"

15 So she went and did according to the word of Elijah: she ate, he and she, and her household [for many] days.

16 The jar of meal did not come to an end and the jug of oil did not fail, according to the word of YHWH that he had spoken through Elijah.

17 Now it happened after these things the son of the woman, the mistress of the house, became sick; and his sickness was so strong that there was no breath left in him.

18 She said to Elijah, "What have [you] against me O man of God, that you have come to me to call to mind my iniquity and to cause the death of my son?"

19 He said to her, "Give me your son." Then he took him from her bosom and carried him to the upper chamber where he was staying and he laid him down upon his bed.

20 Then he called to YHWH and said, "YHWH my God, have you brought evil upon the widow with whom I am staying by causing the death of her son?"

21 Then he stretched himself upon the child three times. There he called upon YHWH and said, "YHWH my God, please let the life of this child come back into him again."

22 YHWH listened to the voice of Elijah, and the life of the child came back into him and he lived.

23 Then Elijah took the child and brought him down from the upper chamber into the house and he gave him to his mother. Elijah said, "See, your son lives."

24 So the woman said to Elijah, "Now I know that you are a man of God and that the word of YHWH in your mouth is truth."

588 Elijah Returns to Ahab
1 Kings 18:1-19

1 Kings 18

1 Now it happened [after] many days, that the word of YHWH came to Elijah in the third year, "Go, show yourself to Ahab and I will send rain upon the face of the ground."

2 So Elijah went to show himself to Ahab; the famine was severe in Samaria.

3 Ahab summoned Obadiah who was in charge of the house; now Obadiah feared YHWH very much.

4 When Jezebel was cutting [down] the prophets of YHWH, Obadiah took a hundred prophets and he hid them, fifty men to a cave, and he nourished them with bread and water.

5 Then Ahab said to Obadiah, "Go through the land to all the springs of water and to all the wadis; perhaps we may find grass and keep alive horse and mule, and not cut down any animal.

6 So they had divided the land between them to pass through it; Ahab went one way by himself, and Obadiah went another way by himself.

7 Now while Obadiah was on the way, suddenly Elijah met him; he recognized him, fell upon his face and said, "Is this you my lord, Elijah?"

8 He said to him, "It is I. Go, say to your lord, 'Elijah is here.'"

9 But he said, "How have I sinned that you would give your servant into the hand of Ahab to put me to death?

10 As YHWH your God lives, there is no nation or kingdom to which my lord [Ahab] has not sent to seek you out and if they said, 'He is not [here],' then he made the kingdom and the nation swear that no one found you.

11 But now you say, 'Go, say to your lord, Elijah is here.'

12 As soon as I go away from you, the spirit of YHWH will carry you I know not where; and when I come to tell Ahab and he does not find you, then he will slay me though your servant has feared YHWH from my youth.

13 Has it not been told to my lord what I did when Jezebel was slaying the prophets of YHWH, that I hid some of the prophets of YHWH, a hundred [of them] fifty[1] men to a cave, and I nourished them with bread and water?

14 Now you say, 'Go, say to your lord, Elijah is here'; he will slay me."

15 Elijah said, "As YHWH of hosts lives, before whom I stand, today I will surely show myself to him."

16 So Obadiah went to meet Ahab and told him; then Ahab went to meet Elijah.

17 When Ahab saw Elijah, Ahab said to him, "Is this you, you troubler of Israel?"

18 But he said, "I have not troubled Israel. Rather you [have] and the house of your father, by forsaking the commandments of YHWH and going after the Baals.

19 Now send, gather all of Israel to me at Mount Carmel, [with] the four hundred and fifty prophets of Baal and the four hundred prophets of Asherah who eat at the table of Jezebel."

---

[1] Literally, "a hundred men, fifty, fifty men in a cave."

Elijah
Sections 586–603

Number	Title	2 Chronicles	1 Kings
586	Elijah Predicts Drought		17:1-7
587	Elijah and the Widow of Zarephath		17:8-24
588	Elijah Returns to Ahab		18:1-19
589	The Contest on Mount Carmel		18:20-40
590	Elijah Prays for Rain		18:41-46
591	Elijah Flees to Horeb		19:1-18
592	The Call of Elisha		19:19-21
593	Ahab Conquers Syria		20:1-43
594	Ahab and Naboth's Vineyard		21:1-29
595	Jehoshaphat's Kingdom Established	17:2-19	
596	Micaiah Prophesies Defeat	18:1-34	22:1-40
597	Prophet Jehu Rebukes Jehoshaphat	19:1-3	
598	Jehoshaphat Appoints Judges	19:4-11	
599	Victory over Moab and Ammon	20:1-30	
600	The Reign of Jehoshaphat	20:31–21:1	22:41-51
601	The Reign of Ahaziah of Israel		22:52-54
602	The Death of Ahaziah		2 Kings 1:1-18
603	Elijah Taken Up to Heaven		2:1-12

589 The Contest on Mount Carmel
1 Kings 18:20-40

1 Kings 18

20 So Ahab sent [word] to all the Israelites and he gathered the prophets at Mount Carmel.

21 Then Elijah drew near to all the people and said, "How long will you stagger[1] over two opinions? If YHWH is God, follow him; but if Baal, follow him." The people did not answer him a word.

22 Then Elijah said to the people, "I alone am left a prophet of YHWH, yet the prophets of Baal are four hundred and fifty men.

23 So let there be given to us two bulls, and let them choose for themselves one bull, cut it into pieces, and put it upon the wood, but do not let them set a fire. And I will make ready the other bull, put it upon the wood, but will not set a fire.

24 Then you call upon the name of your god and I will call on the name of YHWH, and the god who answers with fire, he is God." All the people answered and said, "It is a good idea."

25 So Elijah said to the prophets of Baal, "Choose for yourselves one bull and make [it] ready, for you are the majority; call upon the name of your god, but set no fire."

26 They took the bull that he had given them and they made [it] ready. Then they called upon the name of Baal from morning until noon, "Baal answer us"; but there was no voice, no one answered. They staggered about the altar that he had made.

27 At noon Elijah began mocking them and said, "Call in a loud voice, for he is a god: either he is thinking, or wandering off, or he is on a journey; perhaps he is sleeping and [must] be wakened."

28 They called out in a loud voice and cut themselves, as was their custom, with swords and spears, until blood poured out upon them.

29 As the noontime passed, they prophesied until the offering up of the oblation, but there was no voice, there was no answer, there was no response.

30 Then Elijah said to all the people, "Come near to me," and all the people drew near to him. He repaired an altar of YHWH that had been torn down.

31 Elijah took twelve stones according to the number of the tribes of the sons of Jacob, to whom the word of YHWH had come, saying, "Israel shall be your name."

32 With the stones he built an altar in the name of YHWH, and he made a trench, as would house two measures of grain, surrounding the altar.

33 He arranged the wood, cut the bull in pieces, and put [it] upon the wood.

34 Then he said, "Fill four jars [with] water and pour [it] upon the offering and upon the wood." He said, "A second time," and they did it a second time. He said, "A third time," and they did it a third time,

35 and the waters flowed around the altar and water also filled up the trench.

36 Now when the oblation was being offered, Elijah the prophet drew near and said, "YHWH, God of Abraham, Isaac, and Israel, let it be known today that you are God in Israel, that I am your servant, and that by your word[2] I have done all these things.

37 Answer me, YHWH, answer me! Let this people know that you, YHWH, are God, and that you have turned their heart around."

38 Then the fire of YHWH fell, and consumed the burnt offering, the wood, the stones, and the dust; it licked up the water that was in the trench.

39 When all the people saw [this] they fell upon their faces and said, "YHWH he is God, YHWH he is God."

40 Then Elijah said to them, "Lay hold of the prophets of Baal, do not let one of them escape." So they took hold of them, and Elijah brought them down to the Wadi Kishon, and there he slaughtered them.

---

[1] Literally, "hop."
[2] Reading the Qere.

590 Elijah Prays for Rain
1 Kings 18:41-46

1 Kings 18

41 Then Elijah said to Ahab, "Go up, eat and drink, for there is the sound of rumbling rain."

42 So Ahab went up to eat and to drink. Elijah went up to the top of Carmel, he bent down toward the earth, and he put his face between his knees.

43 Then he said to his servant, "Go up now, look in the direction of the sea." So he went up, looked, and said, "There is nothing." He [Elijah] said, "Return seven times."

44 It happened at the seventh time he said, "Look, a little cloud like a palm of a man's hand is rising from the sea." Then he said, "Go up and say to Ahab, 'Harness [your chariot] and go down, so that the rain may not detain you.'"

45 In a little while the heavens became dark with clouds and wind, and there was a heavy rain. Ahab rode [away] and went to Jezreel.

46 But the hand of YHWH was upon Elijah; so he girded up his loins and ran before Ahab to the entrance of Jezreel.

591 Elijah Flees to Horeb
1 Kings 19:1-18

1 Kings 19

1 When Ahab told Jezebel all that Elijah had done and how he had slain all the prophets with the sword,

2 Jezebel sent a messenger to Elijah, "Thus may the gods do [to me] and more if by this time tomorrow, I [do not] make your life like the life of one of them."

3 As he was afraid, he rose up, and fled for his life: he came to Beersheba which belongs to Judah, and left his servant there.

4 Then he himself went a day's journey into the wilderness and came and sat under a single¹ broom-bush, and asked that he might die. He said, "Enough now, YHWH. Take my life, for I am no better than my ancestors."

5 So he lay down and slept under [the] single broom-bush. Suddenly, a messenger touched him and said to him, "Rise, eat."

6 He looked, and there near his head was a cake [baked on] hot stones and a jug of water. He ate, drank, and lay down.

7 The messenger of YHWH returned a second time and touched him, and said, "Rise, eat, for the journey [will take] a lot out of you."

8 So he rose, ate and drank, and went on [the] strength of that meal forty days and forty nights as far as the mountain of God, Horeb.

9 Then he came to a cave and passed the night there. Suddenly, the word of YHWH came to him and said to him, "What are you [doing] here, Elijah?"

10 He said, "I have been very zealous for YHWH God of hosts, for the Israelites have forsaken your covenant: they have torn down your altars and they have slain your prophets with the sword. I am left, I alone, and they seek my life to take it."

11 He said, "Go out and stand on the mountain before YHWH." Suddenly YHWH was passing by, and a great and strong wind was tearing apart the mountains and shattering the crags before YHWH; but YHWH was not in the wind. After the wind, [there was] an earthquake, [but] YHWH was not in the earthquake.

12 After the earthquake, [there was] a fire, [but] YHWH was not in the fire. After the fire, a still, small sound.

13 When Elijah heard [it] he wrapped his face in his cloak and went out and stood at the entrance of the cave. There came a voice to him and said, "What are you doing here, Elijah?"

14 He said, "I am very zealous for YHWH God of hosts, for the Israelites have forsaken your covenant: they have torn down your altars and they have slain your prophets with the sword. I am left, I alone, and they seek my life to take it."

15 Then YHWH said to him, "Go, return on your way to the wilderness of Damascus. When you arrive you shall anoint Hazael as king over Aram.

16 Moreover you shall anoint Jehu son of Nimshi as king over Israel, and you shall anoint Elisha son of Shaphat from Abel-meholah as prophet in your place.

17 It shall be that anyone who escapes from the sword of Hazael, Jehu shall kill, and anyone who escapes from the sword of Jehu, Elisha shall kill.

18 But I will leave seven thousand in Israel, all the knees that have not bowed down to Baal and every mouth that has not kissed him."

---

[1] Reading the Qere.

592 The Call of Elisha
1 Kings 19:19-21

1 Kings 19

19 So he went from there and found Elisha son of Shaphat. He was ploughing with twelve yoke [of oxen] in front of him; and he was with the twelfth when Elijah passed by him and threw his cloak over to him.

20 Whereupon he left behind the oxen and ran after Elijah, and said, "Please, let me kiss my father and my mother, then I will follow you." So he said to him, "Go, return, for what have I done to you?"

21 He returned from following him, took the yoke of oxen and he sacrificed them. With the [wooden] gear of the oxen he boiled the flesh and gave [it] to the people and they ate. Then he rose, followed after Elijah and served him.

593 Ahab Conquers Syria
1 Kings 20:1-43

1 Kings 20

1 Now Ben-hadad king of Aram gathered all his army; there were thirty-two kings with him [along with] horses and chariots, and he went up and besieged Samaria and he waged war against it.

2 Next he sent messengers to Ahab king of Israel, into the city,

3 and said to him, "Thus says Ben-hadad, 'Your silver and your gold are mine, also your wives and your children, the fairest are mine.'"

4 The king of Israel said in response, "As you say my lord the king, I and all that I have are yours."

5 The messengers returned [again] and they said, "Thus says Ben-hadad, 'Since I sent to you saying, "You must give to me your silver and your gold, your wives and your children,"

6 accordingly, at this time tomorrow I will send my servants to you and they shall search your house and the houses of your servants; and everything that is desirable in your eyes they will pick up in their hand[s] and take away.'"

7 Then the king of Israel called all the elders of the land and said, "Know and see that this [man] is looking for trouble! For he sent to me for my wives and for my children, and for my silver and for my gold and I did not refuse him."

8 Then all the elders and all the people said to him, "Do not obey and do not consent!"

9 So he said to the messengers of Ben-hadad, "Say to my lord the king, 'Everything you commanded your servant at the beginning I will do, but this thing I am not able to do." The messengers went [away] and they brought him [the] word.

10 Ben-hadad sent to him and said, "May [the] gods do so to me and more, if the dust of Samaria will be [enough] handfuls for all the people who follow me."[1]

11 Then the king of Israel said in response, "Tell [him], 'One who dons armor [for battle] should not boast like one who removes [it after battle].'"

12 Now when he heard this message—he had been drinking [with] the kings in the tents—he said to his servants, "Position yourselves [for battle]," and they positioned themselves against the city.

13 Whereupon, a certain prophet drew near to Ahab king of Israel, and said, "Thus says YHWH, 'Have you seen all this great horde? Look, I will give it into your hands today and you shall know that I am YHWH.'"

14 Ahab said, "By whom?" He said, "Thus says YHWH: 'By the young men of the district officers.'" Then he said, "Who shall begin the battle?" He said, "You [shall]."

15 Then he mustered the young men of the district officers, and there were two hundred thirty-two; and after them he mustered all the people, all the Israelites, seven thousand.

16 They went out at noon while Ben-hadad was drinking [himself] drunk in the tents, he and the thirty-two kings supporting him.

17 The young men of the district officers went out first. Ben-hadad had sent out [scouts] and they reported to him, "Men have come out of Samaria."

18 Then he said, "If they have come out for peace, take them alive; and if they have come out for battle, take them alive."

19 But these had already gone out of the city: the young men of the district officers and the army that [came out] after them.

20 Each man struck down his opponent: Aram fled and Israel pursued them. But Ben-hadad king of Aram escaped on a horse as well as [some] horsemen.

21 Then the king of Israel went out and struck down horse and chariot and inflicted a great slaughter upon Aram.

22 The prophet drew near to the king of Israel and said to him, "Go, strengthen yourself, and know and see what you must do, since at the turn of the year the king of Aram will come up against you."

23 Then the servants of the king of Aram said to him, "Their god is a god of the mountains, therefore they were stronger than we; but rather let us fight with them on level ground, surely we shall be stronger than they.

24 Moreover do this thing: remove the kings, each from his position, and put governors in their place.

25 Then you shall measure for yourself an army like the army you have lost— [matching] horse for horse and chariot for chariot—then we will fight them on the level ground and surely we shall be stronger than they." He heeded their voice and did so.

26 At the turn of the year Ben-hadad mustered Aram and went up to Aphek for battle with Israel.

27 Now the Israelites had been mustered and provisioned and they went to challenge them. The Israelites encamped opposite them like two little flocks of goats while Aram filled up the [low]land.

28 A man of God drew near and said to the king of Israel, he said, "Thus says YHWH, 'Since Aram said: "YHWH is a god of the mountains but not a god of the valleys," I shall give all this great horde into your hand and you will know that I am YHWH.'"

29 Now these [forces] were encamped opposite those [forces] for seven days. Then on the seventh day the battle began and the Israelites cut down Aram, one hundred thousand foot soldiers in one day.

30 Those remaining fled to the city of Aphek but the wall fell upon the twenty-seven thousand men remaining; then Ben-hadad fled and entered the city [into] an inner chamber.

31 Then his servants said to him, "Look, we have heard that the kings of the house of Israel, that they are benevolent kings, so let us put sackcloth on our loins and cords on our heads and let us go out to the king of Israel; perhaps he will spare your life."

32 So they tied sackcloths on their loins and cords on their heads and came to the king of Israel, and said, "Your servant Ben-hadad says, 'Spare my life.'" Then he [Ahab] said, "Does he still live? He is my brother."

33 Now the men were looking for a sign and they quickly picked it up from him and said, "[Yes,] Ben-hadad is your brother." Whereupon he said, "Go and fetch him." So Ben-hadad came out to him and he had him come up into the chariot.

34 He said to him, "I will return the cities that my father took from your father and you may establish street markets for yourself in Damascus just as my father has established [them] in Samaria. I will set you free according to the treaty." So he made a treaty with him and set him free.

35 Now a certain man from a prophetic guild said to his comrade by the word of YHWH, "Strike me!" But the man refused to strike him.

36 Then he said to him, "Because you have not heeded the voice of YHWH, now as you go away from me the lion will strike you." He then went away from him and the lion found him and struck him down.

37 So he found another man and said, "Now strike me!" The man struck him, hitting and wounding [him].

38 The prophet went and stood [waiting] for the king along the road, and he disguised himself with a bandage over his eyes.

39 Now as the king passed by, he cried out to the king and said, "Your servant went into the heart of the battle, and a man turned and brought a man to me, and said, 'Guard this man. If he is missing, then it will be your life for his life, or else you must weigh out a talent of silver.'

40 While your servant was about his business here and there, he was gone." Thereupon the king of Israel said to him, "So shall your judgment be: you have fixed [it for yourself]."

41 Then he quickly pulled the bandage away from his eyes and the king of Israel recognized him, that he was one of the prophets.

42 He said to him, "Thus says YHWH, 'Since you have let the man go whom I banned, it will be your life for his life and your people for his people.'"

43 The king of Israel set out for his house sullen and dejected and came to Samaria.

---

[1] Literally, "are at my feet."

Divided Monarchy-2
Sections 590–609

Number	Title	2 Chronicles	1 Kings
590	Elijah Prays for Rain		18:41-46
591	Elijah Flees to Horeb		19:1-18
592	The Call of Elisha		19:19-21
593	Ahab Conquers Syria		20:1-43
594	Ahab and Naboth's Vineyard		21:1-29
595	Jehoshaphat Established	17:2-19	
596	Micaiah Prophesies Defeat	18:1-34	22:1-40
597	Prophet Jehu Rebukes Jehos . . .	19:1-3	
598	Jehoshaphat Appoints Judges	19:4-11	
599	Victory over Moab and Ammon	20:1-30	
600	The Reign of Jehoshaphat	20:31–21:1	22:41-51
601	The Reign of Ahaziah of Israel		22:52-54
602	The Death of Ahaziah		2 Kings 1:1-18
603	Elijah Taken Up to Heaven		2:1-12
604	Elisha Succeeds Elijah		2:12d-25
605	The Reign of Jehoram of Israel		3:1-3
606	Elisha Predicts Victory over Moab		3:4-27
607	The Widow's Oil		4:1-7
608	Elisha and a Shunammite Woman		4:8-37
609	Elisha's Miracles for the Prophets		4:38-44

228

594 Ahab and Naboth's Vineyard
1 Kings 21:1-29

1 Kings 21

1 Now these things happened afterwards. There was a vineyard belonging to Naboth the Jezreelite, that was in Jezreel beside the palace of Ahab king of Samaria.

2 Ahab spoke to Naboth, "Give me your vineyard so it can become a green garden for me since it is right next to my house; and I will give you a better vineyard in its place; [or] if it is good in your eyes, I will give you its price in silver."

3 But Naboth said to Ahab, "May YHWH forbid that I should give you my ancestral inheritance."

4 So Ahab went to his house sullen and dejected over the reply that Naboth the Jezreelite had spoken to him [when] he had said, "I will not give you my ancestral inheritance." So he lay on his bed, turned away his face and did not eat any food.

5 Then Jezebel his wife came to him, and spoke to him, "What is this? Your spirit is resentful and you will not eat food."

6 He spoke to her, "[It is] because I spoke to Naboth the Jezreelite and said to him, 'Give me your vineyard for silver, or if you prefer I will give you a vineyard in its place.' But he said, 'I will not give you my vineyard.'"

7 Jezebel his wife said to him, "You must now exercise kingship over Israel. Get up, eat [some] food and let your heart be joyful. I will give you the vineyard of Naboth the Jezreelite."

8 So she wrote letters in Ahab's name, sealed them with his seal, and dispatched the letters[1] to the elders and to the nobles who were living with Naboth in his city.

9 She wrote in the letters: "Proclaim a fast, and seat Naboth at the head of the people.

10 Then seat two scoundrels[2] opposite him, and let them testify against him saying, 'You have blessed[3] God and king! Then take him out and stone him so that he dies!'"

11 So the men of his city—the elders and the nobles, those who dwelt in his city—did just as Jezebel had ordered, just as it was written in the letters that she had sent them.

12 They proclaimed a fast and they seated Naboth at the head of the people.

13 Then the two scoundrels came in and sat opposite him; the scoundrels testi-fied against Naboth in the presence of the people saying, "Naboth has blessed God and king!" Then they took him outside the city and stoned him with stones so that he died.

14 Then they sent [a message] to Jezebel: "Naboth has been stoned and he has died."

15 As soon as Jezebel heard that Naboth had been stoned and was dead, Jezebel said to Ahab, "Get up! Take possession of the vineyard of Naboth the Jezreelite that he refused to give you in exchange for silver, for Naboth is no longer alive, for [he is] dead."

16 So when Ahab heard that Naboth was dead, Ahab arose to go down to the vineyard of Naboth the Jezreelite to take possession of it.

17 Then the word of YHWH came to Elijah the Tishbite,

18 "Arise, go down to confront Ahab king of Israel who is in Samaria. Look, he is in Naboth's vineyard where he has gone down to take possession.

19 Then you shall speak to him, "Thus says YHWH, 'Have you murdered and also taken possession?'" You shall say to him, "Thus says YHWH, 'In the place where the dogs lapped up the blood of Naboth, the dogs will lap up your blood, yours indeed.'"

20 Then Ahab said to Elijah, "Have you found me my enemy?" Whereupon he said, "I have found [you]. Because you have sold yourself to do what is evil in the eyes of YHWH,

21 I am here to bring[4] disaster on you. I will annihilate you and will cut off from Ahab [every] male, both bound and free, in Israel.

22 I will make your house like the house of Jeroboam son of Nebat and like the house of Baasha son of Ahijah, because of the provocation that you have provoked and [because] you have caused Israel to sin."

23 YHWH also spoke concerning Jezebel, "The dogs shall eat Jezebel within the bounds of Jezreel.

24 Anyone belonging to Ahab [who] dies in the city, the dogs shall eat; and whoever dies in the country, the birds of the air shall eat."

25 (Surely there was never anyone like Ahab who sold himself to do the evil in the eyes of YHWH that Jezebel his wife had incited him to [do].

26 He acted very abominably by going after the idols just as the Amorites had done, whom YHWH had dispossessed before the Israelites.)

27 So when Ahab heard these words he tore his clothes and put sackcloth over his skin. He fasted, lay in sackcloth, and walked about subdued.

28 Then the word of YHWH came to Elijah the Tishbite,

29 "Have you seen how Ahab has humbled himself before me? Because he has humbled himself before me, I will not bring disaster during his days [but] during his son's days I will bring disaster on his house."

---

[1] Reading Kethib in spite of Qere.
[2] Literally, "sons of Belial."
[3] A euphemism for the impossible "curse God."
[4] Reading the Qere.

595 Jehoshaphat's Kingdom Established
2 Chron 17:2-19

2 Chron 17

2 He put a military force in all the fortified cities of Judah and he put deputies in the land of Judah and in the cities of Ephraim that Asa his father had captured.

3 Now YHWH was with Jehoshaphat because he walked in the former ways of David his [fore]father, and had not sought the Baals,

4 rather, he sought the God of his ancestors and walked in his commandments and not according to the deeds of Israel.

5 So YHWH established the kingdom in his hand and all Judah gave tribute to Jehoshaphat, so he had great riches and honor.

6 His heart was exalted in the ways of YHWH, and moreover, he removed the high places and the asherim from Judah.

7 In the third year of his being king he sent his officials, Ben-hail, Obadiah, Zechariah, Nethanel and Micaiah, to teach in the cities of Judah.

8 With them were the Levites: Shemaiah, Nethaniah, Zebadiah, Asahel, Shemiramot, Jehonathan, Adonijah, Tobijah, and Tob-adonijah the Levites, and with them Elishama and Jehoram, the priests.

9 They taught in Judah and the Book of the Torah of YHWH was with them; they went among all the cities of Judah and taught the people.

10 Then a dread of YHWH [fell] upon all the kingdoms of the lands that surrounded Judah so they did not go to war with Jehoshaphat.

11 Some of the Philistines were bringing presents and silver as tribute to Jehoshaphat; also the Arabs were bringing him flocks, seventy-seven thousand rams and seventy-seven thousand he-goats.

12 Now Jehoshaphat was growing exceedingly great and he built fortresses and store-cities in Judah.

13 He had great works in the cities of Judah and had soldiers, valiant warriors, in Jerusalem.

14 This was their muster according to their ancestral houses: for Judah, the commanders of the thousands, Adnah their commander, and with him three hundred thousand valiant warriors;

15 next to him, Jehohanan the commander, and with him two hundred eighty thousand;

16 next to him, Amasiah son of Zichri, a volunteer for YHWH, and with him two hundred thousand valiant men;

17 from Benjamin, a valiant warrior Eliada, and with him armed with bow and shield, two hundred thousand men;

18 next to him Jehozabad, and with him were one hundred eighty thousand men equipped for war.

19 These were serving the king beside those whom the king had put in the fortified cities throughout all Judah.

Jehoshaphat
Sections 595–600

Number	Title	2 Chronicles	1 Kings
595	Jehoshaphat Established	17:2-19	
596	Micaiah Prophecies Defeat	18:1-34	22:1-40
597	Prophet Jehu Rebukes Jehoshaphat	19:1-3	
598	Jehoshaphat Appoints Judges	19:4-11	
599	Victory over Moab and Ammon	20:1-30	
600	The Reign of Jehoshaphat	20:31–21:1	22:41-51

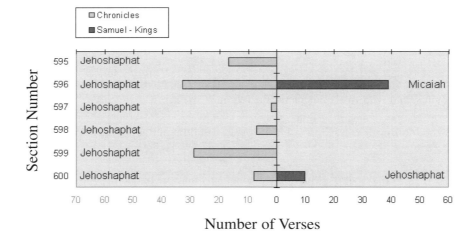

Number of Verses

596 Micaiah Prophesies the Defeat of Ahab and Jehoshaphat
2 Chron 18:1-34 // 1 Kings 22:1-40

2 Chronicles 18

1 Now Jehoshaphat had great riches and honor, and he formed a marriage alliance with Ahab.

2 At the end of [some] years he went down to Ahab at Samaria, and Ahab slaughtered sheep and oxen in great number for him and for the people who were with him. And he incited him to go up to Ramoth-gilead.

3 Ahab king of Israel said to Jehoshaphat the king of Judah, "Will you go along with me to Ramoth-gilead?" And he said to him, "I am as you [are], my people as your people, my horses as your horses."

4 Then Jehoshaphat said to the king of Israel, "Please seek today the word of YHWH."

5 So the king of Israel gathered together the prophets, four hundred of them, and he said to them, "Shall we go up to Ramoth-gilead for battle or shall I hold back?" They said, "Go up; God will deliver [it] into the hand of the king!"

6 But Jehoshaphat said, "Is there not still another prophet of YHWH here that we may inquire of him?"

7 The king of Israel said to Jehoshaphat, "There is still one other man from whom we may inquire of YHWH; but I hate him because he never prophesies good about me, but always for bad—he is Micaiah son of Imla." Jehoshaphat said, "Let not the king say so."

8 Then the king of Israel called to a certain official¹ and said, "Hurry [for] Micaiah the son of Imla!"

9 Now the king of Israel and Jehoshaphat the king of Judah were each sitting on his throne dressed in [their] robes, at the threshing-floor at the entrance of the gate of Samaria, while all the prophets were prophesying before them.

1 Kings 22

1 Three years went by [and] there was no war between Aram and Israel.

2 However in the third year Jehoshaphat king of Judah went down to the king of Israel.

3 The king of Israel said to his servants, "Do you know that Ramoth-gilead belongs to us, yet we do nothing about taking it back from the hand of the king of Aram?"

4 Then he said to Jehoshaphat, "Will you go with me for battle at Ramoth-gilead?" Jehoshaphat said to the king of Israel, "I am as you [are], my people as your people, my horses as your horses."

5 Then Jehoshaphat said to the king of Israel, "Please seek today the word of YHWH."

6 So the king of Israel gathered together the prophets, about four hundred of them, and he said to them, "Shall I go up against Ramoth-gilead for battle, or shall I hold back?" They said, "Go up; my Lord will deliver [it] into the hand of the king!"

7 But Jehoshaphat said, "Is there not still another prophet of YHWH here that we may inquire of him?"

8 The king of Israel said to Jehoshaphat, "There is still one other man from whom we may inquire of YHWH; but I hate him because he will not prophesy good about me, only bad—-Micaiah son of Imlah." Jehoshaphat said, "Let not the king say so."

9 Then the king of Israel called to a certain official² and said, "Hurry quickly [for] Micaiah the son of Imlah!"

10 The king of Israel and Jehoshaphat the king of Judah were each sitting on his throne dressed in [their] robes, at the threshing-floor at the entrance of the gate of Samaria, while all the prophets were prophesying before them.

10 Zedekiah son of Chenaanah made for himself horns of iron, and he said, "Thus says YHWH, 'With these you shall gore Aram until they are finished.'"

11 Now all the prophets were prophesying the same, "Go up to Ramoth-gilead and succeed! YHWH will deliver [it] into the hand of the king."

12 The messenger who had gone to summon Micaiah spoke to him, "Look now, the words of the prophets are at one, favorable to the king, so let your word [be] like one of them, and speak [something] good."

13 But Micaiah said, "As YHWH lives, surely whatever my God shall say, that I will speak."

14 When he came to the king, the king said to him, "Micah, shall we go up to Ramoth-gilead for battle or shall I hold back?" He said, "Go up and succeed (plural), so that they may be delivered into your hand!"

15 Then the king said to him, "How many times must I make you swear that you will speak to me nothing but the truth in the name of YHWH?"

16 Then he said, "I saw all Israel scattered on the mountains, like sheep for whom there is no shepherd; and YHWH said, 'There are no masters for these; let them return, each to his own house in peace.'"

17 Whereupon the king of Israel said to Jehoshaphat, "Did I not say to you, 'He does not prophesy good about me, but only bad?'"

18 Then he said, "Therefore, hear (plural) the word of YHWH, 'I saw YHWH sitting on his throne, and the whole host of heaven standing on his right and on his left.'

19 Then YHWH said, 'Who will entice Ahab king of Israel that he may go up and fall at Ramoth-gilead?' And this one said this and that one said that.

20 One spirit came forward and stood before YHWH and said, 'I will entice him.' YHWH said to it, 'By what means?'

21 It said, 'I shall go forth and become a spirit of deception in the mouth of all his prophets.' And he said, 'You shall entice him and you shall also succeed. Go forth and do it.'

11 Zedekiah son of Chenaanah made for himself horns of iron, and he said, "Thus says YHWH, 'With these you shall gore Aram until they are finished.'"

12 Now all the prophets were prophesying the same, "Go up to Ramoth-gilead and succeed! YHWH will deliver [it] into the hand of the king."

13 The messenger who had gone to summon Micaiah spoke to him, "Look now, the words of the prophets are at one, favorable to the king, let your word³ [be] like a word from one of them, and speak [something] good."

14 But Micaiah said, "As YHWH lives, surely whatever YHWH shall say to me, that I will speak."

15 When he came to the king, the king said to him, "Micaiah, shall we go up to Ramoth-gilead for battle or shall we hold back?" And he said to him: "You go up and succeed (singular), and YHWH will deliver [it] into the hand of the king!"

16 The king said to him, "How many times must I make you swear that you will speak to me nothing but the truth in the name of YHWH?"

17 Then he said, "I saw all Israel being scattered to the mountains, like sheep for whom there is no shepherd; and YHWH said, 'There are no masters for these; let them return, each to his own house in peace.'"

18 Whereupon the king of Israel said to Jehoshaphat, "Did I not say to you, 'He does not prophesy good about me, but only bad?'"

19 Then he said, "Therefore, hear (singular) the word of YHWH, 'I saw YHWH sitting on his throne, and the whole host of heaven standing about him on his right and on his left.'"

20 Then YHWH said, 'Who will entice Ahab so that he may go up and fall at Ramoth-gilead?' One said in this way, and one said in that way.

21 One spirit came forward and stood before YHWH and said, 'I will entice him.' YHWH said to it, 'By what means?'

22 It said, 'I shall go forth and be a spirit of deception in the mouth of all his prophets.' And he said, 'You shall entice him and you shall also succeed. Go forth and do it.'

22 Now see, YHWH has put a spirit of deception in the mouth of these your prophets, and YHWH has spoken evil about you."

23 Then Zedekiah son of Chenaanah came up and he struck Micaiah on the cheek. He said, "Which way did the spirit of YHWH pass from me to speak to you?"

24 Micaiah said, "You will surely see [it] on that day when you go into the inner room to hide yourself."

25 Then the king of Israel said, "Take (plural) Micaiah and return him to Amon the governor of the city, and to Joash son of the king.

26 And you will say (plural), 'Thus says the king: put this one in the prison house; and let them eat the bread of oppression and the water of oppression, until I return in peace.'"

27 But Micaiah said, "If you return in peace, YHWH has not spoken by me." He said, "Hear [this] all peoples."

28 So the king of Israel and Jehoshaphat the king of Judah went up to Ramoth-gilead.

29 The king of Israel said to Jehoshaphat, "Disguise yourself and go into battle, and you wear your robes." So the king of Israel disguised himself and they went into battle.

30 Now the king of Aram had ordered the officers of the chariots with him, "Do not engage in battle the small [or] the great, except the king of Israel alone."

31 So when the officers of the chariots saw Jehoshaphat, they said, "This is the king of Israel"; so they surrounded him to do battle. But Jehoshaphat cried out and YHWH helped him; God lured them away from him.

32 When the officers of the chariots saw that [he] was not the king of Israel, they turned back from following him.

33 But a man drew his bow at random, yet it struck the king of Israel between the solderings and [his] breastplate; so he said to [his] charioteer, "Turn your hand to lead me out of the camp, for I am wounded."

23 Now see, YHWH has put a spirit of deception into the mouth of all these your prophets, and YHWH has spoken evil about you."

24 Then Zedekiah son of Chenaanah came up and he struck Micaiah on the cheek. He said, "Which way did the spirit of YHWH pass from me to speak to you?"

25 Micaiah said, "You will surely see [it] on that day when you go into the inner room to hide yourself."

26 Then the king of Israel said, "Take (singular) Micaiah and return him to Amon the governor of the city, and to Joash son of the king.

27 And you will say (singular), 'Thus says the king: put this one in the prison house; and let them eat the bread of oppression and the water of oppression, until I arrive in peace.'"

28 Then Micaiah said, "If you truly return in peace, YHWH has not spoken by me." He said, "Hear [this] all peoples."

29 So the king of Israel and Jehoshaphat the king of Judah went up [to] Ramoth-gilead.

30 The king of Israel said to Jehoshaphat, "Disguise yourself and go into battle, and you wear your robes." So the king of Israel disguised himself and went into battle.

31 Now the king of Aram had ordered the thirty-two chariot officers of the chariots with him, "Do not engage in battle the small [or] the great, except the king of Israel alone."

32 So when the officers of the chariots saw Jehoshaphat, they said, "Surely he is the king of Israel," so they turned against him to do battle and Jehoshaphat cried out.

33 When the officers of the chariots saw that he [was] not the king of Israel, they turned back from following him.

34 But a man drew his bow at random, yet it struck the king of Israel between the solderings and [his] breastplate; so he said to his charioteer, "Turn your hand and lead me out of the camp, for I am wounded."

34 The battle escalated on that day and the king of Israel was propping himself up in his chariot in view of Aram until the evening; then he died at the going down of the sun.

35 The battle escalated on that day and the king was propped up in his chariot in view of Aram; he died in the evening and the blood from the wound flowed into the inside of the chariot.

36 Then a shout went through the camp as the sun went down, "Each man to his city, each man to his land!"

37 So the king died and came to Samaria and they buried the king in Samaria.

38 As they washed down the chariot by the pool of Samaria, the dogs lapped [up] his blood, and the prostitutes bathed [in it], according to the word of YHWH that he had spoken.

39 Now the rest of the acts of Ahab and all that he did, the house of ivory that he built, all the cities that he built, are they not written in the Book of the Chronicles of the Kings of Israel?

40 When Ahab lay down to rest with his ancestors, Ahaziah his son became king in his place.

---

[1] Literally, "eunuch."
[2] Literally, "eunuch."
[3] Reading the Qere.

597 The Prophet Jehu Rebukes Jehoshaphat
2 Chron 19:1-3

2 Chronicles 19

1 Then Jehoshaphat king of Judah returned to his house in peace, to Jerusalem.

2 But Jehu son of Hanani the seer went out to meet him and he said to King Jehoshaphat, "Should one help the wicked and love those who hate YHWH? For this, wrath is upon you from YHWH.

3 Nevertheless, [some] good things have been found in you since you annihilated the asherim from the land and dedicated your heart to seek God."

598 Jehoshaphat Appoints Judges
2 Chron 19:4-11; Deut 1:16-17; 16:18-20; 10:17

2 Chronicles 19

4 Now Jehoshaphat dwelt in Jerusalem; then he went out again among the people from Beer-sheba to the hill country of Ephraim, and he brought them back to YHWH the God of their ancestors.

5 Next he appointed judges in the land, in all the fortified cities in Judah, city by city,

6 and he said to the judges, "See [to] what you are doing, for you do not judge for humans but for YHWH and [he] is with you in pronouncing judgment.

7 Now let the dread of YHWH be upon you: take care and act, for there is no injustice with YHWH our God, no partiality and no taking of bribes."

8 Further in Jerusalem Jehoshaphat appointed some Levites, priests and ancestral chiefs of Israel for judgment for YHWH and for disputes. Then they returned to Jerusalem.

9 He commanded them saying, "This is how you shall act: in fear of YHWH, in faithfulness and with a whole heart.

10 Every dispute which shall come to you from your kinfolk who live in their cities concerning blood-guilt, between Torah or commandment, statutes or judgment, you shall warn them so that they may not incur guilt before YHWH and his wrath be upon you and upon your kinfolk; if you do this, you shall not incur guilt.

11 See Amariah the chief priest is over you in all matters concerning YHWH, and Zebadiah son of Ishmael the leader of the house of Judah in all matters concerning the king; and the Levites will be officers before you. Act courageously and YHWH will be with the good."

Deuteronomy 1

Parallels concerning justice

16 I commanded your judges at that time, "Hear [cases] between your kinfolk and judge justly between each person and their neighbor whether kinfolk or resident alien.

17 You shall not show partiality in judgment: you shall hear the small and the great alike; you shall not dread any person for the judgment belongs to God. If a matter is too difficult for you, bring it to me and I will hear it.

Deuteronomy 16
18 You shall appoint for yourself judges and officers in all the city-gates which YHWH your God is giving you for your tribes; and they shall give just judgments for the people.

19 You shall not distort judgment, you shall not show partiality; you shall not take a bribe for a bribe blinds the eyes of the wise and perverts the words of the just.

20 Justice, justice you shall pursue so that you might live and possess the land that YHWH your God is giving you.

Deuteronomy 10
17 For YHWH your God is the God of gods and the Lord of lords, the deity who is great and powerful and awesome, who does not show partiality nor take a bribe.

599 The Victory over Moab and Ammon
2 Chron 20:1-30

2 Chronicles 20

1 After this the Moabites, Ammonites and with them some Ammonim came against Jehoshaphat to do battle.

2 So they came and told Jehoshaphat, "A great horde is approaching from beyond-the-sea, from Aram: right now they are at Hazazon-tamar, that is, En-gedi."

3 Jehoshaphat was afraid and he set himself to inquire of YHWH; and he proclaimed a fast over all Judah.

4 Judah gathered together to seek [help] from YHWH; also from all the towns of Judah they came to seek YHWH.

5 Then Jehoshaphat stood in the assembly of Judah and Jerusalem in the house of YHWH, in front of the new court-yard,

6 and he said, "YHWH God of our ancestors, are you not the God in heaven? Do you not rule over all the kingdoms of the nations? In your hand [are] power and might so that none can withstand you.

7 Did you not our God, dispossess the inhabitants of this land from before your people Israel, and give it over to the offspring of Abraham your friend forever?

8 They settled in it and they have built you a temple for your name in it, saying,

9 "If disaster comes upon us, the sword of judgment or pestilence or famine, we will stand before this house and before you—for your name is in this house—and we will cry to you out of our distress and you will hear and you will deliver.

10 Now see the Ammonites and the Moabites and [the people of] Mount Seir, whom you did not allow Israel to go among when they were coming from the land of Egypt, for they turned away from them and did not destroy them.

11 But now they are repaying us, coming to drive us out of your possession which you made our possession.

12 O our God, will you not give judgment against them? For we have no power before this great horde that is coming against us; and we do not know what we should do but our eyes are upon you."

13 All Judah was standing before YHWH, even their little ones, their womenfolk and their children.

14 Jehaziel son of Zechariah, son of Beniah, son of Jeiel, son of Mattaniah, [was] a Levite of the Asaphites, [and] the spirit of YHWH came upon him in the midst of the assembly.

15 He said, "Give heed all Judah and inhabitants of Jerusalem and King Jehoshaphat, thus YHWH says to you, 'Do not be afraid, and do not be dismayed before this great horde, for the battle is not yours but God's.

16 Tomorrow go down against them; see, they will be coming up by the Ascent of Ziz: you will find them at the end of the wadi facing the Wilderness of Jeruel.

17 It is not for you to do battle on this [occasion]. Take your position: stand and see YHWH's deliverance of you O Judah and Jerusalem. Do not be afraid and do not be dismayed. Go out tomorrow before them and YHWH will be with you.'"

18 Then Jehoshaphat bowed down with his face to the ground and all Judah and the inhabitants of Jerusalem fell [down] before YHWH to worship YHWH.

19 The Levites rose up, some Kohathites and some Korahites, to praise YHWH the God of Israel with a very loud voice.

20 Then they started early in the morning and sent out for the Wilderness of Tekoa and as they set out Jehoshaphat stood and said, "Hear me, O Judah and inhabitants of Jerusalem: trust in YHWH your God and you will be upheld; trust in his prophets and prosper!"

21 Moreover, he took counsel with the people and he appointed singers for YHWH to praise [him] in holy array as they went out before the army, saying, "Give thanks to YHWH, for his loving-kindness lasts forever!"

22 At the time when they began singing and praising, YHWH put liers-in-wait against the Ammonites and Moabites and people of Mount Seir who had come against Judah, and they were routed.

23 Then the Ammonites and Moabites took their stand against the inhabitants of Mount Seir to exterminate and annihilate them; when they had finished off the inhabitants of Seir, each one helped to destroy his neighbor.

24 Judah came to the lookout over the wilderness and when they turned toward the horde, there were their corpses fallen to the ground; there was no escape.

25 When Jehoshaphat and his people came to plunder their booty, they found among them in abundance, goods, corpses and precious objects; and they stripped them until there was nothing to carry. They spent three days plundering the booty for it was abundant.

26 On the fourth day they assembled in the Valley of Beracah, for there they blessed YHWH; therefore, the name of this place is called the Valley of Beracah till today.

27 Then all the men of Judah and Jerusalem returned, Jehoshaphat at their head, to return to Jerusalem with joy for YHWH had made them rejoice over their enemies.

28 So they came to Jerusalem with harps, lyres, and trumpets, to the house of YHWH.

29 The dread of God came upon all the kingdoms of the lands when they heard that YHWH had battled against the enemies of Israel.

30 So the kingdom of Jehoshaphat was quiet and his God gave him rest all around.

600 The Reign of Jehoshaphat
2 Chron 20:31–21:1 // 1 Kings 22:41-51

2 Chronicles 20	*1 Kings 22*
31 Jehoshaphat became king over Judah; [he was] thirty-five years old when he became king, and he was king for twenty-five years in Jerusalem. The name of his mother was Azubah daughter of Shilhi.	41 Jehoshaphat son of Asa became king over Judah in the fourth year of Ahab king of Israel.
	42 Jehoshaphat was thirty-five years old when he became king, and he was king for twenty-five years in Jerusalem. The name of his mother was Azubah daughter of Shilhi.

32 He walked in the way of his father Asa, and he did not turn aside from it, doing what was right in the eyes of YHWH.

33 Nevertheless the high places were not removed: and the people still did not direct their heart towards the God of their ancestors.

34 Now the rest of the acts of Jehoshaphat, the first and the last, indeed they are written in the Acts of Jehu son of Hanani, which has been included in the Book of the Kings of Israel.

35 Afterwards, Jehoshaphat king of Judah allied himself with Ahaziah king of Israel; he acted wickedly.

36 He allied himself with him to make ships to go to Tarshish, and they made ships at Ezion-geber.

37 Then Eliezer son of Dodavahu of Mareshah prophesied against Jehoshaphat, saying, "Since you have allied yourself with Ahaziah, YHWH will destroy your work." So the ships were wrecked and were prevented from going to Tarshish.

21:1 When Jehoshaphat lay down to rest with his ancestors, he was buried with his ancestors in the city of David and Jehoram his son became king in his place.

43 He walked in all the ways of Asa his father; he did not turn aside from it, doing what was right in the eyes of YHWH.

44 Nevertheless the high places were not removed: the people were still sacrificing and offering incense on the high places.

45 Jehoshaphat also made peace with the king of Israel.

46 Now the rest of the acts of Jehoshaphat, and his valor that he showed and how he did in battle, are they not written in the Book of the Chronicles of the Kings of Judah?

47 The rest of the male votaries who remained in the days of his father Asa, he exterminated from the land.

48 There was no king in Edom; a deputy was king.

49 And Jehoshaphat made[1] Tarshish ships to go to Ophir for gold; but he did not get [there] because the boats were wrecked[2] at Ezion-geber.

50 Thereupon Ahaziah son of Ahab said to Jehoshaphat, "Let my servants go with your servants in ships." But Jehoshaphat did not consent.

51 When Jehoshaphat lay down to rest with his ancestors, he was buried with his ancestors in the city of David his [fore]father, and Jehoram his son became king in his place.

---

[1] Reading with Qere.
[2] Reading with Qere.

601 The Reign of Ahaziah of Israel
1 Kings 22:52-54

1 Kings 22

52 Ahaziah son of Ahab became king over Israel in Samaria in the seventeenth year of Jehoshaphat king of Judah, and he was king over Israel for two years.

53 He did what was evil in the eyes of YHWH, and walked in the way of his father and in the way of his mother, and in the way of Jeroboam son of Nebat who had caused Israel to sin.

54 He served the Baal and bowed to him, and he provoked YHWH the God of Israel to anger, like all that his father had done.

602 The Death of Ahaziah
2 Kings 1:1-18

2 Kings 1

1 Moab rebelled against Israel after the death of Ahab.

2 Now Ahaziah fell through the window-lattice in his upper chamber that was in Samaria and became sick; so he sent messengers and said to them, "Go, inquire of Baal-zebub the god of Ekron whether I shall recover from this sickness."

3 But the messenger of YHWH spoke to Elijah the Tishbite, "Rise, go up to meet the messengers of the king of Samaria, and say to them, 'Is it because there is no God at all in Israel that you are going to inquire of Baal-zebub the god of Ekron?'

4 Therefore, thus says YHWH, 'You shall not come down from the bed to which you went up, for you shall surely die.'" So Elijah went.

5 When the messengers returned to him, he [Ahaziah] said to them, "Why have you returned?"

6 They said to him, "A man came up to meet us, and he said to us, 'Go, return to the king who sent you, and tell him, Thus says YHWH: Is there no God at all in Israel that you send to inquire of Baal-zebub the god of Ekron? Therefore you shall not come down from the bed to which you went up, but you shall surely die.'"

7 Then he said to them, "What type of man [was he] who came up to meet you and spoke to you these words?"

8 They said to him, "A hairy man, girded with a leather belt around his waist." He said, "It is Elijah the Tishbite!"

9 Then he sent to him a captain of fifty and his fifty men, and he went up to him, and there he was sitting on top of the mountain, and he said to him, "O man of God, the king said, 'Come down!'"

10 But Elijah spoke to the captain of the fifty, "If I am a man of God, let fire come down from the heavens and consume you and your fifty." And fire came down from the heavens and consumed him and his fifty.

11 Again he sent to him another captain of fifty and his fifty, and he answered and said to him, "O man of God, thus says the king, 'Come down quickly!'"

12 Elijah answered him and said to them, "If I am a man of God, let fire come down from the heavens and consume you and your fifty." And fire of God came down from the heavens and consumed him and his fifty.

13 Again he sent to him the captain of a third fifty and his fifty, and the third captain of fifty went up, and came and fell on his knees before Elijah and implored him, and said to him, "O man of God, let my life and the lives of these your fifty servants be precious in your eyes."

15 Thereupon the messenger of YHWH said to Elijah, "Go down with him, do not be afraid of him." So he rose up and went down with him to the king.

16 He said to him, "Thus says YHWH, 'Because you have sent messengers to inquire of Baal-zebub, the god of Ekron—Is it because there is no God at all in Israel to inquire of his word?—therefore you shall not come down from the bed to which you went up, but you shall surely die.'"

17 So he died according to the word of YHWH that Elijah had spoken and Jehoram became king in his place in the second year of Jehoram the son of Jehoshaphat king of Judah, because he had no son.

18 Now the rest of the acts of Ahaziah which he did are they not written in the Book of the Chronicles of the Kings of Israel?

603 Elijah Taken Up to Heaven
2 Kings 2:1-12

2 Kings 2

1 Now when YHWH was about to take Elijah up by a whirlwind into heaven, Elijah and Elisha went forth from Gilgal.

2 Elijah said to Elisha, "Please stay here, for YHWH has sent me as far as Bethel." But Elisha said, "As YHWH lives, and as you yourself live, I will not leave you." So they went down to Bethel.

3 Whereupon the guild of the prophets who were at Bethel came out to Elisha and said to him, "Do you know that today YHWH is about to take your master from being over you?" And he said, "Of course I know; be quiet!"

4 Then Elijah said to him, "Elisha, please stay here, for YHWH has sent me to Jericho." But he said, "As YHWH lives, and as you yourself live, I will not leave you." So they went to Jericho.

5 Whereupon the guild of the prophets who were at Jericho drew near to Elisha, and said to him, "Do you know that today YHWH is about to take your master from being over you?" And he said, "Of course I know; be quiet!"

6 Then Elijah said to him, "Please stay here, for YHWH has sent me to the Jordan." But he said, "As YHWH lives, and as you yourself live, I will not leave you." So the two of them went on.

7 Whereupon fifty men of the guild of the prophets went and stood opposite at a distance while the two of them stood beside the Jordan.

8 Then Elijah took his cloak, rolled it up and struck the waters, and they were parted on this side and on that side, and the two of them crossed over on dry ground.

9 When they had crossed over, Elijah said to Elisha, "Ask what I should do for you before I am taken from you." Elisha said, "Please let a double share of your spirit be mine."

10 He then said, "You have made a difficult request; yet if you see me being taken from you, it will be so for you; but if not, it will not be so."

11 As they kept on walking and talking, a chariot of fire and horses of fire [appeared] and they separated the two of them, and Elijah went up by a whirl-wind into heaven

12 while Elisha was looking on and crying out, "O my father, my father! The chariot of Israel and its horses!" Then he saw him no more.

604 Elisha Succeeds Elijah
2 Kings 2:12d-25

2 Kings 2

12 Then he seized his garments and tore them into two pieces.

13 He lifted up the cloak of Elijah that had fallen from him and went back and stood on the bank of the Jordan.

14 He took the cloak of Elijah that had fallen from him and struck the waters, and said, "Where is YHWH the God of Elijah, even he?" Then he struck the waters; and they were parted on this side and on that side and Elisha passed over.

15 When the guild of the prophets who were in Jericho on the other side saw him, they said, "The spirit of Elijah has come to rest upon Elisha." So they came to meet him and bowed themselves to the ground before him.

16 They said to him, "See now there are with your servants fifty capable men: please let them go and search for your master in the event the spirit of YHWH has carried him off and has thrown him on one of the mountains, or into one of the valleys;[1] but he said, "Do not send [them]!"

17 But they pressed him until he was ashamed and he said, "Send [them]." So they sent fifty men and they searched for three days but they did not find him.

18 When they returned to him, he was staying in Jericho, he said to them, "Did I not say to you: 'Do not go?'"

19 Now the men of the city said to Elisha, "See now, the site of the city is good, as my master sees; but the water is bad and the land barren."

20 He said, "Get me a new bowl and put salt in it." And they took [it] to him.

21 Then he went out to the spring of water and threw salt into it and said, "Thus says YHWH, I have brought healing to this water. No longer shall there be from there death and barrenness."

22 So the water has remained healed to this day according to the word of Elisha that he spoke.

23 He went up from there to Bethel; and while he was going up on the road, some small boys came out from the city and mocked him. They said to him, "Go up, baldy! Go up, baldy!"

24 He turned round and saw them and cursed them in the name of YHWH; and two she-bears came out of the wood and mauled some forty-two of the children.

25 He went from there to Mount Carmel, and from there he returned to Samaria.

---

[1] Reading the Qere.

605 The Reign of Jehoram of Israel
2 Kings 3:1-3

2 Kings 3

1 Jehoram son of Ahab became king over Israel in Samaria in the eighteenth year of Jehoshaphat king of Judah, and he was king for twelve years.

2 He did what was evil in the eyes of YHWH, only not like his father or his mother; he removed the pillar of Baal that his father had made.

3 However, he clung to the sins of Jeroboam son of Nebat which he had made Israel to sin; he did not depart from it.

606 Elisha Predicts Victory over Moab
2 Kings 3:4-27

2 Kings 3

4 Now Mesha king of Moab was a sheep-breeder, and he used to turn over to the king of Israel the wool of a hundred thousand lambs and of a hundred thousand rams.

5 But when Ahab died, the king of Moab rebelled against the king of Israel.

6 King Jehoram went out on that day from Samaria and mustered all Israel.

7 As he went, he sent to Jehoshaphat king of Judah, saying, "The king of Moab has rebelled against me; will you go with me to Moab to battle?" He said, "I will go; I am as you [are]; my people as your people, my horses as your horses."

8 Then he said, "By which road shall we go up?" He said, "The road of the wilderness of Edom road."

9 So the king of Israel, the king of Judah, and the king of Edom went out, and they made a circuit march of seven days, but there was no water for the camp or for the animals that followed him.

10 Then the king of Israel said, "Alas! YHWH surely has summoned these three kings to give them into the hand of Moab."

11 But Jehoshaphat said, "Is there no prophet of YHWH here that we may inquire of YHWH through him?" Then one of the servants of the king of Israel answered and said, "Elisha son of Shaphat is here, who poured water over the hands of Elijah."

12   Whereupon Jehoshaphat said, "The word of YHWH is with him." So the king of Israel, Jehoshaphat, and the king of Edom went down to him.

13   Elisha said to the king of Israel, "What have I to do with you? Go to the prophets of your father and to the prophets of your mother." But the king of Israel said to him, "No, for YHWH has summoned these three kings to give them into the hand of Moab."

14   Then Elisha said, "As YHWH of hosts lives before whom I stand, that if I did not have regard for the face of Jehoshaphat king of Judah, I would not look at you nor [take] notice [of] you.

15   Now fetch me a musician." As the musician played, the hand of YHWH came upon him.

16   He said, "Thus says YHWH, 'This wadi shall make pools, pools!'

17   For thus says YHWH, 'You shall not see wind, nor shall you see rain, yet that wadi shall be filled with water that you may drink, you and your cattle and your animals.'

18   This is a slight thing in the eyes of YHWH; he will also give Moab into your hand.

19   You shall strike down every fortified city and every choice city, you shall fell every good tree and stop up all springs of water and you shall spoil every good parcel of land with stones."

20   So it happened in the morning at the offering up of the meal offering, that water came in from the direction of Edom and the land was filled with water.

21   When all Moab heard that the kings had come up to do battle with them, everyone who could wear a belt and up were called out, and they stood at the border.

22   They rose early in the morning, the sun shone on the water, and Moab saw on the other side the water red as blood.

23   They said, "This is blood; surely the kings have fought together and struck one another. Now, to the spoil Moab!"

24   But when they came to the camp of Israel, Israel rose up and struck down Moab; though they fled from before them, they continued to come on striking[1] Moab down.

25   The cities they destroyed, and into every good parcel [of land] each man threw his stone and filled it; every spring of water they stopped up, and every good tree they felled until there remained only its stones in Kir-hareseth,[2] and the slingers surrounded and struck at it [too].

26   When the king of Moab saw that the battle was too much for him, he took [with] him seven hundred swordsmen to break through to the king of Edom but did not succeed.

27 Then he took his firstborn son, who was to become king in his place, and offered him up as a burnt-offering upon the wall at which point a great wrath [came] upon Israel that they withdrew from him and returned to [their] land.

---

[1] Hebrew obscure.
[2] Hebrew obscure.

607 The Widow's Oil
2 Kings 4:1-7

2 Kings 4

1 Now a certain woman of the wives of the guild of the prophets cried out to Elisha, "Your servant my husband is dead, and you know that your servant feared YHWH but a creditor has come to take my two children as slaves for himself."

2 So Elisha said to her, "What shall I do for you? Tell me what do you have[1] in the house?" She said, "Your maidservant does not have anything at home except a flask of oil."

3 But he said, "Go, ask for yourself vessels from outside from all your neighbors,[2] empty vessels. Do not skimp.

4 Then you shall enter and close the door behind you and behind your children, and pour [oil] into all these vessels. When [one] is full, then remove it."

5 So she went away from him and closed the door behind herself and behind her children: they kept bringing [vessels] to her and she kept on pouring."[3]

6 When the vessels were full, she said to her son, "Bring me another vessel." But he said to her, "There is not another vessel." Thereupon the oil stopped.

7 Then she came and told the man of God, and he said, "Go, sell the oil and you shall pay your debt,[4] and you [and] your children shall live off the rest."

---

[1] Reading the Qere.
[2] Reading the Qere.
[3] Reading the Qere.
[4] Reading the Qere.

Elisha

Sections 604–618 and 628

Number	Title	2 Chronicles	2 Kings
604	Elisha Succeeds Elijah		2:12d-25
605	The Reign of Jehoram of Israel		3:1-3
606	Elisha Predicts Victory over Moab		3:4-27
607	The Widow's Oil		4:1-7
608	Elisha and the Shunammite Woman		4:8-37
609	Elisha's Miracles for the Prophets		4:38-44
610	The Cure of Naaman's Leprosy		5:1-27
611	The Axe-Head Made to Float		6:1-7
612	Elisha and the Syrians		6:8-23
613	Elisha and the Siege of Samaria		6:24–7:20
614	The Shunammite Woman's Land Restored		8:1-6
615	Hazael Becomes King of Syria		8:7-15
616	The Reign of Jehoram of Judah	21:2–22:1	8:16-24
617	The Reign of Ahaziah of Judah	22:2-6	8:25-29
618	Jehu Anointed King of Israel		9:1-13
[628]	Elisha's Final Prophecy and Death		[13:14-25]

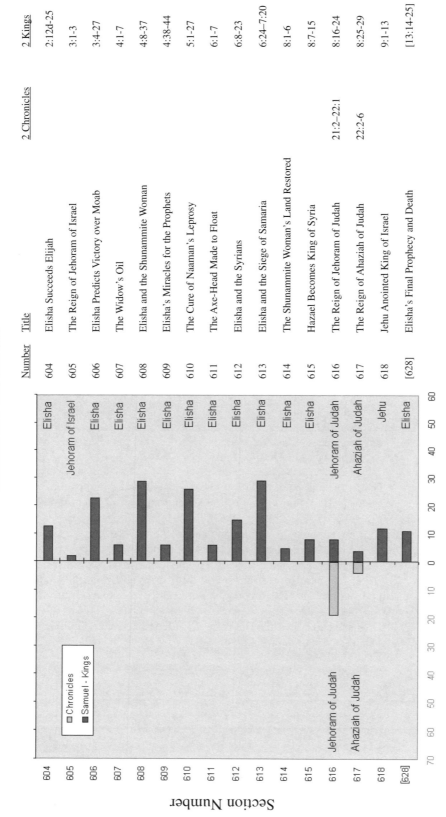

608 Elisha and the Shunammite Woman
2 Kings 4:8-37

2 Kings 4

8 Then there was the day when Elisha passed near Shunem and there was a prominent woman there, and she prevailed on him to eat bread. So it was that as often as he passed by he would turn in there to eat bread.

9 And she said to her husband, "Look, I know for sure that the man of God, the one who regularly passes by us, is a holy man.

10 Let us make a small, walled roof-chamber, and let us put there for him a bed, a table, a chair and a lampstand, and whenever he comes to us, he may turn in there."

11 So there was the day when he came there and turned aside to the roof-chamber and lay down there.

12 He said to Gehazi, his servant, "Call this Shunammite woman." So he called her and she stood before him.

13 Then he said to him, "Say to her, 'Look, you have taken all this care for us. What is there to be done for you? Can a word be spoken on your behalf to the king or to the commander of the army?'" But she said, "I dwell among my people."

14 So he said, "So what is there to be done for her?" Gehazi said, "Well, she has no son and her husband is old."

15 He said, "Call her," so he called her and she stood in the doorway.

16 Then he said, "At this season in due time you[1] shall embrace a son." But she said, "Do not my lord, O man of God, do not deceive your maidservant."

17 So the woman conceived and she bore a son at this season at the appointed time [of] which Elisha had spoken to her.

18 When the child had grown up the day was when he went out to his father to the harvesters.

19 He said to his father, "My head, my head!" He said to the servant, "Carry him to his mother."

20 So he lifted him up and brought him to his mother; [the child] remained on her knees until noon and died.

21 She went up and laid him out on the bed of the man of God, closed [the door] after him and went out.

22 Then she called to her husband and said, "Please send to me one of the servants and one of the she-asses so that I can run to the man of God and return [again]."

23 But he said, "Why are you going² to him today? It is not new [moon], nor is it shabbat." But she said, "It's all right."

24 Then she saddled the she-ass and said to her servant, "Drive [the beast] and keep going! Do not slacken the riding [pace] for me unless I tell you so."

25 So she set out and came to the man of God, to Mount Carmel. When the man of God saw her at a distance, he said to Gehazi his servant, "Look, [there is] that Shunammite woman.

26 Now run [out] to meet her, and say to her, "Is it well with you? Is it well with your husband? Is it well with your child?" She said, "It is well."

27 When she came to the man of God at the mountain she grabbed hold of his feet. Gehazi came near to drive her away, but the man of God said, "Let her alone, for her spirit is bitter, and YHWH has concealed [it] from me and has not told me."

28 Then she said, "Did I ask for a son from my lord? Did I not say, 'Do not mislead me?'"

29 So he said to Gehazi, "Gird your loins and take my staff in your hand and go. If you meet anyone do not bless him, and if anyone blesses you, do not answer him. Then put my staff on the face of the boy."

30 Then the mother of the boy said, "As YHWH lives and as you live, I will not leave you." So he arose and went after her.

31 Now Gehazi had gone on before them and he had put the staff on the face of the boy, but there was no sound nor was there any sign of life, so he turned back to meet him and told him, "The boy has not awakened."

32 Elisha came to the house and there was the boy dead, lying on his bed.

33 So he went in and closed the door behind the two of them and he prayed to YHWH.

34 He went up and lay on the child, and he put his mouth upon his mouth and his eyes upon his eyes and his palms upon his palms,³ and he crouched over him and the child's flesh became warm.

35 He turned away and walked in the house once this way and once that way; then he went up and crouched over him. The boy sneezed all of seven times, and then the boy opened his eyes.

36 He called to Gehazi and said, "Call this Shunammite woman." So he called her and she came to him, and then he said to her, "Take up your son."

37 She came and fell at his feet, and bowed herself down on the ground; then she lifted up her son and went out.

609 Elisha's Miracles for the Prophets
2 Kings 4:38-44

2 Kings 4

38 When Elisha returned to Gilgal, there was famine in the land. Now the guild of the prophets were sitting before him, and he said to his servant, "Set on the large pot and boil [some] pottage for the guild of the prophets."

39 One [of them] went out to the field to gather herbs and he found a vine of the field; he gathered from it field gourds, filling his garment, and came and sliced [them] into the pottage, for they did not know [what they were].

40 So they poured [it] out for the men to eat, but as they were eating from the pottage they cried out and said, "[There is] death in the pot, O man of God!" They were unable to eat [it].

41 Then he said, "Take flour." He threw [it] into the pot and said, "Pour [it] out for the people and let them eat." There was nothing harmful in the pot.

42 A man came from Baal-Shalishah, and he brought the man of God bread of the first fruits, twenty loaves of barley and fresh vegetables in his sack. And [Elisha] said, "Give [it] to the people and let them eat."

43 But his attendant said, "How can I set this before a hundred persons?" He said, "Give it to the people and let them eat, for thus says YHWH, 'They shall eat and leave some remaining.'"

44 So he set [it] out before them and they ate and left some remaining according to the word of YHWH.

Divided Monarchy-3
Sections 610–629

Number	Title	2 Chronicles	2 Kings
610	The Cure of Naaman's Leprosy		5:1-27
611	The Axe-Head Made to Float		6:1-7
612	Elisha and the Syrians		6:8-23
613	Elisha and the Siege of Samaria		6:24–7:20
614	The Shunammite Woman's Land Restored		8:1-6
615	Hazael Becomes King of Syria		8:7-15
616	The Reign of Jehoram of Judah	21:2–22:1	8:16-24
617	The Reign of Ahaziah of Judah	22:2-6	8:25-29
618	Jehu Anointed King of Israel		9:1-13
619	Jehu Kills Joram		9:14-26
620	Jehu Kills Ahaziah	22:7-9	9:27-29
621	The Death of Jezebel		9:30-37
622	Jehu Destroys the House of Ahab		10:1-17
623	Jehu Wipes Out the Worship of Baal		10:18-36
624	Athaliah Usurps the Throne	22:10–23:21	11:1-20
625	The Reign of Jehoash of Judah	24:1-27	12:1-22
626	The Reign of Jehoahaz		13:1-9
627	The Reign of Jehoash of Israel		13:10-13
628	Elisha's Final Prophecy and Death		13:14-25
629	The Reign of Amaziah	25:1–26:2	14:1-22

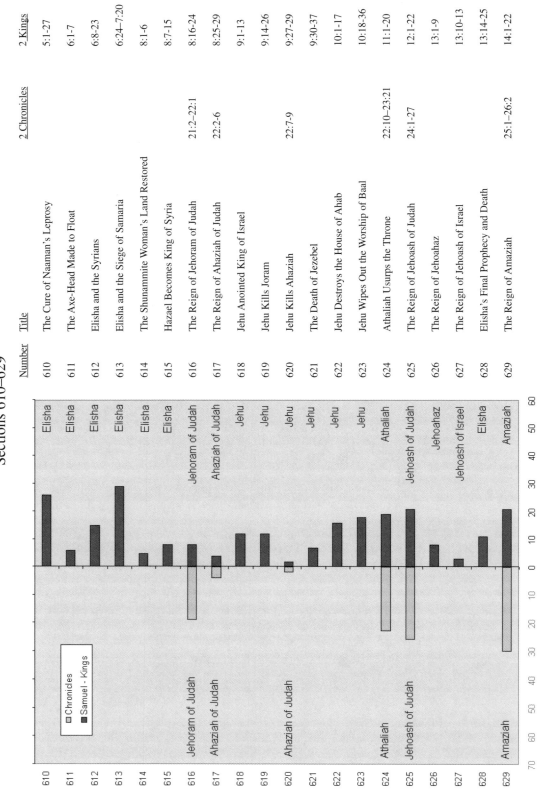

Number of Verses

610 The Cure of Naaman's Leprosy
2 Kings 5:1-27

2 Kings 5

1 Naaman the commander of the army of the king of Aram was a great man before his master and highly regarded because by him had YHWH given victory to Aram; but the man, even [though] a mighty warrior, was a leper.

2 Now Aram had gone out raiding and had taken captive from the land of Israel a young girl; and she served the wife of Naaman.

3 She said to her mistress, "If only my master were in the presence of the prophet who is in Samaria! He would take away his leprosy."

4 So he [Naaman] went and told his master, "Thus and so spoke the girl who [is] from the land of Israel."

5 The king of Aram said, "Go, proceed, and let me send a letter to the king of Israel." So he went and took in his hand ten talents of silver and six thousand [shekels] of gold and ten changes of garments.

6 He brought the letter to the king of Israel which said, "Now, when this letter comes to you, see I have sent to you Naaman my servant, that you may cure him of his leprosy."

7 But when the king of Israel read the letter, he rent his garments and said, "Am I God, to bring death or bring life that this one sends to me to cure a man from his leprosy? Just think and realize that he is seeking a quarrel with me."

8 But when Elisha the man of God, heard that the king of Israel had rent his garments he sent to the king, "Why have you rent your garments? Let him come to me so he may know that there is a prophet in Israel."

9 So Naaman came with his horses[1] and chariots, and he stood at the entryway of Elisha's house.

10 Then Elisha sent to him a messenger, saying, "Go and bathe seven times in the Jordan and your flesh shall return to you and [shall be] clean."

11 But Naaman was angered and he went [away], and said, "I thought, 'Surely he would come out and stand and call on the name of YHWH his God and wave his hand toward the place and cure the leprosy.

12 Are not Abana[2] and Pharpar, rivers of Damascus, better than all the waters of Israel? Could I not bathe in them and then be clean?'" Then he turned and went away in a rage.

13 But his servants came near and spoke to him and they said, "My father, if the prophet had suggested a great thing, would you not have done [it]? How much more when he said to you, 'Wash and be clean?'"

14 So he went down and dipped in the Jordan seven times according to the word of the man of God; and his flesh returned like the flesh of a young lad and he was clean.

15 Then he returned to the man of God, he and his whole company, he came and stood before him and said, "Look now, I know that there is no God in all the earth except in Israel; so now, please take a present from your servant."

16 But he said, "As YHWH lives before whom I stand, I will not take [it]." When he pressed him to take [it], he refused.

17 Then Naaman said, "If not, please let there be given to your servant two mule-loads of earth, for your servant will no longer make burnt offering or sacrifice to gods other than YHWH.

18 For this [one] thing may YHWH forgive your servant, when my master comes into the house of Rimmon to bow down there, while leaning on my arm, and I bow down in the house of Rimmon, when I bow down in the house of Rimmon, may YHWH forgive your servant for this thing."

19 He said to him, "Go in peace." But when he had gone from him a short distance,

20 Gehazi the servant of Elisha the man of God, said [to himself], "Look, my master has spared this Naaman the Aramean by not taking from his hand [that] which he brought. As YHWH lives, I will certainly run after him and I will take something from him."

21 So Gehazi pursued Naaman and [when] Naaman saw [someone] running after him, he jumped down from his chariot to meet him, and he said, "Is all well?"

22 He said, "It is well. My master sent me, saying, 'Just now two young lads have come to me from Mount Ephraim, from the guild of the prophets. Please give them a talent of silver and two changes of garments.'"

23 Naaman said, "Please, take two talents." He pressed him and wrapped up two talents of silver in two bags, with two changes of garments, and he gave them to two of his servants and they carried them in front of him.

24 When he came to the citadel, he [Gehazi] took [them] from their hands and deposited [them] in the house. Then he dismissed the men and they set forth.

25 He came and stood before his master and Elisha said to him, "Gehazi, where[3] [have you come] from?" He said, "Your servant has not gone anywhere."

26 Then he said to him, "Did not my heart go [with you] when a man turned back from his chariot to meet you? Was it a time to take the silver or to take garments, olive orchards and vineyards, sheep, oxen, servants or handmaids?

27 Therefore the leprosy of Naaman shall cling to you and to your descendants forever." So he left his presence leprous like snow.

---

[1] Reading the Qere.
[2] Qere: Amana.
[3] Reading the Qere.

611 The Axe-Head Made to Float
2 Kings 6:1-7

2 Kings 6

1 The guild of the prophets said to Elisha, "Look, the place where we dwell before you is too restricted for us.

2 Let us go to the Jordan and let us each take from there one beam and there let us make for ourselves a place to dwell there." Then he said, "Go ahead."

3 But one [of them] said, "Please go with your servants," and he said, "I will go."

4 So he went with them and they came to the Jordan and they cut down trees.

5 But as one [of them] was felling a beam, the axe-head fell into the water; he cried out and said, "Alas, my master, it was borrowed."

6 Then the man of God said, "Where did it fall?" He showed him the place; whereupon he cut off a piece of wood and threw it there and he made the axe-head float.

7 He said, "Pick it up for yourself," so he stretched out his hand and took it.

612 Elisha and the Syrians
2 Kings 6:8-23

2 Kings 6

8 Now the king of Aram was waging war with Israel and he took counsel with his servants, saying, "At such and such a place [shall be] my encampment."

9 But the man of God sent [a message] to the king of Israel, saying, "Take care not to pass by this place, for the Aram[eans] are descending there."

10 Then the king of Israel sent [a message] to the place about which the man of God had spoken to him. He had warned that it[1] [the place] would be on guard there, [and] not [just] once or twice.

11 The heart of the king of Aram was infuriated concerning this matter, and he called to his servants and said to them, "Will you not tell me who among us [is] for the king of Israel?"

12 Then one of his servants said, "No, my lord the king, for [it is] Elisha the prophet who is in Israel; he relates to the king of Israel the things that you speak in your [own] bedchamber."

13 He said, "Go and see where he is so that I may send and take him." Then it was told him, "Look, he is in Dothan."

14 So he sent there horses and chariots and a heavy force; they came by night and surrounded the city.

15 When the attendant of the man of God arose early and went out, there was a [military] force surrounding the city, horse and chariots, so his servant said to him, "Alas, my master, what shall we do?"

16 But he said, "Fear not, for there are more who are with us than there are with them."

17 Then Elisha prayed and said, "YHWH, please open his eyes that he may see." So YHWH opened the eyes of the servant and he saw, and the mountain was filled with horses and chariots of fire surrounding Elisha.

18 When they [the Arameans] came down against him, Elisha prayed to YHWH and said, "YHWH, please strike this nation with sudden blindness." So he struck them with sudden blindness according to the word of Elisha.

19 Then Elisha said to them, "This is not the road and this is not the city; come after me and let me lead you to the man whom you seek." So he led them to Samaria.

20 As they entered Samaria, Elisha said, "YHWH, open the eyes of these [men] that they may see." YHWH opened their eyes and they saw, and they were right in the center of Samaria!

21 Then the king of Israel said to Elisha, when he saw them, "Shall I really[2] strike [them] down, my father?"

22 But he said, "You shall not strike! Are these [ones] whom you have captured with your sword and with your bow that you would strike [them] down? Put bread and water before them that they may eat and drink and then go to their master."

23 So he prepared a great feast for them: after they ate and drank, he sent them away and they went to their master. And bands of Arameans no longer came raiding into the land of Israel.

---

[1] Reading the Qere.
[2] Hebrew obscure.

613 Elisha and the Siege of Samaria
2 Kings 6:24–7:20

2 Kings 6

24 Some time afterwards Ben-hadad king of Aram gathered all his company and he went up and laid siege to Samaria.

25 There was a great famine in Samaria as they were besieging it to the point that a donkey's head [was going for] eighty [shekels] of silver, and a quarter kab of dove's dung¹ for five [shekels] of silver.

26 Now as the king was passing by upon the wall, a woman cried out to him, "Save [me] my lord the king!"

27 But he said, "No! Let YHWH save you! Where can I save you, from the threshing-floor or from the winepress?"

28 However, the king said to her, "What troubles you?" She said, "This woman said to me, 'Give up your son and we will eat him today, and we will eat my son tomorrow.'

29 So we cooked my son and we ate him, but when I said to her the next day, 'Give up your son and we will eat him,' she hid her son."

30 When the king heard the words of the woman, he tore his garments; now he was passing by upon the wall so the people could see that there was indeed sackcloth on his flesh underneath.

31 Then he said, "Thus may God do to me, and more, if the head of Elisha son of Shaphat remains on him today!"

32 Now Elisha was sitting in his house and the elders were sitting with him. He [the king] had sent a man from his presence. Before the messenger came to him [Elisha], he said to the elders, "Do you see that this murderer has sent [someone] to take off my head? See, when the messenger comes, shut the door and hold the door against him. Is not the sound of his master's feet right behind him?"

33 While he was still speaking with them the messenger was coming down to him. He said, "Look, this evil is from YHWH. Why should I still hope in YHWH?"

7:1 However, Elisha said, "Hear the word of YHWH! Thus says YHWH, 'About [this] time tomorrow a seah of fine flour [will go] for a shekel, and two seahs of barley for a shekel in the gate of Samaria.'"

2 Then the officer who [was assigned] to the king leaned on his arm, answered the man of God and said, "Look, even if YHWH should make windows in the sky, can this thing come to pass?" He said, "You shall be seeing this with your [very own] eyes but you shall not eat from it."

3 Now there were four lepers at the entrance of the [city] gate and they said to one another, "Why do we sit here until we die?

4 If we say, 'Let us enter the city,' there is the famine in the city, and we shall die there; but if we sit here, we shall [also] die. Come now, let us defect to the camp of the Arameans: if they let us live, we shall live and if they put us to death, then we shall die."

5 So they rose up at twilight to go to the camp of the Arameans. Yet when they came to the perimeter of the camp of the Arameans, there was not one person there.

6 But the Lord had made the camp of Arameans hear the sound of chariots, the sound of horse[s], the sound of a great force, so they said to one another, "See, the king of Israel has hired against us the kings of the Hittites and the kings of Egypt to come against us."

7 So they rose up and fled at twilight and left behind their tents, their horses and their donkeys. The camp [stayed] just as it was; they had fled for their lives.

8 When these lepers had come to the perimeter of the camp, they entered one tent and ate and drank and carried away from there silver and gold and garments and they went and concealed [them]. Then they returned and entered another tent, and they carried away [things] from there and went and concealed [them].

9 Then they said to one another, "We are not acting rightly. This day is a day of good news and we are keeping silent: if we wait until the light of morning, guilt will find us. Come now, let us go and report to the house[hold] of the king."

10 So they came and called out to the gate-keeper of the city and reported to them, "We entered the camp of the Arameans and there was not one person there, nor any human voice, except the horse[s] tethered and the donkey[s] tethered, and the tents were just as they [had been]."

11 Then the gatekeepers called out and told the household of the king inside.

12 The king rose up in the night and said to his servants, "Let me tell you what the Arameans have done to us: they know that we are starving so they have gone out of the camp to hide in the field[s],[2] saying, 'When they go out from the city, we shall seize them alive and go into the city.'"

13 Then one of his servants answered and said, "Let them take five of the horses remaining, that have remained in it [the city]; for they are like the whole throng of Israel that has remained in it [the city], they are [just] like the whole throng[3] of Israel that has perished. Let us send out and see."

14 So they took two chariot horses and the king sent [them] after the camp of the Arameans, saying, "Go and see."

15 So they went after them as far as the Jordan and look, the entire road was filled with garments and vessels which the Arameans had thrown away in [their] haste.[4] Then the messengers returned and reported to the king.

16 Then the people went out and looted the camp of the Arameans; so a seah of fine flour [did go] for a shekel and two seahs of barley for a shekel according to the word of YHWH.

17 Now the king had put the officer on whose arm he leaned in charge of the gate, but the people trampled him in the gate and he died just as the man of God had spoken who spoke when the king was coming down to him.

18 For when the man of God had spoken to the king, saying: "Two seahs of barley [will go] for a shekel, and a seah of fine flour for a shekel about [this] time tomorrow in the gate of Samaria,"

19 the officer had answered the man of God and said, "Look, even if YHWH should make windows in the sky, can it come to pass according to this word?" But he said, "You shall be seeing this with your [very own] eyes but you shall not eat from it."

20 So it happened in this way to him: the people trampled him in the [city] gate and he died.

---

614 The Shunammite Woman's Land Restored
2 Kings 8:1-6

2 Kings 8

1 Now Elisha had spoken to the woman whose son he had brought back to life, saying, "Rise up and go, you and your household, and sojourn wherever you can sojourn, for YHWH has called up a famine and it will come into the land for seven years."

2 So the woman rose up and acted according to the word of the man of God: she and her household had gone and sojourned in the land of the Philistines for seven years.

3 At the end of the seven years when the woman returned from the land of the Philistines, she went to cry out to the king for her house and her field.

4 Now the king was speaking with Gehazi the servant of the man of God, saying, "Please relate for me all the great things that Elisha has done."

5 While he was relating to the king how he had brought back a dead person to life, the very woman whose son he had brought back to life [was there] crying out to the king about her house and her field. So Gehazi said, "My lord the king, this is the woman and this is her son whom Elisha brought back to life!"

6 When the king asked the woman [about it], she related [it] to him. Thereupon the king appointed for her a certain official, saying, "Return everything that belonged to her and all the produce of the field from the day that she left the land until now."

615 Hazael Becomes King of Syria
2 Kings 8:7-15

2 Kings 8

7 Now Elisha came to Damascus. Ben-hadad king of Aram was ill and it was reported to him, "The man of God has come here."

8 Then the king said to Hazael, "Take a gift in your hand and go, meet the man of God, so that you may inquire of YHWH from him, saying, 'Shall I recover from this illness?'"

9 So Hazael went to meet him and he took a gift in his hand, and all [the] good things of Damascus, a burden of forty camels. He came and stood before him and said, "Your son, Ben-hadad king of Aram, has sent me to you, saying, 'Shall I recover from this illness?'"

10 Then Elisha said to him, "Go, tell him,[1] 'You shall surely recover'; but YHWH has shown me that he shall surely die."

11 He set his face and held it thus until [he was] ashamed; and the man of God wept.

12 Then Hazael said, "Why is my master weeping?" He said, "Because I know that you will do evil to the Israelites: their fortifications you will set on fire, their young men you will kill by the sword, their children you will dash in pieces, and their pregnant women you will rip open."

13 But Hazael said, "Indeed what is your servant but a dog, that he should do this great thing?" Then Elisha said to him, "YHWH has shown me [that] you will be king over Aram."

14 So he went [away] from Elisha and came to his lord [who] said to him, "What did Elisha say to you?" He said, "He said to me, 'You will surely recover.'"

15 But the next day he [Hazael] took the coverlet, dipped it in water, and spread it over his [Ben-hadad's] face and he [Ben-hadad] died. So Hazael became king in his place.

---

[1] Reading the Qere.

616 The Reign of Jehoram of Judah
2 Chron 21:2–22:1 // 2 Kings 8:16-24

2 Chronicles 21

2 He [Jehoram] had brothers, sons of Jehoshaphat: Azariah, Jehiel, Zechariah, Azariah, Michael and Shepatiah; all these were sons of Jehoshaphat king of Israel.

3 Their father had given them many gifts—of silver and of gold and choice things, together with fortified cities in Judah—but the kingdom he gave to Jehoram, since he was his first-born.

4 When Jehoram had ascended to his father's kingdom and had made himelf strong, he killed all his brothers by the sword, and also some of the officials of Israel.

5 Jehoram was thirty-two years old when he became king, and he was king for eight years in Jerusalem.

6 He walked in the way of the kings of Israel, just as the house of Ahab had done, since the daughter of Ahab was wife to him; and he did what was evil in the eyes of YHWH.

7 But YHWH was not willing to destroy the house of David because of the covenant which he had made with David, and since he had promised that he would give a lamp to him and to his descendants for all the[ir] days.

8 In his days Edom rebelled from under the hand of Judah and they made a king over themselves.

9 Then Jehoram crossed over with his captains and all his chariots with him. He rose up in the night and he struck down Edom, which had surrounded him and the officers of the chariots.

10 So Edom has been in revolt against Judah until this day; also Libnah rebelled at that time from under his hand, for he had forsaken YHWH the God of his ancestors.

11 Moreover he made high places in the mountains of Judah, and he led the inhabitants of Jerusalem into infidelity, and he made Judah go astray.

12 Then there came to him a letter from Elijah the prophet, saying, "Thus says YHWH, the God of David

2 Kings 8

16 In the fifth year of Joram son of Ahab king of Israel, when Jehoshaphat [was] king of Judah, Jehoram son of Jehoshaphat king of Judah, became king.

17 He was thirty-two years old when he became king, and he was king for eight years in Jerusalem.

18 He walked in the way of the kings of Israel, just as the house of Ahab had done since the daughter of Ahab was his wife; and he did what was evil in the eyes of YHWH.

19 But YHWH was not willing to destroy Judah for the sake of David his servant, since he had promised him that he would give a lamp to him and to his descendants for all the[ir] days.

20 In his days Edom rebelled from under the hand of Judah and they made a king over themselves.

21 Then Joram crossed over to Zair and all his chariots with him. He rose up in the night and he struck down Edom which had surrounded him and the officers of the chariots; but the people fled to their tents.

22 So Edom has been in revolt against Judah until this day; also Libnah rebelled at that time.

your [fore]father, 'Because you have not walked in the ways of Jehoshaphat your father and in the ways of Asa king of Judah,

13 but you have walked in the way of the kings of Israel, and have led Judah and the inhabitants of Jerusalem into infidelity, just as the house of Ahab led [Israel] into infidelity, and you have even killed your brothers, [those] of your father's house, who were better than yourself:

14 look, YHWH will strike your people with a great plague, your children, your wives and all your possessions.

15 And you yourself [will have] terrible sickness with a disorder of your bowels until your bowels come out because of the disease, day after day.'"

16 Then YHWH aroused against Jehoram the spirit of the Philistines and the Arabs who are near the Cushites.

17 So they came up against Judah and invaded it and took away all the possessions that were found in the house of the king, even his children and his wives; and no child was left for him, except Jehoahaz, the youngest of his children.

18 After all this, YHWH struck him in his bowels with a disease for [which] there was no cure.

19 After some time, around the time of the passing of two years, his bowels came out because of his disease, and he died of terrible illness. Moreover his people did not make for him a burning [of spices] like the burning for his ancestors.

20 He was thirty-two years old when he became king, and he was king in Jerusalem for eight years; he departed without regret and they buried him in the city of David but not in the tombs of the kings.

23 Now the rest of the acts of Joram and all that he did, are they not written in the Book of the Chronicles of the Kings of Judah?

24 When Joram lay down to rest with his ancestors, he was buried with his ancestors in the city of David. Then Ahaziah his son became king in his place.

22:1 Then the inhabitants of Jerusalem made Ahaziah his youngest son king in his place, since the raiding party that came with the Arabs into the camp had killed all the older ones. So Ahaziah son of Jehoram king of Judah became king.

617 The Reign of Ahaziah of Judah
2 Chron 22:2-6 // 2 Kings 8:25-29 // 2 Kings 9:29, 14-16

2 Chronicles 22	*2 Kings 8*	*2 Kings 9*
2 Ahaziah was forty-two years old when he became king, and he was king for one year in Jerusalem. The name of his mother was Athaliah daughter of Omri.	25 In the twelfth year of Joram son of Ahab, king of Israel, Ahaziah son of Jehoram king of Judah, became king.	29 In the eleventh year of Joram son of Ahab, Ahaziah became king over Judah.
	26 Ahaziah was twenty-two years old when he became king, and he was king for one year in Jerusalem. The name of his mother was Athaliah daughter of Omri king of Israel.	
3 He, too, walked in the ways of the house of Ahab because his mother was his counselor for acting wickedly.	27 He walked in the way of the house of Ahab, and he did evil in the eyes of YHWH, just like the house of Ahab for he was son-in-law to the house of Ahab.	
4 He did evil in the eyes of YHWH just like the house of Ahab for they became his counselors after the death of his father to his destruction.		
5 He also followed their counsel and went with Jehoram son of Ahab king of Israel to battle against Hazael king of Aram at Ramoth-gilead; but the Rameans wounded Joram.	28 He went with Joram son of Ahab to battle with Hazael king of Aram at Ramoth-gilead; but the Arameans wounded Joram.	
		14 Thus Jehu son of Jehoshaphat son of Nimshi, conspired against Joram. Joram had been on guard at Ramoth-gilead, he and all Israel, against Hazael king of Aram.
6 Now he returned to be healed in Jezreel because [of] the wounds which they had inflicted on him at Ramah when he was engaged in battle with Hazael king of Aram	29 Now Joram the king returned to be healed in Jezreel from the wounds which the Arameans had inflicted on him at Ramah when he was engaged in battle with Hazael king of Aram	15 Now Jehoram the king returned to be healed in Jezreel from the wounds which the Arameans had inflicted on him when he was engaged in battle with Hazael king of Aram. So Jehu said, "If [this] is your desire, let no fugitive slip out of the city to go to report[1] it in Jezreel."
and Azariah son of Jehoram king of Judah, went down to see Jehoram son of Ahab at Jezreel because he was ill.	and Ahaziah son of Jehoram king of Judah, went down to see Joram son of Ahab at Jezreel because he was ill.	16 Then Jehu rode in [his chariot] and went to Jezreel since Joram was lying [ill] there, and Ahaziah king of Judah, had gone down to see Joram.

---

[1] Reading the Qere.

618 Jehu Anointed King of Israel
2 Kings 9:1-13

2 Kings 9

1 Then Elisha called one from the guild of the prophets and said to him, "Gird your loins, take this flask of oil in your hand, and go to Ramoth-gilead.

2 When you come there, look there [for] Jehu son of Jehoshaphat son of Nimshi: you shall go and get him away from among his comrades and lead him [to] an inner room.

3 Then you shall take the flask of oil and pour [it] on his head, and say, Thus says YHWH, 'I have anointed you as king over Israel.' Then you shall open the door and flee, you shall not tarry.'"

4 So the young man, the young man[1] the prophet, went to Ramoth-gilead.

5 He came when the commanders of the army were sitting around, and he said, "I have a message for you, O commander." Jehu said, "For which one of us?" So he said, "For you, O commander."

6 So he rose up and went into the house and he poured the oil over his head, and said to him, "Thus says YHWH, the God of Israel, 'I have anointed you as king over the people of YHWH, over Israel.'

7 You shall strike down the house of Ahab your master, so I may avenge the blood of my servants the prophets and the blood of all the servants of YHWH, [shed] by the hand of Jezebel.

8 The whole house of Ahab shall perish, and I will cut off from Ahab [every] male,[2] both the bound and free, in Israel.

9 For I will make the house of Ahab like the house of Jeroboam son of Nebat and like the house of Baasha son of Ahijah.

10 The dogs shall eat Jezebel in the estate of Jezreel and there will be no one to bury [her]." Then he opened the door and fled.

11 Whereupon Jehu went out to the servants of his master, and he said to him, "Is everything all right? Why has this madman come to you?" He said to them, "You know the man and his chatter!"

12 They said, "A lie! Tell us, now!" So he said, "Thus and so he spoke to me: Thus says YHWH, 'I have anointed you as king over Israel.'"

13 Thereupon they made haste and each one took his mantle and placed [it] under him on the bare steps[3] and they blew the shophar, and said, "Jehu is king!"

---

[1] "Young man" does appear twice in the text.
[2] Literally, "[every]one who urinates against the wall."
[3] Hebrew obscure.

619 Jehu Kills Joram
2 Kings 9:14-26

2 Kings 9

14 Thus Jehu son of Jehoshaphat son of Nimshi conspired against Joram. Now Joram had been on guard at Ramoth-gilead, he and all Israel, against Hazael king of Aram.

15 Now Jehoram the king returned to be healed in Jezreel from the wounds which the Arameans had inflicted on him when he was engaged in battle with Hazael king of Aram. So Jehu said, "If [this] is your desire, let no fugitive slip out of the city to go to report[1] it in Jezreel."

16 Then Jehu rode [in his chariot] and went to Jezreel since Joram was lying [ill] there, and Ahaziah king of Judah had gone down to see Joram.

17 Now the lookout was standing on the tower in Jezreel and he saw Jehu's troop as it was coming, so he said, "I see a troop!" Then Jehoram said, "Take a rider and send [him] to meet them, and let him ask 'Is it [for] peace?'"

18 The rider went on horse to meet him, and he said, "Thus says the king, 'Is it [for] peace?'" Jehu said, "What concern is it to you if it is [for] peace? Turn round after me." So the lookout reported, "The messenger reached them, but has not turned back."

19 Then he sent a second horseman and he came to them, and said, "Thus says the king, 'Is it [for] peace?'" Then Jehu said, "What concern is it to you if it is [for] peace? Turn round after me."

20 So the lookout reported, "He reached them, but has not turned back, and the driving is like the driving of Jehu son of Nimshi, for he drives furiously."

21 Then Jehoram said, "Harness up." So someone harnessed up his chariot. Then Jehoram king of Israel went out and [also] Ahaziah king of Judah, each one in his chariot. They went out to meet Jehu, and they found him in the tract [of land] of Naboth the Jezreelite.

22 When Jehoram saw Jehu, he said, "Is it [for] peace, Jehu?" But he said, "How can there be peace as long as the harlotries of Jezebel your mother and her sorceries [are so] many?"

23 Whereupon Jehoram reined up with his [own] hands and fled, and said to Ahaziah, "Treachery, Ahaziah."

24 Then Jehu drew back his bow and he struck Jehoram between his shoulders; the arrow went through his heart and he sank down in his chariot.

25 He said to Bidqar his officer,[2] "Pick him up and throw him in the tract [of land] of the field of Naboth the Jezreelite. For remember how you and I [were] riding as a team behind Ahab his father when YHWH raised up this oracle against him:

26 'As surely as I saw the blood of Naboth and the blood of his sons yesterday,' says YHWH, 'I will pay you back in this [very] tract [of land],' says YHWH. 'So now pick him up [and] throw him on the tract [of land] according to the word of YHWH.'"

---

[1] Reading the Qere.
[2] Reading the Qere.

620 Jehu Kills Ahaziah
2 Chron 22:7-9 // 2 Kings 9:27-29 // 2 Kings 8:25

2 Chronicles 22	*2 Kings 9*	*2 Kings 8*
7 Now Ahaziah's ruin was from God, by [his] going to Joram. When he came he went out with Jehoram to Jehu son of Nimshi whom YHWH had anointed to exterminate the house of Ahab.		
8 It was while Jehu was executing judgment with the house of Ahab that he found the officials of Judah and the sons of the brothers of Ahaziah who were attending Ahaziah; so he killed them.		
9 Then he sought out Ahaziah, and they captured him while hiding away in Samaria; they brought him to Jehu, and they put him to death and they buried him for they said, "He is the son of Jehoshaphat, who sought after YHWH with all his heart." Thus the house of Ahaziah had no one to hold power in the kingdom.	27 When Ahaziah king of Judah saw [this] he fled towards Beth-haggan; but Jehu pursued after him and said, "Shoot him also!" [And they shot him] in the chariot at the Ascent of Gur which was near Ibleam. Then he fled to Megiddo and he died there.	
	28 His servants carried him by chariot to Jerusalem, and they buried him in his [own] tomb with his ancestors in the city of David.	
	29 In the eleventh year of Joram son of Ahab, Ahaziah became king over Judah.	25 In the twelfth year of Joram son of Ahab, king of Israel, Ahaziah son of Jehoram, king of Judah, became king.

621 The Death of Jezebel
2 Kings 9:30-37

2 Kings 9

30 When Jehu came to Jezreel, Jezebel heard [of it] and she painted her eyes with kohl and adorned her head; then she looked through the window.

31 As Jehu came through the gate she said, "Is it [for] peace, [you] Zimri, slayer of his master?"

32 Then he raised his face to the window and said, "Who is with me? Who?" Whereupon two [or] three eunuchs looked down at him.

33 He said, "Throw her down."[1] So they threw her down, and some of her blood splattered on the wall and on the horses, and he trampled on her.

34 Then he went in and ate and drank; he said, "Attend now to this accursed [woman], and bury her, for she is the daughter of a king."

35 So they went to bury her but they did not find her except for the skull, the feet, and the palms of [her] hands.

36 They returned and when they reported [this] to him, he said, "It is the word of YHWH which he spoke through his servant Elijah the Tishbite, 'In the tract [of land] of Jezreel the dogs shall eat the flesh of Jezebel;

37 and the corpse of Jezebel shall be like manure on the surface of the field of the tract [of land] of Jezreel, so that they cannot say, 'This is Jezebel.'"

---

[1] Reading the Qere.

622 Jehu Destroys the House of Ahab
2 Kings 10:1-17

2 Kings 10

1 Now Ahab had seventy sons in Samaria, so Jehu wrote letters and sent [them] to Samaria, to the officials of Jezreel, the elders, and to the guardians [of the sons[1]] of Ahab, as follows,

2 "Now, when this letter reaches you, since the sons of your master are with you, and the chariots, the horses, a fortified city and the weaponry are with you,

3 you should look for the best and most upright of the sons of your master and place him on the throne of his father. Then fight for your master's house!"

4 But they were very, very frightened and said, "Look, two kings could not stand up before him, so how are we to stand?"

5 Then the one over the palace, the one over the city, the elders and the guardians sent to Jehu, saying, "We are your servants, and all that you say to us, we will do: we will not make anyone king. Do what seems best in your eyes."

6 So he wrote them a letter a second time, saying, "If you are with me and you would heed my voice, take the heads of the men of the sons of your master and come to me at this time tomorrow, at Jezreel." Now the king's sons, seventy persons, were with the notables of the city, who were rearing them.

7 As soon as the letter came to them they took the sons of the king, and they slaughtered [the] seventy persons; they put their heads in baskets and sent them to him at Jezreel.

8 Then a messenger came and reported to him, "They have delivered the heads of the king's sons." He said, "Put them [into] two heaps, at the entrance of the gate until morning."

9 When morning came he went out and stood there and he said to all the people, "You are innocent. It was I who conspired against my master and slew him. But who has struck down all these down?

10 Know then that there shall not fall to the ground any of the word that YHWH has spoken against the house of Ahab; for YHWH has done what he spoke through his servant Elijah."

11 So Jehu struck down all those left to the house of Ahab in Jezreel—all notables, his close associates, and his priests, until he left him no survivor.

12 Then he rose up, set out, and went to Samaria. When he was at Beth-eked of the Shepherds on the way,

13 Jehu found the brothers of Ahaziah king of Judah, and he said, "Who are you?" They said, "We are brothers of Ahaziah, and we have come down [to look into] the welfare of the sons of the king and the sons of the queen mother."

14 He said, "Take them alive." So they took them alive, and they slaughtered them at the cistern of Beth-eked, forty-two persons; and he did not spare one of them.

15 When he went from there he encountered Jehonadab son of Rechab [coming] to meet him: he greeted him and said to him, "Is it as constant with your heart as with my heart?" Jehonadab said: "Yes, yes, it is." [Jehu replied²]: "If it is, give [me] your hand." So he gave [him] his hand and [Jehu] pulled him up to himself, into [his] chariot.

16 He said, "Come with me and see my zeal for YHWH!" So they made him ride with him in his chariot.

17 When he came to Samaria he struck down all those who were left to Ahab in Samaria until he wiped it out [his house], according to the word of YHWH that he had spoken to Elijah.

---

¹ Reading with the Septuagint.
² Reading with the Septuagint.

623 Jehu Wipes Out the Worship of Baal
2 Kings 10:18-36

2 Kings 10

18 Then Jehu gathered all the people and said to them, "Ahab served the Baal a little, Jehu will serve a great deal!

19 Now, let all prophets of the Baal, all his servants and all his priests, come to meet me—let no person be absent—for I have a great sacrifice for the Baal. Anyone who absents himself shall not live!" Now Jehu acted with cunning in order to destroy the servants of the Baal.

20 Then Jehu said, "Sanctify a solemn assembly for the Baal," so they proclaimed [it].

21 Then Jehu sent [orders] throughout all Israel, so all the servants of the Baal came, there was no one remaining who did not come, and they came into the house of the Baal so that the house of the Baal was filled from end to end.

22 Then he said to one over the wardrobe, "Bring out vestment[s] for all the servants of the Baal." So he brought out the vestment[s] for them.

23 Then Jehu and Jehonadab son of Rechab entered the house of the Baal, and he said to the servants of the Baal, "Search and see that there are no servants of YHWH here with you, but only servants of the Baal."

24 When they went in to make sacrifices and burnt offerings, Jehu stationed eighty men outside for himself and he said, "Any one who escapes from [among] those men whom I am delivering into your hands, [let it be] his life for his life."¹

25 As soon as he had finished making the burnt offering Jehu said to the Razim and the Shalishim, "Go in and strike them down; let no one get out." So they struck them down with the edge of the sword and the Razim and the Shalishim threw [them] out and then went to the citadel² of the house of the Baal.

26 They brought out the cult-pillars of the house of the Baal and they burned it.

27 They pulled down the cult-pillar of the Baal, and then they pulled down the house of the Baal, and they made it into a cesspool³ until this day.

28 Thus Jehu exterminated the Baal from Israel.

29 Only the sins of Jeroboam son of Nebat, that he caused Israel to sin, Jehu did not turn aside from them, the calves of gold which [were] at Bethel and which [were] at Dan.

30 Then YHWH said to Jehu, "Because you have acted well in doing the right thing in my eyes, and according to all that was in my heart you have done to this house of Ahab, your sons to the fourth generation shall sit on the throne of Israel."

31 But Jehu did not take care to walk in the Torah of YHWH, the God of Israel, with all his heart; he did not turn aside from the sins of Jeroboam that he caused Israel to sin.

32 In those days YHWH began to cut off Israel: and Hazael struck them in all the borders of Israel;

33 from the Jordan eastward, the entire land of Gilead, the Gadites, the Reubenites, and the Manassites, from Aroer, which is by Wadi Arnon, and Gilead and Bashan.

34 Now the rest of the acts of Jehu, everything that he did and all his valor, are they not written in the Book of the Chronicles of the Kings of Israel?

35 When Jehu lay down to rest with his ancestors, they buried him in Samaria. Then Jehoahaz his son became king in his place.

36 The days that Jehu was king over Israel were twenty-eight years in Samaria.

---

[1] Or, "his life [shall be] for the life of him [who escaped]."
[2] Literally, "city."
[3] Reading the Qere.

624 Athaliah Usurps the Throne
2 Chron 22:10–23:21 // 2 Kings 11:1-20

2 Chronicles 22	*2 Kings 11*
10 When Athaliah mother of Ahaziah saw that her son was dead, she rose up and spoke [against] the royal family of the house of Judah.	1 When Athaliah mother of Ahaziah saw[1] that her son was dead, she rose up and destroyed all the royal family.
11 However, Jehoshabeath daughter of the king, took Joash son of Ahaziah, and stole him away from among the king's sons who were about to be put to death; she placed him and his wet-nurse into a bedchamber. Thus Jehoshabeath daughter of King Jehoram [and] wife of Jehoiada the priest, since she was a sister of Ahaziah, concealed him from Athaliah, so that she did not put him to death.	2 However, Jehosheba daughter of King Joram [and] sister of Ahaziah, took Joash son of Ahaziah, and stole him away from among the king's sons who were about to be put to death, him and his wet-nurse, into a bed-chamber; and they concealed him from Athaliah so that he was not put to death.

12 He was with them in the house of God, hidden for six years, while Athaliah was queen over the land.

23:1 But in the seventh year Jehoiada felt strong enough and took the captains over hundreds—that is, Azariah son of Jeroham, Ishmael son of Jehohanan, Azariah son of Obed, as well as Maaseiah son of Adaiah, and Elishaphat son of Zichri—with him into a covenant.

2 Then they went around in Judah and gathered the Levites from all the cities of Judah and the heads of the families of Israel, and they came to Jerusalem.

3 All the assembly then made a covenant in the house of God with the king, and he said to them, "Here is the king's son! Let him be king as YHWH has spoken concerning David's descendants!

4 This is the thing you must do: one third of you who come [on duty] on the sabbath as priests and as Levites [shall be] gatekeepers at the thresholds.

5 [Another] third at the house of the king, and the [remaining] third [shall be] at the gate of the foundation, and all the people [shall be] in the courts of the house of YHWH.

6 No one shall enter the house of YHWH, except the priests and ministering Levites; they may enter since they are holy, but all the people shall keep YHWH's guard.

7 The Levites shall make a circle around the king, each man with his weapons in his hand; anyone who comes near the house shall be put to death. Be with the king in his coming in and his going out."

8 The Levites and all Judah did according to all that Jehoiada the priest had commanded; they each took their men—those coming on duty on the sabbath, along with those going off duty on the sabbath—for Jehoiada the priest had not dismissed the [outgoing] courses.

9 Then Jehoiada the priest gave to the captains of hundreds the spears, the bucklers, and the shields that had been King David's, which were in the house of God.

10 He made all the people stand, each man with his javelin in his hand, from the south corner of the house to the north corner of the house, at the altar and at the house, surrounding the king.

3 He was with her in the house of YHWH, hidden for six years, while Athaliah was queen over the land.

4 But in the seventh year Jehoiada sent [out] and took the captains of hundreds[2] of the Carites and the [royal] guard and had them come to him in the house of YHWH; and he made a covenant with them and bound them by oath in the house of YHWH, and showed them the king's son.

5 Then he commanded them, saying, "This is what you must do: one third of you who come [on duty] on the sabbath [shall] keep charge over the house of the king.

6 [Another] third at the Sur Gate, and the [remaining] third at the gate behind the [royal] guard, and you shall keep guard over the house.[3]

7 The two units among you, all those going off duty on the sabbath, shall keep guard over the house of YHWH for the king.

8 You shall make a circle about the king, each man with his weapons in his hand; anyone who comes near to the ranks shall be put to death. Be with the king in his going out and his coming in."

9 The captains of hundreds did according to all that Jehoiada the priest had commanded; they each took their men—those coming on duty on the sabbath, along with those going off duty on the sabbath—and came to Jehoiada the priest.

10 Then the priest gave to the captains of hundreds the spears and the shields that had been King David's, which were in the house of YHWH.

11 The [royal] guard stood, each man with his weapons in his hand, from the south corner of the house to the north corner of the house, at the altar and at the house, surrounding the king.

11 Then they brought out the son of the king: placed upon him the diadem and the testimony, and they made him king. Jehoiada and his sons anointed him, and they acclaimed, "Long live the king!"

12 When Athaliah heard the sound of the people who were running and praising the king, she came to the people into the house of YHWH.

13 There she saw the king standing by his pillar at the entrance with the captains and the trumpets [sounding] about the king, and all the people of the land rejoicing and sounding trumpets and singers with instruments of music, and songs declaring praise. Athaliah tore her garments and cried, "Treachery, treachery!"

14 Then Jehoiada the priest brought out the captains of hundreds [who had been] appointed over the army, and said to them, "Bring her out from within the ranks: anyone who goes after her shall be put to death by the sword!" For the priest said, "You shall not put her to death in the house of YHWH!"

15 So they laid hands on her and she came into the entry of the horses' gate of the house of the king, and they put her to death there.

16 Jehoiada made a covenant between himself and all the people and the king, that they should be a people to YHWH.

17 Then all the people went to the house of the Baal and broke it down; its altars and its images they smashed and Mattan, the priest of Baal, they killed in front of the altars.

18 Jehoiada placed those appointed [over] the house of YHWH, under the authority of the Levitical priests whom David had assigned over the house of YHWH to offer up burnt offerings [to] YHWH as in the Torah of Moses, with rejoicing and song, according to the direction of David.

19 He also stationed gatekeepers at the gates of the house of YHWH that no one should come in who was unclean in any respect.

20 Further he took the captains of hundreds, the nobles, the rulers over the people, and all the people of the land, and he brought the king down from the house of YHWH; they came through the Upper Gate into the house of the king, and they seated the king upon the throne of the kingdom.

12 Then he brought out the son of the king: placed upon him the diadem and the testimony, and they made him king, anointed him, clapped their hands, and said, "Long live the king!"

13 When Athaliah heard the sound of the [royal] guard [and] the people, she came to the people into the house of YHWH.

14 There she saw the king standing by the pillar, according to custom, with the captains and the trumpets [sounding] for the king, and all the people of the land rejoicing and sounding the trumpets. Athaliah tore her garments and cried, "Treachery, treachery!"

15 Then Jehoiada the priest commanded the captains of hundreds[4] [who had been] appointed over the army, and said to them, "Bring her out from within the ranks: anyone who goes after her put to death by the sword!" For the priest said, "Let her not be put to death in the house of YHWH!"

16 So they laid hands on her and she came by way of the horses' entry to the house of the king, and she was put to death there.

17 Jehoiada made a covenant between YHWH and the king and the people that they should be a people to YHWH, and between the king and the people.

18 Then all the people of the land went to the house of the Baal and broke it down; its altars[5] and its images they smashed completely, and Mattan, the priest of Baal, they killed in front of the altars.

The priest placed those appointed over the house of YHWH.

19 Further he took the captains of hundreds, the Carites, the [royal] guard, and all the people of the land, and they brought the king down from the house of YHWH; they came by way of the Gate of the [Royal] Guard into the house of the king, and he took his seat upon the throne of the king.

21 So all the people of the land rejoiced, and the city was quiet, [once] they had put Athaliah to death by the sword.

20 So all the people of the land rejoiced, and the city was quiet, [once] they had put Athaliah to death by the sword in the house of the king.[6]

---

[1] Reading the Qere, "saw."
[2] Reading the Qere.
[3] The final Hebrew word in the verse is obscure.
[4] Reading the Qere.
[5] Reading the Qere.
[6] Reading the Qere.

625 The Reign of Jehoash of Judah
2 Chron 24:1-27 // 2 Kings 12:1-22

2 Chronicles 24

1 Joash was seven years old when he became king, and he was king for forty years in Jerusalem. The name of his mother was Zibiah from Beersheba.

2 Joash did what was right in the eyes of YHWH all the days of Jehoiada the priest.

3 Jehoiada provided two wives for him and he fathered sons and daughters.

4 Sometime afterwards Joash decided to renovate the house of YHWH.

5 So he gathered the priests and Levites, and said to them, "Go out to the cities of Judah and gather from all Israel money to repair the house of your God year by year, and act quickly on the matter." But the Levites did not act quickly.

2 Kings 12

1 Jehoash was seven years old when he became king.
2 In the seventh year of Jehu, Jehoash became king, and he was king in Jerusalem for forty years. The name of his mother was Zibiah from Beersheba.

3 Jehoash did what was right in the eyes of YHWH all his days while Jehoiada the priest instructed him.

4 However, the high places were not removed; so the people continued sacrificing and burning incense on the high places.

5 Jehoash said to the priests, "All the money for consecrated things that is brought into the house of YHWH—money of assessment for each person, money of each person's valuation [as well as] any money that a person might bring voluntarily into the house of YHWH—

6 let the priests take for themselves, each one from his contributor, that they may repair the dilapidation of the house wherever any dilapidation is found."

7 But by the twenty-third year of King Jehoash the priests [still] had not repaired the dilapidation of the house.

6 So the king summoned Jehoiada the chief [priest], and said to him, "Why have you not required the Levites to bring in from Judah and Jerusalem the tax imposed by Moses, the servant of YHWH, and the assembly of Israel for the Tent of the Testimony?"

7 For Athaliah, wickedness [herself] [and] her sons had broken into the house of God and had even used all the consecrated things of the house of YHWH for the Baals.

8 So the king spoke, and they made a certain chest and they placed it outside the gate of the house of YHWH.

9 They made a proclamation in Judah and Jerusalem to bring in for YHWH the tax of Moses, the servant of God, imposed on Israel in the wilderness.

10 All the officials and all the people rejoiced and they brought [the tax] and dropped [it] into the chest until it was filled up.

11 Whenever the chest was brought to the king's deputies by the hand of the Levites, or whenever they noticed that there was an abundance of money, the king's scribe and the chief priest's deputy would come and empty the chest, and they would then carry it [back] to its place. Thus they did day by day, and so collected money in abundance.

12 Then the king and Jehoiada would give it to the one doing the work of the service of the house of YHWH, and they would hire [stone-] cutters and artisans to renovate the house of YHWH and also artisans in iron and bronze to repair the house of YHWH.

13 So those doing the work kept working; and the work of reclamation proceeded forward in their hand, and they restored the house of God to its [former] condition and reinforced it.

14 As soon as they had finished, they brought before the king and Jehoiada the remainder of the money and they made vessels for the house of YHWH, vessels for ministering and for offering, and dishes and vessels of gold and silver. They were offering up burnt offerings in the house of YHWH continually all the days of Jehoiada.

8 So King Jehoash summoned Jehoiada the priest and the [other] priests and said to them, "Why are you not repairing the dilapidation of the house? Now you shall not take any more money from your contributors but you shall give it [over] for the dilapidation of the house."

9 So the priests agreed not to take [any more] money from the people nor to repair the dilapidation of the house.

10 Then Jehoiada the priest took a certain chest, bored a hole in its lid, and placed it beside the altar on the right side as one enters the house of YHWH, and there the priests guarding the threshold put all the money that was brought to the house of YHWH.

11 Whenever they saw that there was an abundance of money in the chest, the king's scribe and the high priest would come up, bind [it] together, and count the money that was found in the house of YHWH.

12 Then they would put the money that had been measured out into the hands[1] of those doing the work, those appointed over the house of YHWH; and they would give it out to the workers in wood and to the builders who were working on the house of YHWH,

13 and also to the masons and to the stone-cutters, to buy timber and quarried stone, to repair the dilapidation of the house of YHWH as well as for everything [else] that might be laid out on the house for repair.

14 But there were not made for the house of YHWH silver basins, snuffers, bowls, trumpets, [or] any vessels of gold or vessels of silver, from the money that was brought into the house of YHWH,

15 since they were giving it to those doing the work and with it they would repair the house of YHWH.

16 But they did not audit the men into whose hand they had put the money to be given to those doing the work, for they were acting uprightly.

17 Money from guilt-offering[s] and money from sin-offerings was not brought into the house of YHWH; [such] belonged to the priests.

15 When Jehoiada grew old and was full of days, he died; [he was] one hundred and thirty years old at his death.

16 They buried him in the city of David with the kings, for he had done good in Israel, and for God and his house.

17 Now after the death of Jehoiada the officials of Judah came and bowed themselves before the king; then the king listened to them.

18 They forsook the house of YHWH the God of their ancestors, and they served the asherim and the idols. Whereupon [divine] anger came upon Judah and Jerusalem because of this their guilt.

19 Even so, he sent prophets among them, to bring them back to YHWH; they censured them, but they would not heed [them].

20 Then the spirit of God clothed Zechariah son of Jehoiada the priest, and he stood above the people, and said to them, "Thus says God, 'Why do you transgress the commandments of YHWH so that you do not prosper? Because you have forsaken YHWH, he has forsaken you.'"

21 At this they conspired against him, and stoned him with stones at the command of the king in the court of the house of YHWH!

22 Thus Joash the king did not remember the kindness that Jehoiada his father had shown him, but killed his son. As he was dying, he said, "May YHWH see and avenge!"

23 At the turn of the year the army of Aram came up against him; they came into Judah and Jerusalem and destroyed all the officials of the people from [among] the people, and sent all their spoil to the king of Damascus.

18 At this time, Hazael king of Aram came up and fought against Gath and captured it. Then Hazael set his face to go up against Jerusalem;

19 but Jehoash king of Judah took all the consecrated things that Jehoshaphat, Jehoram, and Ahaziah, his ancestors kings of Judah, had consecrated, and his [own] consecrated things, and all the gold that was found in the treasuries of the house of YHWH and the house of the king, and he sent [them] to Hazael king of Aram [who] then went away from Jerusalem.

24 Even though the army of Aram had come with few men, YHWH gave into their hand a larger army because they had forsaken YHWH the God of their ancestors. Thus [the Arameans] carried out judgment upon Joash.

25 Now when they went away from him, for they had left him with many wounds, his servants conspired against him on account of the blood of the sons of Jehoiada the priest, and they slew him upon his bed. So he died; and they buried him in the city of David, but they did not bury him within the tombs of the kings.

26 Those who conspired against him [were] Zabad son of Shimeath, the Ammonite woman, and Jehozabad son of Shimrith, the Moabite woman.

27 Of his sons and the multitude of oracles against him, and the founding of the house of God, these things indeed are written in the Commentary on the Book of Kings, and Amaziah his son became king in his place.

20 Now the rest of the acts of Joash and all that he did, are they not written in the Book of the Chronicles of the Kings of Judah?

21 Moreover, his servants rose up and formed a conspiracy, and they struck Joash down at Beth-millo that leads down to Silla,

22 Jozabad son of Shimeath and Jehozabad son of Shomer his servants, struck him down. So he died; and they buried him with his ancestors in the city of David,

and Amaziah his son became king in his place.

---

¹ Reading the Qere.

626 The Reign of Jehoahaz
2 Kings 13:1-9

2 Kings 13

1 In the twenty-third year of Joash son of Ahaziah, king of Judah, Jehoahaz son of Jehu became king over Israel in Samaria for seventeen years.

2 He did what was evil in the eyes of YHWH, and walked after the sins of Jeroboam son of Nebat who caused Israel to sin; he did not turn away from it.

3 So the wrath of YHWH burned hot against Israel, and he gave them into the hand of Hazael king of Aram and into the hand of Ben-hadad son of Hazael all [their] days.

4 But Jehoahaz implored YHWH and YHWH listened to him, for he saw the oppression of Israel, how the king of Aram oppressed them.

5 Then YHWH gave Israel a deliverer and they led them out from under the hand of Aram; the Israelites then lived in their tents as formerly.

6 Nevertheless they did not turn away from the sins of the house of Jeroboam who caused Israel to sin,[1] he [too] walked in it; the asherah also stood in Samaria.

7 Moreover, he did not leave any militia to Jehoahaz except for fifty horsemen, ten chariots, and ten thousand foot soldiers for the king of Aram had destroyed them, and had made them like chaff at threshing.

8 Now the rest of the acts of Jehoahaz, everything that he did and his valor, are they not written in the Book of the Chronicles of the Kings of Israel?

9 When Jehoahaz lay down to rest with his ancestors, they buried him in Samaria, and Joash his son became king in his place.

---

[1] Reading the Qere.

627 The Reign of Jehoash of Israel
2 Kings 13:10-13 // 2 Kings 14:15-16

2 Kings 13	*2 Kings 14*
10 In the thirty-seventh year of Joash king of Judah, Jehoash son of Jehoahaz became king over Israel in Samaria for sixteen years.	
11 He did what was evil in the eyes of YHWH; he did not turn from all the sins of Jeroboam son of Nebat who caused Israel to sin; he [too] walked in it.	
12 Now the rest of the acts of Joash, everything that he did and his valor with which he fought with Amaziah king of Judah, are they not written in the Book of the Chronicles of the Kings of Israel?	15 Now the rest of the acts of Jehoash that he did and his valor, and how he fought with Amaziah king of Judah, are they not written in the Book of the Chronicles of the Kings of Israel?
13 When Joash lay down to rest with his ancestors, and Jeroboam sat upon his throne, Joash was buried in Samaria with the kings of Israel.	16 When Jehoash lay down to rest with his ancestors, he was buried in Samaria with the kings of Israel, and Jeroboam his son became king in his place.

628 Elisha's Final Prophecy and Death
2 Kings 13:14-25

2 Kings 13

14 Now when Elisha had become sick with his illness from which he would die, Joash king of Israel went down to him and wept before him and said, "My father, my father! The chariot[s] of Israel and its horsemen!"

15 Elisha said to him, "Take a bow and arrows." So he took for himself a bow and arrows.

16 Then he said to the king of Israel, "Put your hand upon the bow"; so he put up his hand [on the bow] and Elisha placed his hands upon the hands of the king.

17 Then he said, "Open the window toward the east"; and he opened [it]. Elisha said, "Shoot!"; and he shot. Then he said, "An arrow of victory for YHWH, and an arrow of victory over Aram, for you shall strike down Aram at Aphek until utterly finished!"

18 He said, "Take the arrows"; and he took [them]. Then he said to the king of Israel, "Beat the ground [with the arrows]"; and he beat [the ground] three times and then stood still.

19 Therefore the man of God was angry with him and said, "Had you beat [the ground] five or six times, then you would have struck down Aram until utterly finished but now you will strike down Aram [only] three times."

20 Then Elisha died and they buried him. Now raiding bands from Moab came into the land as the year came [around].[1]

21 It happened that as they were burying a man, they saw the raiding band, and they threw the man into the grave of Elisha. As soon as the man touched the bones of Elisha, he came to life and stood upon his feet.

22 Now Hazael king of Aram had oppressed Israel all the days of Jehoahaz.

23 But YHWH was gracious to them and had compassion on them and turned toward them because of his covenant with Abraham, Isaac and Jacob. He was not willing to destroy them; so he has not driven them from his presence until now.

24 Then Hazael king of Aram died and Ben-hadad his son became king in his place.

25 Thereupon Jehoash son of Jehoahaz took again the cities from the hand of Ben-hadad son of Hazael, that he had taken in battle from the hand of Jehoahaz his father. Three times Joash struck him down and took back the cities of Israel.

---

[1] Literally, "came the year." The phrase may mean "year by year" or every year at a certain time when raiding was profitable.

629 The Reign of Amaziah
2 Chron 25:1–26:2 // 2 Kings 14:1-22 // Deut 24:16 // 2 Kings 13:12-13

2 Chronicles 25

1 Amaziah was twenty-five years old when he became king, and he was king in Jerusalem for twenty-nine years. The name of his mother was Jehoaddan from Jerusalem.

2 He did what was right in the eyes of YHWH, only not with a whole heart.

3 Now when the kingdom was firmly his, he slew his servants who had struck down the king his father.

4 But their children he did not put to death because as it is written in the Torah in the Book of Moses where YHWH commanded, saying, "Fathers shall not die because of children and children shall not die because of fathers, but each person shall die[1] for his [own] sin."

5 Then Amaziah gathered [the men of] Judah and made them stand by ancestral houses under captains of thousands and captains of hundreds, for all Judah and Benjamin. He mustered those twenty years old and upward and found them [some] three hundred thousand picked men [ready] to go forth to war [and] to handle spear and shield.

6 He also hired from Israel a hundred thousand mighty warriors for one hundred talents of silver.

Deuteronomy 24
16 Fathers shall not be put to death because of children and children shall not be put to death because of fathers, each person shall be put to death for his [own] sin.[3]

2 Kings 14

1 In the second year of Joahaz king of Israel, Amaziah son of Joash, king of Judah, became king.

2 He was twenty-five years old when he became king, [and] he was king in Jerusalem for twenty-nine years. The name of his mother was Jehoaddin from Jerusalem.

3 He did what was right in the eyes of YHWH, only not like David his [fore]father [but] according to all that Joash his father had done, he did.

4 Moreover the high-places were not removed, for the people were still sacrificing and burning incense on the high places.

5 Now when the kingdom was firmly in his hand, he struck down his servants who had struck down the king his father.

6 But the children of those who had struck down [the king] he did not put to death as it is written in the Book of the Torah of Moses where YHWH commanded, saying, "Fathers shall not be put to death because of children and children shall not be put to death because of fathers, but each person shall be put to death for his [own] sin."[4]

7 But a man of God came to him saying, "O king, the army of Israel must not go with you, for YHWH is not with Israel, [not with] all those Ephraimites!

8 Rather you go and act alone; be strong for the battle [otherwise] God will overthrow you in front of the enemy, for God has power to aid or to overthrow."

9 But Amaziah said to the man of God, "And what is to be done about the hundred talents that I have given to the force from Israel?" The man of God answered, "YHWH is able to give you much more than this."

10 So Amaziah discharged them, the force that had come to him from Ephraim, to go back to their homeplace. At this their wrath burned fiercely against Judah and they went back to their homeplace in fierce wrath.

11 However, Amaziah strengthened himself and led his people and went to the Valley of Salt and struck down ten thousand Seirites.

12 The Judahites took another ten thousand alive; they brought them to the top of Sela and flung them down from the top of Sela, and all of them were dashed to pieces.

13 But the men of the force that Amaziah had turned back from going with him to battle, sacked the cities of Judah from Samaria to Beth-horon, struck down three thousand from them and seized much plunder.

14 Now after Amaziah came back from striking down the Edomites, he brought the gods of the Seirites and set them up for himself as gods; he bowed himself down before them and burned incense to them.

7 He struck down ten thousand Edomites in the Valley of Salt,[5] captured Sela in battle and named it Jokthe-el [its name] to this day.

15 YHWH's wrath burned against Amaziah and sent a prophet to him and he said to him, "Why have you looked to the gods of the people who could not deliver their [own] people from your hand?"

16 But while he was still speaking to him, [the king] said to him, "Have we appointed you a counselor to the king? You had better stop now! Why should you be struck down?" So the prophet did stop, but he said, "I know that God has decided to destroy you, because you have done this and not listened to my counsel."

17 Then Amaziah king of Judah took counsel and sent to Joash son of Jehoahaz son of Jehu, king of Israel, saying, "Come,² let us meet face to face."

8 Then Amaziah sent messengers to Jehoash son of Jehoahaz son of Jehu, king of Israel, saying, "Come, let us meet face to face."

18 But Joash king of Israel sent [back] to Amaziah king of Judah saying, "A thistle that was in Lebanon sent to a cedar that was in Lebanon, saying, 'Give your daughter to my son as a wife.' But a beast of the field that was in Lebanon passed by and crushed the thistle.

9 But Jehoash king of Israel sent [back] to Amaziah king of Judah saying, "A thistle that was in Lebanon sent to a cedar that was in Lebanon, saying, 'Give your daughter to my son as a wife.' But a beast of the field that was in Lebanon passed by and crushed the thistle.

19 You say indeed you have struck down Edom and so your heart has lifted you up to brag. Now remain in your house: why look for evil for you shall fall, you and Judah with you?"

10 Certainly you have struck down Edom and so your heart has lifted you up: glory [in it], but stay in your house. Now why look for trouble for you shall fall, you and Judah with you?"

20 But Amaziah did not listen, for it [came] from God so that he could give them into the hand [of Joash], because they had looked to the gods of Edom.

11 But Amaziah did not listen. So Jehoash king of Israel went up and he and Amaziah king of Judah met face to face at Beth-shemesh which is in Judah.

21 So Joash king of Israel went up and he and Amaziah king of Judah met face to face at Beth-shemesh which is in Judah.

22 Judah was overthrown before Israel and everyone fled to their tents.

12 Judah was overthrown before Israel and everyone fled to their tents.

23 Then Joash king of Israel captured Amaziah king of Judah, son of Joash son of Jehoahaz, at Beth-shemesh and brought him to Jerusalem; and made a breach in the wall of Jerusalem from the Ephraim Gate as far as the Poneh Gate, four hundred cubits.

24 Also [he took] all the gold and silver and all the vessels that were found in the house of God with Obed-edom, and the treasures of the house of the king along with hostages, and he returned to Samaria.

2 Kings 13

12 Now the rest of the acts of Joash and all that he did, and the valor with which he fought with Amaziah king of Judah, are they not written in the Book of the Chronicles of the Kings of Israel.

13 When Joash lay down to rest with his ancestors, Jeroboam sat upon his throne. Joash was buried in Samaria with the kings of Israel.

13 Then Jehoash king of Israel captured Amaziah king of Judah, son of Jehoash son of Ahaziah, at Beth-shemesh and came to[6] Jerusalem; and made a breach in the wall of Jerusalem from the Ephraim Gate as far as the Pinnah Gate, four hundred cubits.

14 Also he took all the gold and silver and all vessels that were found [in] the house of YHWH and in the treasuries of the house of the king along with hostages, and he returned to Samaria.

15 Now the rest of the acts of Jehoash that he did, and his valor and how he fought with Amaziah king of Judah, are they not written in the Book of the Chronicles of the Kings of Israel.

16 When Jehoash lay down to rest with his ancestors, he was buried in Samaria with the kings of Israel; and Jeroboam his son became king in his place.

25 Amaziah son of Joash, king of Judah, lived after the death of Jehoash son of Jehoahaz, king of Israel, fifteen years.

26 Now the rest of the acts of Amaziah, from the first to the last, indeed are they not written in the Book of the Kings of Judah and Israel?

27 From the time that Amaziah turned away from following YHWH, they formed a conspiracy against him in Jerusalem, but he fled to Lachish; but they sent after him to Lachish and put him to death there.

28 Then they brought him back on horses and they buried him with his ancestors in the city of Judah.

17 Amaziah son of Joash, king of Judah, lived after the death of Jehoash son of Jehoahaz, king of Israel, [another] fifteen years.

18 Now the rest of the acts of Amaziah, are they not written in the Book of the Chronicles of the Kings of Judah?

19 They formed a conspiracy against him in Jerusalem, but he fled to Lachish; but they sent after him to Lachish and put him to death there.

20 Then they brought him back on horses, and he was buried in Jerusalem with his ancestors in the city of David.

26:1 And all of the people of Judah took Uzziah, who was sixteen years old, and made him king in place of his father Amaziah.

2 He [re]built Eloth and returned it to Judah after the king [Amaziah] lay down to rest with his ancestors.

21 All the people of Judah took Azariah who was sixteen years old, and made him king in place of his father Amaziah.

22 He [re]built Elath and returned it to Judah after the king [Amaziah] lay down to rest with his ancestors.

---

[1] Literally, "They shall die."
[2] Reading the Qere.
[3] Literally, "They shall be put to death."
[4] Reading the Qere.
[5] Reading the Qere.
[6] Reading the Qere.

630　The Reign of Jeroboam II
2 Kings 14:23-29

2 Kings 14

23 In the fifteenth year of Amaziah son of Joash, king of Judah, Jeroboam son of Joash, king of Israel, became king in Samaria for forty-one years.

24 He did what was evil in the eyes of YHWH; he did not turn away from all the sins of Jeroboam son of Nebat that he caused Israel to sin.

25 He restored the frontier of Israel, from Lebo-hamath as far as the Sea of the Arabah, according to the word of YHWH the God of Israel that he spoke through his servant Jonah son of Amittai, the prophet who was from Gath-hepher.

26 For YHWH had seen that the plight of Israel was very rebellious. There was no one, bound or free, no one to help Israel.

27 But YHWH had not said that he would obliterate the name of Israel from under heaven so he delivered them through Jeroboam son of Joash.

28 Now the rest of the acts of Jeroboam and everything that he did, and his valor with which he fought, and how he returned Damascus and Hamath to Judah in Israel, are they not written in the Book of the Chronicles of the Kings of Israel?

29 When Jeroboam lay down to rest with his ancestors, with the kings of Israel, Zechariah his son became king in his place.

Divided Monarchy-4
Sections 630–649

Number	Title	2 Chronicles	2 Kings
630	The Reign of Jeroboam II		14:23-29
631	The Reign of Uzziah (Azariah)	26:3-23	15:1-7
632	The Reign of Zechariah		15:8-12
633	The Reign of Shallum		15:13-16
634	The Reign of Menahem		15:17-22
635	The Reign of Pekahiah		15:23-26
636	The Reign of Pekah		15:27-31
637	The Reign of Jotham	27:1-9	15:32-38
638	The Reign of Ahaz	28:1-27	16:1-20
639	The Fall of Samaria/Captivity of Israel		17:1-23
640	Foreign Resettlement of Samaria		17:24-41
641	The Reign of Hezekiah	29:1-2	18:1-8
642	The Fall of Samaria		18:9-12
643	Hezekiah Restores Service	29:3-36	
644	The Celebration of Passover	30:1–31:1	
645	Hezekiah's Provision for Priests	31:2-21	
646	The Invasion of Sennacherib	32:1-19	18:13-37
647	Judah Delivered from Sennacherib	32:20-23	19:1-37
648	Hezekiah's Sickness	32:24-26	20:1-11
649	Hezekiah Receives Envoys	32:27-31	20:12-19

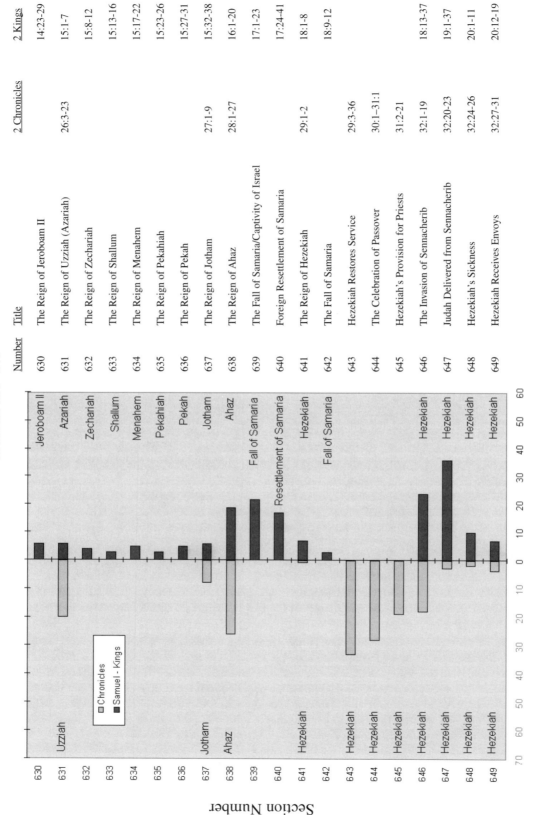

631 The Reign of Uzziah (Azariah)
2 Chron 26:3-23 // 2 Kings 15:1-7

2 Chronicles 26

3 Uzziah [was] sixteen years old when he became king, and for fifty-two years he was king in Jerusalem. The name of his mother was Jecoliah[1] from Jerusalem.

4 He did what was right in the eyes of YHWH according to all that Amaziah his father had done.

5 He set himself to seek God in the days of Zechariah who instructed him in the oracles of God. On the days that he sought YHWH, God made him prosper.

6 He went out and did battle against the Philistines; he breached the wall of Gath, the wall of Jabneh and the wall of Ashdod. He built cities in [the region of] Ashdod and among the Philistines.

7 God helped him against the Philistines, against the Arabs[2] who lived in Gur-baal and [against] the Meunites.

8 Moreover, the Ammonites gave tribute to Uzziah and his fame[3] spread as far as the border of Egypt for he became exceedingly strong.

9 Uzziah built towers in Jerusalem at the Pinnah Gate, at the Valley Gate and at the Angle-Corner, and he fortified them.

10 He also built towers in the wilderness and hewed out many cisterns, for he had large herds of cattle in the Shephelah and in the plain; furthermore, [he had] farmers and vine-dressers in the hills and in the cultivated land for he was one who loved the earth.

11 Further Uzziah had an army ready for battle, to go out to war by divisions according to the enumeration of their muster [made] by Jeiel[4] the scribe and Maaseiah the clerk, under the authority of Hananiah one of the officials of the king.

2 Kings 15

1 In the twenty-seventh year of Jeroboam king of Israel, Azariah son of Amaziah, king of Judah, became king.

2 He was sixteen years old when he became king, and for fifty-two years he was king in Jerusalem. The name of his mother was Jecoliah from Jerusalem.

3 And he did what was right in the eyes of YHWH according to all that Amaziah his father had done.

4 Only the high places were not removed; the people were still sacrificing and burning incense on the high places.

12 The whole enumeration of the heads of ancestral families of mighty warriors was two thousand six hundred.

13 Under their authority was a force of three hundred and seven thousand [and] five hundred, who were ready for battle with mighty power to aid the king against the enemy.

14 Uzziah provided for them, for the entire force: shields, spears, helmets, body-armor, bows and stones for slinging.

15 He made in Jerusalem war machines designed by experts,⁵ to be on the towers and the corners for firing arrows and large stones. Thus his fame went out far and wide, for he was marvelously helped until he was strong.

16 But while growing strong his heart grew proud to his destruction: for he acted unfaithfully toward YHWH his God and entered the sanctuary of YHWH to offer incense on the incense altar.

17 But Azariah the priest went in after him and with him eighty priests of YHWH, men of valor.

18 They stood up to Uzziah the king and said to him, "It is not for you Uzziah to offer incense to YHWH, for that [belongs to] the priests the sons of Aaron who have been consecrated to offer incense. Get out of the holy place, for you have acted unfaithfully; moreover, there is no honor for you from YHWH God.

19 Then Uzziah was enraged; the censer was in his hand ready to offer incense, and in his rage against the priests, leprosy broke out on his brow in front of the priests in the house of YHWH beside the incense altar.

20 When Azariah the chief priest and all the priests looked at him, he was leprous on his brow so they hustled him out from there; in fact, he himself hurried to get out because YHWH had struck him.

21 So Uzziah the king was leprous until the day of his death, and he dwelt [in] a house of isolation⁶ as one leprous, for he was shut out of the house of YHWH while Jotham his son was over the king's house, judging the people of the land.

22 Now the rest of the acts of Uzziah, from the first to the last, Isaiah son of Amoz, the prophet, wrote down.

5 Now YHWH struck the king so that he was leprous until the day of his death; and he lived in a house of isolation⁷ while Jotham, the king's son, was in charge of the house judging the people of the land.

6 Now the rest of the acts of Azariah and all that he did, are they not written in the Book of the Chronicles of the Kings of Judah?

23 When Uzziah lay down to rest with his ancestors, they buried him with his ancestors in a burial ground that belonged to the kings for they said, "he is leprous"; and Jotham his son became king in his place.

7 When Azariah lay down to rest with his ancestors, they buried him with his ancestors in the city of David; and Jotham his son became king in his place.

---

[1] Reading the Qere.
[2] Reading the Qere.
[3] Literally, "name."
[4] Reading the Qere.
[5] Literally, "thought by a thinker."
[6] Reading the Qere.
[7] Literally, "freedom."

632 The Reign of Zechariah
2 Kings 15:8-12

2 Kings 15

8 In the thirty-eighth year of Azariah king of Judah, Zechariah son of Jeroboam became king over Israel in Samaria for six months.

9 He did what was evil in the eyes of YHWH, just as his ancestors had done: he did not turn away from the sins of Jeroboam son of Nebat that he caused Israel to sin.

10 Shallum son of Jabesh conspired against him and struck him down before [the] people and killed him and he became king in his place.

11 Now the rest of the acts of Zechariah, indeed they are written in the Book of the Chronicles of the Kings of Israel.

12 This was the word of YHWH that he had spoken to Jehu, "Your sons to the fourth generation shall sit on the throne of Israel." And so it was.

633 The Reign of Shallum
2 Kings 15:13-16

2 Kings 15

13 Shallum son of Jabesh became king in the thirty-ninth year of Uzziah king of Judah, and was king for one month in Samaria.

14 Menahem son of Gadi went up from Tirzah, came to Samaria, and struck down Shallum son of Jabesh in Samaria and killed him; and he became king in his place.

15 Now the rest of the acts of Shallum, and the conspiracy that he formed, indeed they are written in the Book of the Chronicles of the Kings of Israel.

16 At this time Menahem struck at Tiphsah and everything that was in it, and its territory from Tirzah on. Because it did not open [its gates to him], he struck at [it] [and] sliced open all its pregnant women.

634 The Reign of Menahem
2 Kings 15:17-22

2 Kings 15

17 In the thirty-ninth year of Azariah king of Judah, Menahem son of Gadi became king over Israel for ten years in Samaria.

18 He did what was evil in the eyes of YHWH; he did not turn away from the sins of Jeroboam son of Nebat that he caused Israel to sin all his days.

19 Pul king of Assyria came against the land, and Menahem gave to Pul one thousand talents of silver that his hand might be with him to strengthen his hold on the kingdom.

20 So Menahem laid the silver[-tax] on Israel, on all the men of substance, [who had] to give to the king of Assyria fifty shekels of silver for each man. Then the king of Assyria turned back and did not stay there in the land.

21 Now the rest of the acts of Menahem and all that he did, are they not written in the Book of the Chronicles of the Kings of Israel.

22 When Menahem lay down to rest with his ancestors, Pekahiah his son became king in his place.

635 The Reign of Pekahiah
2 Kings 15:23-26

2 Kings 15

23 In the fiftieth year of Azariah king of Judah, Pekahiah son of Menahem became king over Israel in Samaria for two years.

24 He did what was evil in the eyes of YHWH: he did not turn away from the sins of Jeroboam son of Nebat that he caused Israel to sin.

25 Pekah son of Remaliah, his adjutant, conspired against him and struck him down in Samaria in the citadel of the King's house—with Argob and with Arieh[1]—and with him were fifty men from the Gileadites; so he killed him and became king in his place.

26 Now the rest of the acts of Pekahiah and all that he did, they are indeed written in the Book of the Chronicles of the Kings of Israel.

---

[1] These two names would better fit in the list of Assyrian conquests in 15:29.

636 The Reign of Pekah
2 Kings 15:27-31

2 Kings 15

27 In the fifty-second year of Azariah king of Judah, Pekah son of Remaliah became king over Israel in Samaria for twenty years.

28 He did what was evil in the eyes of YHWH: he did not turn away from the sins of Jeroboam son of Nebat that he had caused Israel to sin.

29 In the days of Pekah king of Israel, Tiglath-pileser king of Assyria came [up] and took Ijon, Abel-beth-maacah, Janoah, Kedesh, Hazor, Gilead and Galilee, all the land of Naphthali; and he exiled them to Assyria.

30 So Hoshea son of Elah formed a conspiracy against Pekah son of Remaliah, struck him down, and killed him, and became king in his place in the twentieth year of Jotham son of Uzziah.

31 Now the rest of the acts of Pekah and all that he did, they are indeed written in the Book of the Chronicles of the Kings of Israel.

637 The Reign of Jotham
2 Chron 27:1-9 // 2 Kings 15:32-38

2 Chronicles 27

1 Jotham was twenty-five years old when he became king, and for sixteen years he was king in Jerusalem. The name of his mother was Jerushah daughter of Zadok.

2 He did what was right in the eyes of YHWH according to all that Uzziah his father had done; only he did not enter the sanctuary of YHWH. However the people continued to corrupt themselves.

3 He built the upper gate of the house of YHWH and built extensively on the city-wall of Ophel.

4 Further he built cities in the hill-country of Judah, and on wooded heights he built citadels and towers.

5 He did battle with the king of the Ammonites and overpowered him. The Ammonites gave him in that year, one hundred talents of silver and ten thousand cors of wheat and ten thousand of barley; the Ammonites handed this over to him in the second and third years.

6 Thus Jotham became strong because he established his ways before YHWH his God.

7 Now the rest of the acts of Jotham and all his battles and his ways, they are indeed written in the Book of the Chronicles of the Kings of Israel and Judah.

8 He was twenty-five years old when he became king, and for sixteen years he was king in Jerusalem.

9 When Jotham lay down to rest with his ancestors, they buried him in the city of David; and Ahaz his son became king in his place.

2 Kings 15

32 In the second year of Pekah son of Remaliah, king of Israel, Jotham son of Azariah, king of Judah, became king.

33 He was twenty-five years old when he became king, and for sixteen years he was king in Jerusalem. The name of his mother was Jerusha daughter of Zadok.

34 He did what was right in the eyes of YHWH according to all that Azariah his father had done.

35 Only they did not remove the high places; the people were still sacrificing and burning incense on the high places. He built the upper gate of the house of YHWH.

36 Now the rest of the acts of Jotham that he did, are they not written in the Book of the Chronicles of the Kings of Judah?

37 In those days YHWH began to send Rezin king of Aram and Pekah son of Remaliah against Judah.

38 When Jotham lay down to rest with his ancestors, he was buried with his ancestors in the city of David his [fore]father; and Ahaz his son became king in his place.

638 The Reign of Ahaz
2 Chron 28:1-27 // 2 Kings 16:1-20 // Isaiah 7:1

2 Chronicles 28

1 Ahaz was twenty years old when he became king, and he was king for sixteen years in Jerusalem. He did not do what was right in the eyes of YHWH like David his [fore]father;

2 but he walked in the ways of the kings of Israel and even made metal images for the Baals.

3 And he offered incense in the valley of the sons of Hinnom, and burned his sons like the abominations of the nations whom YHWH had dispossessed before the Israelites.

4 Moreover he sacrificed and offered incense on the high places and on the hill-tops, and under every verdant tree.

2 Kings 16

1 In the seventeenth year of Pekah son of Remaliah, Ahaz son of Jotham king of Judah became king.

2 Ahaz was twenty years old when he became king, and for sixteen years he was king in Jerusalem. He did not do what was right in the eyes of YHWH his God like David his [fore]father;

3 but he walked in the way of the kings of Israel. He even made his son pass through the fire like the abominations of the nations whom YHWH had dispossessed before the Israelites.

4 Moreover he sacrificed and offered incense on the high places and on the hill-tops, and under every verdant tree.

2 Kings 16
5 Then Rezin king of Aram and Pekah son of Remaliah, king of Israel, went up to Jerusalem to do battle and besieged Ahaz, but they were unable to prevail [against it].

6 At that time Rezin king of Aram recovered Elath for Aram and expelled the Judahites from Eloth, and the Aramaeans came to Elath and settled there to this day.

Isaiah 7:1
1 In the days of Ahaz son of Jotham son of Azariah, king of Judah, Rezin king of Aram and Pekah son of Remaliah, king of Israel, went up to Jerusalem to do battle against it, but he was unable to prevail against it.

2 Kings 14:21-22
21 All the people of Judah took Azariah [who] was sixteen years old, and made him king in place of his father Amaziah.
22 He [re]built Elath and returned it to Judah after the king [Amaziah] lay down to rest with his ancestors.

2 Chronicles 28
5 So YHWH his God gave him into the hand of the king of Aram, and they [the Aramaeans] defeated him and took away from him many captives and brought them to Damascus: he was also given into the hand of the king of Israel and he defeated him with great force.[1]

6 Pekah son of Remaliah slaughtered a hundred and twenty thousand in Judah in one day, all of them men of valor, because they had forsaken YHWH God of their ancestors.

7 Zichri, a warrior of Ephraim, slew Maasieah the king's son and Azrikam, the steward of the [royal] house and Elkanah the king's deputy.

8 The Israelites took away two hundred thousand of their kinsfolk, women, sons and daughters; and they also seized much spoil from them and they brought the spoil to Samaria.

9 However, a prophet of YHWH was there; Oded was his name. He went out to meet the army that had come to Samaria and said to them, "See, because of the rage of YHWH God of your ancestors with Judah, he gave them into your hand; but you have killed them with a fury that has touched heaven.

10 Now you are saying that you will force the people of Judah and Jerusalem to become your slaves and bondwomen. Only, [are] you and they not equal in offenses against YHWH your God?[2]

11 Now listen to me and return the captives whom you have taken away from your kinsfolk; for the fierce anger of YHWH is upon you.

12 Whereupon some of the chief men of Ephraim, Azariah son of Jehohanan, Berechiah son of Meshillemoth, Jehizkiah son of Shallum, and Amasa son of Hadlai rose up against those who were coming [back] from the war,

13 and said to them, "You are not to bring the captives in here, for you are proposing that which will bring us offense against YHWH, to add to our sins and our offenses for our offense is [already] great and [there is] fierce anger upon Israel."

14 So the soldiers released the captives and the spoil in the presence of the officials and all the assembly.

15 Then the men who were selected by name, rose up and took charge of the captives; and all who were naked they clothed from the plunder; thus they clothed them and gave them shoes, fed them and gave them drink, and anointed them; and they convoyed all the feeble upon asses and brought them to Jericho the city of palms beside their kinsfolk. Then they returned to Samaria.

16 At that time King Ahaz sent to the kings of Assyria to help him.

7 Therefore Ahaz sent messengers to Tiglath-pileser king of Assyria saying, "I am your servant and your son. Come up and deliver me from the grasp of the king of Aram and from the grasp of the king of Israel who are rising up against me."

8 Ahaz also took the silver and gold that was found in the house of YHWH and in the treasuries of the house of the king, and sent them to the king of Assyria as a bribe.

9 The king of Assyria listened to him: and the king of Assyria came up to Damascus and captured it; he exiled its population to Kir and Rezin he put to death.

10 When King Ahaz went to meet Tiglath-pileser king of Assyria at Damascus, he saw the altar that was in Damascus. So King Ahaz sent to Uriah the priest a model of the altar and its design in every detail.

11 Uriah the priest built the altar according to all that King Ahaz had sent from Damascus: thus Uriah the priest was at work until King Ahaz came from Damascus.

12 When the king came from Damascus, the king saw the altar. Then the king approached the altar and went up on it.

13 He offered his burnt-offering and his cereal-offering, poured out his drink-offering, and dashed the blood of his peace-offerings against the altar.

14 Further, the bronze altar that was in front of YHWH, he removed from the front of the house, from between the altar and the house of YHWH, and placed it on the north side of his altar.

15 King Ahaz commanded[4] Uriah the priest saying, "Upon the great altar offer the morning burnt-offering and the evening cereal-offering, the burnt-offering of the king and his cereal-offering, and the burnt-offering of all the people of the land, their cereal-offerings and their drink-offerings: all the blood of the burnt-offerings and all the blood of the sacrifice you shall dash against it. But the bronze altar shall be for me to inquire at."

16 So Uriah the priest did according to all that King Ahaz commanded.

17 Then King Ahaz cut off the frames of the pedestals and he removed the basin[5] from them, and took down the Sea from the bronze oxen which were underneath it and put it upon a pediment of stones.

18 The awning[6] for the sabbath which they had built inside the house, and the outer entrance for the king, he removed [from] the house of YHWH out of regard for the king of Assyria.

17 For again the Edomites had come and struck down Judah and had taken away captives.

18 The Philistines also had ravaged the cities of the Shephelah and the Negeb of Judah, and had captured Beth-shemesh, Aijalon, Gederoth, Soco with its villages, Timnah with its villages, and Gimzo with its villages; and they settled there.

19 For YHWH had humbled Judah because of Ahaz king of Israel,[3] for he had acted without restraint against Judah and behaved unfaithfully towards YHWH.

20 So Tilgath-pilneser king of Assyria came up against him; and he oppressed him and did not support him.

21 For Ahaz plundered the house of YHWH and the house of the king and of the officials, and he gave [the spoil] to the king of Assyria; but it did not help him.

22 At the time of his trouble, this king Ahaz became still more unfaithful to YHWH:

23 he sacrificed to the gods of Damascus who had struck him down. For he said, "Since the gods of the kings of Aram aided them, I will sacrifice to them that they may aid me." However, they became his downfall and that of all Israel.

24 Then Ahaz collected the vessels of the house of YHWH and he cut in pieces the vessels of the house of God. Then Ahaz closed the doors of the house of YHWH and made for himself altars at every corner in Jerusalem.

25 In every city and town in Judah he made high places to burn incense to other gods, and thus provoked to anger YHWH the God of his ancestors.

26 Now the rest of his acts and all his ways, from the first to the last, they are indeed written in the Book of the Chronicles of the Kings of Israel and Judah.

19 Now the rest of the acts of Ahaz that he did, are they not written in the Book of the Chronicles of the Kings of Judah?

27 When Ahaz lay down to rest with his ancestors, they buried him in the city of Jerusalem, for they did not bring him into the tombs of the kings of Israel; and Hezekiah his son became king in his place.

20 When Ahaz lay down to rest with his ancestors, he was buried with his ancestors in the city of David; and Hezekiah his son became king in his place.

---

[1] Literally, "He struck him with a great blow."
[2] The Israelites are just as sinful as the Judahites.
[3] "Judah" seems to be what is expected here.
[4] Reading the Qere.
[5] Reading the Qere.
[6] Reading the Qere.

639 The Fall of Samaria and the Captivity of Israel
2 Kings 17:1-23 // 2 Kings 18:9-12

2 Kings 17

1 In the twelfth year of Ahaz king of Judah, Hoshea son of Elah, became king in Samaria over Israel [for] nine years.

2 He did what was evil in the eyes of YHWH only not like the kings of Israel who were before him.

3 Shalmaneser king of Assyria came up against him, and Hoshea became his servant and delivered tribute to him.

4 But the king of Assyria found out that Hoshea [was in] a conspiracy—that he had sent messengers to So king of Egypt, and had not presented tribute to the king of Assyria as [he had] year by year—therefore the king of Assyria restrained him and bound him in prison.

5 Then the king of Assyria came up against all the land; he came up against Samaria and laid siege against it [for] three years.

2 Kings 18

9 In the fourth year of King Hezekiah —it was the seventh year of Hoshea son of Elah, king of Israel—that Shalmaneser king of Assyria came up against Samaria and laid siege against it;

10 and they captured it at the end of three years; in the sixth year of Hezekiah—it was the ninth year of Hoshea king of Israel [when] Samaria was captured.

6 In the ninth year of Hoshea, the king of Assyria captured Samaria and exiled Israel to Assyria. He settled them in Halah, on the Habor, the river of Gozan, and [in] the cities of the Medes.

7 [This] happened because the Israelites had sinned against YHWH their God who had brought them up from the land of Egypt, from under the hand of Pharaoh king of Egypt. They had feared other gods,

8 and had walked in the customs of the nations whom YHWH had dispossessed from before the Israelites, and [in accordance with the customs of] the kings of Israel that they had done.

9 Now the Israelites had done things secretly that were not proper against YHWH their God: they built for themselves high places in all their cities from watchmen tower to fortified city;

10 they erected for themselves pillars and asherim upon every high hill and under every verdant tree;

11 they burned incense there at every high place like the nations whom YHWH had exiled before them; and they did evil things to provoke YHWH to anger.

12 They served the idols of which YHWH had said to them, "You shall not make this thing!"

13 Indeed, YHWH had warned Israel and Judah through each prophet and[1] each seer, saying, "Turn back from your evil ways and keep my commandments, my statutes, according to all the Torah that I commanded your ancestors and that I sent to you through my servants the prophets.

11 Then the king of Assyria exiled Israel to Assyria, set them down in Halah, and on the Habor, the river of Gozan and [in] the cities of the Medes

12 because they had not listened to the voice of YHWH their God, but had transgressed his covenant: all that Moses the servant of YHWH had commanded they did not listen to and they did not do.

14 They did not listen, but stiffened
their neck like the neck of their
ancestors who had not stood firm in
YHWH their God.

15 Moreover they rejected his
statutes and his covenant that he had
made with their ancestors, and
[also] to his testimonies with which
he admonished them. They went
after false gods and served futility,
following[2] the nations that surrounded them whom YHWH had
commanded them that they should
not act like them.

16 They forsook all the commandments of YHWH their God and
made for themselves molten
image[s] of two calves: they made
an asherah and bowed themselves
before all the host of heaven and
served the Baal.

17 Also they made their sons and
daughters to pass through the fire
and they practiced divination and
sought omens and they sold themselves to do what was evil in the
eyes of YHWH so as to provoke
him [to anger].

18 So YHWH became very angry
against Israel and removed them
from his presence; none remained
except the tribe of Judah alone.

19 Even Judah did not keep the
commandments of YHWH their
God, but walked in the customs that
Israel had practiced.

20 Thus YHWH rejected every
descendant of Israel and oppressed
them and gave them into the hand of
looters until he cast them from his
presence.

21 When he had torn Israel from
the house of David and they made
Jeroboam son of Nebat king,
Jeroboam enticed[3] Israel away from
YHWH and caused them to sin
great sin.

22 The Israelites walked in all the
sins that Jeroboam had done. They
did not turn from it

23 until YHWH had removed Israel
from his presence as he had spoken
through all his servants the
prophets. So he exiled Israel from
its land to Assyria until this day.

---

[1] Reading the Kethib but connecting the waw currently attached to "prophet" with the following word "each."
[2] Reading the waw on "after" as dittography.
[3] Reading the Qere.

640 Foreign Resettlement of Samaria
2 Kings 17:24-41

2 Kings 17

24 The king of Assyria brought [people] from Babylon, from Cuthah, from
Avva, from Hamath, and Sepharvaim and settled [them] in the cities of Samaria
in place of the Israelites; they took possession of Samaria and settled in its
cities.

25 But it happened at the beginning of their settling there that they did not
reverence YHWH, so YHWH sent lions against them which were killing them.

26 So they said to the king of Assyria, "The nations that you exiled and settled
in the cities of Samaria do not know the way of the god of the land: and he has
sent lions against them, and they are surely killing them because they do not
know the way of the god of the land."

27 Then the king of Assyria commanded, "Send there one of the priests whom
you exiled from there, that they may go and dwell there and he will teach them
the way of the god of the land."

28 So one of the priests whom they exiled from Samaria came and dwelt in
Bethel, and he taught them how they should reverence YHWH.

29 But every nation kept making its gods and placing [them] in the shrine of
the high places that the Samaritans had made, every nation, in the cities where
they were dwelling.

30 The Babylonians made Succoth-benoth; the Cuthites made Nergal; the
Hamathites made Ashima;

31 and the Avvites made Nibhaz and Tartak; and the Sepharvites burned their
children in the fire to Adrammelech and Anammelech, the gods of Sepharvaim.[1]

32 They were also reverencers of YHWH and made for themselves from their number, priests for the high places; and they were acting for them in the shrine of the high places.

33 So they were reverencing YHWH but they continued serving their gods according to the way of the nations from whence they [Assyrians] had exiled them.

34 To this day they are acting according to the former ways. They are not reverencing YHWH and they are not acting according to the statutes, or their customs, or the Torah, or the commandment that YHWH commanded the descendants of Jacob [upon] whom he put his name Israel.

35 YHWH had made a covenant with them, and he commanded them, "You shall not reverence other gods or bow yourselves down to them; you shall not serve them or sacrifice to them:

36 But you shall reverence only YHWH who brought you up from the land of Egypt with great power, and with outstretched arm, to him you shall bow yourselves down, and to him you shall sacrifice.

37 Also the statutes, the decrees, the Torah and the commandment that he wrote for you, you shall take care to do all [your] days. You shall not reverence other gods:

38 and the covenant that I made with you, you shall not forget. You shall not reverence other gods,

39 but, you shall reverence only YHWH your God; and he will rescue you from the hand of all your enemies.

40 But they did not listen; they simply went on acting according to their former ways.

41 So these nations were reverencing YHWH, but they were also serving their own images. Even their children and their children's children, as their ancestors had done, continue so doing to this day.

---

[1] Reading the Qere.

641 The Reign of Hezekiah
2 Chron 29:1-2 // 2 Kings 18:1-8

2 Chron 29

1 Hezekiah became king at twenty-five years of age and for twenty-nine years he was king in Jerusalem. The name of his mother was Abijah daughter of Zechariah.

2 Kings 18

1 In the third year of Hoshea son of Elah, king of Israel, Hezekiah son of Ahaz, king of Judah, became king.

2 He did what was right in the eyes of YHWH according to all that David his [fore]father had done.

2 He was twenty-five years old when he became king, and for twenty-nine years he was king in Jerusalem. The name of his mother was Abi daughter of Zechariah.

3 He did what was right in the eyes of YHWH according to all that David his [fore]father had done.

4 He removed the high places and broke down the pillars and cut down the asherah. He broke up into pieces the bronze serpent that Moses had made because until those days, the Israelites were offering incense to it; it was called Nehushtan.

5 In YHWH God of Israel, he trusted; and after him there was none like him among all the kings of Judah, or [among those] who were before him.

6 For he held firmly to YHWH; he did not turn away from him but kept his commandments that YHWH had commanded Moses.

7 Therefore YHWH was with him; in all that he undertook he was successful. He rebelled against the king of Assyria and would not serve him.

8 He struck down the Philistines as far as Gaza and its borders, from watchmen's tower to fortified city.

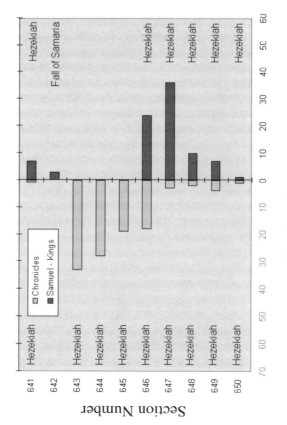

Hezekiah
Sections 641–650

Number	Title	2 Chronicles	2 Kings
641	The Reign of Hezekiah	29:1-2	18:1-8
642	The Fall of Samaria		18:9-12
643	Hezekiah Restores Service	29:3-36	
644	The Celebration of Passover	30:1–31:1	
645	Hezekiah's Provision for Priests	31:2-21	
646	The Invasion of Sennacherib	32:1-19	18:13-37
647	Judah Delivered from Sennacherib	32:20-23	19:1-37
648	Hezekiah's Sickness	32:24-26	20:1-11
649	Hezekiah Receives Envoys	32:27-31	20:12-19
650	The Death of Hezekiah	32:32-33	20:20-21

642 The Fall of Samaria
2 Kings 18:9-12

2 Kings 18

9 In the fourth year of King Hezekiah—it was the seventh year of Hoshea son of Elah, king of Israel—Shalmaneser king of Assyria came up against Samaria and laid siege against it;

10 and they captured it at the end of three years; in the sixth year of Hezekiah—it was the ninth year of Hoshea king of Israel [when] Samaria was captured.

11 Then the king of Assyria exiled Israel to Assyria, set them down in Halah, and on the Habor the river of Gozan, and [in] the cities of the Medes

12 because they had not listened to the voice of YHWH their God, but had transgressed his covenant: all that Moses the servant of YHWH had commanded they did not listen to and they did not do.

643 Hezekiah Restores the Service of the House of the Lord
2 Chron 29:3-36

2 Chron 29

3 In the first year of his being king, in the first month, he opened the doors of the house of YHWH and repaired them.

4 Then he brought the priests and the Levites and assembled them in the square on the east.

5 He said to them, "Listen to me, O Levites, consecrate yourselves now, and consecrate the house of YHWH the God of your ancestors and take out what is impure from the sanctuary.

6 For our ancestors have acted unfaithfully and they have done what was evil in the eyes of YHWH our God; they have forsaken him, and they have turned their faces from the dwelling place of YHWH and have turned [their] back [on it].[1]

7 They also have closed the doors of the porch and extinguished the lamps; and they have not burned an incense offering or offered up a burnt offering in the sanctuary to the God of Israel.

8 Therefore the anger of YHWH has been upon Judah and Jerusalem as he has given them [over] to trembling,[2] to horror and to hissing as you see with your [own] eyes.

9 Look, our ancestors have fallen by the sword; our sons, our daughters and our wives are in captivity because of this.

10 Now it is in my heart to make a covenant to YHWH God of Israel so that he may turn from us the fierceness of his wrath.

11 My sons, do not now be negligent because YHWH has chosen you to stand before him to minister to him and to be his ministers and those who offer incense.

12 Then the Levites rose up: Mahath son of Amasai, and Joel son of Azariah, from the Kohathites; from the Merarites: Kish son of Abdi, and Azariah son of Jahallelel; from the Gershonites: Joah son of Zimmah, and Eden son of Joah;

13 from the sons of Elizapan: Shimri and Jeuel; from the sons of Asaph: Zechariah and Mataniah;

14 from the sons of Heman: Jehuel and Shimei; and from the sons of Jeduthun: Shemaiah and Uzziel.

15 They assembled their brothers, consecrated themselves, and went in at the command of the king by the words of YHWH to purify the house of YHWH.

16 The priests went in to purify the innermost part of the house of YHWH. They brought out every unclean thing that they found in the temple of YHWH to the court of the house of YHWH. Then Levites received [them] to carry [them] outside to the wadi Kidron.

17 They began on the first day of the first month to consecrate and on the eighth day of the month they came to the porch of YHWH: then they consecrated the house of YHWH for eight days and on the sixteenth day of the first month they finished.

18 So they went inside to Hezekiah the king and said, "We have purified all the house of YHWH, the altar of burnt offering and all its vessels, and the table for rows [of bread] and all its vessels.

19 All the vessels which king Ahaz had rejected during his kingship in his unfaithfulness, we have set up and consecrated; see, they are in front of the altar of YHWH."

20 Then Hezekiah the king rose early and assembled the officials of the city and went up to the house of YHWH.

21 They brought seven oxen, seven rams, seven lambs and seven male-goats as a sin-offering for the kingdom, for the sanctuary, and for Judah. He ordered the sons of Aaron, the priests, to offer [them] on the altar of YHWH.

22 So they slaughtered the cattle, and the priests received the blood and dashed [it] against the altar; they slaughtered the rams and dashed the blood against the altar; and they slaughtered the lambs and dashed the blood against the altar.

23 Then they brought forward male-goats for a sin-offering before the king and the assembly. They laid their hands on them,

24 and the priests slaughtered them and made their blood a sin-offering at the altar to atone for all Israel. For the king said that the burnt offering [should be] for all Israel.

25 He made the Levites stand [in] the house of YHWH with cymbals, with stringed instruments and with lyres at the commandment of David, and of Gad the seer of the king, and of Nathan the prophet, for the commandment was from YHWH through his prophets.

26 So the Levites stood with the [musical] instruments of David and the priests with trumpets.

27 Then Hezekiah ordered the offering of the burnt offering at the altar. At the time the burnt offering began, there began the song of YHWH and the trumpets with the playing of the [musical] instruments of David king of Israel.

28 All the assembly bowed themselves down as songs were sung and trumpets blown,[3] all until the completion of the burnt offering.

29 When the burnt offering was completed, the king and all who were present with him knelt and bowed themselves down.

30 Then Hezekiah the king and the officials ordered the Levites to offer praise to YHWH in the words of David and Asaph the seer, and they praised to the point of rejoicing, did obeisance and bowed down.

31 And Hezekiah gave answer and said, "Now you have consecrated yourselves[4] to YHWH; come forward and bring sacrifices as thank offerings to the house of YHWH. So the assembly brought sacrifices as thank offerings[5]; and all who were of generous heart [brought] burnt offerings.

32 The number of the burnt offering that the assembly brought was seventy cattle, one hundred rams, two hundred lambs—all these for a burnt offering to YHWH.

33 The consecrated offerings were six hundred cattle, and three thousand sheep.

34 Only there were too few priests and they were not able to flay all the burnt offerings, so their brothers the Levites assisted them until the completion of the work and until [additional] priests had consecrated themselves, since the Levites were more conscientious[6] in consecrating themselves than the priests.

35 In addition to the abundance of burnt offering[s] there was fat for peace offerings, and libations for the burnt offering[s]. Thus the service of the house of YHWH was restored

36 and Hezekiah and all the people rejoiced because of what God had [re]established for the people; for the work happened quickly.

---

[1] Literally, "given the neck."
[2] Reading the Kethib.
[3] Reading the Qere.
[4] Literally, "You have filled your hands."
[5] Reading the waw connected to "thank offerings" epexigetically.
[6] Literally, "upright in heart."

644 The Celebration of Passover
2 Chron 30:1–31:1

2 Chron 30

1 Then Hezekiah sent throughout all Israel and Judah, and also he wrote letters to Ephraim and Manasseh, to come to the house of YHWH in Jerusalem to keep passover for YHWH the God of Israel.

2 The king, his officials and all the assembly in Jerusalem had taken counsel to keep passover in the second month

3 because they were unable to keep it at that time since the priests had not consecrated themselves in sufficient number and the people had not assembled to Jerusalem.

4 Moreover the plan seemed right in the eyes of the king and in the eyes of all the assembly.

5 So they set up the means to spread [his] announcement in all Israel, from Beer-sheba to Dan, to come to keep passover to YHWH God of Israel in Jerusalem, for not many had done as [it was] written.

6 The couriers went with letters from the hand of the king and his officials into all Israel and Judah; and according to the command of the king, they said, "Israelites return to YHWH, God of Abraham, Isaac, and Israel, that he may return to the remnant among you who escaped from the grasp of the kings of Assyria.

7 Do not be like your ancestors and your kindred who acted unfaithfully against YHWH God of their ancestors, that he gave them over to destruction as you see.

8 Now, do not stiffen your neck like your ancestors but submit yourselves to YHWH[1] and come to his sanctuary that he has consecrated forever, and serve YHWH your God that the heat of his anger may turn from you.

9 For when you return to YHWH, your kindred and your children [will find] mercy before their captors to return to this land. For YHWH your God is gracious and merciful. He will not turn [his] face from you if you return to him.

10 As the couriers were passing from city to city in the land of Ephraim and Manasseh, and as far as Zebulun, they were laughing at them and ridiculing them.

11 Only, people from Asher and Manasseh and from Zebulun, did humble themselves and come to Jerusalem.

12 Also the hand of God was in Judah to give them one heart to keep the command of the king and the officials by the word of YHWH.

13 A great many people were assembled in Jerusalem to keep the Feast of Unleavened Bread in the second month, a very great assembly.

14 They rose up and removed the altars that were in Jerusalem, and all the incense altars they removed and threw into the wadi Kidron.

15 Then they slaughtered the passover [lamb] on the fourteenth of the second month, and the priests and the Levites were ashamed so they consecrated themselves and brought burnt offerings [into] the house of YHWH.

16 They stood in their accustomed positions according to the Torah of Moses the man of God; the priests were dashing the blood [they received] from the hand of the Levites.

17 Since there were many in the assembly who had not consecrated themselves, the Levites took charge of the slaughter of the passover [lambs] for all those [who were] not pure in order to consecrate [them] to YHWH.

18 For a multitude of the people—many from Ephraim and Manasseh, Issachar and Zebulun—had not purified themselves, yet they ate the passover contrary to what was written, but Hezekiah prayed on their behalf saying, "May the good YHWH make atonement for[2]

19 each one who sets his heart to seek the God YHWH God of his ancestors, even though not according to the purity of the sanctuary."

20 And YHWH listened to Hezekiah and healed the people.

21 So the Israelites who were present in Jerusalem kept the Feast of Unleavened Bread seven days with great joy; and the Levites and the priests were praising YHWH day by day with loud instruments for YHWH.

22 Hezekiah spoke from the heart [to] all the Levites who performed with great skill for YHWH. They ate the [food of] the festival seven days, sacrificing peace offerings and giving thanks to YHWH God of their ancestors.

23 Then all the assembly decided to keep [the festival] seven days more. So they kept [the festival another] seven days [with] joy,

24 for Hezekiah king of Judah contributed for the assembly a thousand oxen and seven thousand sheep, and the officials contributed for the assembly a thousand oxen and ten thousand sheep. Priests in large numbers consecrated themselves.

25 So all the assembly of Judah, the priests and the Levites, and all the assembly that had come from Israel and the resident aliens who came from the land of Israel and who were living in Judah, rejoiced.

26 There was great joy in Jerusalem, for since the days of Solomon son of David, king of Israel, there had been nothing like this in Jerusalem.

27 Then the priests, the Levites,[3] rose up and blessed the people; and their voice was heard as their prayer went to his holy dwelling place, to heaven.

31:1 When all this was finished, all Israel who were present went out to the cities of Judah and broke down the pillars, hewed down the asherim, and pulled down the high places and altars from all Judah and Benjamin, and in Ephraim and Manasseh, completely. Then all the Israelites returned each to his holding [and] to their cities.

---

[1] Literally, "give hand."
[2] Reading as continuing into the next verse in spite of MT versification.
[3] Or, "Levitical priests." Many versions read "priests and Levites." The MT has no *waw* between priest and Levite.

645 Hezekiah's Provision for the Priests and Levites
2 Chron 31:2-21

2 Chron 31

2 Hezekiah set up the work-rotations[1] of the priests and of the Levites by their divisions—each one according to his service, for the priests and for the Levites—for burnt offering and for peace offerings to minister and to give thanks and to praise in the gates of the encampments of YHWH.

3 The portion of the king's livestock [was for] the burnt offering of morning and evening, the burnt offerings for the sabbaths, for the new moons and for the festivals as it is written in the Torah of YHWH.

4 Then he ordered the people, the inhabitants of Jerusalem, to give the portion due the priests and the Levites that they might hold firmly on the Torah of YHWH.

5 So when the word spread, the Israelites brought great quantities of the first fruits of grain, new wine, fresh oil, honey, and all the produce of the field; the tenth of the whole they brought in abundance.

6 The Israelites and Judahites who were dwelling in the cities of Judah, they too, brought a tenth of cattle and sheep and a tenth of consecrated things that had been consecrated to YHWH their God, and they piled them up in heaps.

7 In the third month they began to pile up the heaps and in the seventh month they finished.

8 When Hezekiah and the officials came and saw the heaps, they blessed YHWH and his people Israel.

9 And Hezekiah inquired of the priests and the Levites concerning the heaps.

10 Azariah the chief priest of the house of Zadok said to him, "Since they began bringing the contribution [to] the house of YHWH, there is enough to eat and to satisfy and an abundance left over, for YHWH has blessed his people that this abundance is left over."

11 Then Hezekiah ordered storerooms to be set up in the house of YHWH and they set [them] up.

12 They brought in faithfully the contribution, the tithes and the consecrated things. Over them in charge was Conaniah the Levite and Shimei his brother, second [in rank]

13 with Jehiel, Azaziah, Nahath, Asahel, Jerimoth, Jozabad, Eliel, Ismachiah, Mahath, and Benaiah, deputies under Conaniah and Shimei his brother, an appointment by Hezekiah the king and Azariah of the house of God.

14 Kore son of Imnah, the Levite, the gatekeeper of the East Gate, was in charge of the free-will offerings for God to give the contribution to YHWH and the consecrated things.

15 Under him [were] Eden, Miniamin, Jeshua, Shemaiah, Amariah and Shecaniah in the cities of the priests, faithfully distributing to their kindred by divisions, great and small alike;

16 besides those enrolled by genealogy—males beginning at three years of age and above—all who came to the house of YHWH for their daily task as required for their service in their watch according to their divisions.

17 The priests were enrolled by genealogy according to their ancestral houses; and the Levites, from twenty years of age and above, according to their watches by their divisions.

18 Enrolled by genealogy were all their young children, their wives, their sons and daughters, for the whole assembly, because in their faithfulness they kept themselves holy.

19 As for the sons of Aaron, the priests, [who were] in the fields of common land [around] their cities, in each city [by] city people were designated by name to distribute portions to every male among the priests, and to all enrolled by genealogy among the Levites.

20 Hezekiah did thus throughout all Judah: so he did what was good and right and true before YHWH his God.

21 And in every work that he undertook in the service of the house of God or the Torah or Commandment to seek out his God, he did with all his heart; and he prospered.

---

[1] Literally, "divisions."

646 The Invasion of Sennacherib
2 Chron 32:1-19 // 2 Kings 18:13-37 // Isa 36:1-22

2 Chron 32	*2 Kings 18*	*Isaiah 36*

2 Chron 32

1 After these faithful deeds,[1] Sennacherib king of Assyria came. Moreover he came into Judah and encamped against the fortified cities that he thought to break into [them] for himself.

2 When Hezekiah saw that Sennacherib had come with his face set for battle against Jerusalem,

3 he took counsel with his officials and his warriors to stop up the waters of the springs which were outside the city, and they assisted him.

4 Many people were gathered and they stopped up all the springs and the wadi that was flowing through the land, saying, "Why should the kings of Assyria come and find abundant water?"

5 Moreover he [Hezekiah] strengthened and rebuilt each broken wall and erected on the towers and outside [it], another wall and strengthened the Millo of the city of David. Then he made spear[s] in abundance, and shields.

6 He appointed officers for battles over the people and gathered them to him in the open place at the gate of the city, and he spoke to their hearts, saying,

7 "Be strong and be courageous. Do not fear and do not be dismayed before the king of Assyria or before all the horde that is with him for with us there is one greater than with him.

8 With him is an arm of flesh; but with us is YHWH our God to help us and to fight our battles." So the people were encouraged by the words of Hezekiah king of Judah.

2 Kings 18

13 In the fourteenth year of King Hezekiah, Sennacherib king of Assyria came up against all the fortified cities of Judah and seized them.

Isaiah 36

1 It happened in the fourteenth year of King Hezekiah that Sennacherib king of Assyria came up against all the fortified cities of Judah and seized them.

14 Then Hezekiah king of Judah sent to the king of Assyria to Lachish, saying, "I have done wrong; turn back from me and whatever you place on me, I will bear." So the king of Assyria imposed upon Hezekiah king of Judah three hundred talents of silver and thirty talents of gold.

15 Hezekiah gave [him] all the silver that was found in the house of YHWH and in the storehouses of the house of the king.

16 At that time Hezekiah stripped the doors of the temple of YHWH and the doorposts that [he], Hezekiah king of Judah had overlaid, and gave them to the king of Assyria.

9 After this Sennacherib king of Assyria sent his servants to Jerusalem—while he [went up] against Lachish, all his entourage with him—against Hezekiah king of Judah and against all of Judah who were in Jerusalem, saying,

17 Nevertheless the king of Assyria sent the Tartan, the Rab-saris, and the Rabshakeh from Lachish to King Hezekiah with a substantial force [to] Jerusalem. They went up and came to Jerusalem. When they had come up, they came and stood at the channel of the upper pool that was on the public road to [the] Fuller's Field.

2 Then the king of Assyria sent the Rabshakeh from Lachish to Jerusalem to King Hezekiah with a substantial force. He stood at the channel of the upper pool on the public road to [the] Fuller's Field.

18 They called to the king and there came out to them Eliakim son of Hilkiah who was over the palace, Shebnah the scribe, and Joah son of Asaph the recorder.

3 There came out to him Eliakim son of Hilkiah who was over the palace, Shebna the scribe, and Joah son of Asaph the recorder.

10 Thus says Sennacherib king of Assyria, "On what are you trusting while living under siege in Jerusalem?

19 Then the Rabshakeh said to them, "Say now to Hezekiah, 'Thus says the great king of Assyria: What is this trust that you have trusted?

4 Then the Rabshakeh said to them, "Say now to Hezekiah, 'Thus says the great king of Assyria: What is this trust that you have trusted?

20 Are you really saying that simply a word from lips [is] strategy and power for battle? Now, upon whom have you trusted that you have rebelled against me?

5 Am I really saying that simply a word from lips [is] strategy and power for battle? Now, upon whom have you trusted that you have rebelled against me?

21 Now look, you trust yourself on the staff of this crushed reed, on Egypt—which, when anyone would

6 Look, you trust on the staff of this crushed reed, on Egypt—which, when anyone would support himself

support himself on it, will enter his palm and pierce it: thus is Pharaoh king of Egypt to all who trust in him.

on it, will enter his palm and pierce it: thus is Pharaoh king of Egypt to all who trust in him.

11 Is not Hezekiah leading you astray giving you over to death by famine and thirst saying, 'YHWH our God will deliver us from the grasp of the king of Assyria?'

22 But if you should say to me, 'In YHWH our God we trust,' is it not he whose high places and altars Hezekiah has removed? And [is it not he who] said to Judah and to Jerusalem, 'Before this altar you shall bow yourselves down in Jerusalem.'

7 But if you should say to me, 'In YHWH, our God, we trust,' is it not he whose high places and altars Hezekiah has removed? And [is it not he who] said to Judah and to Jerusalem, 'Before this altar you shall bow yourselves down.'

12 Has not he, Hezekiah, removed his high places and his altars, and said to Judah and to Jerusalem, 'Before one altar you shall bow yourselves down and upon it you shall offer incense.'

13 Do you not know what I and my ancestors did to all the peoples of the lands? Were the gods of the nations of the lands able to deliver their land from my hand?

14 Who among all the gods of these nations whom my ancestors utterly destroyed is able to deliver his people from my hand, that your gods should be able to deliver you from my hand?

23 So now make a wager with my master, with the king of Assyria: I will give to you two thousand horses if you are able to put riders on them.

8 So now make a wager with my master the king of Assyria: I will give to you two thousand horses if you are able to provide riders for them.

24 But how can you turn away one captain of the lesser servants of my master when you entrust yourself to Egypt for chariotry and for horsemen?

9 But how can you turn away one captain of the lesser servants of my master when you entrust yourself to Egypt for chariotry and for horsemen.

25 Now is it without YHWH [that] I have come up against this place to destroy it? YHWH said to me, 'Go up against this land and destroy it.'"

10 And now is it without YHWH [that] I have come up against this land to destroy it? YHWH said to me, 'Go up to this land and destroy it.'"

26 Then Eliakim son of Hilkiah, Shebnah, and Joah said to the Rabshakeh, "Speak, please, to your servants [in] Aramaic because we understand [it], but do not speak with

11 Then Eliakim, Shebna and Joah said to the Rabshakeh, "Speak, please, to your servants [in] Aramaic because we understand [it], but do not speak to us [in] Judahite

us [in] Judahite [directly] in the ears of the people who are on the wall."

within the hearing of the people who are on the wall."

27 But the Rabshakeh said to them, "Is it against your master and to you that my master sent me to speak these words [and] not against the people who are sitting on the wall, [destined] to eat their excrement[2] and to drink their urine[3] with you?"

12 But the Rabshakeh said, "Is it to your master and to you that my master sent me to speak these words? Is it not against the people who are sitting on the wall, [destined] to eat their excrement[4] and to drink their urine[5] with you?"

28 Then the Rabshakeh stood and called out in a loud voice, [in] Judahite. He spoke and said, "Hear the word of the great king, king of Assyria.

13 Then the Rabshakeh stood and called out in a loud voice, [in] Judahite. He said, "Hear the words of the great king, king of Assyria.

15 So now do not let Hezekiah deceive you and do not let him mislead you in this way, and do not trust him, for no god of any nation or kingdom is able to deliver his people from my hand or from the hand of my ancestors. How much less shall your gods deliver you from my hand!"

29 Thus says the king, 'Do not let Hezekiah deceive you because he is not able to deliver you from his hand.'

14 Thus says the king, 'Do not let Hezekiah deceive you because he is not able to deliver you.'

16 His servants spoke still more against YHWH God and against Hezekiah his servant.

30 Moreover do not let Hezekiah make you trust in YHWH, saying, 'Surely YHWH will deliver us, and this city will not be given into the hand of [the] king of Assyria.'

15 Moreover do not let Hezekiah make you trust in YHWH saying, 'Surely YHWH will deliver us, and this city will not be given into the hand of the king of Assyria.'

17 He also wrote letters to insult YHWH the God of Israel to speak against him, saying, "Just as the gods of nations of [other] lands, who did not deliver their people from my hand, so the God of Hezekiah will not deliver his people from my hand."

18 They called out in a loud voice, [in] Judahite, to the people of Jerusalem who were on the city wall to frighten them and terrify them that they might capture the city.

31 Do not listen to Hezekiah for thus says the king of Assyria, 'Make peace with me and come out to me: then everyone shall eat [from] his vine and everyone [from] his fig-tree, and everyone shall drink water from his cistern

16 Do not listen to Hezekiah for thus says the king of Assyria, 'Make peace with me and come out to me: then everyone shall eat [from] his vine and everyone [from] his fig-tree and everyone shall drink water from his cistern

32 until I come and take you to a land like your land, a land of grain and new wine, a land of bread and vineyards, a land of olive, oil and honey, that you may live, and not die. But do not listen to Hezekiah because he would mislead you, saying, 'YHWH will deliver us.'

17 until I come and take you to a land like your land, a land of grain and new wine, a land of bread and vineyards.

19 They also spoke regarding the God of Jerusalem like the gods of the peoples of the earth, the work of human hands.

33 Did the gods of the nations ever really deliver anyone's land from the hand of the king of Assyria?

18 Lest Hezekiah mislead you, saying, 'YHWH will deliver us.' Did the gods of the nations deliver anyone's land from the hand of the king of Assyria?

34 Where are the gods of Hamath and Arpad? Where are the gods of Sepharvaim, Hena and Ivvah? Did they deliver Samaria from my hand?

19 Where are the gods of Hamath and Arpad? Where are the gods of Sepharvaim? Did they deliver Samaria from my hand?

35 Who among all the gods of the lands has delivered their land from my hand that YHWH should deliver Jerusalem from my hand?"

20 Who among all the gods of these lands has delivered their land from my hand that YHWH should deliver Jerusalem from my hand?"

36 The people were silent and they did not answer him a word because it was the command of the king, "You will not answer him."

21 They were silent and they did not answer him a word because it was the command of the king, "You will not answer him."

37 Then Eliakim son of Hilkiah who was over the palace, Shebna the scribe, and Joah son of Asaph the recorder, came to Hezekiah [with] garments torn, and they recounted to him the words of the Rabshakeh.

22 Then Eliakim son of Hilkiah who was over the palace, Shebna the scribe, and Joah son of Asaph the recorder, came to Hezekiah [with] garments torn, and they recounted to him the words of the Rabshakeh.

---

[1] Reading as hendiadys; literally, "deeds and faithfulness."
[2] Reading the Qere.
[3] Reading the Qere.
[4] Reading the Qere.
[5] Reading the Qere.

647 Judah Delivered from Sennacherib
2 Chron 32:20-23 // 2 Kings 19:1-37 // Isa 37:1-38

2 Chron 32	*2 Kings 19*	*Isaiah 37*
20 So Hezekiah the king and Isaiah son of Amoz the prophet prayed concerning this and they cried out [to] heaven.	1 As soon as King Hezekiah heard, he tore his garments, covered himself in sackcloth, and went to the house of YHWH.	1 As soon as King Hezekiah heard, he tore his garments, covered himself in sackcloth, and went to the house of YHWH.
	2 And he sent Eliakim who was over the palace, and Shebna the scribe, and the elders of the priests, covered in sackcloth to Isaiah the prophet, son of Amoz.	2 And he sent Eliakim who was over the palace, and Shebna the scribe, and the elders of the priests, covered in sackcloth to Isaiah son of Amoz, the prophet.
	3 They said to him, "Thus says Hezekiah, 'A day of distress, rebuke, and contempt is this day, for children are coming to the mouth of the womb but there is no strength to give birth.'	3 They said to him, "Thus says Hezekiah, 'A day of distress, rebuke, and contempt is this day, for children are coming to the mouth of the womb but there is no strength to give birth.'
	4 Perhaps YHWH your God will listen to all the words of the Rabshakeh whom his master the king of Assyria has sent to insult the living God, and will rebuke the words that YHWH your God has heard. So you should offer up a prayer on behalf of the remnant that is present."	4 Perhaps YHWH your God will listen to the words of the Rabshakeh whom his master the king of Assyria has sent to insult the living God, and will rebuke the words that YHWH your God has heard. So you should offer up a prayer on behalf of the remnant that is present."
	5 When the servants of King Hezekiah came to Isaiah,	5 When the servants of King Hezekiah came to Isaiah,
	6 Isaiah said to them, "Thus you shall say to your master, 'Thus said YHWH: Do not be afraid because of the words which you have heard with which the servants of the king of Assyria have blasphemed me.	6 Isaiah said to them, "Thus you shall say to your master, 'Thus said YHWH: Do not be afraid because of the words which you have heard with which the servants of the king of Assyria have blasphemed me.
	7 Look, I am putting in him a spirit, and he will hear a report and return to his land and I will make him fall by the sword in his land.'"	7 Look, I am putting in him a spirit, and he will hear a report and return to his land and I will make him fall by the sword in his land.'"
	8 The Rabshakeh returned and found the king of Assyria fighting against Libnah, for he had heard that he had withdrawn from Lachish.	8 The Rabshakeh returned and found the king of Assyria fighting against Libnah, for he had heard that he had withdrawn from Lachish.

9 When he heard about Tirhakah king of Cush: "Look, he has set out to do battle with you," he returned and sent messengers to Hezekiah, saying,

10 "Thus shall you say to Hezekiah king of Judah, 'Let not your god in whom you are trusting deceive you, saying: Jerusalem will not be given into the hand of the king of Assyria.

11 Look, you have heard what kings of Assyria have done to all the lands, exterminating them. Will you be delivered?

12 Did the gods of the nations deliver them [the nations] that my ancestors destroyed: Gozan, Haran, Rezeph, and the Edenites who were in Telassar?

13 Where is the king of Hamath, the king of Arpad, the king of the city of Sepharvaim, Hena, and Ivvah?'"

14 Then Hezekiah took the letters from the hand of the messengers, read them, and went up to the house of YHWH; and Hezekiah spread it before YHWH.

15 And Hezekiah prayed before YHWH, and he said, "YHWH God of Israel, sitting [upon] the cherubim, you are God, you alone of all the kingdoms of the earth. You made the heavens and the earth.

16 YHWH, incline your ear and hear. YHWH, open your eyes and see; hear the words of Sennacherib that he has sent to insult the living God.

17 It is true YHWH, the kings of Assyria have laid waste the nations and their land,

9 He heard concerning Tirhakah the king of Cush: "He has set out to do battle with you." When he heard he sent messengers to Hezekiah, saying

10 "Thus shall you say to Hezekiah king of Judah, 'Let not your god in whom you are trusting deceive you, saying: Jerusalem will not be given into the hand of the king of Assyria.

11 Look, you have heard what the kings of Assyria have done to all the lands, exterminating them. Will you be delivered?

12 Did the gods of the nations deliver them [the nations] that my ancestors destroyed: Gozan, Haran, Rezeph, and the Edenites who were in Telassar?

13 Where is the king of Hamath, the king of Arpad, and the king of the city of Sepharvaim, Hena, and Ivvah?'"

14 Then Hezekiah took the letters from the hand of the messengers, read [them], and went up to the house of YHWH; and Hezekiah spread it before YHWH.

15 And Hezekiah prayed to YHWH, saying,

16 "YHWH of hosts, God of Israel, sitting [upon] the cherubim, you are God, you alone of all the kingdoms of the earth. You made the heavens and the earth.

17 YHWH, incline your ear and hear. YHWH, open your eyes and see; hear all the words of Sennacherib that he has sent to insult the living God.

18 It is true YHWH, the kings of Assyria have laid waste all the lands, and their land,

18 and they put their gods into the fire—for they are not gods, but only a work of human hands, wood and stone—and they destroyed them.

19 So now, YHWH our God, save us I pray, from his hand that all of the kingdoms of the earth may know that you, YHWH, are God, you alone."

20 Then Isaiah son of Amoz sent to Hezekiah saying, "Thus says YHWH the God of Israel: 'What you have prayed to me concerning Sennacherib king of Assyria I have heard.'"

21 This is the word which YHWH spoke against him:

"She despises you, she mocks you, virgin daughter, Zion; behind you she tosses her head, daughter, Jerusalem.

22 Whom have you insulted and blasphemed? Against whom have you raised [your] voice and lifted on high your eyes? Against the Holy One of Israel!

23 By means of your messengers you have insulted my Lord; and you say,

'With the great number of my chari- otry I have gone up the heights of the mountains, the summits of Lebanon. I cut down its tallest cedars, the best of its cypresses.

I entered its remotest refuge,[1] its rich woodlands. 24 I dug wells and drank water of foreigners. I dried up with the sole of my feet all the water courses of Egypt.'

25 Have you not heard from afar that I did it? From days of old I planned it and I have brought it to pass,

19 and they put their gods into the fire—for they are not gods, but only a work of human hands, wood and stone—and they destroyed them.

20 So now YHWH our God, save us from his hand that all of the kingdoms of the earth may know that you are YHWH, you alone."

21 Then Isaiah son of Amoz sent to Hezekiah saying, "Thus says YHWH the God of Israel: 'What you have prayed to me concerning Sennacherib king of Assyria.'"

22 This is the word which YHWH spoke against him:

"She despises you, she mocks you, virgin daughter, Zion; Behind you she tosses her head, daughter, Jerusalem.

23 Whom have you insulted and blasphemed? Against whom have you raised [your] voice and lifted on high your eyes? To the Holy One of Israel!

24 By means of your servants you have insulted my Lord; and you say,

'By the great number of my chari- otry I have gone up the heights of the mountains; the summits of Lebanon. I cut down its tallest cedars, the best of its cypresses.

I entered its remotest height, its rich woodlands. 25 I dug wells and drank water.

I dried up with the sole of my feet all the water courses of Egypt.'

26 Have you not heard from afar that I did it? From days of old I planned it and I have brought it to pass,

that you make fortified cities
fall into ruined heaps;
26 their inhabitants, powerless, dismayed and withered;

they have become as vegetation of
the field, as a green shoot of grass,
as grass of roofs,
and a blighted thing before standing
[grain].

27 But your sitting down, your
going out
and your coming in, I know,
and your raging against me

28 Because you have raged against
me and your boasting has come up
into my ears,
I will place my hook into your nose
and my bridle through your lips;
and I will make you return on the
way
by which you came.

29 Now this shall be a sign for you:
you shall eat for the year that which
grows of itself; and in the second
year the grain that will grow from
that; then in the third year, sow,
reap, and plant vineyards, and eat
their fruit.

30 The remaining survivors of the
house of Judah shall again take root
downward, and produce fruit upward;

31 for from Jerusalem will go forth
a remnant, and survivors from
Mount Zion. The zeal of YHWH
will do this.

32 Therefore thus says YHWH to
the king of Assyria: He shall not
come to this city, and he shall not
shoot an arrow there, nor shall he
come before it [with] a shield, nor
pile up siege mound against it.

33 By the way that he will come he
will return, and to this city he will
not come: Oracle of YHWH.

that you make fortified cities
fall into ruined heaps;
27 their inhabitants powerless, dismayed and withered;

they have become as vegetation of
the field, as a green shoot of grass,
as grass of roofs,
and a blighted thing before standing
[grain].

28 But your sitting down, your
going out
and your coming in, I know,
and your raging against me

29 Because you have raged against
me and your boasting has come up
into my ears,
I will place my hook into your nose
and my bridle through your lips;
and I will make you return on the
way
by which you came.

30 Now this shall be a sign for you:
you shall eat for the year that which
grows of itself; and in the second
year the grain that will grow from
that; then in the third year, sow,
reap, and plant vineyards, and eat
their fruit.[2]

31 The remaining survivors of the
house of Judah shall again take root
downward, and produce fruit upward;

32 for from Jerusalem will go forth
a remnant, and survivors from
Mount Zion. The zeal of YHWH of
Hosts will do this.

33 Therefore thus says YHWH to
the king of Assyria: He shall not
come to this city, and he shall not
shoot an arrow there, nor shall he
come before it [with] a shield, nor
pile up siege mound against it.

34 By the way that he came he will
return, and to this city he will not
come: Oracle of YHWH.

21 And YHWH sent a messenger and annihilated every mighty warrior and commander and officer in the camp of the king of Assyria.

Whereupon he returned with shameful face to his land.

When he entered the house of his god, some of his own offspring brought him down with the sword.

22 So YHWH saved Hezekiah and the inhabitants of Jerusalem from the hand of Sennacherib king of Assyria and from the hand of all [others]; and he gave them rest all around.

23 Many brought tribute to YHWH, to Jerusalem and precious things to Hezekiah king of Judah; and he was exalted in the eyes of all the nations thereafter.

34 I will defend this city to save it for my own sake and for the sake of David my servant."

35 It was on that same night that the messenger of YHWH went forth and struck down one hundred eighty-five thousand in the camp of Assyria. When they [the Jerusalemites] rose early in the morning, all of them were dead carcases.

36 Then Sennacherib king of Assyria hurried and went [home], and dwelt in Nineveh.

37 As he was worshiping in the house of Nisroch his god, Adramelech and Sharezer struck him down with a sword; and they escaped to the land of Ararat. Then Esar-haddon his son became king in his place.

35 I will defend this city to save it for my own sake and for the sake of David my servant."

36 Then the messenger of YHWH went forth and struck one hundred eighty-five thousand in the camp of Assyria. When they [the Jerusalemites] arose early in the morning, all of them were dead carcases.

37 Then Sennacherib king of Assyria hurried and went [home], and dwelt in Nineveh.

38 As he was worshiping in the house of Nisroch his god, Adramelech and Sharezer, his sons, struck him down with a sword; and they escaped to the land of Ararat. Then Esar-haddon his son became king in his place.

---

[1] Reading the Qere.
[2] Reading the Qere.

648 Hezekiah's Sickness
2 Chron 32:24-26 // 2 Kings 20:1-11 // Isa 38:1-22

2 Chron 32	*2 Kings 20*	*Isaiah 38*
24 In those days Hezekiah became sick to [the point] of death, so he prayed to YHWH and he [YHWH] spoke to him and he gave him a sign.	1 In those days Hezekiah became sick [to the point] of death. Isaiah son of Amoz, the prophet, came to him and said to him, "Thus says YHWH: 'Set your house in order because you are going to die and you shall not live.'"	1 In those days Hezekiah became sick to [the point] of death. Isaiah son of Amoz, the prophet, came to him and said to him, "Thus says YHWH: 'Set your house in order because you are going to die and you shall not live.'"
	2 Thereupon he turned his face to the wall and prayed to YHWH, saying,	2 Thereupon Hezekiah turned his face to the wall and prayed to YHWH
	3 "O YHWH, remember I pray how I have walked before you in truth with a whole heart, and the good I have done in your eyes." Then Hezekiah wept profusely.[1]	3 and said, "O YHWH, remember I pray how I have walked before you in truth with a whole heart, and the good I have done in your eyes." Then Hezekiah wept profusely.
	4 Now Isaiah had not gone out of the middle court[2] when the word of YHWH came to him:	4 Then the word of YHWH came to Isaiah, saying,
	5 "Turn back and you shall say to Hezekiah, leader of my people, 'Thus says YHWH the God of David your [fore]father: I have heard your prayer. I have seen your tears. See, I am going to heal you; on the third day you shall go up to the house of YHWH;	5 "Go and say to Hezekiah, 'Thus says YHWH the God of David your [fore]father: I have heard your prayer, I have seen your tears. See I am going to add on to your days, fifteen years.
	6 and I shall add on to your days, fifteen years. From the grasp of the king of Assyria I will deliver you and this city, and I will defend this city for my sake and for the sake of David my servant."	6 From the grasp of the king of Assyria I will deliver you and this city, and I will defend this city."
	7 Then Isaiah said, "Take a poultice of figs." And they took and put [it] on the boil and he recovered.[3]	21 Then Isaiah said, "Let them bring a poultice of figs." They rubbed [it] on the boil and he recovered.[4]
	8 Hezekiah said to Isaiah, "What sign [is there] that YHWH will heal me and that I shall go up on the third day to the house of YHWH?"	22 Hezekiah said, "What sign [is there] that I shall go up to the house of YHWH?"
	9 Isaiah said, "This shall be the sign for you from YHWH, for YHWH will do the thing that he has	7 And this shall be the sign for you from YHWH, that YHWH will do this thing which he said.

said. The shadow has gone ten steps [forward], shall it now turn back ten steps?"

10 Then Hezekiah said, "It is easy for the shadow to extend ten steps, not for the shadow to turn backwards ten steps."

11 Isaiah the prophet cried out to YHWH; and he turned the shadow on the steps that had gone down on the steps of Ahaz, backwards ten steps.

8 "See I am returning the shadow on the steps that has gone down on the steps of Ahaz, with the sun, backwards ten steps." So the sun turned back ten steps, on the steps where it had gone down.

25 But Hezekiah did not respond according to the benefit [shown] him for his heart became proud and so there was anger against him and against Judah and Jerusalem.

26 Then Hezekiah humbled himself in the pride of his heart—he and the inhabitants of Jerusalem—so the wrath of YHWH did not come against them during the days of Hezekiah.

9 A composition of Hezekiah king of Judah, when he was sick and had recovered from his sickness:

10 I said: "In the quiet of my days
I must be gone:
to the gates of Sheol
I have been assigned [for] the rest of my years."

11 I said, "I will not see YHWH
in the land of the living.
I shall not look upon humanity again
among the inhabitants of the land of decease.

12 My time is pulled up and removed from me like the tent of my shepherd;
I have rolled up my life like a weaver,
from the loom he cuts me off.

From day until night you make an end of me,
13 I compose [myself] until morning.

Like a lion thus he breaks all my
bones:
from day until night you make an
end of me.

14 Like a swallow, a crane, thus I
peep;
I moan like a dove.
My eyes languish at the height.
My Lord, I am oppressed; give me
certainty.

15 What can I say? Now he has
spoken to me and he has acted.
I shall walk slowly all my years
because of the bitterness of my soul.

16 My Lord, because of these
[things] they will live;
and for all in them is the life of my
spirit.
May you restore me to health
and make me live.

17 See, for my well-being I had
bitterness, bitterness;
but you have lovingly saved my life
from the pit of extinction;
for you have cast behind your back
all my sins.

18 For Sheol does not praise you,
[nor] Death extol you,
those who go down into the pit
cannot hope for your faithfulness.

19 The living, the living, he praises
you
as I do today.
A father makes known to [his] sons
your faithfulness.

20 YHWH [has promised] to save
us[5]
that we may play our[6] stringed
instruments
all the days of our lives,
before the house of YHWH.

---

[1] Literally, "a great weeping."
[2] Reading the Qere.
[3] Literally, "lived."
[4] Literally, "lived."
[5] Literally, "me."
[6] Literally, "my."

649 Hezekiah Receives Envoys from Babylon
2 Chron 32:27-31 // 2 Kings 20:12-19 // Isa 39:1-8

2 Chron 32	*2 Kings 20*	*Isaiah 39*

2 Chron 32

27 Now Hezekiah had very much wealth and honor. So he made treasure-houses for himself, for silver and gold, for precious stone[s] and aromatic spices, for shields and for all costly weapons;

28 and storehouses for the produce of grain, of new wine, and fresh oil, and stalls for all cattle and livestock for folds.

29 He also made cities for himself and a large number of flocks and herds, because God had given him very many possession[s].

30 This Hezekiah stopped up the spring of the waters of the Upper Gihon and made them flow straight¹ downwards, west to the city of David. So Hezekiah was successful in all his deed[s],

31 even with respect to the representatives of the officials of Babylon who were sent to him to inquire about the sign that had occurred in the land, [when] God had forsaken him to test him, to know all [that was] in his heart.

2 Kings 20

12 At that time Berodach-baladan son of Baladan king of Babylon, sent emissaries and a gift to Hezekiah because he had heard that Hezekiah had been ill.

13 When Hezekiah heard concerning them he showed them all the house of his treasury—the silver and gold, the spices and the good oil, his armory and all that was found in his treasure-houses. There was not a thing which Hezekiah did not let them see in his house, and in all his realm.

14 Then Isaiah the prophet came to king Hezekiah and said to him, "What did these men say? From where did they come to you?" Hezekiah said, "From a distant land, they came from Babylon."

Isaiah 39

1 At that time Merodach-baladan son of Baladan king of Babylon, sent emissaries and a gift to Hezekiah, for he had heard that he had been ill and grew stronger.

2 When Hezekiah rejoiced concerning them he let them see the house of his treasury—the silver and gold, the spices and the good oil, all his armory and all that was found in his treasure-houses. There was not a thing which Hezekiah did not let them see in his house, and in all his realm.

3 Then Isaiah the prophet came to king Hezekiah and said to him, "What did these men say? From where did they come to you?" Hezekiah said, "From a distant land, they came to me from Babylon."

15 He said, "What did they see in your house?" Hezekiah said, "They have seen all that is in my house: there is not a thing which I have not let them see in my treasure-houses."

16 Then Isaiah said to Hezekiah, "Listen to the word of YHWH:

17 'Look, the days are coming when all that is in your house and that which your ancestors stored up until this day shall be carried into Babylon. Not a thing will be left,' says YHWH.

18 'Moreover, some of your sons who will come forth from you, whom you have fathered, they shall take and they will become eunuchs in the palace of the king of Babylon.'"

19 Then Hezekiah said to Isaiah, "The word of YHWH which you have spoken is good." But he said [to himself], "Will there not be peace and security in my days?"

4 He said, "What did they see in your house?" Hezekiah said, "They have seen all that is in my house: there is not a thing which I have not let them see in my treasure-houses."

5 Then Isaiah said to Hezekiah, "Listen to the word of YHWH of hosts:

6 'Look, the days are coming when all that is in your house and that which your ancestors stored up until this day shall be carried [to] Babylon. Not a thing will be left,' says YHWH.

7 'Moreover, some of your sons who will come forth from you, whom you have fathered, they shall take and they shall become eunuchs in the palace of the king of Babylon.'"

8 Then Hezekiah said to Isaiah, "The word of YHWH which you have spoken is good." But he said [to himself], "that there will be peace and security in my days."

---

[1] Reading the Qere.

650 The Death of Hezekiah
2 Chron 32:32-33 // 2 Kings 20:20-21

2 Chron 32

32 Now the rest of the acts of Hezekiah and his faithful acts, indeed they are written in the Vision of Isaiah son of Amoz, the prophet, in the Book of the Kings of Judah and Israel.

33 When Hezekiah lay down to rest with his ancestors, they buried him on the ascent to the tombs of the descendants of David, and all Judah and the inhabitants of Jerusalem did honor to him when he died. And Manasseh his son became king in his place.

2 Kings 20

20 Now the rest of the acts of Hezekiah and all his valor, and what he made—the pool and the channel—and how he brought the water into the city, are they not written in the Book of the Chronicles of the Kings of Judah?

21 When Hezekiah lay down to rest with his ancestors, Manasseh his son became king in his place.

Divided Monarchy-5
Sections 650–667

Number	Title	2 Chronicles	2 Kings
650	The Death of Hezekiah	32:32-33	20:20-21
651	The Reign of Manasseh	33:1-20	21:1-18
652	The Reign of Amon	33:21-25	21:19-26
653	The Reign of Josiah and Early Reform	34:1-7	22:1-2
654	The Torah Book Discovered	34:8-33	22:3–23:3
655	Josiah's Reforms		23:4-20
656	Josiah Keeps the Passover	35:1-19	23:21-23
657	YHWH's Persistent Anger against Judah		23:24-27
658	The Death of Josiah	35:20–36:1	23:28-30
659	The Reign of Jehoahaz	36:2-4	23:31-35
660	The Reign and Dethronement of Jehoiakim	36:5-8	23:36–24:7
661	Jehoiachin and Babylonian Captivity	36:9-10	24:8-17
662	The Reign of Zedekiah	36:11-17	24:18-20
663	The Fall of Jerusalem		25:1-7
664	The Captivity of Judah	36:18-21	25:8-21
665	The Remnant Flee to Egypt		25:22-26
666	Jehoiachin Released and Honored		25:27-30
667	The Proclamation of Cyrus	36:22-23	

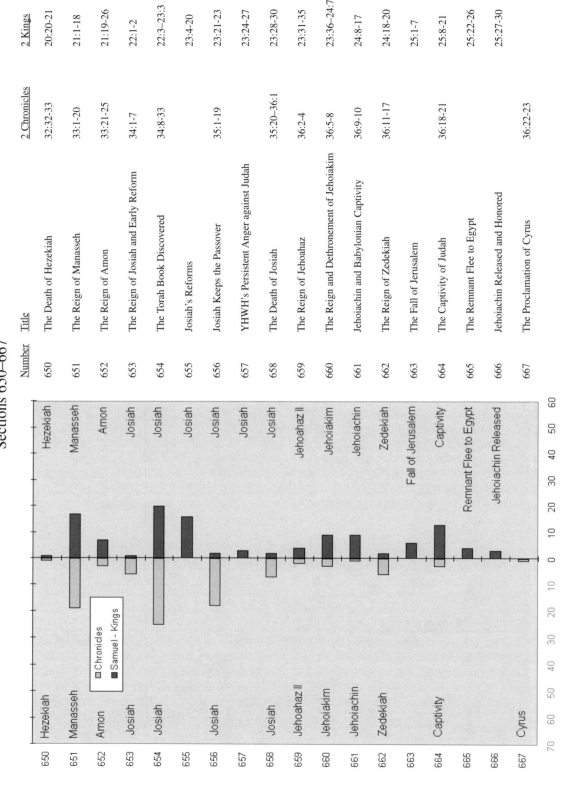

Number of Verses

Section Number

322

651 The Reign of Manasseh
2 Chron 33:1-20 // 2 Kings 21:1-18

2 Chron 33	*2 Kings 21*
1 Manasseh was twelve years old when he became king and he was king for fifty-five years in Jerusalem.	1 Manasseh was twelve years old when he became king, and he was king for fifty-five years in Jerusalem. The name of his mother was Hephzibah.
2 He did what was evil in the eyes of YHWH like the abominations of the nations whom YHWH had dispossessed before the Israelites.	2 He did what was evil in the eyes of YHWH like the abominations of the nations whom YHWH had dispossessed before the Israelites.
3 For he rebuilt¹ the high places that Hezekiah his father had pulled down; and he set up altars to the Baalim and he made asheroth: they bowed themselves down to all the host of heaven and he served them.	3 For he rebuilt the high places that Hezekiah his father had destroyed; and he set up altars to Baal, and he made [an] asherah as Ahab king of Israel had done: they bowed themselves down to all the host of heaven and he served them.
4 He built altars in the house of YHWH of which YHWH said, "In Jerusalem my name will be forever."	4 He built altars in the house of YHWH of which YHWH had said, "In Jerusalem I will put my name."
5 He also built altars to all the host of heaven in the two courts of the house of YHWH.	5 He also built altars for all the host of heaven in the two courts of the house of YHWH.
6 It was he who made his sons pass through the fire in the Valley of Ben Hinnom. And he engaged in soothsaying, divination, and sorcery and he practiced necromancy and wizardry. He added much more that was evil in the eyes of YHWH to provoke him to anger.	6 He made his son pass through the fire; and he engaged in soothsaying and divination and practiced necromancy and wizardry. He did much more that was evil in the eyes of YHWH to provoke [him] to anger.
7 He set up the carved idol, the statue that he had made, in the house of God of which God had said to David and to Solomon his son, "In this house and in Jerusalem which I have chosen out of all the tribes of Israel, I will place my name forever.	7 He set up the carved idol of asherah that he had made in the house of which YHWH had said to David and to Solomon his son, "In this house and in Jerusalem, which I have chosen out of all the tribes of Israel, I will place my name forever;
8 I will not make the foot of Israel turn aside anymore from upon the ground that I have established for your ancestors, if only they would take care to do according to all that I have commanded them according to all the Torah, the statutes, and the customs [given] through Moses."	8 I will not make the foot of Israel wander anymore from the ground that I gave to their ancestors, if only they would take care to do according to all that I have commanded them and according to all the Torah that my servant Moses has commanded them."
9 But Manasseh caused Judah and the inhabitants of Jerusalem to err, to do more evil than the nations that YHWH had destroyed before the Israelites.	9 But they did not listen: so Manasseh caused them to err, to do more evil than the nations that YHWH had destroyed before the Israelites.
10 YHWH spoke to Manasseh and his people, but they did not give heed.	

11 So YHWH brought against them the officers of the army that belonged to the king of Assyria and they took Manasseh captive in shackles and bound him in bronze fetters, and brought him to Babylon.

12 Now as he was distressed, he sought the favor from YHWH his God and he humbled himself greatly before the God of his ancestors.

13 He prayed to him and his supplication was received. He [God] heard his petition and returned him [to] Jerusalem, to his kingdom. Then Manasseh knew that YHWH was God indeed.

14 After this, he built an outer wall for the city of David west of Gihon in the wadi, [reaching] to the entrance of the Fish Gate, and he ordered the wall to encircle the Ophel and he made it very high. Also he put officers of the army in all the fortified cities of Judah.

15 He removed the foreign gods, the statue from the house of YHWH and all the altars which he had built on the mountain of the house of YHWH and in Jerusalem, and he cast them outside the city.

16 Then he set up[2] the altar of YHWH and sacrificed upon it peace offerings and a thank offering; and he ordered Judah to serve YHWH the God of Israel.

17 But the people still kept sacrificing in the high places, only to YHWH their God.

10 Then YHWH spoke through his servants the prophets, saying,

11 "Because Manasseh king of Judah has done these abominations, and has caused more evil than all that the Amorites did who were before him and has made Judah also to sin with his idols,

12 therefore, thus says YHWH the God of Israel: 'See, I am bringing [such] evil against Jerusalem and Judah, that anyone who hears [of] it[3] will have his two ears tingle.

13 For I will stretch out against Jerusalem the plumbline of Samaria and the level of the house of Ahab and I will wipe out Jerusalem as one wipes a dish, wiping [it] and turning it upside down.

14 Thus I will cast off the remnant of my inheritance and will give them into the hand of their enemies, and they will become spoil and booty to all their enemies

15 because they did what was evil in my eyes and have been provoking me to anger from the day when their ancestors went out from Egypt to this day.

16 Furthermore, Manasseh poured out so much innocent blood until he filled Jerusalem from end to end, besides the sin that he caused Judah to sin, to do what was evil in the eyes of YHWH.

18 Now the rest of the acts of Manasseh, and his prayer to his God, the words of the seers who spoke to him in the name of YHWH the God of Israel, indeed they are in the Annals of the Kings of Israel.

17 Now the rest of the acts of Manasseh, and all that he did, and his sin that he sinned, are they not written on the Book of the Chronicles of the Kings of Judah?

19 Also his prayer, how his supplication was received, and all his sin, his unfaithfulness, the places on which he built high places, set up the asherim and the idols, before he was humbled, indeed, they are written in the Words of Hozai.

20 When Manasseh lay down to rest with his ancestors, they buried him in his house; and Amon his son became king in his place.

18 When Manasseh lay down to rest with his ancestors, he was buried in the garden of his house, in the garden of Uzza; and Amon his son became king in his place.

---

¹ Reading as hendiadys. Literally, "returned and built."
² Reading the Qere.
³ Reading the Qere.

652 The Reign of Amon
2 Chron 33:21-25 // 2 Kings 21:19-26

2 Chron 33

21 Amon was twenty-two years old when he became king, and he was king for two years in Jerusalem.

2 Kings 21

19 Amon was twenty-two years old when he became king, and he was king for two years in Jerusalem. The name of his mother was Meshullemeth daughter of Haruz from Jotbah.

22 He did what was evil in the eyes of YHWH as Manasseh his father had done. Also Amon sacrificed to all the idols that his father had made and served them.

20 He did what was evil in the eyes of YHWH as Manasseh his father had done.

21 He walked in all the way that his father had walked and served the idols that his father had served; and they bowed themselves down to them:

23 He did not humble himself before YHWH as Manasseh his father had humbled himself, rather he, Amon, increased [his] guilt.

22 he forsook YHWH the God of his ancestors and did not walk in the way of YHWH.

24 His servants conspired against him and put him to death in his house.

25 But the people of the land struck down all the conspirators against King Amon; and the people of the land made Josiah his son king in his place.

23 The servants of Amon conspired against him and put the king to death in his house.

24 But the people of the land struck down all the conspirators against King Amon; and the people of the land made Josiah his son king in his place.

25 Now the rest of the acts of Amon that he did, are they not written in the Book of the Chronicles of the Kings of Judah?

26 They buried him in his tomb in the garden of Uzza; and Josiah his son became king in his place.

Josiah
Sections 653–658

Number	Title	2 Chronicles	2 Kings
653	The Reign of Josiah and Early Reform	34:1-7	22:1-2
654	The Torah Book Discovered	34:8-33	22:3–23:3
655	Josiah's Reforms		23:4-20
656	Josiah Keeps the Passover	35:1-19	23:21-23
657	YHWH's Persistent Anger		23:24-27
658	The Death of Josiah	35:20–36:1	23:28-30

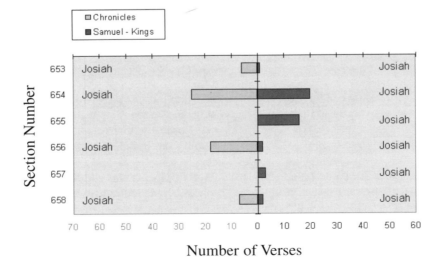

653 The Reign of Josiah and Early Reform
2 Chron 34:1-7 // 2 Kings 22:1-2

2 Chron 34

1 Josiah was eight years old when he became king, and he was king in Jerusalem for thirty-one years.

2 He did what was right in the eyes of YHWH and walked in the ways of David his [fore]father, and did not turn to the right or left.

3 In the eighth year of his kingship, while he was yet a youth, he began to seek the God of David his [fore]father; and in the twelfth year he began to cleanse Judah and Jerusalem of the high places, the asherim and the carved images and cast metal idols.

4 They broke down in his presence the altars of the Baalim, and the incense-altars that were on top of them. He cut down the asherim; the carved images and cast metal idols he smashed and pulverized, and scattered [them] on top of the tombs[1] of those who had sacrificed to them.

5 The bones of the priests he burned on their[2] altars and cleansed Judah and Jerusalem.

6 Also in the cities of Manasseh, Ephraim and Simeon and as far as Naphtali, on the hill of their shrines all around,[3]

7 he broke down the altars and the asherim; and the cast metal idols he beat to powder, and all of the incense-altars he cut down throughout all the land of Israel. Then he returned to Jerusalem.

2 Kings 22

1 Josiah was eight years old when he became king, and for thirty-one years he was king in Jerusalem. The name of his mother was Jedidah daughter of Adaiah from Bozkath.

2 He did what was right in the eyes of YHWH and walked in all the way of David his [fore]father, and did not turn to the right or left.

---

[1] The Massoretic Text may preserve here an enclitic mem.
[2] Reading the Qere.
[3] Hebrew uncertain.

654 The Torah Book Discovered
2 Chron 34:8-33 // 2 Kings 22:3–23:3

2 Chron 34	*2 Kings 22*
8 In the eighteenth year of his kingship, [after] purifying the land and the house, he sent Shaphan son of Azaliah, and Maaseiah the officer of the city, and Joah son of Joahaz the recorder, to repair the house of YHWH his God.	3 It happened in the eighteenth year of King Josiah, that the king sent the scribe Shaphan son of Azaliah son of Meshullam, to the house of YHWH, saying,
9 They came to Hilkiah the high priest, and they gave [him] the money that had been brought into the house of God that the Levites, guardians of the threshold, had collected from the hand of Manasseh and Ephraim, and from all the remnant of Israel and from all Judah and Benjamin and from the inhabitants[1] of Jerusalem.	4 "Go up to Hilkiah the high priest that he may tally the money that has been brought into the house of YHWH that the guardians of the threshold have collected from the people;
10 They gave it into the hand of the one doing the work, those appointed over the house of YHWH, and they gave it [to] those doing the work who were working in the house of YHWH to mend and to repair the house.	5 and let them put it[4] into the hand of those doing the work, those appointed over the house of YHWH and let them [in turn] give it to those doing the work who are in the house of YHWH to repair the dilapidation of the house,
11 They gave [it] to the craftsmen and the builders to purchase quarried stone and timber for joists and to cross-beam the buildings that the kings of Judah had let fall into decay.	6 [that is], to the craftsmen, the builders and the masons, to purchase timber and quarried stone to repair the house.
12 The men worked honestly on the undertaking. Over them were appointed Jahath and Obadiah the Levites of the sons of Merari, and Zechariah and Meshullam of the sons of Kohath, to act as supervisors; and Levites all skilled in instruments of song,	7 But the money with them that was put into their hand is not to be audited, for they are working honestly."
13 [were] over the laborers and acted as supervisors over all engaged in the undertaking; some of the Levites [were] scribes, officials, and gatekeepers.	
14 As they were bringing out the money that had been brought into the house of YHWH, Hilkiah the priest found the Book of Torah of YHWH given through Moses.	
15 Hilkiah responded and said to Shaphan the scribe, "I have found the Book of the Torah in the house of YHWH"; and Hilkiah gave the book to Shaphan.	8 Hilkiah the high priest said to Shaphan the scribe, "I have found the Book of Torah in the house of YHWH"; and Hilkiah gave the book to Shaphan and he read it.
16 Shaphan then brought the book to the king, and he further informed the king, saying, "All that was put into the hand of your servants they are doing.	9 Then Shaphan the scribe went to the king and informed the king, and he said, "Your servants have emptied out the money that was found in the house and have put it into the hand of those doing the work, those appointed over the house of YHWH."

17 They have emptied out the money that was found in the house of YHWH, and have put it into the hand of those appointed [supervisors] and into the hand of those doing the work."

18 Shaphan the scribe told the king, saying, "Hilkiah the priest has given me a book." Shaphan then read aloud in it before the king.

19 When the king heard the words of the Torah, he tore his garments.

20 Then the king commanded Hilkiah, Ahikam son of Shaphan, Abdon son of Micah, Shaphan the scribe, and Asaiah the king's servant, saying,

21 "Go, inquire of YHWH on my behalf, and on behalf of the remnant in Israel and in Judah concerning the words of the book that has been found, for great is the wrath of YHWH that has been poured out against us because our ancestors did not keep the word of YHWH to do according to all that is written in this book."

22 So Hilkiah and those [with²] the king went to Huldah the prophetess wife of Shallum son of Tokhath³ son of Hasrah, the keeper of the garments—she dwelt in Jerusalem in the Second Quarter—and they spoke to her accordingly.

23 She said to them, "Thus says YHWH, the God of Israel: Tell the man who sent you to me,

24 'Thus says YHWH, See, I am about to bring evil upon this place and upon its inhabitants all the curses which are written in the book, that they have read before the king of Judah.

25 Because they have forsaken me and have burned incense to other gods, so as to provoke me against all the works of their hands, therefore my wrath shall be poured out against this place and it will not be quenched.'

26 But to the king of Judah who has sent you to inquire of YHWH, thus you shall say to him, 'Thus says YHWH, the God of Israel: [With respect to] the words which you have heard,

27 because your heart has been penitent and you have humbled yourself before God when you heard his words against this place and against its inhabitants and

10 And Shaphan the scribe told the king, "Hilkiah the priest has given me a book." Shaphan then read it aloud before the king.

11 When the king heard the words of the Book of the Torah he tore his garments.

12 Then the king commanded Hilkiah the priest, Ahikam son of Shaphan, Achbor son of Micaiah, Shaphan the scribe, and Asaiah the king's servant, saying,

13 "Go, inquire of YHWH on my behalf, and on behalf of the people, and on behalf of all Judah concerning the words of this book that has been found, for great is the wrath of YHWH which has been kindled against us because our ancestors did not listen to the words of this book to do according to all that is written concerning us."

14 So Hilkiah the priest, and Ahikam, Achbor, Shaphan, and Asaiah went to Huldah the prophetess wife of Shallum son of Tikvah son of Harhas, the keeper of the garments—-she dwelt in Jerusalem in the Second Quarter—and they spoke to her.

15 She said to them, "Thus says YHWH the God of Israel: Tell the man who sent you to me,

16 'Thus says YHWH, See, I am about to bring evil on this place and upon its inhabitants all the words of the book that the king of Judah has read.

17 Because they have forsaken me and have burned incense to other gods, so that they have provoked me with all the work of their hands, therefore my wrath shall be kindled against this place and it will not be quenched.'

18 But to the king of Judah who has sent you to inquire of YHWH, thus you shall say to him, 'Thus says YHWH, the God of Israel: [With respect to] the words which you have heard,

19 because your heart has been penitent and you have humbled yourself before YHWH when you heard what I spoke against this place and against its inhabitants

[because] you have humbled yourself before me, and have torn your garments and wept before me, so I also have heard—Oracle of YHWH.

28 See, I will gather you to your ancestors; you shall be gathered to your [ancestral] tombs in peace; your eyes shall not look on all the evil that I am about to bring on this place and on its inhabitants.'" Then they reported back to the king.

29 Then the king sent and he gathered all the elders of Judah and Jerusalem.

30 The king went up to the house of YHWH and all the men of Judah and the inhabitants of Jerusalem, the priests and the Levites, and all the people from great to small, and he read in their ears all the words of the Book of the Covenant that had been found [in] the house of YHWH.

31 The king stood upon his spot and enacted the covenant before YHWH to walk after YHWH and to keep his commandments, his testimonies, and his statutes with all his heart and with all his life, to do the words of the covenant, written in this book.

32 Then he made all who were present in Jerusalem and Benjamin stand up for it; so the inhabitants of Jerusalem did according to the covenant of God, the God of their ancestors.

33 Further, Josiah removed all the abominations from all the lands which belonged to the Israelites and he made all who were present in Israel serve YHWH their God. All his days they did not turn away from following YHWH the God of their ancestors.

that they should become a desolation and a curse, and [because] you have torn your garments and wept before me, so I also have heard—Oracle of YHWH.

20 Therefore, see, I will gather you beside your ancestors; you shall be gathered to your [ancestral] tombs in peace; your eyes shall not look on all the evil that I am about to bring upon this place.'" Then they reported back to the king.

23:1 Then the king sent, and all the elders of Judah and Jerusalem gathered to him.

2 The king went up to the house of YHWH and all the men of Judah and all the inhabitants of Jerusalem with him, the priests and the prophets, and all the people from small to great, and he read in their ears all the words of the Book of the Covenant that had been found in the house of YHWH.

3 The king stood by the pillar and enacted the covenant before YHWH to walk after YHWH and to keep his commandments, his testimonies, and his statutes with all [his] heart and with all [his] life, to affirm the words of this covenant that were written in this book; and all the people pledged [themselves] to the covenant.

---

[1] Reading the consonants of the Kethib instead of the Qere.
[2] Hebrew obscure.
[3] Reading the Qere.
[4] Reading the Qere.

655 Josiah's Reforms
2 Kings 23:4-20

2 Kings 23

4 The king commanded Hilkiah the high priest, the priests of the second rank and those guarding the threshold, to bring out from the temple of YHWH all the vessels made for the Baal, for the asherah, and for all the host of heaven; and he burned them outside Jerusalem in the fields of the Kidron and carried their ashes to Bethel.

5 He did away with the idol-priests whom the kings of Judah had installed to burn incense[1] on the high places in the cities of Judah and surrounding Jerusalem, and those also who burned incense to the Baal, the sun and the moon, the constellations and to all the host of heaven.

6 He brought out the asherah from the house of YHWH, outside Jerusalem, to the Wadi Kidron, and burned it at the Wadi Kidron, pounded [it] to dust, and threw its dust over the burial ground of the common people.

7 Moreover, he pulled down the shrines of the male votaries who were in the house of YHWH where the women were weaving things[2] for asherah.

8 He brought out all the priests from the cities of Judah, and rendered unclean the high places where the priests had burned incense, from Geba to Beersheba; he also tore down the high places of the gates that were at the entrance of the gate of Joshua the prefect of the city, that were on a person's left side at the gate of the city.

9 However, the priests of the high places did not come up to the altar of YHWH in Jerusalem; instead they ate unleavened bread among their brothers.

10 He rendered unclean Topheth which is in the Valley of the Ben[3] Hinnom, so that no one could make his son or daughter pass through the fire of Molech.

11 He also did away with the horses that the kings of Judah had given to the sun, at the entrance to the house of YHWH by the chamber of Nathan-melech the eunuch that was in the colonnades; and he burned the chariots of the sun with fire.

12 The altars that were on the roof—the upper story of Ahaz—that the kings of Judah had made, as well as the altars that Manasseh had made in the two courts of the house of YHWH, the king tore down and removed quickly from there and cast their dust into the Wadi Kidron.

13 The high places that were east of Jerusalem, to the south of the Mount of Destruction that Solomon the king of Israel had built for Ashtoreth the vile thing of the Sidonians, and for Chemosh the vile thing of Moab, and for Milcom the abomination of the Ammonites, the king also polluted.

14 He also broke down the pillars and cut down the asherim and filled their place with human bones.

15 Also, the altar that was in Bethel, the high place that Jeroboam son of Nebat had made, who made Israel to sin, even that altar and high place he tore down and burned the high place [and] pounded [it] to dust; he also burned [the] asherah.

16 As Josiah turned, he saw the tombs there on the mount; he sent and took the bones from the tombs and he burned [them] on the altar and thus polluted it according to the word of YHWH that the man of God had proclaimed who had proclaimed these things;

17 and he said, "What is that cairn that I see?" The men of the city told him, "The tomb of the man of God who came from Judah and proclaimed these things that you have done against the altar at Bethel."

18 So he said, "Let him rest; let no one move his bones." So they left his bones alone with the bones of the prophet who had come from Samaria.

19 Also all the shrines of the high places that were in the cities of Samaria that the kings of Israel had made to provoke [YHWH] to anger, Josiah removed; and he did to them all the things that he had done at Bethel:

20 he slaughtered all the priests of the high places who were there upon the altars and burned human bones upon them. Then he returned to Jerusalem.

---

¹ Literally, "and he burned incense."
² Literally, "houses."
³ Reading the Qere.

656 Josiah Keeps the Passover
2 Chron 35:1-19 // 2 Kings 23:21-23

2 Chron 35	*2 Kings 23*
1 Josiah kept [the] Passover to YHWH in Jerusalem; and they slaughtered the Passover [lamb] on the fourteenth day of the first month.	21 Now the king commanded all the people, saying, "Keep [the] Passover to YHWH your God as it is written in this Book of this Covenant."
2 He set up priests over their watches and supported them in the service of the house of YHWH.	
3 He said to the Levites who taught¹ all Israel, those consecrated to YHWH, "Place the holy ark in the house that Solomon son of David, king of Israel, built: you need not carry it on your shoulder [any longer]. Now serve YHWH your God and his people Israel.	

4 Arrange yourselves[2] according to your ancestral
houses, according to your divisions, following the writing of David king of Israel and the writing of Solomon
his son.

5 Stand in the sanctuary according to the groupings of
ancestral houses for your brothers, the common people,
and let there be a share of an ancestral house for the
Levites.

6 Slaughter the Passover [lamb] and consecrate yourselves and arrange for your brothers to act according to
the word of YHWH through Moses.

7 Josiah presented to the common people flocks, lambs
and kids, all for Passover offerings; for all who were
present to the amount of thirty thousand and three
thousand head of cattle—these were from the king's
own livestock.

8 His officials also presented voluntarily to the people,
to the priests, and to the Levites. Hilkiah, Zechariah
and Jehiel, the chief officers of the house of God, gave
to the priests for the Passover offerings two thousand
six hundred [small cattle] plus three hundred large
cattle.

9 Also Conaniah[3] and Shemaiah and Nethanel his
brothers, and Hashabiah, Jeiel, and Jozabad, the chiefs
of the Levites, presented to the Levites for Passover
offerings five thousand [small cattle] and five hundred
large cattle.

10 When the service was arranged, the priests stood at
their station and the Levites by their divisions, according to the command of the king.

11 Then they slaughtered the Passover [lamb]; the
priests dashed [the blood that they received] from their
hand while the Levites did the flaying.

12 Next they set aside the burnt offering[s] for their
distribution to the groupings of the ancestral house[s]
of the common people for offering up to YHWH in
accord with what is written in the Book of Moses. And
[so they did] with the large cattle.

13 They cooked the Passover [lamb] with fire according to the ordinance; they cooked the sacred offerings
in pots, in caldrons and pans, and then carried them
quickly to all the common people.

14 Afterward they made arrangements for themselves and for the priests, since the priests the sons of Aaron, [were busy] at the offering up the burnt offering[s] fat pieces until night; so the Levites made arrangements for themselves and for the priests the sons of Aaron.

15 The singers the sons of Asaph, were at their station according to the command of David, as well as Asaph, Heman, and Jeduthun, the king's seer. The gatekeepers were likewise at each gate: it was not necessary for them to leave off their service since their brothers the Levites made arrangements for them.

16 So all the service of YHWH was established on that day to enact the Passover and to offer up burnt offerings on the altar of YHWH according to the commandment of King Josiah.

17 The Israelites who were present kept the Passover at that time and the Feast of Unleavened Bread for seven days.

18 No Passover like it had been kept in Israel since the days of Samuel the prophet; nor did any of the kings of Israel keep such a Passover as was kept by Josiah, the priests and the Levites, and all Judah and Israel who were present and the inhabitants of Jerusalem.

19 In the eighteenth year of the reign of Josiah this Passover was kept.

22 For nothing like this Passover had been kept since the days of the judges who judged Israel or [during] all the days of the kings of Israel or of the kings of Judah.

23 However, in the eighteenth year of King Josiah, this Passover was kept to YHWH in Jerusalem.

---

[1] Reading the Qere.
[2] Reading the Qere.
[3] Reading the Qere.

657 YHWH's Persistent Anger against Judah
2 Kings 23:24-27

2 Kings 23

24 Moreover the mediums, the wizards, the household gods, the idols, and all the loathsome things that were seen in the land of Judah and in Jerusalem, Josiah burned so that he might affirm the words of the Torah written in the book which Hilkiah the priest had found [in] the house of YHWH.

25 There had been no king like him before him who turned to YHWH with all his heart, with all his being, and with all his might according to all the Torah of Moses; and after him there did not arise his like.

26 Nonetheless, YHWH did not turn from the fierceness of his great wrath whereby his wrath was kindled against Judah on account of all the provocations with which Manasseh had provoked him.

27 Therefore YHWH said, "I will remove Judah also from before me as I have removed Israel, and I will cast off this city that I have chosen, Jerusalem and the house of which I said, 'My name shall be there.'"

658 The Death of Josiah
2 Chron 35:20–36:1 // 2 Kings 23:28-30

2 Chron 35

20 After all this when Josiah had set up the house, Neco king of Egypt went up to do battle at Carchemish on the Euphrates, and Josiah went out to meet him.

21 But he dispatched envoys to him, saying, "What is there between me and you, king of Judah? I am not [coming] against you today, but rather against the house with which I am at war; and God has told me to hurry on. For your part, stop [opposing] God who is with me so that he will not destroy you."

22 But Josiah did not turn his face from him but he did disguise himself to do battle with him. He did not listen to the words of Neco from the mouth of God and went up to do battle on the plain of Megiddo.

23 The archers shot at King Josiah and the king said to his servants, "Take me away for I am severely wounded."

24 So his servants took him out of [his] chariot and bore him on a second chariot belonging to him, and conveyed him [to] Jerusalem. He died and he was buried in the tombs of his ancestors, and all Judah and Jerusalem mourned for Josiah.

25 Jeremiah also lamented for Josiah, and all the male and female singers have spoken of Josiah in their lamentations until today; they have made them an institution in Israel—indeed they are written in the Laments.

26 Now the rest of the acts of Josiah and his loyalties according to what is written in the Torah of YHWH,

2 Kings 23

[29 In his days Pharaoh Neco king of Egypt went up to the king of Assyria at the river Euphrates, and King Josiah went to meet him and he [Pharaoh Neco] killed him at Megiddo when he saw him.

30 His servants bore him by chariot dead from Megiddo and brought him to Jerusalem, and they buried him in his [own] tomb. Then the people of the land took Jehoahaz son of Josiah, and they anointed him and made him king in place of his father.]

28 Now the rest of the acts of Josiah, and all that he did, are they not written in the Book of the Chronicles of the Kings of Judah?

27 and his acts, the first and the last, they are indeed written in the Book of the Kings of Israel and Judah.

29 In his days Pharaoh Neco king of Egypt went up to the king of Assyria at the river Euphrates, and King Josiah went to meet him and he [Pharaoh Neco] killed him at Megiddo when he saw him.

30 His servants carried him by chariot dead from Megiddo and brought him to Jerusalem, and they buried him in his [own] tomb. Then the people of the land took Jehoahaz son of Josiah, and they anointed him and made him king in place of his father.

36:1 Then the people of the land took Jehoahaz son of Josiah and made him king in place of his father in Jerusalem.

659 The Reign and Dethronement of Jehoahaz
2 Chron 36:2-4 // 2 Kings 23:31-35

2 Chron 36

2 Joahaz was twenty-three years old when he became king, and he was king for three months in Jerusalem.

3 But the king of Egypt deposed him in Jerusalem, and laid upon the land a tribute of a hundred talents of silver and a talent of gold.

4 Then the king of Egypt made Eliakim his brother king over Judah and Jerusalem and changed his name to Jehoiakim, and Neco took Joahaz his brother and brought him to Egypt.

2 Kings 23

31 Jehoahaz was twenty-three years old when he became king, and he was king for three months in Jerusalem. The name of his mother was Hamutal daughter of Jeremiah from Libnah.

32 He did what was evil in the eyes of YHWH according to all that his ancestors had done.

33 Pharaoh Neco imprisoned him at Riblah in the land of Hammath that he might not be king[1] in Jerusalem, and imposed a tribute upon the land of a hundred talents of silver and a talent of gold.

34 Then Pharaoh Neco made Eliakim son of Josiah king in place of Josiah his father, and changed his name to Jehoiakim; and took Jehoahaz, and he [Jehoahaz] went to Egypt and died there.

35 Moreover, Jehoiakim gave to Pharaoh the silver and the gold; only he had to tax the land to give the money at the bidding of Pharaoh; according to each person's valuation he exacted the silver and the gold together with the people of the land to give [it] to Pharaoh Neco.

---

[1] Reading the Qere.

660 The Reign of Jehoiakim
2 Chron 36:5-8 // 2 Kings 23:36–24:7 // Dan 1:1-2

2 Chron 36

2 Kings 23

Daniel 1

5 Jehoiakim was twenty-five years old when he became king, and he was king for eleven years in Jerusalem. He did what was evil in the eyes of YHWH his God.

36 Jehoiakim was twenty-five years old when he became king, and he was king for eleven years in Jerusalem. The name of his mother was Zebidah[2] daughter of Pedaiah of Rumah.

37 He did what was evil in the eyes of YHWH according to all that his ancestors had done.

6 Nebuchadnezzar king of Babylon, came up against him, and bound him in bronze fetters to lead him to Babylon;

24:1 In his days Nebuchadnezzar king of Babylon came up, and Jehoiakim became his servant for three years; then he turned and rebelled against him.

1 In the third year of the kingship of Jehoiakim king of Judah, Nebuchadnezzar king of Babylon came to Jerusalem, and laid siege to it.

7 and some of the vessels of the house of YHWH Nebuchadnezzar brought to Babylon and put them in his temple[1] in Babylon.

2 Adonay gave Jehoiakim king of Judah into his hand along with part of the vessels of the house of God, and he brought them to the land of Shinar, to the house of his god, and he brought the vessels into the treasure-house of his god.

2 So YHWH sent against him bands of Chaldeans, bands of Arameans, bands of Moabites, and bands of Ammonites, and he sent them against Judah to destroy it according to the word of YHWH that he had spoken through his servants the prophets.

3 Surely this came upon Judah on the order of YHWH, so as to remove [them] from before his face for the sins of Manasseh according to all that he had done.

4 There was also the blood of the innocent that he had shed and had filled Jerusalem with innocent blood; so YHWH was not willing to pardon [him].

8 Now the rest of the acts of Jehoiakim, and his abominations that he did and what was found against him, indeed they are written in the Book of the Kings of Israel and Judah; and Jehoiachin his son became king in his place.

5 Now the rest of the acts of Jehoiakim and all that he did, are they not written in the Book of the Chronicles of the Kings of Judah?

6 When Jehoiakim lay down to rest with his ancestors, Jehoiachin his son became king in his place.

7 The king of Egypt did not come again out from his land, for the king of Babylon had taken from the Brook of Egypt to the River Euphrates all that belonged to the king of Egypt.

---

[1] Alternative translation: "in his palace."
[2] Hebrew Qere reads "Zebudah."

661 Jehoiachin and Officials Are Led into Babylonian Captivity
2 Chron 36:9-10 // 2 Kings 24:8-17

2 Chron 36

9 Jehoiachin was eight years old when he became king, and he was king in Jerusalem for three months and ten days. He did what was evil in the eyes of YHWH.

2 Kings 24

8 Jehoiachin was eighteen years old when he became king, and he was king in Jerusalem for three months. The name of his mother was Nehushta daughter of Elnathan from Jerusalem.

9 And he did what was evil in the eyes of YHWH according to all that his ancestors had done.

10 At that time the servants of Nebuchadnezzar king of Babylon came up[1] [to] Jerusalem, and the city came under siege.

11 Nebuchadnezzar king of Babylon came to the city as his servants were besieging it.

12 Then Jehoiachin king of Judah went out to the king of Babylon—he, his mother, his servants, his officers, and his officials—and the king of Babylon took him in the eighth year of his being king.

13 He [the king of Babylon] carried away from there all the treasures of the house of YHWH and the treasures of the house of the king; and he cut into pieces all the vessels of gold in the temple of YHWH that Solomon king of Israel had made, just as YHWH had spoken.

14 He exiled all Jerusalem, all the officers and all the warriors, ten[2] thousand captives, and every craftsman and smith. None remained, except the poor of the people of the land.

15 He exiled Jehoiachin to Babylon; the mother of the king, the wives of the king, his officials, and the elite[3] of the land he led into exile from Jerusalem to Babylon.

16 Also all the men of the army, seven thousand, and [every] craftsman and smith, one thousand, all strong men fit for battle—these the king of Babylon brought into exile to Babylon.

10 At the return of the year King Nebuchadnezzar sent and brought him to Babylon along with the choicest vessels of the house of YHWH, and made Zedekiah his brother king over Judah and Jerusalem.

17 Then the king of Babylon made Mattaniah his uncle king in his place, and changed his name to Zedekiah.

---

[1] Reading the Qere.
[2] Reading the Qere.
[3] Following the Kethib rather than the Qere.

662 The Reign of Zedekiah
2 Chron 36:11-17 // 2 Kings 24:18-20 // Jer 52:1-3

2 Chron 36	*2 Kings 24*	*Jeremiah 52*
11 Zedekiah was twenty-one years old when he became king, and he was king for eleven years in Jerusalem.	18 Zedekiah was twenty-one years old when he became king, and he was king for eleven years in Jerusalem. The name of his mother was Hamutal[3] daughter of Jeremiah from Libnah.	1 Zedekiah was twenty-one years old when he became king, and he was king for eleven years in Jerusalem. The name of his mother was Hamutal daughter of Jeremiah from Libnah.
12 He did what was evil in the eyes of YHWH his God. He did not humble himself before Jeremiah the prophet [who spoke] from the mouth of YHWH.	19 He did what was evil in the eyes of YHWH according to all that Jehoiakim had done.	2 He did what was evil in the eyes of YHWH according to all that Jehoiakim had done.

13 He also rebelled against King Nebuchadnezzar who had made him swear by God, and he stiffened his neck and hardened his heart against returning to YHWH the God of Israel.

14 Also all the leaders of the priests and the people increasingly acted unfaithfully[1] according to all the abominations of the nations; and they polluted the house of YHWH that he had consecrated in Jerusalem.

15 Now YHWH the God of their ancestors had sent to them early and often through his messengers because he had compassion on his people and on his dwelling place.

16 But they kept mocking the messengers of God, despising his words and ridiculing his prophets, until the rage of YHWH mounted against his people to the point of no cure.

17 He [God] brought up against them the king of the Chaldeans,[2] and he killed their young men with the sword in the house of their sanctuary, and had no pity on young man or virgin, the old or the grey-haired; all he gave into his hand.

20 Indeed, the wrath of YHWH mounted against Jerusalem and against Judah until he cast them away from his presence. Zedekiah also rebelled against the king of Babylon.

3 Indeed, the wrath of YHWH mounted against Jerusalem and Judah until he cast them away from his presence. Zedekiah also rebelled against the king of Babylon.

---

[1] Reading the Qere.
[2] Reading the Qere.
[3] Reading the Qere.

663 The Fall of Jerusalem
2 Kings 25:1-7 // Jer 52:4-11 // Jer 39:1-7

2 Kings 25	*Jeremiah 52*	*Jeremiah 39*
1 So in the ninth year of his being king, in the tenth month, on the tenth day of the month, Nebuchadnez-zar king of Babylon, he and all his army, came against Jerusalem, and he encamped against it; and they built a siege-wall against it all around.	4 So in the ninth year of his being king, in the tenth month, on the tenth day of the month, Nebuchadnez-zar king of Babylon, he and all his army, came against Jerusalem, and they encamped against it; and built a siege-wall against it all around.	1 In the ninth year of Zedekiah king of Judah in the tenth month, Neb-uchadnezzar king of Baby-lon and all his army came against Jerusalem and be-sieged it.
2 The city was under siege until the eleventh year of King Zedekiah.	5 The city came under siege until the eleventh year of King Zedekiah.	2 In the eleventh year of Zedekiah, in the fourth month, on the ninth day of the month, the city was breached.
3 On the ninth day of the month the famine had taken such a hold in the city that there was no bread for the people of the land.	6 In the fourth month, on the ninth day of the month, the famine had taken such a hold in the city that there was no bread for the people of the land.	
		3 All the officers of the king of Babylon came and they sat in the Middle Gate: Nergal-sharezer, Samgar-nebo, Sar-sechem the Rabsaris, Nergal-sarezer the Rabmag, and all the rest of the officers of the king of Babylon.
4 Then the city [wall] was breached and all the men of war [fled] by night by way of the gate between the two walls, that [is] beside the garden of the king though the Chaldeans were [all] around the city. He went by way of the Arabah.	7 Then the city [wall] was breached and all the men of war fled and went out from the city by night by way of the gate between the two walls, that is beside the garden of the king though the Chaldeans were [all] around the city. They went by way of the Arabah.	4 When Zedekiah king of Judah and all the men of war saw them, they fled and went out by night from the city by way of the garden of the king through the gate between the two walls. They went out by way of the Arabah.
5 But the army of the Chaldeans pursued after the king and overtook him	8 But the army of the Chaldeans pursued after the king and overtook	5 But the army of the Chaldeans pursued after them and overtook

on the plains of Jericho and all his army was scattered from him.	Zedekiah on the plains of Jericho and all his army was scattered from him.	Zedekiah on the plains of Jericho.
6 Then they captured the king and brought him up to the king of Babylon to Riblah, and they pronounced judgment upon him.	9 Then they captured the king and brought him up to the king of Babylon, at Riblah, in the land of Hamath, and he pronounced judgments on him.	Then they took him and brought him up to Nebuchadnezzar king of Babylon at Riblah, in the land of Hamath, and he pronounced judgments on him.
7 They slaughtered the sons of Zedekiah before his eyes, and then he put out the eyes of Zedekiah, bound him in bronze fetters, and brought him [to] Babylon.	10 The king of Babylon slaughtered the sons of Zedekiah before his eyes; and he also slaughtered all the officers of Judah at Riblah.	6 The king of Babylon slaughtered the sons of Zedekiah at Riblah before his eyes; the king of Babylon also slaughtered all the nobles of Judah.
	11 Then he put out the eyes of Zedekiah, bound him in bronze fetters, and the king of Babylon brought him to Babylon, and put him into house arrest until the day of his death.	7 Then he put out the eyes of Zedekiah, and bound him in bronze fetters in order to bring him to Babylon.

664 The Captivity of Judah
2 Chron 36:18-21 // 2 Kings 25:8-21 // Jer 52:12-30 // Jer 39:8-10

2 Chron 36	*2 Kings 25*	*Jeremiah 52*	*Jeremiah 39*
	8 In the fifth month, on the seventh day of the month—it was the nineteenth year of King Nebuchadnezzar king of Babylon—Nebuzaradan the captain of the guardsmen, a servant of the king of Babylon, came [to] Jerusalem.	12 In the fifth month, on the tenth day of the month—it was the nineteenth year of King Nebuchadnezzar king of Babylon—Nebuzaradan the captain of the guardsmen, who stood before the king of Babylon, came to Jerusalem.	
18 All the vessels of the house of God, great and small, and the treasures of the house of YHWH and the treasures of the king and his officials, all he brought to Babylon.			

19 They burned the house of God, and they pulled down the wall of Jerusalem, and they burned all its palaces with fire and all its precious vessels were destroyed.

9 He burned the house of YHWH and the house of the king and all the houses of Jerusalem; every great house he burned with fire.

10 The walls around Jerusalem, all the army of the Chaldeans who were [with] the captain of the guardsmen, pulled down.

11 Then the rest of the people who remained in the city, and the deserters who deserted to the king of Babylon, and the rest of the multitude, Nebuzaradan the captain of the guardsmen carried into exile.

12 But some of the poor of the land the captain of the guardsmen left behind to be vinedressers and cultivators.

13 The pillars of bronze which were in the house of YHWH, and the stands and the sea of bronze that were in the house of YHWH, the Chaldeans broke to pieces and they carried the bronze to Babylon.

14 The pots, the shovels, the snuffers, the dishes, and all the vessels of bronze with which they had served, they took away,

15 as well as the firepans and the basins. What was of gold, [for its] gold, and what was of silver, [for its]

13 He burned the house of YHWH and the house of the king and all the houses of Jerusalem; every great house he burned with fire.

14 All the walls around Jerusalem, all the army of the Chaldeans who were with the captain of the guardsmen, pulled down.

15 Then some of the poor of the people, and the rest of the people who were left in the city, and the deserters who deserted to the king of Babylon, and the rest of the masterworkmen, Nebuzaradan the captain of the guardsmen carried into exile.

16 But some of the poor of the land Nebuzaradan the captain of the guardsmen left behind to be vinedressers and cultivators.

17 The pillars of bronze which belonged to the house of YHWH, and the stands and the sea of bronze which were at the house of YHWH, the Chaldeans broke to pieces and carried all the bronze to Babylon.

18 The pots, the shovels, the snuffers, the basins, the dishes, and all the vessels of bronze with which they had served, they took away

19 as well as the bowls, the firepans, the basins, the pots, the lampstands, the dishes, and sacrificial

8 The house of the king and the house of the people the Chaldeans burned with fire, and the walls of Jerusalem they pulled down.

9 The rest of the people who remained in the city, and the deserters who deserted to him, and the rest of the people who were left, Nebuzaradan the captain of the guardsmen carried into exile to Babylon.

10 But some of the poor people who had nothing Nebuzaradan the captain of the guardsmen left behind in the land of Judah and gave them vineyards and fields in that day.

silver, the captain of the guardsmen took away.

vessels. What was of gold, [for its] gold, and what was of silver, [for its] silver, the captain of the guardsmen took away.

16 As for the two pillars, the single sea, and the stands that Solomon had made for the house of YHWH, there was no [possible] weighing of the bronze in all these vessels.

20 As for the two pillars, the single sea, and the twelve bronze oxen which were under [the sea, and the] stands that King Solomon had made for the house of YHWH, there was no [possible] weighing of the bronze in all these vessels.

17 The height of a single pillar was eighteen cubits, and upon it there was a capital of bronze; the height of the capital was three cubits; a network and pomegranates, all of bronze, were upon the capital round about, and the same for the second pillar including the network.[1]

21 As for the pillars, the height of a single pillar was eighteen cubits, its circumference was twelve cubits, and its thickness was four fingers, [and it was] hollow.

22 Upon it there was a capital of bronze, and the height of a single capital was five cubits; a network and pomegranates, all of bronze, were upon the capital round about, and the same for the second pillar along with pomegranates.

23 There were ninety-six pomegranates on a side; all the pomegranates on the surrounding network were a hundred.

18 The captain of the guardsmen took Seraiah the chief priest, and Zephaniah the second priest, and three keepers of the threshold;

24 The captain of the guardsmen took Seraiah the chief priest, and Zephaniah the second priest, and three keepers of the threshold;

19 and from the city he took one officer who had been in charge of the men of war, five men from

25 and from the city he took one officer who had been in charge of the men of war, seven men from

those who had access to the king who were found in the city, the scribe [of] the commander of the army who conscripted the people of the land, and sixty men from the people of the land who were found in the city.

those who had access to the king who were found in the city, a scribe of the commander of the army who conscripted the people of the land, and sixty men of the people of the land who were found inside the city.

20 He [Nebuchadnezzar] took into exile to Babylon those left who survived the sword, and they became servants to him and to his sons until the rule of the kingdom of Persia

20 Nebuzaradan the captain of the guardsmen took them, and led them over to the king of Babylon at Riblah.

26 Nebuzaradan the captain of the guard took them, and led them to the king of Babylon at Riblah.

21 The king of Babylon struck them down and put them to death in Riblah in the land of Hamath. So Judah went into exile from its land.

27 And the king of Babylon struck them down and put them to death in Riblah in the land of Hamath. So Judah went into exile from its land.

21 to fulfill the word of YHWH from the mouth of Jeremiah, until the land had accepted its sabbaths. All the days of desolation it kept sabbath to fulfill [the] seventy years.

28 These are the people whom Nebuchadnezzar took into exile: in the seventh year three thousand and twenty-three Jews;

29 in the eighteenth year of Nebuchadnezzar, from Jerusalem: eight hundred and thirty-two persons;

30 in the twenty-third year of Nebuchadnezzar, Nebuzaradan the captain of the guardsmen, took into exile seven hundred and forty-five Jews; all the persons were four thousand and six hundred.

---

¹ Literally, "on the network."

665 The Remnant Flee to Egypt
2 Kings 25:22-26 // Jer 40:1–41:3, 43:7

2 Kings 25	*Jeremiah 40*

Jeremiah 40

1 The word which came to Jeremiah from YHWH after Nebuzaradan the captain of the guardsmen had set him free from Ramah, when he took him—and he was bound in chains—along with all the [other] captives of Jerusalem and Judah who were being exiled to Babylon.

2 The captain of the guardsmen took Jeremiah and said to him, "YHWH your God pronounced this evil upon this place;

3 and YHWH has brought [it] and has done as he spoke. Because you have sinned against YHWH and have not listened to his voice, this thing has come upon you.

4 Now see I have freed you today from the chains that are on your hands. If it seems good in your eyes to come with me to Babylon, come, and I will keep my eye on you, but if it seems wrong in your eyes to come with me to Babylon, do not. See, the whole land is before you: go wherever it seems good and right in your eyes to go."

22 And as for the people who were left behind in the land of Judah whom Nebuchadnezzar king of Babylon had left behind, he appointed over them Gedaliah son of Ahikam son of Saphan.

5 But he would not go back— "Then return to Gedaliah son of Ahikam son of Saphan, whom the king of Babylon has appointed over the cities of Judah, and stay with him among the people, or go any-where in your eyes it is right to go." Then the captain of the guardsmen gave him a food allowance and a present and set him free.

6 Thereupon Jeremiah went to Gedaliah the son of Ahikam at Mizpah, and stayed with him among the people who remained behind in the land.

23 When all the commanders of the forces, they and [their] men, heard that the king of Babylon had appointed Gedaliah, they came to Gedaliah at Mizpah: that is, Ishmael son of Nethaniah, Johanan son of Kareah, Seraiah son of Tanhumeth the Netophathite and Jaazaniah son of the Maacathite, they and their men.

7 When all the commanders of the forces that were in the field, they and their men, heard that the king of Babylon had appointed Gedaliah son of Ahikam over the land, and that he had assigned to him men, women, and children, and some of the poor of the land from those who had not been exiled to Babylon,

8 they came to Gedaliah at Mizpah: that is, Ishmael son of Nethaniah, Johanan and Jonathan sons of Kareah, Seraiah son of Tanhumeth, sons of Ephai the Netopathite, and Jezaniah son of the Maacathite, they and their men.

24 And Gedaliah swore to them and to their men, and said to them, "Do not be afraid of the servants of the Chaldeans. Stay in the land, and serve the king of Babylon, and it will go well with you."

9 And Gedaliah son of Ahikam son of Saphan swore to them and to their men, "Do not be afraid to serve the Chaldeans. Stay in the land and serve the king of Babylon, and it will go well with you.

10 As for me, see I am staying at Mizpah to stand before the Chaldeans who will come to us, but you gather the wine and summer fruits, and oil, and put [them] in your vessels and stay in your cities that you have taken over.

11 Also, when all the Jews who were in Moab and among the Ammonites, in Edom, and all [other] lands heard that the king of Babylon had left a remnant in Judah and that he had appointed over them Gedaliah son of Ahikam son of Saphan,

12 then all the Jews returned from all the places to which they had been driven and came to the land of Judah, to Gedaliah at Mizpah, and they gathered the wine and summer fruits in great abundance.

13 Now Johanan son of Kareah and all the commanders of the forces that were in the field came to Gedaliah at Mizpah,

14 and they said to him, "Do you not realize that Baalis king of the Ammonites, has sent Ishmael son of Nethaniah to take your life?" But Gedaliah son of Ahikam did not believe them.

15 Then Johanan son of Kareah spoke in secret to Gedaliah at Mizpah, "Let me go now and strike down Ishmael son of Nethaniah and no one need know. Why should he take your life, that all the Jews who have gathered to you would be scattered and all the remnant of Judah perish?"

16 But Gedaliah son of Ahikam said to Johanan son of Kareah, "You shall not do this thing, for you are telling a lie about Ishmael."

25 But in the seventh month, there came Ishmael son of Nethaniah son of Elishama of the royal family, and ten men with him, and they struck down Gedaliah so that he died as well as the Jews and the Chaldeans who were with him at Mizpah.

41:1 But in the seventh month, there came Ishmael son of Nethaniah son of Elishama of the royal family, and the counselors of the king, and ten men with him, to Gedaliah the son of Ahikam at Mizpah, and they ate bread together there at Mizpah.

2 Then Ishmael son of Nethaniah and the ten men who were with him rose up and they struck down Gedaliah son of Ahikam son of Shaphan with the sword. He killed him whom the king of Babylon had appointed over the land;

3 and all the Jews who were with Gedaliah at Mizpah and the Chaldeans who were found there, the men of war, [these also] Ishmael struck down.

[Jeremiah 43

26 Then all the people, from small to great, and the leaders of the forces rose up and went to Egypt, for they were afraid of the Chaldeans.

7 And they went into the land of Egypt since they had not listened to the voice of YHWH, and they went as far as Tahpanhes.]

666 Jehoiachin Released and Honored in Babylon
2 Kings 25:27-30 // Jer 52:31-34

2 Kings 25	*Jeremiah 52*
27 Now in the thirty-seventh year of the exile of Jehoiachin king of Judah, in the twelfth month on the twenty-seventh day of the month, Evil-merodach king of Babylon in the year of his becoming king, raised up the head of Jehoiachin king of Judah [and brought him] out of prison;	31 In the thirty-seventh year of the exile of Jehoiachin king of Judah, in the twelfth month on the twenty-fifth day of the month, Evil-merodach king of Babylon in the year of his obtaining kingship, raised up the head of Jehoiachin king of Judah and brought him out of prison confinement;
28 and he spoke kindly to him and set his seat above the seat of the kings who were with him in Babylon.	32 and he spoke kindly to him and set his seat above the seat of the kings[1] who were with him in Babylon.
29 So he [Jehoiachin] changed his prison garments and ate bread regularly before him all the days of his life.	33 So he changed his prison garments and ate bread regularly before him all the days of his life.
30 As for his allowance, a regular allowance was given him by the king, a portion day by day all the days of his life.	34 As for his allowance, a regular allowance was given him by the king of Babylon, a portion day by day until the day of his death all the days of his life.

[1] Reading the Qere.

667 The Proclamation of Cyrus
2 Chron 36:22-23 // Ezra 1:1-4

2 Chron 36	*Ezra 1*
22 In the first year of Cyrus king of Persia, to complete the word of YHWH by the mouth of Jeremiah, YHWH stirred up the spirit of Cyrus king of Persia, that he made a proclamation throughout all his kingdom and also in writing, saying,	1 And in the first year of Cyrus king of Persia, to complete the word of YHWH from the mouth of Jeremiah, YHWH stirred up the spirit of Cyrus king of Persia, that he made a proclamation throughout all his kingdom and also in writing, saying,

23 "Thus says Cyrus king of Persia: All the kingdoms of the earth YHWH the God of heaven, has given to me, and he has charged me to build for him a house in Jerusalem which is in Judah. Who among you [is] from any of his people? May YHWH his God [be] with him, and let him go up."

2 "Thus says Cyrus king of Persia: All the kingdoms of the earth YHWH the God of heaven, has given to me, and he has charged me to build for him a house in Jerusalem which is in Judah.

3 Who among you [is] from any of his people? May his God be with him, and let him go up to Jerusalem which is in Judah and let him build the house of YHWH the God of Israel—he is the God who is in Jerusalem—

4 and any [returning] survivor from any of the places where he may reside, let the men of his place assist him with silver and gold and with goods and with [pack-] animals, along with the freewill offering[s] for the house of God that is in Jerusalem.

Appendix

Synoptic Parallels in Chronicles and Samuel-Kings

With the following chart, readers may use either Chronicles or Samuel-Kings as the lead text. Both columns are for the most part in chronological order. When a text is out of sequence, it will be bracketed.

David
Sections 494–551

#	Title	1 Chronicles	1 Samuel	Page
494	The Death of Saul and His Sons	10:1-14	31:1-13	51
495	David Learns of Saul's Death		2 Sam 1:1-16	52
496	David's Lament over Saul and Jonathan		1:17-27	53
497	David Made King over Judah		2:1-7	54
498	David Fights the House of Saul		2:8–3:1	55
499	David's Sons Born at Hebron	[3:1-4a]	3:2-5	57
500	Abner Plans a Covenant with David		3:6-21	57
501	Joab Murders Abner		3:22-39	59
502	The Assassination of Ish-bosheth		4:1-12	60
503	David Made King in Israel	11:1-3	5:1-5	61
504	David Captures Zion	11:4-9	5:6-10	62
[535]	David's Mighty Men	11:10-47	[23:8-39]	62
[536]	David's Helpers at Ziklag	12:1-23		65
[537]	David's Army at Hebron	12:24-41		66
[508]	David Proposes to Bring Ark to Jerusalem	13:1-4		67
[509]	David Goes to Bring the Ark	13:5-14	[6:1-11]	68
505	Hiram's Recognition of David	14:1-2	5:11-12	69
506	David's Children Born at Jerusalem	14:3-7	5:13-16	69
507	David Defeats the Philistines	14:8-17	5:17-25	70
508	David Proposes to Bring Ark to Jerusalem	[13:1-4]		71
509	David Goes to Bring the Ark	[13:5-14]	6:1-11	71
510	The Ark Brought to Jerusalem	15:1–16:6	6:12-19a	73

Solomon
Sections 552–569

Divided Monarchy
Sections 570–667